Exploring the History of Statistical Inference in Economics

T0311470

Exploring the History of Statistical Inference in Economics

Annual Supplement to Volume 53
History of Political Economy

Edited by Jeff Biddle and Marcel Boumans

Duke University Press
Durham and London 2021

Contents

Inference without a Cause

Exploring the History of Statistical Inference in Economics: Introduction

Jeff Biddle and Marcel Boumans

We had two motivations that made us decide that an exploration of the history of statistical inference could be productive. One was related to John Maynard Keynes's distinction between two different functions that he observed in statistical research, and the other is that existing histories of empirical analysis seem to miss an important part of existing research practices in economics.

Keynes, in his *Treatise on Probability*, made a distinction between the descriptive function of the theory of statistics, which involved devising ways to represent and summarize large amounts of data, and the inductive function, which "seeks to extend its descriptions of certain characteristics of observed events to the corresponding characteristics of other events that have not been observed" (Keynes [1921] 1973: 359). This second part of statistics he called the theory of statistical inference. When looking at any given example of statistical research in economics, one is likely to see both what Keynes called description and what he called inference; indeed, it is not always obvious where one ends and the other begins. The researcher will have made decisions about how best to summarize statistical data, and

We would like to thank all participants of the conference at which these papers were discussed for the first time. Besides the contributors to this volume, they were Kevin Hoover, Jennifer Jhun, and Steven Medema. We are very grateful to our external reviewers for their valuable and constructive reports: Maria Bach, H. Spencer Banzhaf, Beatrice Cherrier, Erwin Dekker, Federico D'Onofrio, Verena Halsmayer, Catherine Herfeld, Steven Medema, Theodore Porter, and Gerardo Serra.

History of Political Economy 53 (annual suppl.) DOI 10.1215/00182702-9414747

also decisions about what generalizations can be made, with what level of confidence, based on the information in the sample. These two sets of decisions are often related: the choice of how to summarize the sample information is influenced by beliefs about which summary measures provide the firmest bases for the types of generalizations the researcher hopes to make. But Keynes's distinction is a real and important one, nonetheless. Crossing the line from description of the information in a sample to inference about things beyond the sample, no matter how inconspicuous the act of crossing may be, necessarily involves making assumptions, implicitly or explicitly, about the relationship between the data in the sample and the phenomena outside the sample about which generalizations are being made. If one accepts that Keynes's distinction is a meaningful one, it follows that bound up with the history of statistical analysis in economics, there is a distinguishable history of statistical inference, a history of the ways in which economists have gone about generalizing from statistical data.

The second motivation can also be clarified by a distinction. Edward Leamer (1978: vi) observed a wide gap between the formal textbook approach, "taught on the top floor (the third)," and its practiced variant, "done in the basement of the building": "I was perplexed by the fact that the same language was used in both places. Even more amazing was the transmogrification of particular individuals who wantonly sinned in the basement and metamorphosed into the highest of high priests as they ascended to the third floor." The people in the basement are sinners because their research does not meet the high standards of the discipline, often presented more generally as the standards of science. It seemed to us that most histories are written about the good works of these high priests, with little attention to the works of Leamer's "sinners."

There may be a reason why we do not have so many histories of sinful research. It is smudgy and messy and therefore does not lend itself to "seamless accounts to make it comprehensible," for which one has to "paper over the knots and holes in scientific life" (Morgan 2012: xv). More generally, the study of research practices faces distinct and substantial challenges. In a reflection on practice-oriented studies, which often are case studies, Andrea Woody discusses two of these challenges. The first, obvious challenge in case study research is how to generalize from a particular case, "how to avoid getting stuck at a level of particularity that evades any reasonable effort to generalize" (Woody 2014: 124). The more vexing challenge, however, has to do with normativity, that is, the issue of the abovementioned sinning. In our assessments of a practice, we build on strong intuitions and a priori reasoning: "In effect, the normativity of the analysis is built in from the get-go" (125). Although Woody focuses only on philosophical assessments, we believe that this built-in normativity also restricts the kinds of practices that are studied by historians. A priori concepts of "good science" influence the selection of historical cases of economic research that historians find worthwhile to investigate. In this sense, history of economic science reflects contemporaneous philosophy of science.[1] Tjalling Koopmans's (1947) negative review of the work done at the National Bureau of Economic Research (NBER), which he criticized as "measurement without theory," did not only set the scientific standards of empirical research in economics for decades; it also blinded historians to many practices that did not meet Koopmans's standards for proper research (see also Stapleford, this volume). The result is that there are relatively few historical studies of the work of Irma Adelman, Wassily Leontief, or Simon Kuznets, even though the latter two are Nobel laureates.

A number of interesting narrative threads, involving varied and changing inferential methods and strategies, can be discerned in the history of empirical economic research. One that has gotten a fair amount of attention (although mostly indirectly, in the context of histories of econometrics) involves the process through which the use of inferential procedures derived from probability theory, and designed to measure the possible impact of sampling error on the reliability of statistical estimates, came to be ubiquitous in empirical research in economics.

To be more specific, by the last decades of the twentieth century, a broad consensus had developed in the economics profession that statistical inference required the use of these procedures. A rather recent econometric textbook, *Econometric Analysis* (Greene 1999) even labeled this consensus "classical theory of inference," thus suggesting that this consensus is old and lasting, which is an important feature of standards. According to this standard for statistical inference, a plan for data analysis typically begins with a set of assumptions about the joint distribution of random variables of interest in a population of interest. This joint distribution is characterized by fixed parameters that embody important but

1. This normativity was explicitly vindicated by Imre Lakatos, aptly summarized by his dictum that "history of science without philosophy is blind." While this view on history today is only embraced by a very few historians, we nevertheless believe that scientific norms and standards still play an important role in the selection of what is interesting or relevant to study. For a detailed discussion of the relationship of the image of science and history of econometrics, see Boumans and Dupont-Kieffer 2011.

unknown facts about some phenomenon of interest. The assumptions are usually patterned on one of a set of canonical "statistical models" with well-understood properties, such as the linear regression model.

It is also assumed that the set of observations of the relevant variables is a *random sample* of observations taken from the population of interest. Statistical inference is, then, a matter of applying formulas to this sample information. A formula produces estimates of the parameters, and other formulas produce measures of the reliability of those estimates—"standard errors" and so forth. These formulas have been derived from probability theory, and there is a set of procedures—also derived from probability theory—for using the estimates produced by the formulas to test hypotheses about the parameters.

The work of Trygve Haavelmo and the Cowles Commission econometricians, in particular Koopmans, in the 1940s and early 1950s was crucial to the eventual widespread acceptance by economists of this approach to statistical inference. The Cowles group's justification of the application of probability theory to economic data is found in Haavelmo's "Probability Approach in Econometrics." Koopmans (1947) based his "measurement without theory" attack on the nonprobabilistic approach to the analysis of business cycles of Arthur F. Burns and Wesley C. Mitchell (1946) on his interpretation of the major message of Haavelmo's 1944 "probability approach," namely, that for *scientific* statistical inference, probability theory is essential. By the early 1970s, a standardized set of inferential methods justified by probability theory—methods of producing estimates, of assessing the reliability of those estimates, and of testing hypotheses—was being taught to the majority of economics graduate students. The phrase *statistical inference* had come to mean, in the minds of economists, the application of a set of techniques derived from probability theory (Biddle 2017), and for many economists the term *econometric* was reserved for empirical research that employed these methods and the methods of estimation that they accompanied (Biddle 2021: 280).

There is a robust historical literature about the activities of Haavelmo, Koopmans, and other early Cowles Commission econometricians and the subsequent development of the approach to statistical analysis that by the late twentieth century had inherited the title "econometrics" (Boumans, Dupont-Kieffer, and Qin 2011; De Marchi and Gilbert 1989; Epstein 1987; Morgan 1990; Qin 1993, 2013). This literature necessarily deals with the development of inferential methods based on probability theory. However, one of our motivations for organizing this conference is that the "history of statistical inference" that emerges from this literature leaves out much that is important and interesting.

For example, despite the fact that discussions of some of the principles and procedures of the "classical theory of inference" could be found in standard textbooks on economic statistics in the 1920s, prior to World War II very few empirical economists in the United States made any use of these tools of statistical inference to draw conclusions from statistical data. In the immediate postwar decades, as the use of the inferential tools derived from probability theory was coming to be regarded as the scientific standard for empirical research in economics, nonprobabilistic approaches to inference persisted in the common practice of empirical economics, and new nonprobabilistic approaches to inference were being developed. These modes of inference were in a sense put on the defensive, however, by the increasing popularity of the "econometric" approach. They became less visible, and we believe less studied, by historians of economics partly because many of the economists who practiced and taught them were not working on Leamer's "top floor" but in the "basements" of the academic departments of economics, and often outside academics altogether in government or the private sector,[2] and also because the dominance of the probabilistic approach was confused with its dispersion. It was assumed that coverage of the probabilistic approach would be sufficient to understand the history of postwar empirical research.

Thus, as we began to organize the conference, we were hoping for contributions that would bring these practices more to the foreground and show how widespread they actually were in the latter decades of the twentieth century, as well as contributions that would throw light on the many nonprobabilistic approaches to inference found in the work of economists writing before 1940. We were not disappointed.

With the support of Duke University Press and the editors of this journal, we invited a number of scholars with an interest in the history of empirical research in economics to contribute papers on episodes in or aspects of that history that would highlight the various ways in which Keynes's "statistical inference"—generalizing from evidence provided by a set of statistical data to statements about phenomena not described in those data—manifested itself. We particularly invited them to explore those practices that did not meet Koopmans's standards.

---

2. Histories of nonprobabilistic approaches can be found in *HOPE* conference volumes covering more general themes and a longer time period, such as Klein and Morgan 2001 and Maas and Morgan 2012.

The conference was scheduled for April 2020. By March, however, it became apparent that because of the COVID-19 pandemic, a traditional style of conference should not be held, so a "virtual" conference was planned instead. We anticipated with some disappointment the loss of certain attractive features of traditional conferences: the spontaneous and informal discussions between sessions and over meals of topics and questions raised during the formal sessions, and the chance to renew old acquaintances and talk about shared interests. And these things were indeed missed. But the conference sessions, though mediated by internet technology and involving participants in locations (and time zones) from Berlin to Berkeley, were orderly and stimulating. Further discussions between participants took place by email between the closing of one day's sessions and the opening of the next and continued in the days after the conference as participants turned to the task of revising their papers. There was wide agreement that the conference had worked out well.

The conference papers and discussions provided strong indications of the existence of a promising area for research. There was a general consensus that attention to inference as an analytically separable aspect of research involving statistical data could be a fruitful perspective from which to understand the history of empirical economics. Throughout the conference, participants introduced, and elaborated through discussion, several potentially useful ways to understand "statistical inference" and conceptual frameworks for thinking about it. And the papers themselves provided an indication of the fascinating variety of topics and themes that could ultimately be comprehended as part of the history of inferential methods and practices in economics.

The resulting chapters can be grouped together by three general themes: Inferences in the Field (Burnett, Biddle, and Samuel), Inference in Time (Morgan, Lenel, Stapleford), and Inference without a Cause (Boumans, Velkar, Akhabbar, and Maas). The concept of field has several connotations that are relevant for the cases studied in the first three chapters. It refers to research not done in Leamer's building at all but outside academic institutions and universities. Field, of course, can also be taken literally, and the chapters of this first section discuss research in agricultural economics and economic development. The concept of time plays a central role in the cases of the next three chapters but in two different ways. Mary S. Morgan and Laetitia Lenel discuss research on economic developments in time, such as trends and cycles, while Thomas A. Stapleford discusses the development of statistical research in time. The final four chapters discuss inferences made with a cause, but where the achievement of this cause or the cause itself was questioned.

Thinking about Statistical Inference: Themes Emerging from the Conference

The conference proposal shared with the contributors was centered on Keynes's 1921 definition of inference and his opposition between statistical description (within a sample) and statistical inference (making statements about things not observed in the sample on the basis of the information in the sample). As drafts of papers circulated and discussions began, however, it became clear that an idea of inference based on Keynes's presentation was, for several reasons, unduly narrow.

First, Keynes's concept of statistics was a twentieth-century concept. As G. U. Yule (1911) explained, the meaning of *statistics* had evolved over the eighteenth and nineteenth centuries, originally referring to expositions, largely verbal, of noteworthy characteristics of a state. Only gradually did the word *statistics* come to be associated with numerical information, lose its close association with information about a state, and acquire the meaning that Yule and Keynes attributed to it. So, as a historical matter, the evidence with which statistical inference has dealt is not limited to the numerical information that Keynes had in mind.[3] Accordingly, in this volume, we have Morgan's account of Thomas Robert Malthus's use of narrative in making inferences from evidence that was *statistical* in the eighteenth-century sense of the word, while Marcel Boumans describes Francis Galton's project of applying concepts from nineteenth-century statistics to draw inferences from photographs, based on the assumption that a collection of photographs will have some of the same properties as the collections of measurements that make up conventional statistical samples.

Second, Keynes's distinction between description and inference leaves out what is a necessary element of any statistical project in economics, the collection of the statistical data. And just as the decisions about how to describe data already collected are often influenced by a consideration of what sorts of inferences one hopes to make using the data, so are decisions about the data collection process—how concepts will be defined, how they will be measured, the composition of the sample, and so on. In

3. According to Yule (1911: 3), at the founding of the Royal Statistical Society in 1834, *statistics* was still being used to describe both numerical and nonnumerical information.

Harro Maas's chapter in this volume, for example, one sees how debates over the credibility of inferences presented in contingent valuation studies often focused on details of how the data were gathered, while Jeff Biddle's chapter describes how the US Department of Agriculture's economists reacted to past errors in forecasting crop and livestock production by redesigning data collection instruments and sampling procedures.

Third, Keynes's discussion of inference often referred to the "sample-universe" framework for thinking about inference: if one had a sample of statistical data, how could one best use it to make generalizations about some universe or population of interest beyond the sample? This way of thinking required the investigator to explore whether the members of the sample in hand had actually belonged to the universe of interest, how "representative" of the universe the sample was, in what specific sense a sample might not be representative of the universe, and so on. The sample-universe conceptualization was part and parcel of the project of developing techniques of statistical inference based on probability theory and is almost taken for granted in modern discussions of statistical inference. But it was just becoming familiar to empirical economists at the time Keynes wrote. Yule (1911) made use of it in his *Introduction to the Theory of Statistics*, and it would be discussed in the leading books on statistical methods for economists published in the United States in the 1920s (Biddle 2017). However, one finds in economists' writings of that and the next several decades ample evidence of a belief that the sample-universe framework was not a good one for thinking about how to draw credible inferences from many of the types of data with which empirical economists were working. The chapters by Biddle and Laetitia Lenel in this volume discuss the strong opinion of economists in the 1920s and 1930s that it was not useful to regard time series as samples from a universe, especially when forecasting was the goal of inference. Amanar Akhabbar (this volume) shows that Leontief made little use of sample-universe thinking in developing inferential procedures for his early input-output analyses, and he was unmoved by the opinion of econometricians, whose "indirect" methods of inference he criticized, that he would do better to reconceive his project of estimating input-output coefficients in a sample-universe framework. And much of the statistical material used in national income accounting and related efforts to describe national economies still does not lend itself to a sample-universe way of thinking, as is clear from Boris Samuel's chapter in this volume.

As noted above, conference discussions led to the elaboration and refinement of several potentially useful heuristics and conceptual frameworks for historians examining the role and nature of statistical inference in empirical economics. A first is a simple observation by Morgan that inference is a verb as well as a noun and that one could be interested in understanding a process or in the outcome of that process. In her chapter in this volume, Morgan observes that the terminology of inference nowadays seems to just refer to the outcome, not the process, of drawing the inference from the evidence. Halfway through the twentieth century, the various informal and tacit practices of inferences came to be replaced by more formal statistical inference based on explicit rules and procedures with clear criteria to ensure the reliability of the process. It seems that when such processes became rule bound, the process of making the inference and the statement of the inferential outcome somehow became conflated, with the consequence that the process of inference became less visible.

It is valuable to develop a clear understanding of the question or goal that motivated an inferential process, who was asking it, and why. Failure to do so risks missing the forest among the trees that are the often complicated statistical and inferential procedures that economists employ. Aashish Velkar's chapter in this volume produces interesting insight into the nature of statistical inference by looking at the use of the same basic descriptive statistical technique—the construction of a price index number—to answer two different questions: Stanley Jevons's attempt to measure changes in the value of the monetary standard versus the British Board of Trade's efforts to measure changes in workers' cost of living. The question behind the inferential activities described in both Biddle's and Lenel's chapters is easily grasped—the economists were making forecasts of future economic activity, and they adjusted their inferential procedures over time as their forecasting errors were revealed. But in two of the chapters, the relationship between the question motivating the research and the process and outcome of inference are less straightforward. In Boumans's chapter, we see that Galton's method of handling photographs did not allow him to make the sorts of inferences he had hoped to make about the facial characteristics of racial or criminal types, but it did surprise him by pointing to an inference about a different question: the relationship between facial "beauty" and the individual irregularities of appearance among the photographed subjects. In Samuel's chapter, we see that an accurate description of past macroeconomic conditions or forecasts of future ones for the purposes of recommending policy was only one of many goals sought by International Monetary Fund economists in their work with data, with the result that they adopted inferential practices that they understood to be less effective than others that they could have used.

The idea of inferential gaps, an expansion of a concept of "inferential distance" employed by Kevin D. Hoover and Michael Dowell (2001), seemed to the conferees a promising one. In one sense, inference is necessitated by the existence of *a* gap, that between the statistical data one has in hand, known with complete certainty, and the phenomenon about which one wants to generalize, which is unknown. This gap can also be felt to be very large (the "distance" can be very long), in particular when the phenomenon is not part of our daily experiences and hence is conceived of as "strange," as Burns and Mitchell (1946: 17) described the result of their inferences that led to a conceptualization of the business cycle:

> Thus the concept of business cycles ties together in our minds, and gives meaning to, a host of experiences undergone by millions of men, few of whom think of themselves as influenced by cyclical pressures and opportunities. The concept, as we develop it, is itself a symbol compounded of less comprehensive symbols representing the cyclical behavior characteristic of many unlike activities. In turn, these symbols are derived by extensive technical operations from symbolic records kept for practical ends, or combination of such records. We are, in truth, transmuting actual experience in the workaday world into something new and strange.

Inference is, in a sense, the attempt to bridge this gap; it is what happens "between evidence and expression," as Stapleford put it at the conference. But a sense developed at the conference that it was perhaps better to be on the lookout for many types of inferential gaps that might arise in an empirical research project and the strategies employed to bridge them in the process of creating plausible inferences.

An analogy with a bridge, however, can be misleading with respect to the problems that the empirical researchers were facing. A bridge goes from *known* to *known*. For Haavelmo (1944: iii), it was "a conjunction of economic theory and actual measurements, using the theory and technique of statistical inference as a bridge pier." His "Probability Approach in Econometrics" aimed at building such a bridge. But often the other side of an inferential gap could not be seen.

Gaps can originate for various reasons. Gaps arise from data quality problems, when the measures available to the researcher of the things he or she wants measured are inaccurate or imprecise. There is concept mismatch: the thing that was measured (well or badly) is not exactly the thing that the researcher wanted to make inferences about. There is sample-universe mismatch: the sample is representative of one environment, but the researcher wanted to draw an inference about a different environment. And there is sampling bias and sampling error in samples that come from the environment the researcher cared about. In Velkar's contribution to this volume, one sees still another inferential gap: that between the inferences about the cost of living to which the available data and the accredited statistical procedures lead the experts and the inferences of ordinary citizens based on their experiences—a gap that involves the strangeness referred to in the Burns and Mitchell quotation above. Having identified the inferential gaps that faced a researcher or researchers, it is then worth asking how much attention was given to each of these problems and what steps were taken to solve them.

It was suggested that when considering the history of statistical inference more broadly, one might be able to identify certain inferential strategies common to a number of historical episodes. A familiar example is the strategy of trying to quantify the extent to which a sample statistic, say a regression coefficient, might differ from the unknown population value it is meant to estimate. The tactics associated with this strategy are based on probability theory and taught as a matter of course to aspiring economists. But other common strategies have long been employed by economists. Maas and Morgan discuss the strategy of *triangulation*. The strategy is based on the idea that we can have more trust in an inference when information derived from different methods and sources are found to be congruent and consistent with the same conclusion. Inferences based on descriptive statistics of a certain sample of data may be bolstered by evidence from other types of samples and statistical materials, from interviews, from surveys, and so forth. The agricultural economists in Biddle's paper "triangulated" by comparing the forecasts of production they derived from the reports of volunteers in the agricultural areas with the later reports of railroads about volumes of freight carried. Paul Burnett's chapter in this volume describes how Zvi Griliches used interviews with seed company executives to make sense of the shapes of empirical curves derived from data on hybrid corn adoption. The triangulation tactic of interviewing experts as an aid to drawing good inferences also appears in

Lenel's account of the Harvard Economic Service's increasing reliance on the opinions of bankers and businessmen along with its statistical model in developing forecasts.

Another inferential strategy involves the use of theory and assumed theoretical relationships to go from observed and measured phenomena to unobserved phenomena of interest. Using data on trends in wages along with the marginal productivity theory of distribution to infer trends in productivity would be one example, and Samuel (this volume) describes how IMF economists use the quantity theory of money and the monetary approach to the balance of payments to derive estimates of unmeasured macroeconomic quantities from the data available to them.

Morgan's contribution to the volume makes the intriguing proposal that the construction of narratives might be a process through which researchers arrive at inferences, which would make narrative an inferential strategy worth looking for in the history of empirical economics. Burnett's chapter on Theodore Schultz's (1964) discussion of statistical evidence in *Transforming Traditional Agriculture* provides a fascinating analysis of what may be another general inferential strategy. He describes how Schultz assembled and interpreted a small assortment of statistical studies, making each, with the help of basic neoclassical theory, into a "statistical parable" that supported his arguments in a controversy with other development economists in the late 1950s and early 1960s.

Toward a Broader View of the History of Statistical Inference in Economics

What follows is a selective sketch of the history of statistical inference in economics in the twentieth century, meant to place the better-known narrative thread centered on the development and growing prominence of inferential tools derived from probability theory into the wider context provided by the variety of approaches to statistical inference being used throughout the period. In doing so we highlight the contributions of the chapters in this volume to fleshing out that broader history and suggest some further opportunities for research.

Although this sketch focuses on the twentieth century, statistical inference as an activity of economists is older than that, as Morgan, Boumans, and Velkar remind us. At the turn of the nineteenth century, Malthus was engaging in statistical inference when "statistics" meant something altogether different than it does now. At the end of the 1800s, Galton was experimenting with ways to draw "statistical" inferences from collections of photographs. By the early twentieth century, the price index number was a well-enough-established statistical device that the government of the United Kingdom was maintaining a cost-of-living index, which became the basis of conflicting inferences about trends in British living standards and appropriate economic policies. Probability theory, however, had no significant role in the economic approaches of the nineteenth and early twentieth century. It was believed that probabilistic laws governed only errors and deviations, and the methods and procedures of inferences that were used were based on this belief. In other words, the methods were designed to deal with uncertainty in terms of ignorance; in economics the deterministic worldview was still dominant.

During the first two decades of the twentieth century, there were a few economists (e.g., Arthur Bowley [1920], F. Y. Edgeworth [1913], Yule [1911]) who explained how probability theory could be used to generalize from statistical data. However, the measures associated with these inferential procedures (e.g., the *probable errors* of means and correlation coefficients) are rarely seen in the statistical work of the time. Keynes's 1921 *Treatise on Probability* included an explicit and detailed rejection of probability theory as a basis for statistical inference, and his arguments proved influential. Several US economists embraced and built on them, and during the 1920s and 1930s, popular statistics textbooks and essays on statistical methodology quoted Keynes in passages dismissing the usefulness of the probability-theory-based measures (Biddle 2017, this volume; Lenel, this volume). A common theme in this American literature was that time series data, the type of data most often used in empirical research in economics in the first half of the twentieth century, did not fit the assumptions on which the inferential measures derived from probability theory were based. It was implausible, so the argument went, to regard a time series as a random sample from a larger universe characterized by stable relationships between variables. Further, even if one were willing to accept this characterization of a time series, the individual observations in a single time series sample were almost never independent of one another, a situation that contradicted one of the key assumptions underlying the probabilistic inferential methods of the time (Klein 1997). The rejection of the assumptions necessary for application of those inferential methods to time series data necessitated the development of alternative methods.

Along with his rejection of probability theory, Keynes offered an alternative framework for thinking about statistical inference. His central theme was that the logic underlying good statistical induction (a phrase Keynes considered synonymous with statistical inference) was similar to the more familiar logic of universal induction, that is, the process of reasoning on the basis of multiple instances of observation to formulate and build confidence in conclusions claiming universality, for example, "all swans are white." Both forms of induction relied on what Keynes called the method of analogy. Inductive arguments in support of universal statements were built on numerous instances of observation. The characteristics shared by a set of instances constituted a *positive analogy* of the set (each involved a swan, in each the swan was white), while differences in characteristics across the instances constituted a *negative analogy* (swans of different sizes, observed in different seasons, on different continents).

Keynes argued that it was through careful consideration of the positive and negative analogy in sets of observations that one refined and/or built confidence in inductive generalizations. An additional observation of a white swan on a new continent would, in Keynes's terms, "strengthen the negative analogy" of one's set of instances and strengthen confidence in the universality of the positive analogy "all swans are white"; observing a black swan in Australia would narrow the scope of the generalization that the set of observations could support ("all swans outside Australia are white"), and so forth. The ultimate goal of Keynes's discussion, however, was to show how the same logic could be applied to the problem of statistical inference, that is, reasoning from samples of statistical data to probabilistic generalizations about events or relationships of the form "if A, then a 20 percent chance of B."

In statistical inference, one built general conclusions not on sets of individual observational instances but on sets of samples of statistical data. Each sample was like previous samples in some ways (the positive analogy) and unlike those samples in other ways. Further, any given sample was being used to draw conclusions about some "universe," with which it would share some characteristics but from which it would differ in certain ways. Building strong inferences on the basis of statistical measures required careful attention to the circumstances surrounding the generation of the data used to calculate the measures and the circumstances surrounding the phenomena about which one wished to draw conclusions. Keynes illustrated this point with the example of drawing an inference about the relationship between age and the probability of death on the basis of a sample of deceased individuals:

We note the proportion who die at each age, and plot a diagram which displays these facts graphically. We then determine by some method of curve fitting a mathematical frequency curve which passes with close approximation through the points of our diagram. . . . In providing this comprehensive description the statistician has fulfilled his first function. But in determining the accuracy with which this frequency curve can be employed to determine the probability of death at a given age in the population at large, he must pay attention to a new class of considerations and must display a different kind of capacity. He must take account of whatever extraneous knowledge may be available regarding the sample of the population which came under observation, and of the mode and conditions of the observations themselves. Much of this may be of a vague kind, and most of it will be necessarily incapable of exact, numerical, or statistical treatment. (Keynes [1921] 1973: 372)

That Keynes's rejection of the inferential measures derived from probability theory was consistent with his positive heuristics for statistical inference can be seen in the quoted passage because the measures he rejected claimed to be able to provide reliable conclusions about phenomena outside the sample based only on information from the sample itself—without considering "extraneous knowledge" regarding the sample and considering only those characteristics of the sample members amenable to mathematical treatment. Keynes understood the arguments from probability theory that justified the use of these inferential measures, but he believed that the assumptions on which those arguments were based were seldom met in data from the social world (e.g., 418–19). Before one could arrive at an inference, one needed to ascertain the commonalities in the data that created a positive analogy, which Keynes in his *Treatise* called "uniformity" and in his controversy with Tinbergen on the econometric method, "homogeneity" (Boumans 2019). This aspect also played a decisive role on the justification of Galton's pictorial inference (Boumans, this volume): inferences from samples whose members did not have something in common—for example, belonging to the same "natural class"—would be meaningless. In biology, when drawing inferences from observations of the same species, for example, the requirement of uniformity could be justified. But with respect to economic or social phenomena this was an open question that first needed to be investigated (Klein 1997).

As with the rejection of probability-based inference, one finds in the US literature that explicitly addresses appropriate empirical methods echoes of Keynes's constructive advice on *statistical induction*, sometimes accompanied by references to his *Treatise*. Biddle (this volume) shows how the inferential practices of an important group of empirical economists, those employed by the US Department of Agriculture in the 1920s and early 1930s, exemplified Keynes's ideas and admonitions about statistical inference.

More generally, during the prewar period economists employed a wide variety of strategies for developing methods for the statistical estimation of such things as the course of the price level, the effectiveness of various farming practices, and the relationship between the cyclical movements of different economic activities. In the early 1920s, the NBER was founded, and across the decades researchers associated with the NBER developed a distinctive methodology of empirical research, supplementing their publications with detailed descriptions of their inferences.[4] The NBER researchers were also instrumental in the development of the techniques of national income accounting, devising clever methods for estimating unknown quantities from observable data and assessing the reliability of those estimates. Many of these methods, which have little relationship to probability theory, remain part of national income accounting today. And, as Akhabbar (this volume) describes, Leontief created new methods of statistical inference for use with his interindustry or input-output analyses.

In the early 1940s, in the introduction to his "Probability Approach in Econometrics," Haavelmo (1944: iii) acknowledged, and promised to refute, the prevalent opinion among empirical economists that applying probability models was a "crime in economic research" and "a violation of the very nature of economic data." At the center of his refutation was an ingenious reconceptualization of the inferential problem presented by a sample of statistical data. In response to the doubts expressed by the leading statistical economists of the 1920s and 1930s about the wisdom of regarding a time series as a sample drawn from some known, fixed *universe*, Haavelmo proposed the idea of the time series as a set of observations generated by a mechanism, one capable of generating an infinity of observations. The mechanism could be characterized by a probability law, and the task of statistical inference was to discover that probability law (iii, 48). Haavelmo's reconceptualization of the economists' inferential problem was embraced by the Cowles Commission econometricians of

---

4. Stapleford's contribution to this volume revisits the ideas about the proper approach to statistical analysis and the role of that analysis in economics espoused and modeled by the NBER's intellectual leader, Mitchell.

the 1940s and early 1950s, who employed an array of established and new inferential procedures derived from probability theory.

This universe created by Haavelmo implied, however, a specific ontology: it was Nature's "enormous laboratory" that produced a "stream of experiments" (14). In this universe, samples are the outcomes of repeated experiments. This is a different universe than that of Keynes, which consists of people's beliefs and expectations and implies a different concept of probability. By putting statistical inference in an experimental setting, it created, according to Leamer (1983), the myth of empirical research being objective and free of personal prejudice.

After World War II, inspired by Keynes's *General Theory* and aided by newly developed methodologies, including national income accounting, macro-econometric modeling, and input-output analysis, economic policy-making was increasingly based on statistical analyses. One sees both probabilistic and nonprobabilistic inferential methods being employed in this work. Data-based approaches to economic policy development and implementation were being designed and further developed at national levels but also at newly founded international organizations like the United Nations, the World Bank, and the International Monetary Fund. There are of course institutional histories of these organizations, but they give relatively little attention to the statistical approaches on which they based their policy programs (but see Samuel, this volume, and references cited therein).

The early 1960s mark something of a turning point in the pedagogy of statistics and econometrics, after which graduate students in economics would routinely be taught to understand statistical estimation and inference as an application of probability theory, whether in the context of a Cowles-style presentation of simultaneity, identification, and so forth, or simply more prosaic instruction in constructing confidence intervals and testing ordinary least squares regression coefficients for *statistical significance*. In the 1950s, however, the amount of systematic instruction in methods of statistical inference based in probability theory available to interested economics graduate students, not to say average economics graduate students, depended on where they were being trained. For example, it was not until 1962 that a departmental committee at Columbia University, home of one of the largest economics PhD programs in the United States, recommended that econometrics be offered as a field for graduate students (Rutherford 2004).

At the University of Chicago, site of another major US graduate program and home of the Cowles Commission until 1955, the situation was complicated. Griliches came to Chicago in 1954, took classes from Henri Theil and Haavelmo, among others, and began teaching graduate econometrics there himself in 1957. Among his students in the early 1960s was the future econometrician G. S. Maddala, who considered writing a dissertation in econometric theory before opting for a more empirically oriented topic. But Maddala reports that econometrics at Chicago was very "low key." Neither Maddala nor any other student in his cohort who was writing an empirical dissertation used anything more complicated than ordinary least squares regression. High-tech methods were eschewed for actual empirical work (Krueger and Taylor 2000; Lahiri 1999). So, what did inference look like in these empirical dissertations and in the work of the Chicago economists who supervised them?

Burnett (this volume) provides a good account of the inferential method employed by one leading University of Chicago economist, Theodore Schultz, and in the dissertation of Griliches, one of Schultz's most successful students. Schultz reported standard errors and formal hypothesis tests, but they were almost irrelevant to his arguments. The same can be said of the inferential arguments found in the work of other influential contributors to the "Chicago Economics" of that era, including Milton Friedman, H. Gregg Lewis, and Jacob Mincer (Biddle 2017). More research that took a close look at the techniques of statistical inference taught and employed at the University of Chicago during this period would be welcome.

Just as it took time for the inferential methods associated with Cowles-style econometrics to dominate economic pedagogy, it took time for those methods to spread through the empirical literature in economics. In the 1940s and 1950s, most empirical articles in economics did not use regression methods, much less report standard errors or tests of statistical significance (Backhouse 1998; Biddle 1999). By the 1960s, regression analysis had become the preferred method of detecting and measuring the economic relationships involved in theoretical analyses, but a number of influential empirical studies that used regression analysis made little use of inferential techniques derived from probability theory. This is due partly, no doubt, to simple inertia—even by 1960, empirical economics was dominated by people who had little or no formal training in the use of the Cowles-inspired inferential methods and did not see a need to learn them. But, as Biddle (2017) argues, neither Haavelmo's essay nor the empirical methods used by the Cowles Commission econometricians provided convincing answers for several important elements of the preexisting case against applying probability theory to economic data, and many empirical economists of the 1940s and 1950s may have carefully considered the increasingly popular inferential procedures and consciously decided against using them. Kuznets (1950), Leontief, and Millard Hastay (1951) were among the prominent empirical economists who explicitly expressed doubts about the value of the new methods (Akhabbar, this volume).

Nonetheless, by the 1970s, there was a broad consensus in the profession that inferential methods justified by probability theory—methods of producing estimates, of assessing the reliability of those estimates, and of testing hypotheses—were not only applicable to economic data but a necessary part of almost any attempt to generalize on the basis of economic data. In discussing the nature of this consensus, and how it differed from the reigning opinions on statistical inference held by the empirical economists of thirty years earlier, it is helpful to make use of the concept of mechanical objectivity introduced by Lorraine J. Daston and Peter Galison (1992) in their writings on the history of scientific objectivity and fruitfully applied to the history of quantification in the social sciences by Theodore Porter in his 1995 book *Trust in Numbers*.

Statistical inference is about using samples of statistical data as a basis for drawing conclusions about what is true, or probably true, in the world beyond the sample. In this setting, mechanical objectivity means employing a set of explicit and detailed rules and procedures to produce conclusions that are objective in the sense that if many different people took the same statistical information, and followed the same rules, they would come to exactly the same conclusions. The trustworthiness of the conclusion depends on the quality of the method. *Statistical inference* as defined and described in post-1960 econometrics textbooks is a prime example of this sort of mechanical objectivity.

Porter contrasts mechanical objectivity with an objectivity based on the "expert judgment" of those who analyze sample data. The analyst's expertise is acquired through a training process sanctioned by a scientific discipline, as well as through experience making similar decisions using similar data subject to the surveillance of other experts. One's faith in the analyst's conclusions depends largely on one's assessment of the quality of his or her disciplinary expertise but also on his or her commitment to the ideal of scientific objectivity.

Speaking in these terms, we would argue that in the 1920s and 1930s, the importance and propriety of applying expert judgment in the process of statistical inference was explicitly acknowledged by empirical economists. At the same time, mechanical objectivity was valued—it is easy to find examples of empirical economists employing rule-oriented, replicable procedures for drawing conclusions from economic data. The rejection of the tools of inference based on probability theory during this period was simply a rejection of one particular technology for achieving mechanical objectivity. In the post-1970s consensus regarding statistical inference in economics, however, application of this one particular form of mechanical objectivity became an almost required part of the process of drawing conclusions from economic data, taught in a standardized way to every economics graduate student.

Also, although there is a fundamental tension between the desire for mechanically objective methods and the belief in the importance of expert judgment in arriving at and communicating statistical results, it would be wrong to characterize what happened to statistical inference between the 1940s and the 1970s as a displacement of procedures requiring expert judgment by mechanically objective procedures. In the 1920s and 1930s there was disagreement over whether the phrase *statistical inference* should be applied to all aspects of the process of drawing conclusions based on statistical data, or whether it meant only the use of formulas derived from probability theory to create estimates from statistical data, measure the reliability of those estimates, and use those estimates to test hypotheses. The econometrics textbooks published after 1960 explicitly or implicitly accepted this second, narrower, definition, and their instruction on statistical inference was largely limited to instruction in the mechanically objective procedures based on probability theory. It was understood, however, that expert judgment was still an important part of empirical economic analysis, particularly in the specification of the economic models to be estimated. But the disciplinary knowledge needed for this task was to be taught in other classes, using other textbooks.

And something else was left largely unspoken in the descriptions of procedures for statistical inference found in the econometric textbooks from this period: even after choosing the statistical model, calculating the estimates and standard errors, and conducting the hypothesis tests, there was room for an empirical economist to exercise a fair amount of judgment, based on his or her specialized knowledge, before drawing conclusions from the statistical results. Indeed, no procedure for drawing conclusions from data, no matter how algorithmic or rule bound, can dispense entirely with the need for expert judgment (Boumans 2015: 84–85). And few empirical economists after 1970 would deny that the interpretation of statistical results, even those produced and assessed using the methods that had come to be called "econometrics," often involved a good deal of expert judgment. These "broader" inferential skills, such as those endorsed by Keynes, however, became a sort of craft knowledge picked up by economists from thesis advisers or other mentors, often referred to as an "art," thereby separating it from science itself.

This does not mean that the near ubiquity of a set of standard inferential tests and measures associated with probability theory in the empirical economics literature since the 1970s was simply a change in style or rhetoric. When application of these inferential procedures became a necessary part of economists' analyses of statistical data, the results of applying those procedures came to act as constraints on the set of claims that a researcher could credibly make to his or her peers on the basis of that data. For example, if a regression analysis of sample data yielded a large and positive partial correlation, but the correlation was not *statistically significant*, it would simply not be accepted as evidence that the *population* correlation was positive. If estimation of a statistical model produced a significant estimate of a relationship between two variables, but a statistical test led to rejection of an assumption required for the model to produce unbiased estimates, the evidence of a relationship would be heavily discounted. And once an author had justified an empirical model with a theoretical argument, a presentation and discussion of the coefficient estimates and significance tests associated with one or two versions of the empirical model was often a sufficient amount of *interpretation of results* to satisfy journal editors and referees.

So, we believe that in the latter half of the twentieth century, a mechanically objective procedure to generalize on the basis of statistical measures went from being a choice determined by the preferences of the analyst to a professional requirement, one that had real consequences for what economists would and would not assert on the basis of a body of statistical evidence. At the same time, the results produced by the procedure were still only part of the argument, to be combined with theory and other forms of evidence. This raises the question of whether one can discern implicit, but widely observed, *canons of inference* in the post-1970 empirical literature of this period. Arguably, the *credibility revolution* in the empirical microeconomic literature of the 1990s (Angrist and Pischke 2010), recently examined by Matthew T. Panhans and John D. Singleton (2017), represents among other things a significant change in these implicit canons of inference.

Stapleford (this volume) raises another interesting possibility, suggesting that the period during which the use of probability-based inferential tools is regarded as a necessary part of empirical research in economics may be an interlude in the history of economics that is coming to an end. Looking at the methodological statements and research practices of economists associated with the *data revolution* that commenced in the late twentieth century, he makes the case that the approach to empirical research being adopted by modern economists working with *big data* bears a resemblance to one promoted by Mitchell at the NBER, in which there was little place for tools and methods based in probability theory.

Finally, one still finds in the last decades of the twentieth century many examples of statistical inference without probability. Input-output models, computational general equilibrium models, and macroeconomic models with calibrated parameter values all represent techniques for using data to generate estimates of economic quantities and relationships. The growth accounting methods developed in the 1950s and 1960s to explain past economic growth, and applied to understand the productivity slowdown of the 1970s and 1980s, were seen to be largely *noneconometric* in nature (Biddle 2021: chap. 6). National income accounts continued to be updated, and international agencies like the IMF and the World Bank continued to create statistical pictures of national economies to guide their decisions (see Samuel, this volume). Economists working with all these empirical approaches faced the inferential problems of determining the reliability and the generalizability of the estimates they produced. For the most part, however, the nonprobabilistic inferential methods these researchers developed were not part of the formal econometrics curriculum of typical graduate programs in economics. Instead, they were taught in optional courses in places where an expert in the area might be part of the faculty, or picked up as the young PhDs found themselves in need of apprentice-like instruction from members of the established community of researchers working with those methods. Again, this situation has rendered these methods less visible to historians, and the question of how economists using these models did inference, and how their inferences were regarded by a profession that was for the most part committed to the probability-based approach, seems well worth pursuing.

References

Angrist, Joshua, and Jörn-Steffen Pischke. 2010. "The Credibility Revolution in Empirical Economics: How Better Research Design Is Taking the Con out of Econometrics." *Journal of Economic Perspectives* 24, no. 2: 3–30.

Backhouse, Roger. 1998. "The Transformation of US Economics, 1920–1960, Viewed through a Survey of Journal Articles." In *From Interwar Pluralism to Postwar Neoclassicism*, edited by Mary S. Morgan and Malcolm Rutherford. *History of Political Economy* 30 (supplement): 85–107.

Biddle, Jeff E. 1999. "Statistical Economics, 1900–1950." *History of Political Economy* 31, no. 4: 607–52.

Biddle, Jeff E. 2017. "Statistical Inference in Economics, 1920–1965: Changes in Meaning and Practice." *Journal of the History of Economic Thought* 39, no. 2: 149–74.

Biddle, Jeff E. 2021. *Progress through Regression: The Life History of the Empirical Cobb-Douglas Production Function*. Cambridge: Cambridge University Press.

Boumans, Marcel. 2015. *Science outside the Laboratory*. Oxford: Oxford University Press.

Boumans, Marcel. 2019. "Econometrics: The Keynes-Tinbergen Controversy." In *The Elgar Companion to John Maynard Keynes*, edited by Robert W. Dimand and Harald Hagemann, 283–89. Cheltenham, UK: Edward Elgar.

Boumans, Marcel, and Ariane Dupont-Kieffer. 2011. "A History of the Histories of Econometrics." In Boumans, Dupont-Kieffer, and Qin 2011: 5–31.

Boumans, Marcel, Ariane Dupont-Kieffer, and Duo Qin, eds. 2011. *Histories on Econometrics*. Supplemental issue to vol. 43 of *History of Political Economy*. Durham, NC: Duke University Press.

Bowley, Arthur. 1920. *Elements of Statistics*. 4th ed. London: P. S. King and Son.

Burns, Arthur F., and Wesley C. Mitchell. 1946. *Measuring Business Cycles*. New York: National Bureau of Economic Research.

Daston, Lorraine J., and Peter Galison. 1992. "The Image of Objectivity." In "Seeing Science." Special issue, *Representations* 40: 81–128.

De Marchi, Neil, and Christopher Gilbert, eds. 1989. *History and Methodology of Econometrics*. Oxford: Oxford University Press.

Edgeworth, F. Y. 1913. "On the Use of the Theory of Probabilities in Statistics Relating to Society." *Journal of the Royal Statistical Society* 76, no. 2: 165–93.

Epstein, R. 1987. *A History of Econometrics*. Amsterdam: North-Holland.

Greene, William H. 1999. *Econometric Analysis*, 4th ed. Englewood Cliffs, NJ: Prentice Hall.

Haavelmo, Trygve. 1944. "The Probability Approach in Econometrics." *Econometrica* 12 (supplement): iii–115.

Hastay, M. 1951. Review of *Statistical Inference in Dynamic Economic Models*, edited by J. Marschak and T. Koopmans. *Journal of the American Statistical Association* 46, no. 255: 388–90.

Hoover, Kevin D., and Michael Dowell. 2001. "Measuring Causes: Episodes in the Quantitative Assessment of the Value of Money." In *The Age of Economic Measurement*, edited by Judy L. Klein and Mary S. Morgan. *History of Political Economy* 33 (supplement): 137–61.

Keynes, John Maynard. (1921) 1973. *A Treatise on Probability*. London: Macmillan.

Klein, Judy L. 1997. *Statistical Visions in Time: A History of Time Series Analysis, 1662–1938*. Cambridge: Cambridge University Press.

Klein, Judy L., and Mary S. Morgan, eds. 2001. *The Age of Economic Measurement.* Supplemental issue to vol. 33 of *History of Political Economy.* Durham, NC: Duke University Press.

Koopmans, Tjalling C. 1947. "Measurement without Theory." *Review of Economics and Statistics* 29, no. 3: 161–72.

Krueger, Alan B., and Timothy Taylor. 2000. "An Interview with Zvi Griliches." *Journal of Economic Perspectives* 14, no. 2: 171–89.

Kuznets, Simon. 1950. "Conditions of Statistical Research." *Journal of the American Statistical Association* 45, no. 249: 1–14.

Lahiri, K. 1999. "The ET Interview: G. S. Maddala." *Econometric Theory* 15, no. 5: 753–76.

Leamer, Edward E. 1978. *Specification Searches: Ad Hoc Inferences with Nonexperimental Data.* New York: Wiley.

Leamer, Edward E. 1983. "Let's Take the Con out of Econometrics." *American Economic Review* 73, no. 1: 31–43.

Maas, Harro, and Mary S. Morgan, eds. 2012. *Observing the Economy.* Supplemental issue to vol. 44 of *History of Political Economy.* Durham, NC: Duke University Press.

Morgan, Mary S. 1990. *The History of Econometric Ideas.* Cambridge: Cambridge University Press.

Morgan, Mary S. 2012. *The World in the Model: How Economists Work and Think.* Cambridge: Cambridge University Press.

Panhans, Matthew T., and John D. Singleton. 2017. "The Empirical Economist's Toolkit: From Models to Methods." In *The Age of the Applied Economist: The Transformation of Economics since the 1970s,* edited by Roger E. Backhouse and Béatrice Cherrier. *History of Political Economy* 49 (supplement): 127–57.

Porter, Theodore. 1995. *Trust in Numbers: The Pursuit of Objectivity in Science and Public Life.* Princeton, NJ: Princeton University Press.

Qin, Duo. 1993. *Formation of Econometrics: A Historical Perspective.* Oxford: Oxford University Press.

Qin, Duo. 2013. *A History of Econometrics: The Reformation from the 1970s.* Oxford: Oxford University Press.

Rutherford, Malcolm. 2004. "Institutional Economics at Columbia University." *History of Political Economy* 36, no. 1: 31–78.

Schultz, Theodore W. 1964. *Transforming Traditional Agriculture.* New Haven, CT: Yale University Press.

Woody, Andrea I. 2014. "Chemistry's Periodic Law: Rethinking Representation and Explanation after the Turn to Practice." In *Science after the Practice Turn in the Philosophy, History, and Social Studies of Science,* edited by Léna Soler, Sjoerd Zwart, Michael Lynch, and Vincent Israel-Jost, 123–50. New York: Routledge.

Yule, G. U. 1911. *Introduction to the Theory of Statistics.* London: Charles Griffen.

Inferences in the Field

Statistical Parables: Agricultural Economists, Development Discourse, and Paths to Modernization during the Cold War

Paul Burnett

Social scientists face a critical challenge in applying their research to the more general domains of social policy: how to make the knowledge gained in one site—with its specific data and local conditions—portable, applicable, and replicable in other sites. After World War II, the push to conceptualize and act on the problem of economic development encouraged economists to think about how to bridge what they knew about one set of instances to what they might encounter in other, unfamiliar spaces with different cultures, histories, and factor endowments. The first obstacle to such a transfer of knowledge was the lack of reliable data. The second problem was the conceptualization of the object of development. For example, could there be gradual modifications and small-scale investments that would yield outsized benefits, or did there need to be a root and branch extirpation of either a colonial superstructure and/or a transformation of the customs and habits of the developing economy's denizens for any type of modernization to take place? Finally, depending on the object of development, what types of intervention would yield economic growth?

During the 1950s and 1960s, the field of development economics emerged from crumbling colonial empires, the rise of the United States as a global hegemon, and the consolidation of two separate spheres of influence of

History of Political Economy 53 (annual suppl.) DOI 10.1215/00182702-9414761

the Cold War.[1] The task of this applied economics was to consider the most fruitful path to economic growth, especially for an emerging "Third World" of states aligned with neither the West nor the Soviet Union. One strategy utilized by its practitioners was to modify classical economics, which focused on an early "stage" of now-developed economies. Structuralist development economists such as W. Arthur Lewis and Raul Prebisch posited that the homogeneous structure and low standard of living of developing countries were consequences of secular declining terms of trade between industrialized and developing countries, describing the existing structure of international trade between them as a main cause of the "underdevelopment" of developing countries.

There were other economists, however, whose life experiences and disciplinary identity did not accord with the notion of either a state-controlled reorganization of social and economic affairs or a laissez-faire continuation of existing trade relationships between rich and poor countries. Many agricultural economists were engaged directly in technical assistance to developing countries, though few offered to contend with the macroeconomic formulations favored by the development economists. American agricultural economists who took up senior positions either in government program administration or in advising sometimes ran afoul of political pressures, which is what led the economist Theodore Schultz to leave Iowa State College to set up an office of agricultural economics at the University of Chicago (Burnett 2011a).

This article explores Schultz's use of statistical case studies as normative and even moral exemplars for shaping economic and social policy in this larger arena, beyond narrow technical assistance. In *Transforming Traditional Agriculture*, Schultz used these "statistical parables,"[2] his own

1. The literature on the history of economic development is substantial. Suffice it to say that the postcolonial, Cold War competition for the minds of planners in the global South is central to understanding the framing of the knowledge produced in this context as well as the inferences drawn therefrom. See Tribe 2018, Easterly 2001, Leys 1996, and Hunt 1989.

2. *Statistical parables* is inspired by the term *exemplary cases* coined by Mary Morgan (2019: 9), as examples "which have potential to speak to new questions and new problems for recognizably similar objects in the same broad domain." The term *statistical parables* conveys the sense that there was a normative valence to these cases. They were meant to instruct, not necessarily in the narrow academic or technical sense, but in the broader arena of policy advocacy and governance. A statistical parable, though rooted in data and produced from inferential interpretation, need not be particularly robust, especially if the available data underlying it are neither reliable nor in abundance. It is, like all parables, a narrative that circulates over time and stands for an orientation to behavior. And in Morgan's use of the term in the social-scientific domain, it can serve to crystallize programs and research in that orientation.

and those of others, to develop an alternative to the dominant conceptions of the determinants of economic development. Statistical parables are case studies used in contexts in which the lack of reliable data inclines researchers toward their preferred theoretical frameworks. The parables might take the form of a limited analysis that seeks to rupture existing assumptions about phenomena, or they might be a case imported from another context in which the data are more robust and thus serve as an "exemplary case," in the historian Mary Morgan's sense, of a path for possible action. The purpose of a statistical parable is not primarily academic or even scientific; it is to edify or sow skepticism among those who work in the domain of state policy.

The germ of the notion of a statistical parable emerged from conversations I had with surviving members of the agriculture/development group at the University of Chicago from this period, including Arnold Harberger and George S. Tolley. We talked about Schultz many times, both informally and as part of recorded oral history interviews. I was struck by the way in which discussions about Schultz would invariably touch on his study of the Indian experience of the influenza pandemic after World War I. Harberger spoke with admiration of the study and also spoke repeatedly, in a parallel fashion, about the prime audience of his technical assistance work: the beleaguered government official or bureaucrat who was responsible for helping run a national economy. These interviews helped me understand a puzzle about Schultz's reputation and that of his most influential work, *Transforming Traditional Agriculture*. Both the reputation and the book were less visible in the academic journals than one should expect given his eventual award of the Bank of Sweden Prize in Economics in 1979. The expected audience for that book—functionaries and political authorities—shaped the narrative structure of the arguments. Moreover, the durability of the storytelling around the arguments in that book helped me to think about the nature of statistical parables.

Statistical inferences are made with some kind of audience or user in mind. That audience is usually given by the medium or organ of communication of a bounded scientific community, such as a specific journal of record or an annual conference. The statistical parable, by contrast, is an instance in which the logical, economic inference alone is insufficient to reach an intended audience that is adjacent to the scientific community in which the statistical research is being done. The statistics, and the inferences drawn therefrom, need to be packaged in some legible way in order to "travel fruitfully" beyond the normal scientific community in question

(Morgan 2011: 18). It is not clear that the parable does epistemic work in the sense of Morgan's narratives (explored in this volume), but in applied research—such as agricultural economics or development work—there are multiple communities that will apply this knowledge and need to be convinced of its merits among the din of competing narratives about how to proceed. But neither is it clear that the parable is mere rhetorical expression. It is certainly not "science popularization" or vulgarization. There is a specific audience for the statistical parable, with an intended outcome.

Others have suggested that the term *fable* captures both the didactic and the moral dimensions of certain forms of scientific reasoning and communication (Cartwright and Le Poidevin 1991: 62). I use the term *parable* to emphasize the narrative, didactic, and normative qualities of the arguments around Schultz's statistical inferences. The parable is often a story of the inversion of a conventional understanding or moral order that, through its establishment as a cultural or religious trope in a community, comes to stand for and reinforce a new moral orientation. A parable is not definitive in this disruption of conventional thinking but generative of a new understanding, the potential beginning of a new orientation of the disciple. This is not at all to suggest that Schultz was some Christlike shepherd in development circles. However, by the time *Transforming Traditional Agriculture* was published in 1964, he was an important thought leader in the American technical assistance community, including among American universities, State Department programs, and a number of economics graduate training programs that he established in several countries in South America and later on in Asia. That year, Schultz's Chile Project for training economists ended, which then seeded other economics programs in Argentina, Brazil, and elsewhere down to the present day. Schultz's intervention in development economics has become a story in itself. If Christ's parables are bound up with the biblical metanarrative of the telling of the parable and the effects it had on the disciples, so have Schultz's parables acquired a secondary narrative on the effects they had among those working in development policy.

There were three assumptions in development economics that Schultz challenged with these parables. First, there was the prevalent notion that a large proportion of the rural labor force was un- or underemployed, the so-called doctrine of the zero marginal productivity of labor, also known as disguised unemployment. Second, many development economists believed that efforts to increase agricultural productivity were undermined by declining terms of trade and that consequently the real growth potential lay in the industrial sector. Third, assuming a developing country's agricultural sector could be transformed, it had to be subordinated to policies of industrialization and land reform. All these assumptions had at their root the notion of the farmer as the passive recipient of change that would need to be imposed from outside.

To challenge these three conventions, Schultz identified exemplary cases of economic phenomena about the nature of agricultural labor, rational agency among poor farmers, and the institutional and cultural mechanisms by which new forms of production could be learned and adopted. First, he challenged the concept of disguised unemployment in developing countries with a case study of the abrupt removal of part of the labor supply, an analysis of the flu epidemic in India in 1918 and its effects on agricultural output. Second, he used field studies by the anthropologist Sol Tax and the economist David Hopper to argue that poor farmers could and did respond to market incentives, although such new incentives might not be visible or accessible to those farmers without assistance. Third, Schultz provided an analogous case of how the mechanisms by which economic growth in the agricultural sector was fostered in the United States might be transferred to farmers in developing countries. For this case, he deployed his student Zvi Griliches's analyses of the adoption of more productive techniques in agriculture and rates of return on investments in research, education, and agricultural extension.

According to Schultz, development economists had adapted elements of classical political economy—as passed down through Marx—to model the developing economy. To the structuralists, the problem of agriculture was that it was frozen in the stage of primitive accumulation, with its class relations of rent-extracting landowners and peasants. Only by redistributing land and rationalizing its use could agriculture be made more productive (Schultz 1964: 9–11). To do so necessitated land reform, in some cases the aggregation of agricultural workers on larger farms, and state inducement to move a surplus labor population from the countryside to the cities. By contrast, Schultz argued that land was not the limiting factor, nor was capital the primary engine of growth; it was human capital and the institutions that could support the adoption of more productive techniques. The human agent became the center of the Schultz development story, as opposed to the state's redistribution of land or the reorganization of the relations of production.

But there is also a larger context for Schultz's selection of evidence, theoretical frameworks, and statistical tests, which had to do with his training and identity as an economist. Among his group that focused on agricultural economics at Chicago, there was an ethic of service. In the agricultural economics of the land-grant system, service was mostly to the farmers and agribusiness operations of their state. For the Chicago agriculture group, however, accountability was more to a public that they chose and defined. They wanted to be free from the demands of any outside interest to shape their policy advice, and Schultz sought support from multiple sources of private foundations, federal research organs, and international research institutions to secure that freedom. In Schultz's view, the Chicago group's scientific questions and conclusions flowed from the data, not from their politics. Schultz and Griliches were also scientists of the state in the sense of providing special expertise in the measurement of the objects of government policy and of the effectiveness of the techniques of public services.

Schultz's expertise in agricultural modernization and international trade made him a natural fit for a national and international role as a policy adviser. In 1950, he was invited to join a group of experts charged by the secretary general of the United Nations with producing a report titled *Measures for the Economic Development of Under-developed Countries.* Schultz was the only member of the committee whose primary experience was in the economic problems of underdeveloped portions of a highly industrialized country. Among the others was Lewis, a professor of political economy at the University of Manchester who had begun his career in economic analysis at the Colonial Office of St. Lucia before the war.

It was with Lewis that Schultz would have the most intense disagreements over the nature of economic development and ultimately the nature of economic analysis. According to the historian Robert Tignor (2006: 84), Lewis had the greatest role in shaping the final report, which applied a new concept to the problem of economic development in poor countries. Although Schultz put his signature to the report, he was disturbed by Lewis's framing of the term *disguised unemployment,* which Lewis defined as "those persons who work in their own account and who are so numerous relative to the resources with which they work that if a number of them were withdrawn for work in other sectors of the economy, the total output of the sector from which they were withdrawn would not be diminished" (United Nations 1951: 7). According to this theory, a paucity of land and weak demand for overabundant supplies of labor were the cause of this underemployment in the countryside of developing countries. The solution was to be an emphasis on investment in urban industrialization rather than in agriculture, at a ratio of between 50 percent more in Latin America and six to one in East Asia (74–77). This was in line with the "Big Push" economic development proposals advocated by economists such as Paul Rosenstein-Rodan, whose 1943 paper "Problems of Industrialization in Eastern and Southeastern Europe" was obliquely referenced in the UN report. In this paper, Rosenstein-Rodan estimated a "surplus" population of underemployed in agriculture of 20 to 25 percent. Since almost all the available land was owned or under cultivation, the only apparent options for developing countries were rapid industrialization and land reform.[3] Essentially, this approach involved taxing the countryside by various means to finance rapid urban industrial development. Although the report warned against planning for the whole economy, one of the recommended interventions was in the domain of price controls, against which many in the Chicago economics department were already inveighing by this time (United Nations 1951: 66). But Schultz appeared to be most alarmed by the emphasis on exploiting agriculture as a lever of industrial development.

Lewis adapted concepts from classical economics to offer a different framework for understanding the sources of growth than those found in neoclassical or even Keynesian concepts. In Lewis's "dual sector" model, there is a capitalist sector and a subsistence sector. Rooted in his experiences in poorer countries, and particularly former colonial spaces, Lewis noted the apparent surplus of underemployed or unemployed people— from large farming families on small plots of land to large numbers of day laborers scrambling to get a single available job—and argued that the capital-intensive modernization in the cities would siphon off this surplus labor without an increase in wages. Further, he noted the legacy of imperialism, which set wages at the subsistence level in order to preserve peasants' dependence on the plantations.

Lewis did not claim that the subsistence sector was to be ignored. In fact, he argued that some kind of agricultural revolution always accompanied its industrial counterpart. But in his reading of the history of the development of Japan and the USSR, the surplus from this additional

3. Salim Rashid argues that the primary message of the UN report was land reform: "In many under-developed countries, the cultivators of the soil are exploited mercilessly by a landlord class which performs no useful social function. . . . In such countries land reform, abolishing this landlord class, is an urgent pre-requisite of agricultural progress" (United Nations 1951: 21). Elsewhere in the report, Schultz introduced more moderate language, but he did put his name to the report. His hostility to this prescription of agricultural modernization grew with its popularity. See Rashid 2018.

productivity was captured for use in capital formation by the industrial sector through taxation and others means: "This also defines for us the case in which it is true to say that it is agriculture which finances industrialization. . . . If the capitalist sector depends on the peasants for food, it is essential to get the peasant to produce more, while if at the same time they can be prevented from enjoying the full fruit of their production, wages can be reduced relatively to the capitalist surplus" (Lewis [1954] 2008: 434). Productivity increases in farming in an open-economy developing country would help plantation owners, not subsistence farmers, Lewis argued. That a proportion of workers in the agricultural sector displayed zero marginal productivity meant that they could profitably be transferred to the capitalist sector without affecting agricultural production significantly. In India, Lewis (1955: 327) wrote, "At least a quarter of the agricultural population is surplus to requirements," the same proportion identified by Rosenstein-Rodan for eastern and southern Europe.

Schultz was dismayed by the marginalization of the agricultural sector in Lewis's dual-sector model. He had spent the first half of his career analyzing the deep imbrication of agriculture and industry in the United States and the profound structural imbalances between the two sectors. The sectors were connected, in that an industrial-scientific-educational complex furnished and demonstrated technical innovations to farmers that increased agricultural productivity. The imbalance lay in the inelasticity of demand for agricultural products compared to industrial products, meaning greater income and supply challenges for farmers, especially smallholders, labor opportunities in the cities that went begging, all complicated by political pressure to enact policies that restored price relationships from a bygone era. Although this imbalance was the problem of an advanced industrial nation, it pointed to the centrality of agriculture to all processes of modernization. This freer-market framework was not laissez-faire capitalism; it included a crucial role for the state in fostering and sustaining this connection between the agricultural and industrial sectors, via the land-grant colleges, entrepreneurs, and extension services. Most important, it showed the mechanisms of transmission of modern knowledge and its uptake and adoption by farmers. So far, this assessment of imbalance could imply an approach similar to the "Big Push," capital-investment take-off theses that were rife in development economics in the 1950s. But the key to Schultz's analysis, in keeping with Chicago tradition, was respecting the operation of prices in the economy. And this very imbalance in the economy held out the prospect of *complementary* rather than exploitative growth in the two sectors.

The Parable of the Indian Flu

This concept of surplus agricultural labor in development economics, Schultz argued, had its roots in the misinterpretation of statistics concerning precisely this imbalance between the farm sector and the industrial sector of countries like the United States during the Great Depression. In *Transforming Traditional Agriculture*, Schultz claimed first that there was a misapprehension among development economists of the seasonal nature of agricultural labor.

> The tap root of this doctrine has been a set of bad statistical estimates that emerged from playing the game of treating agricultural production as if it could be organized to employ all agricultural workers ten hours a day the year round (Sundays and holidays off, of course), or of taking the combination of factors of production and the higher labor outputs that had been achieved in a technically more advanced country and applying the mix of factors to the poor agricultural country. (Schultz 1964: 58)

Schultz was in effect claiming that the observations of these growth economists indulged in theory at the expense of evidence, to the point that they ignored the low-level equilibrium of much agriculture in developing countries and the long-term disequilibria that arose from recent processes of agricultural modernization, from which the United States was itself still emerging. He argued that the claim of zero marginal productivity of labor in agriculture began to have consequences as it was applied to policy in developing countries. Despite the fact that in many low-income countries agriculture was the largest economic sector, they were either industrializing "without taking comparable measures to increase agricultural production" or were doing so at the expense of agriculture. To respond to this narrative, Schultz devoted a chapter of *Transforming Traditional Agriculture* to a study he and his students conducted to demonstrate that the zero marginal productivity of agricultural labor was a myth.

In his view, most of the disguised-unemployment advocates pointed to processes where capital was substituted for labor over time, or, as claimed earlier, they misinterpreted the seasonal nature of agricultural labor. Data during wartime were so distorted as to be nearly useless, undermining Rosenstein-Rodan's work on planning for a postwar Europe, for example. If disguised unemployment was a theory falsely supported by gradual substitutions of other inputs for agricultural labor, Schultz needed a kind of natural experiment that was much more sudden, so as to exclude confounding factor substitutions. A true test required a sudden change in circumstances in normal years of production. Schultz found such an experiment in the data on agricultural production in British India for two years, one before the flu epidemic of 1918–19 and one after. The agricultural labor force was reduced by 8 percent as a result of the epidemic, while acreage sown dropped from 265 million to 228 million from 1916–17 to 1917–18. But the following year's acreage was still 10 million below 1916–17.

Schultz asked what part of this change was due to the subtraction of labor from the countryside due to influenza. He began by pointing out that recent sample surveys of Indian agriculture indicated that the elasticity of output with respect to labor was .4, meaning a 10 percent reduction in labor would result in a 4 percent decrease in agricultural output, whereas the zero-marginal-productivity-of-labor hypothesis would suggest an elasticity of zero. He then chose one preepidemic year and one postepidemic year from the data for British India as a whole, explaining how his choice of which years to compare helped control for the impact of confounding weather events and other variational noise. His metric of agricultural productivity was acreage sown, which was both better measured and less sensitive to changes in labor supply than yield, offering a more decisive test. In the data for India as a whole, acreage had fallen by 3.8 percent, very close to the decline one would expect following an 8 percent decrease in labor supply if the relevant elasticity were .4. Then, to create a test that would allow an assessment of statistical significance, Schultz created a sample of province-level data for the two years, took death rates for each state, and adjusted them for the reported increase in mortality that was specific to working-age farmers to estimate the decline in each province's agricultural labor force. Following a suggestion of Dale Jorgensen, he correlated the state-level decline in labor supply with the decline in acreage sown from the preepidemic to the postepidemic year. The resulting estimate of the elasticity of acreage sown with respect to labor supply was .349 with a standard error of .076, an estimate, Schultz argued, that was statistically different from zero but not from the estimate of .4 for that elasticity from the more recent surveys.

Here Schultz was comparing just two years and three variables in order to provide a negative instance that he hoped would scuttle a popular tenet of development economics. If up to one quarter of the rural workforce had been surplus to the needs of the agricultural economy, he inferred that a sudden reduction in the working-age population would not have so closely matched the reduction in acreage sown. Moreover, the fact that these variables correlated so closely even as they varied from state to state lent credence to his analysis.

Of course, there are and were questions about the reliability of the data on which this inference was based, a point that Schultz himself raised in another context. One of his minor statistical criticisms in *Transforming Traditional Agriculture* was a cautionary tale about a paper given by a former student at Iowa State, Earl O. Heady. In Heady's Cobb-Douglas analysis of six classes of farms across India, Schultz argued that the returns to land, labor, and capital varied so extremely that there could be no explanation save for unreliable data. Schultz then deployed Hopper's account of the problems with data in India to draw his conclusion: "It is no wonder that the results of working with such data are so meaningless" (quoted in Heady 1960).

Schultz's flu parable, by contrast, was not the analysis of some secular trend but the comparison of two years of data. He was not in a position to know the comparability of the data on the composition of the workforce and the population from which the death rates were calculated, despite his best efforts to count only adults of working age. However, the care with which he chose his variables and the tight fit between them, even as production and market conditions varied from state to state, aimed to improve the persuasive power of his argument. The choice of India as a site for this test was apt, as the zero marginal productivity of labor doctrine was apparently especially favored by economists there (Bhagwati and Chakravarty 1969: 55). In this case, the parable here was that his carefully constructed and controlled statistical inference was an elegant refutation of the assumption, derived from structuralist theory, that there was surplus labor in agriculture due to low productivity and a superabundant population. This inference became a parable, the moral of which was that assumptions about the special nature of the development space needed to be carefully examined. This parable of the Indian flu, which could be reduced to a story of a few sentences, made possible a new orientation to the problem of economic development in low-income countries.

The Anthropology of "Poor but Efficient"

Having demonstrated that the agricultural labor market in a developing country was in fact quite tight, and that there was no significant idle proportion of the population waiting to be directed toward new factories in the cities, Schultz needed to find evidence for the agency of poor farmers who were capable of making rational decisions under new circumstances. Despite Schultz's years of experience running technical assistance programs in Latin America, Schultz turned to anthropologists to draw conclusions from two cases of low-income farmers in developing countries. Tax's *Penny Capitalism* gave Schultz some evidence to legitimate his conception of rational choice in a low-level equilibrium context. Noting the thrift and work ethic of farmers in developing countries, Schultz (1964: 28) argued that "incentives to work more than these people do are weak because the marginal productivity of labor is very low; and incentives to save more than they do are weak because the marginal productivity of capital is also very low." But Schultz's "sample" of the allocative efficiency of poor farmers was one village in Guatemala and another in India, which drew from the fieldwork of Tax and Hopper, respectively. It was not that traditional farmers were inefficient, the corollary of the disguised-unemployment narrative; rather, it was that they were as efficient as could be given the resources and knowledge they had, which made them potentially receptive to further education, research, and new technology. However, once a new input was introduced, the lags to adoption by farmers in low-income areas could be comparable to those of American farmers, as a fellow of the Chicago agriculture group, Raj Krishna (1963), found in his study of the Punjab in the 1930s.

Schultz's use of field studies is curious. Why would place and cultural practice matter to an economist steeped in neoclassical conceptions of economic behavior, who was more comfortable in the realm of statistical analysis than cultural anthropology? One could argue that there was an issue of the paucity of data on the subject of low-income farmers in developing countries. But the early 1960s was also a time of the boundary-blurring activities of economists, especially at Chicago. Indeed, the historian Philip Mirowski (2000: 928) argued that it was the excitement of the development decade of the 1960s that fueled a disciplinary expansion on the part of neoclassical economists into myriad policy and political domains, including that of anthropology: "Culture, initially posited as the residual category that the economy was not, was repeatedly and predictably absorbed back into the realm of the economic as the demands of consultancy and the exigencies of intellectual fashion permitted." If the domain of anthropology included the features of culture and custom rooted in the local, Schultz wished to show that rational responses to changes in the market as defined by economists were not outside culture and could challenge the anthropologist's penchant for explorations of complex, nonmonetary systems of gifting or mutual obligations. If the local knowledge claim ruptured the universal, Schultz turned this approach around. For example, he argued that in local instances in developing countries, rent was sometimes low or, if high, a function of a return to capital invested in the land (Schultz 1964: 97–99). The pattern in all of these examples is that each undercut the dominant view of agricultural stagnation in developing countries. Although these two cases, both of Tax and of Hopper, looked at cultural and economic practices in a locality, they both collected economic data, which showed that people reacted to changes in prices, for example. The statistical parable in these cases was that economic analysis using neoclassical tools in the development space was possible and productive. Schultz's packaging of these cases suggested a different orientation to the problem of development that did not require special economic theory to understand how low-income farmers behaved.

The Parable of the (Publicly Supported) Entrepreneurial Farmer

The fulcrum to Schultz's framework in *Transforming Traditional Agriculture* was the agent who could learn and adapt. In classical and neoclassical theory, there was land, labor, and capital as discrete categories. By contrast, the agriculture group at Chicago focused on investment in the recently articulated concept of human capital—used by both Schultz and recent Chicago PhD Gary Becker—which blurred the distinction between capital and labor. Schultz and others had in fact been using the term for years, if not decades. He worked with a number of graduate students, such as Griliches, on the returns to investments in technology and education and adapted Milton Friedman's idea of permanent income streams to the challenge of getting low-income farmers to invest in new techniques and technology. But the key piece was Griliches's work, which Schultz (1961) began showcasing in his publications from the beginning of the 1960s, which treated all techniques, research, and education as "industries" that produced new forms of capital.

Lewis, for one, was doubtful that research on returns to investment in education alone in developed countries was applicable to the challenges of poverty in developing countries. In 1961, he wrote:

> Some confusion has been caused by applying to these countries the conclusions of statisticians who try to measure the yield of education in rich countries, and who emerge with such conclusions as that the yield of

investment in humans exceeds the yield of investment of physical resources. In the first place, investment in humans is not to be equated with education, as normally conceived in institutional terms. Human capacity is improved by education, by public health, research, invention, institutional change, and better organization of human affairs, whether in business or in private or in public life. To attribute all improvement in productivity to education would therefore be more than a little naïve. Secondly, rich countries have a greater capacity to absorb the products of schools than have poor countries; so even if we could isolate the average yield of various types of education in rich countries, this would throw no light on the marginal yield of similar types in poor (or for that matter in rich) countries. (Lewis 1961: 114)

If this was a critique of Chicago economics research on returns to investment in education, it is a misinterpretation, as all the additional factors that Lewis points to are included in Schultz's conception of "investment in humans." But Lewis did identify the weakness of other parts of Schultz's argument: applying inferences from statistical research in agriculture in the United States to the development space.

Although *Transforming Traditional Agriculture* challenged the shibboleth of disguised unemployment with inferences from the case of the Indian flu, it appeared to proceed from another fundamental tenet, supported more by assumption than evidence: that poor farmers are rational, efficient actors who respond to prices. Schultz acknowledged that the rationality of extreme poverty already looked different from that in developed countries. The cost of adopting new techniques or inputs was almost always prohibitively high, leading to a correspondingly rational aversion to risk among the very poor. The key, he argued, was investment in research to develop techniques that could be adapted to the needs of low-income farmers and demonstrated and supported to overcome the risk of adoption.

Schultz was attempting to provide counternarratives to structuralist economic plans promoted by any number of development economists, but he was not averse to planning per se. In fact, he had spent the previous two decades working for think tanks that promoted policy planning for the state support of market-oriented agricultural development in the United States (Burnett 2011b). At the beginning of the United Nations Decade of Development, however, both education and the rural sector took a back seat to industrialization. All eyes were on the planners in the 1960s, and Schultz sought more and better evidence for the importance of human capital in development. He turned his student Griliches toward the question of the residual "technological change" in growth models, such as those of Robert M. Solow, and Griliches set about developing statistical strategies to identify the drivers of technological change in the data. One of Griliches's landmark contributions to statistics and development economics was based on his dissertation, in which he created plots of the rate of hybrid corn adoption against time for a number of states and then fit logistic curves to those graphs. Examining the graphs, he noted the lags in both the time at which the hybrid corn technology became available and its uptake by farmers in each state. What is often noted about this research is that certain assumptions needed to fit the logistic curves were not made arbitrarily; they were assigned based on detailed and numerous conversations and observations with experiment station scientists and farmers. Chicago colleagues Harberger, Tolley, and Lester Telser repeatedly described their research as involving direct experience of the markets, labor factors, and technological systems under study in order to guide the development of statistical tests and their interpretation (Tolley 2020: 45).

What Griliches found was that the lags in adoption represented a careful calculus on the part of the seed producers to gauge the size of the prospective market, the cost of marketing, the cost of innovating for the target area, and the rate of acceptance. Some of his statistical innovations were in fact derived from those metrics used by the seed companies themselves to estimate the marketability of their product in a given area. Market size was measured not by geographic area but by a variable that indicated the average corn acreage in an area multiplied by the target adoption rate of hybrid corn divided by the total land in farms in that area. By running multiple regressions, Griliches found the strongest association between the date the technology became available and market density. In other words, the seed companies first rolled out their innovations in the areas that were likely to be the most profitable: "While these results may not be too conclusive, together with information gathered in conversations with executives in the industry and a graphical survey of the data, they leave little doubt in my mind that the development of hybrid corn was largely guided by expected pay-off, 'better areas' being entered first, even though it may be difficult to measure very well the variables entering into those calculations" (Griliches 1957: 515).

There are two striking lessons detailed in the paper's final footnotes: the extraordinary returns to public investment in the hybrid corn seed industry—on which he elaborated in a paper the following year—and his conclusion that the economic variables overwhelmed the sociological variations in the process of technological change (Griliches 1957: 522). Griliches had earlier noted that the adoption rate on "marginal farms"— farms that planted a low proportion of corn to their total plantings, that were more dispersed, and that were therefore harder to reach by both seed companies and extension services—was much lower than on the early- adopter farms. Such plantings were also harder to track statistically, since only a portion was used for market, the rest being used for feed or family consumption. Such a farm would be more analogous to many of the farms in developing countries, but Schultz was undeterred by his enthusiasm for the promise and significance of Griliches's research. The adoption rates were slower and lower but still profitable if adopted. The lags and varia- tion in adoption pointed to the importance of sustained public and private applied research in adapting and marketing new technologies. And for profitable technologies, the ultimate extent of adoption was rather uniform across multiple sociological criteria, hinting at the greater prevalence of rational economic decision-making across farm size, types, capitalization, and location. The lesson in this parable was that farmers respond to dem- onstrations of profitable new techniques and technologies despite varia- tions in level of income, distance from markets, or other factors.

Accounting for Growth

Schultz had long argued for the returns to investment in research in agri- culture and had attempted some calculations of these at the national level in *The Economic Organization of Agriculture* in 1953. What Griliches did in his 1958 paper was to quantify the social returns to public investment: "Almost none of the calculated social returns from hybrid corn were appropriated by the hybrid seed industry or by producers. They were passed on to consumers in the form of lower prices and higher output." Public investment in agricultural research and extension worked in har- mony with the inelasticity of demand for important crops that was part of Schultz's framework for the imbalance of modern agriculture. A compar- atively modest investment in human capital produced tremendous social returns through the operation of the market. But the investment needed to be public, as the "incentive for private investment was very much smaller than implied by the social rate of return," given the difficulty of securing the intellectual property rights of the seeds or any kind of long-run monopoly position (Griliches 1958: 430).[4]

With the evolving body of work of Griliches and other students, Schultz believed he had the evidence to investigate and clarify the problems with the growth models, particularly Solow's. In *Transforming Traditional Agriculture*, Schultz cited recent work by Griliches that was part of his long-range econometric study of the sources of productivity growth. In this work, Griliches had pointed out the difficulties in accurately aggregating measurements in growth models and argued that much of the residual variable in production functions could be explained if variables were properly specified, measured, and weighted. In studying the sources of productivity growth in US agriculture, Griliches found that the conventional approach to studying the sources of economic growth contained incorrect assumptions about the relative importance of growth in the capital stock and growth in the labor force in their contributions to overall growth, in part because they ignored the imbalances between the agricultural and industrial economies that Schultz had been documenting for the previous two decades. Rather than assuming the values for these elasticities of output with respect to labor and capital, Griliches derived them from a statistically estimated production function for the agricultural sector, finding values that were quite different from those assumed in the conventional approach. After correcting for these differences, Griliches (1963: 332) could explain the mysterious residual "technical change" of Solow-type growth models, after all, by improvements in the quality of labor as a result of education; improvements in the quality of machinery services; underestimation of the contribution of capital and overestimation of the contribution of labor to output growth; and economies of scale. With a production function that now stressed the more specific factors that appeared to make the most difference in agricultural modernization, Schultz (1964: 143) advocated that "in order to break this dependency, farmers situated in traditional agriculture must somehow acquire, adopt, and learn how to use effectively a profitable new set of factors." The lesson Schultz draws from this statistical parable is that investment in human capital is not just an important aspect of economic growth; it is the most important factor.

---

4. Historians have subsequently pointed out that the breeding of hybrid varieties is itself a form of intellectual property protection, as seed-saving of hybrids by farmers results in losses of the initial gains from the hybrid variety, and the hybrid plants have already lost the distinguishing characteristics that made plant breeding by farmers possible (Fitzgerald 1993).

Transforming Traditional Agriculture marked an inflection point in the trajectory of development economics. The field, like agricultural economics, had defined itself as a set of theories and policy tools to deal with a specific historical context. Agricultural economics in the United States was born as a policy science even before it was an academic discipline. An active Bureau of Agricultural Economics in the US government was founded in the post–World War I agricultural depression, just three years after the establishment of the *Journal of Farm Economics* in 1919.[5] Development economics emerged from the crisis of the Cold War, postcolonial world. Both of these applied subdisciplines of economics evolved to cope with the problem of inequality generated by the structural and structured imbalance between the agricultural and industrial sectors of countries. In both cases, because these imbalances had arisen partly through international trade, the solution was often understood to be the state management of international trade to reduce inequality and provide opportunities for disadvantaged groups. Economists of each subdiscipline were asked to provide solutions to give a prescribed "just" outcome: a fair price for wheat pegged to an index of prices pre–World War I, or a five-year plan for the construction of a steel industry in India.

Members of the Chicago agriculture group had already had decades of experience dealing with mechanisms to provide "economic justice" for farmers in US agriculture and saw familiar dead ends when they looked to the nascent development economics. They were now fully engaged in both domestic agriculture and international development and concluded that markets did not generate the injustice; they were the medium through which long-run problems of modernization were to be addressed. This is what their market fundamentalism meant to them: to identify the forces of modernization and move societies more or less in harmony with them. Schultz declared the peasant farmer *homo economicus*, capable of discernment and action and economic progress. This did not translate to laissez-faire policy advocacy, however. Much has been made of some Chicago economists' opposition to the substantial foreign aid programs of the 1950s and 1960s, and Friedman on several occasions called for the dismantling of the US Department of Agriculture (Strassman 1976: 70). But Schultz's agriculture group did not deny the importance of state invest-

---

5. For more on the sophistication and reach of the Bureau of Agricultural Economics, see Biddle, this volume. The early importance of agricultural economists as bureaucrats in the US government contrasts with the later ascendance of the general economics profession in the US government during and especially after World War II. See Bernstein 2001; and Burnett 2008: 46–62.

ment in agriculture, either domestically or abroad; on the contrary, they promoted aid and government support as essential to economic growth. The emphasis, however, was on education and extension in the domains in which the recipient economies had potential.

What emerges from this portrait of Schultz is a basic policy orientation that shaped his use and interpretation of statistics. First, he possessed a great skepticism of newer models of mixed-market and command economies. He was opposed to development economics on principle, as it presupposed the creation of special economic tools to understand what he viewed to be classical and neoclassical problems of international trade and project management. True, he was trained as an agricultural economist, but he was also an expert in international trade and macroeconomics and understood his discipline to be a set of tools rather than a particular domain of application. Second, Schultz considered the state an essential midwife of market-oriented development. As a corollary to this, he and his colleagues revived and repurposed nineteenth-century tools of benefit-cost analysis to facilitate governance that was more consonant with market forces. They embraced simple but powerful ways to understand specific economic problems, partly because some of them believed that policymakers would be more likely to use them. Third, long experience with policy failures taught them to support gradual and cautious policy interventions. This is why statistical parables in *Transforming Traditional Agriculture* took the form they did. The chief audience and client of the agriculture group was the bureaucrat at the State Department, the foundation head, the economist at the World Bank, or the future finance minister of Chile or of Taiwan.[6]

In the 1960s, Lewis and Schultz formed two significant points in the constellation of development economics. By then, the capital-intensive, industry-centered growth economics had already begun to suffer setbacks as the imbalances of this approach began to reveal themselves and as the world economy tumbled into economic crisis in the 1970s. Lewis himself became deeply involved in advising the Ghanaian government on the Akosombo Dam project, which was plagued by debt, construction, and marketing problems (Tignor 2006: 195–97). Meanwhile, the Green Revolution

---

6. "I believe that in order for us to have influence in those discussions, we absolutely have to talk a language that these other guys can understand. And we cannot think that they're all graduates of Harvard, and MIT, and Stanford. They are people, some of whom have never had a course in economics, and some may have had one or two, and very few will have had more. We have to be able to make them understand what we're talking about" (Schultz quoted in Harberger 2016: 125).

proved at least a partial and temporary vindication for Schultz's vision for development through investment in training, demonstration, and a suite of modern agricultural inputs. The Chicago agriculture group consulted more and more for governments around the world. Harberger seeded an Argentinian economics program with Chilean economists and personally trained dozens of finance ministers of various countries. Tolley advised South Korea on rice price policy, and D. Gale Johnson and Schultz were active in Taiwan and China after 1978, bringing a succession of Chinese cohorts to Chicago in the 1980s to be students of Tolley and Johnson, and informal mentees of Schultz, who had officially retired in 1967. Over the years, *Transforming Traditional Agriculture* was translated into many languages, including Mandarin, with a softcover edition published in China in 2000. Schultz's last student, Justin Yifu Lin, went on to become chief economist at the World Bank and to write several books on Chinese agricultural development that contained several of the basic frameworks that Schultz outlined decades ago. It is perhaps a sign of the apotheosis of the Chicago agriculture group's advocacy that William Easterly's (2001, 2006) critical histories of development economics in the 2000s were governed by the agriculture group's critical framework, with no mention of any of them.

In the end, both Lewis and Schultz were partly right. Both were intervening in a sector with scarce data and were extrapolating from complex statistical relationships and time series of better-known phenomena. Developing countries with more highly developed state infrastructure and the right natural endowments were better able to take on some of the transformations described by Schultz. Other countries had a level of poverty, higher rates of population growth, and a paucity of natural endowments that made such transformations more of a challenge, as Lewis had warned in the 1950s (Otsuka 2006). Lewis ([1954] 2008: 413) thought that fine-grained statistical tests and analysis were neither possible nor useful in countries that lacked good information about producers on the margins of society. It is perhaps fitting that both economists shared the Bank of Sweden Prize in Economic Sciences in Memory of Alfred Nobel, even if their ideas about economic development were difficult to reconcile. Lewis was a champion of the special considerations needed to deal with the challenges of extremely poor, mostly rural countries. Schultz argued for his part that even the poorest of economies could do much better if the right combination of supports were in place to take advantage of the increased productivity afforded by new technological systems with which the West had only recently become familiar.

Schultz's use of his own and Griliches's cases revealed a strong desire to inject rigor into a world of what they viewed as political imaginaries of rapid change, whether capitalist or socialist. Although I take seriously their belief that their conclusions derived from their scientific interpretation of the data, it is also understood in the history of science that researchers' backgrounds and life experiences shape their approach to scientific work, even if this influence results in a steadfast commitment to an understanding of objectivity and truth that is isolated or isolable from the world of mundane politics or ideology. I have already mentioned the defining crucible of the Chicago agriculture group in the exodus of Schultz, Johnson, and others from Iowa State College to Chicago. But there is also Schultz's coming of age in a poorer farm state of South Dakota during the catastrophic agricultural recession after World War I, and his encounters with collective farms in the Soviet Union. Johnson and Arcadius Kahan spent decades studying the economics of Soviet agriculture, which reinforced their dim view of command agricultural planning. There is Griliches, a Lithuanian immigrant who had suffered the terror of the advancing Soviet Army before being placed in a Jewish ghetto by the Nazis. And there is Tolley, whose father, Howard, ran the Bureau of Agricultural Economics during its most controversial period during World War II and who was fired for the bureau's conduct of politically inconvenient social research in the South. Each of these social scientists had direct life experience with the heavy hand of either the state or organized private interests, and most of them had grown up witnessing the challenges of agricultural modernization. The pursuit of a development policy because it appeared to mimic the capital-intensive developmentalism of the Soviets was uninteresting to them, as was lending economic legitimacy to this or that demand for rapid social change. Statistics was partly a refuge, a way to transform politically insoluble challenges into tractable problems that might be solved over the longer run.

Given this background, there is a question about the influence and uptake of *Transforming Traditional Agriculture*. For whom were these statistical parables exemplary and instructive? Certainly, despite his sharing the Bank of Sweden economics prize with Lewis for his contributions to development economics, Schultz is more or less absent from academic histories of economic development, which tend to focus on the achievements and conversations among academic departments of development studies or among particular disciplines perceived to be more closely associated with development. The journal of record of agricultural economists in the United States, for example, all but ignored the book save for an ambivalent review by Walter Falcon twenty-four years after its publication: "The book was widely discussed because it was controversial. Scholars debated Schultz because the data that shaped his findings were meager and because his arguments were often made by a combination of assertion and faith." The data were indeed meager, but this is partly because *Transforming Traditional Agriculture* is a didactic text containing statistical parables. It is largely a narrative exposition of the problems with conventional narratives of governance and technical assistance in the development space. Falcon's (1988: 199) criticisms point to the book's nature as a compendium of statistical studies explained as parables to inform policy: "One of the volume's appealing aspects was its readability. There were no equations, little jargon, and few numbers." Schultz (1964: 115) himself wrote, "Even when an investigator is not carried away by doctrinal drifts, he will find it hard to navigate his inquiry through the tangled empirical float." This was Schultz's audience: the educated bureaucrat who needed to implement policy in an international institution or in a developing country. The parables challenged the poverty of existing theory with empirical data and warned against drawing conclusions based on assumptions or on unreliable data. They represented Schultz's experience with the transformative power of research, technology, entrepreneurship, and extension that produced American agricultural modernity. But they also distracted attention from whatever social and cultural factors might shape or determine a particular farmer's access to land, resources, credit, and education.

As scientists of the state, there was a relatively strong consensus among agricultural economists after World War II about which aspects of society were appropriate areas to investigate. The development of techniques to measure the social costs and benefits of state-funded research and extension in agriculture were part of the mission. By contrast, investigations of race relations in the South resulted eventually in the dismantling of the Bureau of Agricultural Economics in 1953, despite Schultz's vocal protests to stop this slow death of economic intelligence-gathering in the US Department of Agriculture. The personal risks of doing such research were simply too high for economists who wished to have influence at the highest levels of government.[7]

7. To be clear, there were agricultural economists who worked on land reform and other economic justice issues. Paul S. Taylor of UC Berkeley, for example, worked for years to study and assist the farmworkers movement in California. This field of study is considered rural sociology. For more on agricultural economics and the politics of redistribution in farming in the United States, see Gilbert 2015.

Esther Duflo (2006) wrote that development discourse revolved around Schultz's "poor but efficient hypothesis" about farmers in developing countries for years after its publication, only to be superseded in the 1990s by a renewed exploration of the particular economic considerations of the poor, beyond risk aversion. There are, of course, established cultural and institutional norms that frame who gets access to which resources. It is a glaring blind spot in *Transforming Traditional Agriculture*, even though some of Schultz's colleagues had already begun to look at the impact of race, for example, on the tendency of American farmers to stay in farming and take advantage of new techniques and technologies (Tolley and Hjort 1963; Tolley 1970). But the fact of Schultz's tentative embrace of some anthropology in the early 1960s was a precursor to Duflo's more fully integrated and critical economic anthropology of poverty. And the inference from the research of Griliches—that poor farmers could respond to incentives given the right opportunities, education, and mechanisms to overcome their aversion to risk—found partial confirmation in Duflo's social experiments with extension work. What her research revealed is that the intensity required of these human capital investments that Schultz recommended has proved far greater than anticipated and in many cases are overshadowed by the social factors that were beyond his framework.

Schultz's parables in *Transforming Traditional Agriculture* served as exemplars, especially with respect to the agricultural sectors of middle-income developing countries in South America and Asia, through three conduits: the training of economists who then served as organic intellectuals in state institutions of developing countries; direct consulting by the Chicago agriculture group economists with leaders of state agencies, especially in China, Taiwan, South Korea, Chile, Argentina, Brazil, and numerous other countries; and the harmony between the focus of Schultz's multidecade research program and the evaluative exigencies of American and international aid institutions. The state has difficulty engaging with those at the margins of its reach, about whom the least is known and against whom the most is projected. It is a point made repeatedly by anthropological critiques of development economics (Escobar 1995; Scott 1999; Ferguson 1990). Taken as a whole, the statistical parables in *Transforming Traditional Agriculture* served as the advocacy of an antipolitics machine (Ferguson 1990), elevating science-based, state-led investment in education and technical assistance in rural areas in place of redistributive schemes or plans rooted in what they viewed as excessively theoretical abstraction. These parables were more effective as narrative vehicles for the dissemination of a set of values and policy orientations than as proof of the effectiveness of a suite of techniques and technologies.

References

Bernstein, Michael. 2001. *A Perilous Progress: Economists and Public Purpose in Twentieth-Century America.* Princeton, NJ: Princeton University Press.

Bhagwati, Jagdish N., and Sukhamoy Chakravarty. 1969. "Contributions to Indian Economic Analysis: A Survey." *American Economic Review* 59, no. 4: 1–73.

Burnett, Paul. 2008. *The Visible Land: Agricultural Economics, US Export Agriculture, and International Development, 1918–65.* PhD diss., University of Pennsylvania.

Burnett, Paul. 2011a. "Academic Freedom or Political Maneuvers: Theodore W. Schultz and the Oleomargarine Controversy Revisited." *Agricultural History* 85, no. 3: 373–97.

Burnett, Paul. 2011b. "The Price Is Not Right: Theodore W. Schultz, Policy Planning, and Agricultural Economics in the Cold-War United States." In *Building Chicago Economics: New Perspectives on the History of America's Most Powerful Economics Program*, edited by Robert Van Horn, Philip Mirowski, and Thomas Stapleford, 67–92. Cambridge: Cambridge University Press.

Cartwright, Nancy, and Robin Le Poidevin. 1991. "Facts and Fables." *Proceedings of the Aristotelian Society, Supplementary Volumes* 65: 55–82.

Duflo, Esther. 2006. "Poor but Rational?" In *Understanding Poverty*, edited by A. Banerjee, R. Benabou, and D. Mukerjee, 367–78. Oxford: Oxford University Press.

Easterly, William. 2001. *The Elusive Quest for Growth: Economists' Adventures and Misadventures in the Tropics.* Cambridge, MA: MIT Press.

Easterly, William. 2006. *The White Man's Burden: Why the West's Efforts to Aid the Rest Have Done So Much Harm and So Little Good.* New York: Penguin.

Escobar, Arturo. 1995. *Encountering Development: The Making and Unmaking of the Third World.* Princeton, NJ: Princeton University Press.

Falcon, Walter. 1988. Review of "Transforming Traditional Agriculture." *American Journal of Agricultural Economics* 70, no. 1: 198–200.

Ferguson, James. 1990. *The Anti-Politics Machine: "Development," Depoliticization, and Bureaucratic Power in Lesotho.* New York: Cambridge University Press.

Fitzgerald, Deborah. 1993. "Farmers Deskilled: Hybrid Corn and Farmers' Work." *Technology and Culture* 34, no. 4: 324–43.

Gilbert, Jess. 2015. *Planning Democracy: Agrarian Intellectuals and the Intended New Deal.* New Haven, CT: Yale University Press.

Griliches, Zvi. 1957. "Hybrid Corn: An Exploration in the Economics of Technological Change." *Econometrica* 27, no. 4: 501–22.

Griliches, Zvi. 1958. "Research Costs and Social Returns: Hybrid Corn and Related Innovations." *Journal of Political Economy* 66, no. 5: 419–31.

Griliches, Zvi. 1963. "The Sources of Measured Productivity Growth: United States Agriculture, 1940–60." *Journal of Political Economy* 71, no. 4: 331–46.

Harberger, Arnold. 2016. "Sense and Economics: An Oral History with Arnold Harberger." Conducted by Paul Burnett in 2015 and 2016. Oral History Center, Bancroft Library, University of California, Berkeley.

Heady, Earl O. 1960. "Techniques of Production, Size of Productive Units, and Factor Supply Conditions." Paper presented at the Social Science Research Council on Relations between Agriculture and Economic Growth, Stanford University,

Hunt, Diana. 1989. *Economic Theories of Development: An Analysis of Competing Paradigms.* Savage, MD: Barnes & Noble.

Krishna, Raj. 1963. "Farm Supply Response in India-Pakistan: A Case Study of the Punjab Region." *Economic Journal* 73, no. 21: 477–87.

Leys, Colin. 1996. *The Rise and Fall of Development Theory.* Bloomington: Indiana University Press.

Lewis, W. Arthur. (1954) 2008. "Economic Development with Unlimited Supplies of Labor." In *On Models of Development: Unpublished Manuscripts,* edited by Phil Leeson. Manchester: University of Manchester.

Lewis, W. Arthur. 1955. *The Theory of Economic Growth.* London: Allen and Irwin.

Lewis, W. Arthur. 1961. "Education and Economic Development." *Social and Economic Studies* 10, no. 2: 113–37.

Mirowski, Philip. 2000. "Exploring the Fault Lines: Introduction to the Minisymposium on the History of Economic Anthropology." *History of Political Economy* 32, no. 4: 919–32.

Morgan, Mary. 2011. "Travelling Facts." In *How Well Do Facts Travel? The Dissemination of Reliable Knowledge,* edited by Peter Howlett and Mary Morgan, 3–39. New York: Cambridge University Press.

Morgan, Mary. 2019. "Exemplification and Use-Values in Cases and Case-Studies." *Studies in the History and Philosophy of Science* 78 (2019): 5–13.

Otsuka, Keijiro. 2006. "Why Can't We Transform Traditional Agriculture in Sub-Saharan Africa?" *Review of Agricultural Economics* 23, no. 3: 332–37.

Rashid, Salim. 2018. "From Anxiety to Nonchalance: 'Neoclassical Economic Development' from 1950 to 2000." In *The Political Economy of Development Economics: A Historical Perspective,* edited by Michele Alacevich and Mauro Boianovsky. *History of Political Economy* 50 (supplement): 286–302.

Rosenstein-Rodan, P. N. 1943. "Problems of Industrialization in Eastern and Southeastern Europe." *Economic Journal* 53, nos. 210–11: 202–11.

Schultz, Theodore. 1953. *The Economic Organization of Agriculture.* New York: McGraw-Hill.

Schultz, Theodore. 1961. "Investment in Human Capital." *American Economic Review* 51, no. 1: 1–17.

Schultz, Theodore. 1964. *Transforming Traditional Agriculture.* New Haven, CT: Yale University Press.

Scott, James C. 1999. *Seeing Like a State: How Certain Schemes to Improve the Human Condition Have Failed.* New Haven, CT: Yale University Press.

Strassmann, Paul W. 1976. "Development Economics from a Chicago Perspective." *Journal of Economic Issues* 10, no. 1: 63–80.

Tax, Sol. 1953. *Penny Capitalism: A Guatemalan Indian Economy.* Washington, DC: Smithsonian Institution, Institute of Social Anthropology.

Tignor, Robert. 2006. *W. Arthur Lewis and the Birth of Development Economics.* Princeton, NJ: Princeton University Press.

Tolley, George S. 1970. "Management Entry into US Agriculture." *American Journal of Agricultural Economics* 52, no. 4: 485–93.

Tolley, George S. 2020. "George S. Tolley: From Agricultural to Resource, Urban, and Health Economics at the University of Chicago," conducted by Paul Burnett in 2018, Oral History Center, Bancroft Library, University of California, Berkeley.

Tolley, George S., and H. W. Hjort. 1963. "Age-Mobility and Southern Farmer Skill: Looking Ahead for Area Development." *Journal of Farm Economics* 45, no. 1: 31–46.

Tribe, Keith. 2018. "The Colonial Office and British Development Economics, 1940–60." In *The Political Economy of Development Economics: A Historical Perspective,* edited by Michele Alacevich and Mauro Boianovsky. *History of Political Economy* 50 (supplement): 97–113.

United Nations. 1951. *Measures for the Economic Development of Under-Developed Countries.* New York: United Nations Department of Economic Affairs.

Statistical Inference in Economics in the 1920s and 1930s: The Crop and Livestock Forecasts of the US Department of Agriculture

Jeff Biddle

Broadly speaking, statistical inference refers to the process by which one uses information obtained from samples of statistical data to draw conclusions about phenomena beyond those recorded in the samples. Since the 1970s, statistical inference in economics has almost invariably involved, as a central element, inferential measures derived from probability theory, such as the standard error of a regression coefficient. Prior to World War II, however, even the most technically sophisticated empirical economic researchers were reluctant to make these measures an important part of their argument when using descriptive statistics calculated from sample data to make claims about the wider world (Biddle 2017). This lack of confidence in inferential measures based on probability theory was typically an element of a broader positive approach to statistical inference. Researchers in this period occasionally articulated principles to follow in assessing the reliability of sample statistics as indicators of characteristics of more general economic phenomena. More often, however, one must discern the prevailing guidelines for conducting statistical inference by examining economists' practices.

In this article I provide a case study of the approach to statistical inference adopted by an important group of empirical economists working in the 1920s and 1930s—those employed by the Bureau of Agricultural

The article has benefited from the comments of the participants in the *HOPE* conference on the history of statistical inference, as well as those of Spencer Banzhaf.

History of Political Economy 53 (annual suppl.) DOI 10.1215/00182702-9414775

Economics (BAE) in the US Department of Agriculture. This group of economists had a knowledge of statistical theory and method well beyond that of the average empirical economist of the time. They also had access to a great deal of economic data and to resources needed to process those data. BAE economists of the 1920s and 1930s were involved in a variety of empirical research projects in the service of the bureau's broad mission of "disseminating information of current interest and immediate value to farmers" while also conducting "studies of long time problems" intended to "form the basis of wise policies for future agricultural developments" (USDA 1924–35: 1925 report, 1).

One of the more important activities of the BAE, at least in terms of the resources devoted to it, was the production of crop and livestock estimates and forecasts. The BAE was responsible for making, on a regular basis, "estimates" of the quantities of numerous agricultural products that had actually been harvested or marketed in the very recent past and also "forecasts" of the quantities of various crops and animals likely to be brought to market in the near future. In 1923, the BAE made about fifty thousand such estimates and forecasts at a cost of four hundred thousand dollars, or about six million dollars in today's currency (Pearson 1924), and the scope of the program grew steadily through the 1920s.

In this article, I focus on the problem of making crop and livestock forecasts. In particular, I describe the BAE's program for forecasting hog production, which relied on sample data from surveys of farmers about the number of pigs recently born on their farms, and the BAE's procedures for forecasting crop yields, which used data provided by knowledgeable observers about the health of a crop in their area to predict the eventual yield per acre of that crop. Both of these tasks are clearly examples of statistical inference as defined at the start of this article—the use of sample data to draw conclusions about phenomena not described in the sample.

Statistical forecasting, at least when the quantity being forecast is easily observable, is a form of statistical inference with an interesting feature: comparisons between what is forecast and what is actually realized provide a repeated test of the materials and methods used as the basis of inference. Persistent deviations between the forecast and reality can lead to a reassessment of materials and methods; this was certainly true for the BAE crop and livestock forecasting program, as illustrated below.

Another peculiarity of the case of crop and livestock forecasting as an example of statistical inference in economics bears mentioning. The problem of creating good crop and livestock forecasts was, for these empirical economists, almost entirely a problem of applied statistics, and involved very little in the way of applying economic theory.[1] So, by choosing to examine crop and livestock forecasting, I am sidestepping some important questions that would be central in most case studies of how economists have done statistical inference, such as: What role did economic theory play in their process of statistical inference? How did it affect economists' decisions about what sample statistics would provide the firmest basis for making inferences about the phenomena of interest? How did it influence the generalizations they were actually willing to make on the basis of those statistics? An advantage of looking at this case, however, is that the absence of major economic theoretical considerations allows a clearer view of how economists of this period handled the more purely statistical problems involved in making generalizations from sample data.

My article has two major purposes. The first is to describe, and illustrate through examples, a general approach to statistical inference that dominated the practice of empirical economics in the United States during the interwar period. The second is to portray the nature of empirical economic research at this time, that is, how researchers creatively employed statistical analysis to answer the questions that intrigued them.

In the next section, I provide some institutional background for my case study, first describing the origin and purposes of the USDA's crop and livestock estimation program, and then the emergence of the BAE in the 1920s as a leading center for applied statistical research. I next describe the general approach to statistical inference shared by BAE economists. This approach is consistent with, and was demonstrably influenced by, ideas found in J. M. Keynes's *Treatise on Probability* on statistical inference. I summarize Keynes's arguments and document the presence of the same arguments in the writings of BAE economists and other economists in the 1920s and early 1930s. This is followed by my accounts of methods of statistical inference developed for two of the BAE's forecasting activities: forecasting hog production and forecasting crop yields.

---

1. This is in contrast, for example, to the case of price forecasting, another inferential activity of the BAE. Price forecasting required the economist to make assumptions about which of many measurable factors might be related to the price of an agricultural product and to develop a strategy to measure those relationships. An important source for such assumptions was the general theory of supply and demand, augmented by further theorizing about how the relationships portrayed in the general theory would be mediated by the institutions of specific agricultural markets. See Haas and Ezekiel 1926 for a leading example and Banzhaf 2006 for a historian's account of BAE price forecasting.

The Crop and Livestock Forecasts of the USDA

When the US Department of Agriculture was established in 1862, it was understood that one of its duties would be to collect and disseminate agricultural statistics, including estimates and forecasts of the nation's production of important crops and livestock varieties.[2] The stated justifications for having this be a responsibility of the federal government remained fairly consistent up through the 1920s. One common argument was that ignorance of the true planted acreage and condition of certain major crops in the field fueled speculation in the markets for those crops. Asymmetric information was a problem as well: "middlemen" were believed to be able to obtain privately at least some information on actual and prospective supplies of various farm commodities, giving them an advantage in bargaining over their "individual and isolated countrymen" working on farms. The collection and general dissemination of accurate information by a trusted and objective agency, it was held, would significantly mitigate these problems.

It was also argued that accurate information on likely agricultural output would help farmers operate more profitably, leading them to shift away from the production of crops likely to be in surplus and toward crops for which demand looked to be high relative to supply. This argument supported efforts to produce ever earlier forecasts of likely production, so as to allow farmers time to change plans in response to indications of impending surpluses and shortages. (It was not lost on USDA crop forecasters that success in altering the plans of farmers would lead to inaccuracy in the forecasts.)

And, the argument went, farmers were not the only economic decision-makers who would benefit from accurate estimates of the quantities produced of various crops. Bankers in rural counties considering loan applications, railroads allocating cars to the movement of harvested crops, and dealers in agricultural commodities making decisions about inventories all had reason to want better estimates of the amount of the various agricultural commodities being brought to market.

The idea that frequent wide swings in the prices of agricultural commodities was a problem for the nation as a whole, and one that could be ameliorated by accurate crop and livestock forecasts, was present in the rhetoric of the Department of Agriculture from its founding and grew in importance as time went on. A chief cause of unstable farm prices was

---

2. This section draws on Taylor and Taylor 1952: chap. 12; and USDA 1969: 18–65.

believed to be the tendency of farmers to base the coming year's production decisions on the previous year's prices, so that a high price last year led to overproduction and a low price this year. With agricultural prices being an important determinant of income for a large share of the American population, these price fluctuations could have harmful reverberations throughout the economy. If, rather than reacting to last year's prices, farmers acted on the basis of accurate forecasts of other farmers' initial production intentions (demand being believed to be relatively stable over time), the instability of agricultural prices would be reduced.

From its establishment in the 1860s, the USDA collected the data on which it based its crop and livestock estimates and forecasts from an army of volunteer "reporters" who would provide information on such things as acreage planted, the "condition of the crops," or the change in livestock populations in their area. Ideally, reporters would be knowledgeable about agriculture and their local community and engaged in farming or some farm-related occupation. A much smaller group of paid employees of the USDA and the state agricultural agencies would collate the reported information and maintain regular communication with the reporters, in hopes of providing guidance that improved the quality of the information flow. As of the 1920s and 1930s, the USDA was relying on the voluntary efforts of tens of thousands of local reporters to provide the raw data underlying the crop and livestock forecasts.[3]

Overall, the history of the crop and livestock forecasting activities of the USDA prior to 1920 is marked by many successful efforts to improve methods in light of inaccurate forecasts. However, in the 1920s, the whole way of thinking about making and improving crop forecasts at the USDA changed significantly, as the task became the responsibility of a remarkable group of empirical economists gathered at the newly created Bureau of Agricultural Economics.

Agricultural Economics and the Creation of the Bureau of Agricultural Economics

Over the first three decades of the twentieth century in the United States, social scientists self-identifying as "agricultural economists" became a distinct professional group, believed to possess expertise highly relevant

---

3. For an excellent description of the USDA's data collection program during 1890–1930, see Didier 2012.

to the making of agricultural policy.[4] One point of entry for economists into teaching and research in the nations' agricultural colleges was a field known as "farm management." In the early 1900s, a wide range of applied scientists—plant geneticists, soil scientists, entomologists, and so forth—contributed to this field, teaching courses and doing research intended to help farmers solve practical problems and make more money. The pioneering agricultural economists employed two successful arguments as to why the study of economics should also be considered an essential part of the farm management curriculum. A first was that economists had developed an effective analytic framework, the neoclassical theory of the firm, for thinking about how the farmer should make decisions regarding inputs, production methods, and outputs to maximize profits. The second was that a key determinant of farmers' ultimate economic fortunes was the prices prevailing in markets for their most important inputs and outputs. A farmer with a better understanding of the forces that determined these prices would be in a position to make more profitable decisions. Moreover, policies intended to increase the prosperity of the nation's farmers should be based on a sound understanding of these market forces. Economists had the expertise required to teach about, and conduct research to build knowledge of, how prices were determined in markets.

The newly emerging subfield of agricultural economics was much more empirically oriented than the economics discipline in general. Agricultural economists had access to decades' worth of government-collected data on agricultural prices and production. Further, the USDA, the state departments of agriculture, and the land grant colleges and universities all had a mission of supporting research that would help make life better for farmers, and in practice this often meant research that involved the collection and analysis of farm-related data. As a result, to be an effective agricultural economist almost required one to have some training in statistical methods.

A leading figure behind the rising influence of economists in the world of agricultural education, research, and policy was Henry C. Taylor, who was the nation's first professor of agricultural economics and the author of the first textbook on agricultural economics. Taylor was a master of academic politics, skilled at recruiting allies, neutralizing opponents, and persuading potential patrons to support various initiatives for building the new field. He used his talents to establish the first department of agricultural economics in 1909 (at the University of Wisconsin) and aided those

---

4. Harry McDean (1983) and Spencer Banzhaf (2006) describe how this came about. A key participant's account is found in Taylor and Taylor 1952.

creating such departments at other major institutions. For several years he worked to establish a lasting professional association of agricultural economists, a goal that was accomplished with the formation in 1919 of the American Farm Economic Association, with over three hundred members, annual meetings, and a regularly published scholarly journal, the *Journal of Farm Economics*.

A highlight, if not the culmination, of Taylor's efforts on behalf of the new field of agricultural economics was the establishment of the Bureau of Agricultural Economics within the USDA in 1922, with Taylor in charge. Harry McDean (1983) provides a detailed account of the complicated maneuvers by which Taylor, as chief of the USDA's Office of Farm Management managed an "administrative coup," through which his office gained "complete control over all statistical information issued from the USDA," and eventually succeeded in creating the BAE, making it the home for a number of existing USDA programs along with several new ones. More important than his reshuffling of the USDA's organizational chart, however, were the changes in USDA personnel that Taylor was able to bring about. Taylor interviewed existing staff, ascertained their interest in economics and their potential for economic research, suggested transfer or resignation to those who came up short, and offered programs for additional training to those with the appropriate interest but not the required knowledge. New personnel were recruited from the nation's PhD programs in agricultural economics, and economists and statisticians were lured away from other governmental positions. What Taylor started was imitated by his lieutenants and immediate successors. As a result of this aggressive and deliberate personnel strategy, by the mid-1920s the BAE was a leading center for empirical research in agricultural economics and the hub of a network of researchers spread throughout academe and the state agricultural agencies. It was also home to what was probably the most able and technically advanced team of statisticians and empirical economists in the United States.[5]

Ideas about Statistical Inference at the BAE in the 1920s and 1930s

The ideas of the leading US empirical economists of the 1920s about how best to draw inferences from statistical data strongly resembled, and were obviously influenced by, arguments about statistical inference found in

---

5. This claim is well documented in Fox 1986 and Rutherford 2011, among others.

Keynes's *Treatise on Probability* (Biddle 2017). In the *Treatise*, Keynes made a distinction between the descriptive function of the theory of statistics, which involved devising ways to summarize large amounts of data, and the inductive function, which "seeks to extend its descriptions of certain characteristics of observed events to the corresponding characteristics of other events that have not been observed." This part of statistics he called the theory of statistical inference, and he noted that it was currently understood to be "closely bound up with the theory of probability" (Keynes 1921: 327). The theory of probability provided the basis for using sample information to calculate probable errors for statistical measures like the mean and the correlation coefficient, and it justified the use of those probable errors in making inferences about unobserved phenomena on the basis of descriptive statistics calculated for a sample. But Keynes believed that this approach to statistical inference was an unsound basis for drawing conclusions from statistical data. As he stated at one point, "To apply these methods to material, unanalyzed in respect to the circumstances of its origin, and without reference to our general body of knowledge, merely on the basis of arithmetic and those characteristics of our material with which the methods of descriptive statistics are competent to deal, can only lead to error and delusion" (384).

Keynes's critique of the inferential measures derived from probability theory was embedded in a more positive discussion about what he believed to be the appropriate approach to statistical inference. According to Keynes, reliable statistical inferences about some phenomenon of interest would be the product of a comparative analysis of information from several samples of data on the phenomenon, with careful attention to similarities and differences in the circumstances surrounding the generation of the sample data, informed by one's "general knowledge" of the phenomenon from other sources. Keynes was thus dubious about the value of the inferential measures derived from probability theory, as these measures claimed to provide reliable conclusions about phenomena outside the sample based only on information from the sample itself—without considering the provenance of the sample or nonstatistical knowledge of the phenomena.[6]

During the 1920s, one can find important themes from Keynes's discussion of statistical inference, sometimes with explicit reference to

6. For a more detailed discussion of Keynes's arguments about good inferential procedures, see Biddle and Boumans, this volume.

Keynes, in essays on statistical methodology by leading empirical economists in the United States, and in the most popular US textbooks on statistical methods for economists (Biddle 2017). It is also clear that Keynes's ideas on inference were widely embraced in the community of agricultural economists. As a group, the agricultural economists of the 1920s had little use for the probability-based inferential measures. This comes through clearly, for example, in the 1928 report "Research Method and Procedure in Agricultural Economics" sponsored by the Social Science Research Council and put together by a committee of prominent agricultural economists, based on contributions from active researchers.[7] Early in the section of the report devoted to "statistical method," the committee noted that

> economic statisticians . . . generally take the position that the mathematics of sampling and error and inference thus far developed, which holds rigorously only for pure chance and simple samples of entirely unrelated events, is inadequate for the needs of economic phenomena, and that there is little prospect of mathematical analysis soon being developed that will be adequate. Once the assumptions of pure chance are violated, inference has to proceed along other lines than those based on simple mathematical probability. (Advisory Committee 1928: 38)

The message that the data of agricultural economics did not meet the assumptions required for probability-based inference was repeated by other contributors to the report. The section on sampling explained that most samples in agricultural economics did not fill the requirements of random sampling. The author of the section of the report devoted to statistical inference included another common objection of the time to the use of "the mathematics of sampling error and inference": even if an economist was working with a sample that was drawn in such a way as to be representative of some "universe," it would seldom be the universe about which the economist wished to draw conclusions.[8]

During the late 1920s and early 1930s, the BAE economist Charles F. Sarle taught statistics courses to USDA and other government employees through the USDA's graduate education program.[9] Sarle joined the BAE

---

7. The committee members were John Black, E. G. Nourse, L. C. Gray, and H. R. Tolley.

8. The section on inference (270–86 in Advisory Committee 1928) was largely written by Elmer J. Working, who spent a portion of his career at the BAE.

9. For a description of the activities of the USDA graduate school during this period, see Rutherford 2011.

shortly after its formation, having previously served as the agricultural statistician for the State of Iowa.[10] A set of notes from Sarle's 1932 statistics course survives. In the lectures on the "theory and application of sampling," students were introduced to the concept of the standard error and the formulas for calculating the standard error of the mean for various types of samples. Emphasis was placed on the assumptions required for these measures to be valid, and during lectures devoted to the problem of statistical inference, students were cautioned to think about, and if possible test, those assumptions in their data. They were warned that the samples that come into the hands of the analyst might not be representative of the universe of interest—indeed, "many surveys are made without any very clear idea of what the universe of inquiry is really supposed to be" (Sarle 1932b: 56).[11] Statisticians were encouraged to look for "check data," such as data from the periodic federal agricultural censuses, or from tax records, or shipping records from railroads, that might contain some of the same variables as the sample at hand for the desired universe. Differences between the distribution of common variables in the samples and in the check data would indicate possible bias in the sample. And, Sarle noted, "few if any farm management surveys can be said to be representative with respect to time." The universe about which one hoped to make generalizations had likely changed since the time the sample was collected, so one had to consider "the 'dynamic' aspects of the problem . . . the influence of factors that change materially with time" (41, 57). When possible, a study of successive samples taken in the past from the same or similar universes might give the analyst insight into these dynamic aspects. Sarle's advice to his students on statistical inference, then, is consistent with Keynes's admonition that strong statistical inferences required the study of several samples, with attention to the manner in which and circumstances under which the samples were drawn, along with consideration of one's general knowledge of the subject.[12]

In the following two sections I describe how BAE economists developed procedures for using statistical data to generate two of the many types of forecasts issued by the USDA in the 1920s and 1930s. It is my contention that these examples show that the practice of BAE statisticians

10. For more on Sarle's career, see King 1966.

11. Page references to Sarle 1932b refer to the downloadable PDF version. The original is not consistently paginated.

12. See also Sarle's observations on statistical inference on pages 12–38 of Sarle 1932a, a USDA technical bulletin that also served as his doctoral dissertation. In these pages Sarle quotes Keynes's *Treatise* at four points.

reflected the ideas and admonitions about statistical inference summarized in this section.

The Pig Survey and Forecasting Hog Production

Shortly after the Division of Crop and Livestock Estimation was integrated into the newly created BAE, a high priority was assigned to the project of expanding the range of livestock-related estimates and forecasts reported by the USDA.[13] Along with the expansion of the range of statistics to be produced came a plan for improving their quality.

Prior to the war, estimates of the likely growth or decline in livestock populations throughout the country were based on "judgment estimates" provided by the USDA's volunteer reporters, who were asked for their opinions on how much, in percentage terms, populations of various types of livestock on farms in their area had changed since the previous year. There was a consensus among BAE economists, however, that more reliable information could be obtained by asking a random sample of farmers in an area to report on changes in their own livestock holdings. The procedure eventually adopted for gathering the information required to construct such "individual farm estimates" involved using rural mail carriers to collect data from individual farmers and was first implemented for the "pig survey" of 1922.[14] Mail carriers were given cards to distribute to farmers along their route. One side of the card contained instructions for the carrier, including, "The farms reported upon should be such as to give a good average picture or sample of all farms on the route. The surest way of obtaining a fair sample is to get reports from every farm along a portion of the route—owned and rented, large and small, good and poor, etc.— just as they come" (Taylor and Taylor 1952: 248). The other side of the card, reproduced below as figure 1, contained the questions for farmers.

As figure 1 shows, farmers were asked how many sows on their farm had farrowed (given birth to litters) or were expected to farrow during the first six months of the current year, and how many had farrowed during the first six months of the previous year. They were also asked for the average litter size this year and last year. The information was used to create a forecast of the percentage change from last year to this year in the number of fattened pigs (hogs) that would be brought to market during the

13. Becker and Harlan 1939: 815–21, the main source for the next two paragraphs, includes an explanation of why this was a high priority at the time.

14. The story of the origin of agricultural data collection by rural mail carriers is told (in slightly different ways) in Taylor and Taylor 1952: 246–47 and Becker and Harlan 1939: 817.

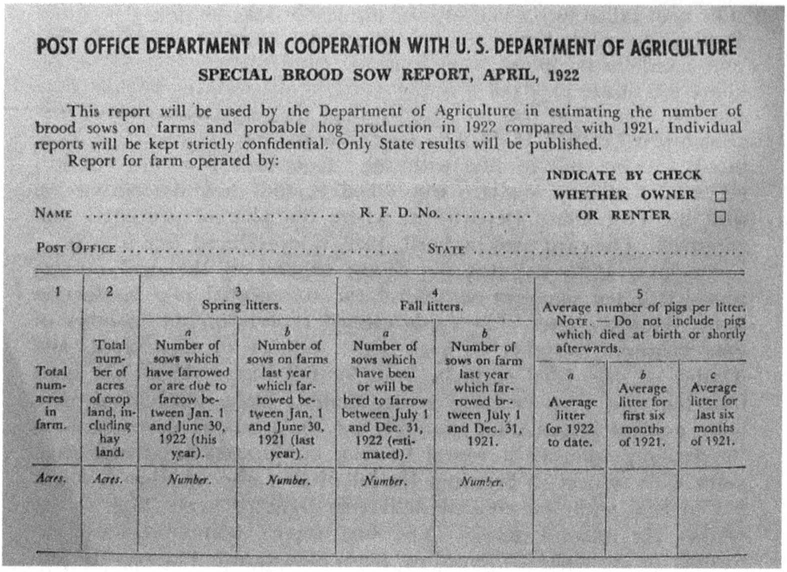

POST OFFICE DEPARTMENT IN COOPERATION WITH U. S. DEPARTMENT OF AGRICULTURE

SPECIAL BROOD SOW REPORT, APRIL, 1922

This report will be used by the Department of Agriculture in estimating the number of brood sows on farms and probable hog production in 1922 compared with 1921. Individual reports will be kept strictly confidential. Only State results will be published.

Report for farm operated by:

INDICATE BY CHECK WHETHER OWNER ☐ OR RENTER ☐

NAME .... R. F. D. No. ....

POST OFFICE .... STATE ....

1	2	3 Spring litters.		4 Fall litters.		5 Average number of pigs per litter. NOTE.—Do not include pigs which died at birth or shortly afterwards.		
Total num-acres in farm.	Total number of acres of crop land, including hay land.	a Number of sows which have farrowed or are due to farrow between Jan. 1 and June 30, 1922 (this year).	b Number of sows on farms last year which farrowed between Jan. 1 and June 30, 1921 (last year).	a Number of sows which have been or will be bred to farrow between July 1 and Dec. 31, 1922 (estimated).	b Number of sows on farm last year which farrowed between July 1 and Dec. 31, 1921.	a Average litter for 1922 to date.	b Average litter for first six months of 1921.	c Average litter for last six months of 1921.
Acres.	*Acres.*	*Number.*	*Number.*	*Number.*	*Number.*			

Figure 1 Card distributed to farmers for the 1922 pig survey.

fall and winter.[15] The pig survey became a semiannual activity (corresponding to the two pig-breeding seasons per year) for the next several years. The forecasts derived from the pig surveys were perceived by the USDA to be of great value to farmers and others whose business decisions depended on what was going on in the agricultural sector (USDA 1924–35: 1932 report, 3), and improving the accuracy of the forecast was an ongoing concern of the economists and statisticians at the BAE.[16]

An early analysis of the reliability of the data from the pig survey samples as a basis for forecasts of hogs brought to market is found in a 1924 internal

15. The cards also asked about the farmer's plans for the fall breeding season, which would produce hogs to be brought to market in the following spring. This information would form the basis of the first "intentions" report for pigs. The reports based on farmers' intentions to produce hogs in the upcoming season (and similar "intentions to plant" reports for major crops that the USDA began to issue in 1923) were not meant as forecasts. Indeed, the USDA hoped that they would often prove inaccurate as forecasts, by leading farmers to modify their plans when the intentions reports suggested a likely surplus or shortage (USDA 1924–35: 1926 report, 2). I do not discuss the BAE's work with intentions data.

16. The first two BAE annual reports made strong claims for the accuracy of the forecasts constructed from the pig survey data (USDA 1924–35: 1924 report, 3, 11; 1925 report, 4), but internally, the researchers saw much room for improvement, with Sarle commenting in the second half of the 1920s (in Advisory Committee 1928: 130, 136) that memory bias was a serious problem for pig estimates and that outside the corn belt, the sample sizes obtained from the rural carrier surveys were often too small to produce a reliable estimate of the likely change in the number of hogs brought to market.

memo by Bradford B. Smith and Mordecai Ezekiel.[17] The key statistical measure produced by the pig survey at that time was the ratio of the sample mean of sows farrowed this year to the sample mean of sows farrowed last year, which was taken as a forecast of the "hog crop to come" this year as a proportion of the known hog crop last year. The memo summarized an analysis designed to assess the "statistical accuracy" of this ratio, with an eye toward determining the appropriate sample size for future surveys.

Smith and Ezekiel first applied probability theory to the problem. Defining X_1 as the sample mean of sows farrowed this year and X_2 as the sample mean of sows farrowed last year, they presented the theoretical formula for the standard error the ratio X_1/X_2:

$$\left[\frac{M_1^2}{M_2^2} \left(\left(\frac{\sigma_1^2}{M_1^2} \right) - 2r_{12} \frac{\sigma_1}{M_1} \frac{\sigma_2}{M_2} + \left(\frac{\sigma_2^2}{M_2^2} \right) \right) \right]^{\frac{1}{2}}$$

M_j equaled the population mean of X_j, σ_j equaled the population standard deviation of X_j, and r_{12} equaled the correlation of X_1 and X_2 in the population. Since the actual values of the Ms, σs, and r_{12} could not be obtained, they were replaced with sample estimates of these values.

The authors then described their empirical tests of whether this calculable approximation to the theoretical standard error formula was suitable for data from the pig survey. The tests were done using a sample of eight thousand survey cards from Iowa. The main test was this: sixty random samples were drawn from the eight thousand cards. From these sixty samples it was possible to calculate a standard deviation for the sixty sample values of X_1/X_2, the ratio of sows farrowed this year to sows farrowed last year. Then a subsample of the eight thousand cards was used to calculate values to stand in for the Ms and the σs in the standard error formula above (e.g., M_1 was replaced by a sample average of X_1). If the resulting calculated standard error was sufficiently close to the observed standard deviation of the sixty means of X_1/X_2 from the sixty random subsamples, then the (feasibly calculable) theoretical standard error provided an acceptable measure of how far a sample mean value of X_1/X_2 might deviate from the true population value. As a matter of fact, the standard deviation of the mean of this ratio across the sixty samples was about twice the value of the standard error calculated using the theoretical formula.

17. Ezekiel spent most of his career working for the federal government and the United Nations. His research on statistical methods and agricultural economics led to his selection as a fellow of the American Statistical Association, the American Association of Agricultural Economists, and the Econometric Society (Wells 1975). Smith left the USDA in the late 1920s after publishing several influential articles on statistical forecasting. He spent most of his career as the chief economist for US Steel.

The failure of the theoretical formula, the authors argued, likely lay in the fact, evident from their data, that both X_1 and X_2 had highly skewed distributions, while the theoretical standard error applied to a ratio of (approximately) normally distributed random variables. Their recommendation for those wishing to gauge the statistical accuracy of the mean ratios derived from the pig survey was to calculate the standard error of the ratio using the theoretical formula and then double it.

The theoretical formulas assumed that the sample was representative, another assumption that Smith and Ezekiel tested. One concern was that farmers who returned completed cards to their mailboxes might be the more progressive, successful farmers, and for that reason might make breeding decisions that differed from those of the average farmer. Under the assumption that successful farmers would tend to have larger farms, the authors looked at three hundred cards from their sample and calculated the correlation between the size of the farm and X_1/X_2, and found it to be negligible.

Check Data

In their 1924 memo, Smith and Ezekiel evaluated the likely reliability of a sample estimator by studying the characteristics of the sample itself. This was the approach to inference that Keynes had criticized as inadequate, although Smith and Ezekiel went well beyond simply using the sample data to calculate a standard error of the estimate. However, the dominant method employed by the crop and livestock forecasters of the BAE to assess the reliability of their forecasts involved the use of "check data," that is, alternative sources of data from which one could estimate the realized value of the forecast quantity. A great deal of effort was spent identifying and analyzing possible sources of check data for all the crop and livestock estimates and forecasts made by the bureau. The decennial agricultural censuses, which aimed at a complete enumeration of the production of various agricultural products by the nation's farmers, were an important source of check data, as were tax assessor's reports from the various states.[18] The BAE also received check data from an array of businesses and other government agencies, with the railroads being the most important among the cooperating businesses. The 1928 annual report of the BAE, discussing the role of the railroads in providing check data for forecasts of fruit crops, explained that

18. The federal Census of Agriculture became quinquennial in 1925.

daily telegraphic reports are received at Washington from several hundred transportation lines, showing the number of cars originating in each division superintendent's territory. . . . Approximately 400 individual division superintendents or other reporting officials send daily wires in season. . . . About 15,000 local freight and express agents send monthly (station) reports by mail, covering a greater number of products than those in the daily wires. (USDA 1924–35: 1928 report, 15)

Since the early 1920s, the BAE had been building a historical record of the actual production and movement between states of livestock, relying on "information obtained . . . from stockyards, packing plants, railroads, and other agencies actively engaged in the process of marketing livestock" (USDA 1924–35: 1924 report, 12), soon supplemented by "records of brand inspections or sanitary board inspections of livestock . . . and local records of livestock slaughter" (USDA 1933: 15). This program provided the check data used for the forecasts derived from the pig survey.

Most check data sources were "fragmentary," covering only part of the total production of a product but taken together form(ed) an extensive list (15). And for many purposes, partial coverage was sufficient. If the goal, as in the pig survey, was to forecast a percentage increase or decrease in total production, then it was only necessary that the part of total production covered by the check data remained fairly stable from year to year. But this condition did not always hold. Not long after the beginning of its program for estimating livestock production, the proportion of slaughtered livestock going direct to packers without moving through stockyards began to increase steadily, which required the BAE to develop new data sources, including the packers themselves. By the end of the 1930s, the growing use of trucks rather than railcars to transport a wide variety of agricultural products was undermining the reliability of a large number of the BAE's check data series, again prompting the development of new sources and methods (Becker and Harlan 1939: 819–20; USDA 1933: 14). For reasons such as these, a 1933 discussion by BAE statistical staff on the use of check data in crop and livestock estimation explained that "check data are not always considered conclusive, or better than estimates based on the sample data" but also that "regardless of such limitations of check data in their original form, they frequently reflect major changes in acreage and production that may not be fully indicated by the established sampling methods. Thus they may serve as a warning that for some one commodity the sampling process needs to be extended and given more detailed analysis or supplemented by additional inquiry" (USDA 1933: 15).

Diagnosing and Correcting Problems
with the Pig Survey

BAE economists spoke of two general classes of problems in sample data that might lead to consistent deviations between sample-based measures and what was revealed by the check data: unrepresentativeness and bias. An "unrepresentative" sample was simply one that did not properly represent the "universe" of interest, with the ideal benchmark being the well-understood concept of a simple random sample from that universe.[19] "Bias" typically referred to errors in the measurement of variables that occurred during the data collection process.[20]

Poorly designed questionnaires could be a source of bias, and several times during the 1920s the BAE discovered problems with the pig survey questionnaire. As the questionnaire was expanded to include questions about other types of livestock, the wording of the questions also changed. At one point, respondents were asked three questions in sequence:

1. Number of sows which farrowed on your farm between December 1, 1927, and June 1, 1928.
2. Total number of pigs saved on your farm between December 1, 1927, and June 1, 1928.
3. Number of sows which farrowed on your farm between December 1, 1926, and June 1, 1927.

After the cards arrived in Washington, however, it was realized that many farmers had answered question 3 with the number of pigs saved during the previous spring, rather than the number of sows that had farrowed. The solution for this problem was to add a fourth question about the number of pigs saved from all litters during the previous season.

Using the terminology of "pigs saved" when trying to determine average litter size also proved problematic, as it was discovered that this phrase had a different meaning in different regions of the country. In the "corn belt" it meant the number of pigs that lived to weaning age. Elsewhere it might mean pigs that the farmer raised but did not sell, but it was "often difficult to determine what the reporter actually (had) in mind." The discovery of a problem with a questionnaire, however, created a

19. Check data, for example, information from the most recent agricultural census, could be used to assess the representativeness of samples. For example, the original pig survey card (fig. 1) asked about farm size and whether the farm was rented or owned, and the sample distribution of these variables could be compared with information from the census. The census also served as a source of weights for correcting unrepresentativeness.

20. The BAE distinction between unrepresentativeness and bias appears, among other places, in Sarle 1932a: 19.

dilemma, because BAE economists had learned that "great caution is needed in changing the wording of schedules, both because the new schedule may turn out to be no better than the old, and because the comparability of the returns for the two years may be affected" (Callander 1928: 245; Advisory Committee 1928: 119–21).

For many crops, the indications provided by samples would be corrected for known and fairly constant biases that had been revealed by analyses of check data, but for the first ten years of the pig survey, the BAE did not believe that it had accumulated enough check data to make such corrections at the state level. So the forecast of the increase or decrease in the hog crop would simply be the percentage change in pigs calculated from farmers' reports of the number of pigs "saved" this year and last year. However, there were increasing complaints from those who used the forecasts about their accuracy at the state level and about the fact that the percentage change forecasts were not informative as to the absolute numbers of hogs expected to come to market. By 1932 the BAE was ready to revise its method of hog forecasting in a way that incorporated new information and several lessons learned over the preceding years (Becker and Harlan 1939: 819–20; USDA 1933: 14).[21]

The 1930 agricultural census included questions about actual and planned pig breeding between January and June that were comparable to the questions found on the annual pig surveys. After the census data from these questions were "studied in relationship to information from the surveys as to pigs saved per litter . . . , it was decided that they gave a basis for making actual numerical estimates of sows farrowed and pigs saved" (USDA 1933: 54). Thus, starting in 1932, the USDA hog forecast was expressed in terms of actual numbers of pigs, applying each year's increase or decrease estimated from the pig surveys cumulatively to the absolute numerical estimates provided by the 1930 census.

The method of calculating percentage changes from the annual surveys was also changed. Starting in the late 1920s, BAE researchers began to investigate the possible value of analyzing "identical farm" samples, that is, samples limited to farms that had returned the survey cards for the same season two years in a row.[22] With identical farm samples, one could compare the answers given in a current year, say 1931, with the answers about 1931 given by the same farmer in the following year.

21. The remainder of this section is based on Becker and Harlan 1939: 819; and USDA 1933: 53–54.

22. Research on the value of identical farm samples is first mentioned in the BAE annual report for the 1928–29 fiscal year (USDA 1924–35: 1929 report, 12).

The analysis of the identical farm samples revealed memory errors on the part of farmers when asked about last year's pig production but also something BAE researchers called "intentional bias" (called "cash crop bias" in other contexts): farmers gave conservative (downward biased) reports of current production, presumably believing that a smaller quantity estimate would lead to higher market prices. More problematic was evidence that the bias only existed in some states and varied from year to year with economic conditions.

These discoveries prompted the BAE to develop a new method of forecasting the likely change in the hog crop, which it called the "ratio-relative" method. The basic measures of change from one year's spring or fall season to the next were now the ratios of mean number of sows farrowed / pigs saved *per farm* and *per one hundred acres* this year, reported on this year's cards, to the same per farm and per acre measures reported for last year, on last year's cards. The new measures avoided memory errors and also any intentional bias that was constant from year to year. According to BAE staff, "The studies conducted before it was finally decided to make this change showed that the ratio-relatives of sows farrowed per farm and per hundred acres, and the percentage changes in these items from the identical farm tabulations, gave better indications of actual changes, as checked by records of marketings and slaughter, than did the current to historic changes in which the apparent bias from year to year was not constant" (USDA 1933: 54).

In the methods used by BAE economists to improve the forecasts obtained by the pig survey, there are two elements of Keynes's recommended approach to statistical inference. The comparative analysis of successive samples from the same or similar "universes" was an important aspect of the process, with attention to the similarities and differences in the origins of the samples—successive surveys from different years, with different wordings, were compared, "identical farm" subsamples compared with full cross-section samples, survey data compared with census data, and so on. Also, nonstatistical "general knowledge" of matters such as regional dialects and farmers' motivations for misreporting had a role to play as well.

Forecasting Crop Yields Based on Condition Estimates

BAE forecasts of the production of field crops such as cotton, wheat, and corn were the product of two underlying forecasts: acreage to be harvested and yield per acre. The making of each of these types of forecast required different methods and materials and raised different problems for the statisticians. The raw materials used to forecast yield per acre for a crop variety were samples that included "judgment estimates" of voluntary reporters on the "condition" of the crop as it was growing in the fields in their area. These condition estimates had been collected by the USDA since its establishment, but in 1912, the department began to implement a method of converting condition estimates into numerical yield per acre forecasts.

The practice as of 1923, when these yield forecasts became the responsibility of the newly formed BAE, was to convert condition reports into yield forecasts using the "par method." Each month during the growing season for a particular crop, reporters were asked to assess the condition of that crop on the farms in their area as a percentage of what was "normal" for that month. Reporters were provided with a definition of "normal":

> A normal condition is not an average condition, but a condition above the average, giving promise of more than an average crop. Furthermore, a normal condition does not indicate a perfect crop, or a crop that is or promises to be the very largest in quantity and the very best in quality that the region reported upon may be considered capable of producing. The normal indicates something less than this, and thus comes between the average and the possible maximum, being greater than the former and less than the latter. The normal may be described as a condition of perfect healthfulness, unimpaired by drought, hail, insects, or other injurious agency, and with such growth and development as may be reasonably looked for under these favorable conditions. (Callander and Becker 1923: 187)

The sample average value of the monthly condition reports in an area would be calculated and would be used to create an (unadjusted) yield per acre forecast using the formula

$$Y = C \left(\frac{Y_m}{C_m} \right)$$

where Y was the yield forecast, C the average condition number, Y_m the average over the most recent ten years of yields per acre in that area, and C_m the ten-year average of condition reports for that month in that area. In other words, the long-term relationship between a particular month's average condition estimate and the actual yield at harvest was used to convert a current condition report into a yield forecast.[23] The fraction (Y_m/C_m) was the "par," or more technically, the "equivalent 100% yield."

---

23. Y_m was calculated using the department's past estimates of actual yield per acre, which were based on the reports made after the harvest by farmers and other in the agricultural community, perhaps adjusted based on analyses of various sources of check data.

The unadjusted yield per acre forecast was given to the Crop Reporting Board, a group made up mainly of USDA economists. The board was permitted to adjust the par factor if it saw fit, for example, if a par based on the most recent five years was very different from that produced by the ten-year average. Members of the Crop Reporting Board also knew that the linear relationship between eventual yield and reported condition assumed by the par method did not hold for unusually high or low condition estimates, and might make an adjustment for that (Callander and Becker 1923; USDA 1933: 24).

Not surprisingly, in 1923 the statistically oriented agricultural economists brought to the BAE by Taylor were already launching research projects designed to improve the yield forecasts. One experiment asked the reporters to include a "probable yield" estimate along with the condition estimate each month. It was found that these probable yield estimates could, in certain identifiable circumstances, outperform the condition estimates, and Crop Reporting Boards adopted the practice of using the probable yield estimates to adjust the par when these circumstances obtained. A longer-term project involved the investigation of how weather conditions during the growing season would influence the relationship between condition and eventual yield (USDA 1933: 32).

In 1923, there had already been some initial experiments using linear regression analysis to estimate the relationship between condition estimates and yield, but it was recognized that linear regression and correlation would not help with one of the more pressing problems of the par system, that is, its inaccuracies when the relationship between condition estimates and yield was not linear. Over the next several years BAE economists developed new techniques for using regression analysis to estimate "curvilinear" relationships, and this work led to a complete overhaul of the bureau's yield forecasting methodology.

Yield Forecasting with "Dot Charts"

The new method, phased in and refined between 1927 and 1930, involved the use of a graphical tool referred to at the BAE as a "dot chart." In the case of yield forecasting, the dot chart was a scatter plot, specific to a month, a state, and a crop, with the average condition estimate on the horizontal axis and actual yield on the vertical. The "dots" were the plotted combinations of average condition and eventual yield of that crop for

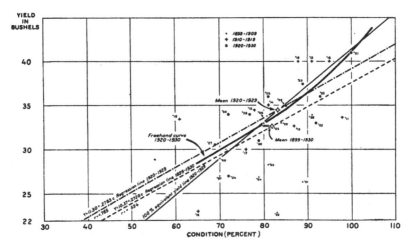

Figure 2 A "dot chart" for making a corn yield forecast.

past years in that state and that month. Figure 2 shows a dot chart for the July 1 condition estimates for corn in Minnesota. Each dot is labeled according to the year of the condition-yield pair that it represents. The "100% equivalent yield line" represents the "par" relationship between condition and yield. The two dotted lines come from linear regressions of yield on condition—one based on data from 1899–1930, the other based on data from 1920–29. The user of the dot chart could compare these two lines to see that the yield corresponding to any given condition had been moving up. The solid "freehand curve 1920–1930" was meant to reflect the nature of the nonlinearity in the relationship between Minnesota's July 1 condition report and its eventual average yield.

Typically, when a member of the Crop Reporting Board received a dot chart for the crop-month-state combination for which a forecast needed to be made, it had only the par line on it, and he was free to draw in whatever additional lines he might consider helpful in coming to a yield forecast to go along with the condition report for that month. The BAE saw the following "distinct advantages" in the "graphic method of forecasting" using dot charts:

(1) Lines of best fit (to be used as a basis for forecasting) may be established freehand or mathematically before the current data are available.

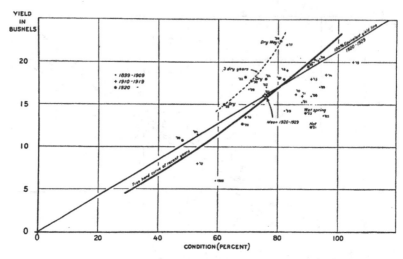

Figure 3 A "dot chart" used for forecasting the yield of winter wheat.

(2) The method is not limited to linear relationships.

(3) Years that fall "off the line" stand out and can be studied separately or in connection with other similar years.

(4) Frequently one or more distinct "levels" of relationship are observed. Research into similarities in years on the several levels make it possible to improve the forecasts.

(5) The method is not limited to condition-yield relationships but can be used with any measurable data.

(6) Several factors may be related to yield by graphical multiple correlation methods. (USDA 1933: 25)

Some of these features are illustrated by figure 3, a dot chart for the May 1 condition reports for winter wheat in Ohio, with lines of the sort that might be added by a member of the Crop Reporting Board.

By 1930, it was known based on past research that reporters' condition estimates for winter wheat would not properly account for the effect of growing-season weather on eventual yield. So this chart identified dots from years with unusual weather, revealing that a dry season moved the condition-yield relationship to a different level. Freehand curves were drawn through the three "dry years" and also through dots for all recent years, with the second curve helping the dot chart user to adjust for nonlinearity. A board member might have added a regression line based on the 1899–1920 data, to see if the condition-yield relationship was trending up.

Research to Improve Crop Yield Forecasts

It is hard to find words to express the amount of time and effort involved, month in and month out, in the BAE's crop reporting program. With a focus only on the forecasting of crop yields, consider that in 1923, the new BAE was issuing monthly reports throughout the growing season for over one hundred crops, usually for several states, and that the number of yield forecasts expanded through the 1920s and into the early 1930s.[24] On top of that, basic research designed to improve the forecasts was ongoing at the BAE throughout the 1920s and early 1930s.

One major research effort was devoted to developing general procedures for uncovering and incorporating into the forecasts both nonlinearities in the condition-yield relationship and the influence on yields of factors besides reported condition, particularly the weather. This research led to the development of new techniques for applying multiple regression and correlation analysis to nonlinear relationships, including graphical techniques for estimating and displaying those relationships.[25] It should also be remembered that for each crop, for each month, in each state, there was potentially a different relationship between crop yield and reported condition and a different set of additional factors that might influence the condition-yield relationship. Considerable research went into understanding the causes of these differences. Multiple regression techniques could be useful in measuring the impact on yields of factors not captured in the condition estimates, but the identification of what factors to consider in the first place often required knowledge of the agronomy of a particular crop in a particular region, or the reasoning of an economist as to how farmers might behave differently in different circumstances.

Adjusting the very important cotton yield forecasts for the impact of the boll weevil proved to be a complicated task. In the early twentieth century the boll weevil spread unevenly through the cotton-producing states, and infestations were worse in some years than in others, sometimes due to predictable weather factors. It also appeared that about three years after the arrival of the weevil in a region, cotton crop reporters' concept of a "normal" condition would begin to change. Ultimately, BAE economists determined that if they asked cotton crop reporters to estimate the percentage reduction in the cotton crop they expected due to boll weevils in

24. For all the crop and livestock forecasts and estimates being issued by the BAE as of 1932, see USDA 1933: 6–8.

25. USDA 1969: 73. Mordecai Ezekiel and Louis H. Bean were the leaders of this effort. The techniques are explained in Ezekiel 1930.

their area that year, the responses could be used to construct a "boll weevil index" that explained a significant amount of the variation of actual yields around yields predicted solely on the basis of reported condition. After 1929, the basic tool for predicting cotton yield was a curvilinear regression of past yields on past values of condition and this boll weevil index (USDA 1933: 24, 34–35; Callander and Becker 1923).[26]

Another problem for cotton forecasters was "cash crop bias" in reporters' probable yield estimates. The reporters, who were usually cotton farmers themselves, tended to give probable yield estimates that underpredicted actual yield. However, historically this bias diminished as more of the cotton crop in an area was processed, or "ginned," each season. The BAE economists eventually included a question asking reporters for their estimate of the percentage of the cotton crop in their area that had already been ginned. The answer to this question was sufficiently correlated with the bias in the probable yield estimates that it markedly improved the forecasts of actual yields when included in a regression along with probable yield.

The crop forecasting approach that had developed at the BAE by the end of the thirties thus exemplifies a number of Keynes's heuristics for statistical inference. The dot chart itself was a simultaneous display of statistical results from successive samples taken from similar, but not identical, universes. Comparison of dots within a chart and comparisons of charts pertaining to the same crop variety being grown in different regions were standard methods for understanding how the relationship between actual yields and reported conditions differed across regions, over time, with different types of weather conditions, and in different economic circumstances. And while a dot chart, or a regression analysis for that matter, might help uncover how the condition-yield relationship was influenced by various factors that differed across samples, explaining why the differences existed, which was understood to be as essential to good statistical forecasting as knowing that they did exist, required the resort to Keynes's "general knowledge," that is, information beyond what could be found in any of the samples. For BAE economists, this was, inter alia, agronomic knowledge and economic reasoning about how the profit motive might affect farmer behavior.

26. Note that although the extent of a boll weevil infestation might be related to many measurable and unmeasurable factors, with this solution the local knowledge of cotton farmers about boll weevil infestations, their correlates, and their determinants was relied on to produce a single measure reflecting many factors. Having a single adequate measure of the joint impact of many variables was important in an era when regression calculations were done by hand.

Concluding Remarks

In the introduction I mentioned that one feature of forecasting as a species of statistical inference is that those making forecasts often have the ability to compare them with reliable measures of the quantities they are attempting to forecast. I close with some thoughts occasioned by a consideration of how this may have affected the approach to inference employed by the BAE's crop and livestock forecasters.

BAE economists obviously valued their ability to compare their forecasts with an eventually revealed reality, thus getting feedback that could be used to analyze and improve the materials and methods underlying their forecasts. As a result, they emphasized and devoted substantial resources to expanding and improving their collections of check data.

However, during the time that statistical analysis has been an important part of economic research, it has much more often been the case that researchers who made generalizations on the basis of samples of statistical data did not expect that they would have consistent and reliable feedback on the accuracy of their inferences. This is true of economists doing something as straightforward as estimating the unemployment rate, to say nothing of those using sample data to estimate more subtle quantities like the elasticity of male labor supply with respect to changes in the wage, or of aggregate investment with respect to changes in the interest rate.

I believe that this circumstance might help explain why the approaches to inference employed in crop and livestock forecasting at the BAE differed from those employed by certain communities of economic researchers working in the second half of the twentieth century. Start with the proposition that when examining the empirical research of communities of economists over the past century, one typically finds instances of all the various approaches to building stronger, more convincing inferences that were employed by the agricultural economists of the BAE, including the careful scrutiny of procedures used to collect samples, comparative analysis of the results obtained from samples collected under different circumstances, the application of "general knowledge," including formal economic theory, to the interpretation of sample results, and so on, but also the use of inferential measures based in probability theory and research applying that theory to develop new measures suitable to a wider range of data environments. The important question, then, is not whether a community of researchers engages in each of these activities but the priority placed on them in the community's implicit and explicit canons of inference. For example, is a particular inferential practice used as a matter of course whenever one is using sample data to establish a generalization or test a hypothesis, or is the practice only resorted to after one's inference has been challenged, or in challenging the inference of another? Given that time and resources available for research are limited, it is reasonable to think there will be some logic in decisions about allocating those resources among various potential inferential procedures, logic based on the type of inference the researcher is making along with assorted constraints he faces in doing so.

The BAE's crop and livestock forecasters knew that they would often be able to repeatedly apply the same forecasting method to different samples taken from similar universes, and that the potential existed to measure the accuracy of those forecasts against reality to gain information that could be used to improve the forecasting method. Under these circumstances, it made sense for them to place a high priority on the development of better check data, and to make the comparative analysis of results from different samples a central element of their forecasting research. Compare this to the situation of researchers who have no realistic expectation of receiving clear signals from the world beyond their samples that sample-based measures are or are not reliable indicators of truth, and for whom the collection of other samples from similar universes is very costly. For such researchers, the promise offered by the inferential measures derived from probability theory—the ability to say, on the basis only of information from the sample in hand, that the true value of a quantity estimated with the sample data was almost certain to fall within a particular range of values—would be very attractive. Reporting such a range along with sample estimates would become routine. The development of procedures for obtaining samples that met the assumptions required to justify those reported ranges would be given a high priority, as would theoretical research that revealed how such ranges could be calculated under an ever-widening range of assumptions about the characteristics of the sample and the universe from which it was drawn. These trends, of course, are important general features of the development of empirical economics in the second half of the twentieth century.

References

Advisory Committee on Economic and Social Research in Agriculture of the Social Science Research Council. 1928. *Research Method and Procedure in Agricultural Economics.* 2 vols. New York: Social Science Research Council.

Banzhaf, H. Spencer. 2006. "The Other Economics Department: Demand and Value Theory in Early Agricultural Economics." In *Agreement on Demand: Consumer Theory in the Twentieth Century*, edited by D. Wade Hands and Philip Mirowski. *History of Political Economy* 38 (supplement): 9–30.

Becker, Joseph and C. L. Harlan. 1939. "Developments in Crop and Livestock Reporting since 1920." *Journal of Farm Economics* 21, no. 4: 799–827.

Biddle, Jeff E. 2017. "Statistical Inference in Economics, 1920–1965: Changes in Meaning and Practice." *Journal of the History of Economic Thought* 39, no. 2: 149–73.

Callander, W. F. 1928. "Problems in Crop and Livestock Estimating." *Journal of Farm Economics* 10, no. 2: 232–46.

Callander, W. F., and Joseph A. Becker. 1923. "The Use of 'Pars' and 'Normal' in Forecasting Crop Production." *Journal of Farm Economics* 5, no. 4: 185–97.

Didier, Emmanuel. 2012. "Cunning Observation: US Agricultural Statistics in the Time of Laissez-Faire." In *Observation and Observing in Economics*, edited by Haaro Maas and Mary S. Morgan. *History of Political Economy* 44 (supplement): 25–43.

Ezekiel, Mordecai. 1930. *Methods of Correlation Analysis*. New York: John Wiley.

Fox, Karl A. 1986. "Agricultural Economists as World Leaders in Applied Econometrics, 1917–33." *American Journal of Agricultural Economics* 68, no. 2: 381–86.

Haas, G. C., and Mordecai Ezekiel. 1926. *Factors Affecting the Price of Hogs*. Department Bulletin No. 1440. Washington, DC: US Department of Agriculture.

Keynes, J. M. 1921. *A Treatise on Probability*. London: Macmillan.

King, Arnold J. 1966. "Charles F. Sarle." *American Statistician* 20, no. 4: 43.

McDean, Harry. 1983. "Professionalism, Policy, and Farm Economists in the Early Bureau of Agricultural Economics." *Agricultural History* 57, no. 1: 64–82.

Pearson, F. A. 1924. "Discussion." *Journal of Farm Economics* 6, no. 2: 156–63.

Rutherford, Malcolm. 2011. "The USDA Graduate School: Government Training in Statistics and Economics, 1921–1945." *Journal of the History of Economic Thought* 33, no. 4: 419–47.

Sarle, Charles F. 1932a. *Adequacy and Reliability of Crop-Yield Estimates*. Technical Bulletin 311. Washington, DC: USDA.

Sarle, Charles F. 1932b. *Statistics*. Bound typescript, Albert R. Mann Library, Cornell University. Digitized version, babel.hathitrust.org/cgi/pt?id=coo.31924013703693.

Smith, Bradford B., and Mordecai Ezekiel. 1924. *Size of Sample Study, with Particular Reference to the Pig Survey of the Bureau of Agricultural Economics*. Washington, DC: US Bureau of Agricultural Economics. Bound typescript, Albert R. Mann Library, Cornell University. Digitized version, babel.hathitrust.org/cgi/pt?id=coo.31924013938224;view=1up;seq=3.

Taylor, Henry C., and Anne Dewees Taylor. 1952. *The Story of Agricultural Economics in the United States, 1840–1932*. Ames: Iowa State College University Press.

USDA (United States Department of Agriculture). 1924–35. *Report of the Chief of the Bureau of Agricultural Economics*. Washington, DC: US Government Printing Office. Annual reports bound in a single volume, Albert R. Mann Library, Cornell University. Digitized version, babel.hathitrust.org/cgi/pt?id=coo.31924052806951.

USDA (United States Department of Agriculture). 1933. *The Crop and Livestock Reporting Service of the United States*. Miscellaneous Publication No. 171. Washington, DC: US Government Printing Office.

USDA (United States Department of Agriculture). 1969. *The Story of U.S. Agricultural Estimates*. Washington, DC: US Government Printing Office.

Wells, Oris V. 1975. "In Memoriam: Mordecai J. B. Ezekiel, 1899–1974." *American Statistician* 29, no. 2: 106.

False Accounting as Formalizing Practices: The Computation of Macroeconomic Aggregates in African Countries since Structural Adjustment

Boris Samuel

Studies of the historical sociology of quantification have described the search for "good economic measurements" in Africa since the late colonial period: experts and statisticians have striven to overcome difficulties involved in collecting data, conducting surveys, compiling social and demographic statistics, and building macroeconomic aggregates to put African realities into numbers (see, e.g., Morgan 2011; Speich 2011; Samuel 2013, 2016; Bonnecase 2014; Davie 2015; Serra 2015). This literature has also described the formally satisfying but often deceptive numbers produced in Africa, due to the historical weakness of most of the statistical administrations, inadequate data, the distant relations of many experts to the African economies, and the embeddedness of statistical and economic works in social or political relations (see Hibou 2000; Samuel 2011; Jerven 2013).

The historical examination of the quantification of African economies thus poses a challenge. Whereas Mary Morgan (2008, 2011) described how Wolfgang Stolper's gathering and combination of data helped Nigeria build a "consistent" plan after independence, in which economic aggregates held together individual actions in a common and coherent frame directed toward economic development, it seems that in many historical situations, the efforts of economists and statisticians have not been chiefly motivated by the search for accuracy, reliability, or veracity. How should we characterize the methods, the validation criteria, and in sum, the types

History of Political Economy 53 (annual suppl.) DOI 10.1215/00182702-9414789

of inferential activities involved in the production of these quantified economic discourses?

The present article reflects on this issue by studying economic quantification in Mauritania in the 2000s, which led in 2004 and 2005 to the denunciation of a *statistical lie* orchestrated by the Mauritanian government and to sanctions by the International Monetary Fund (IMF) for "misreporting." In many African countries macroeconomic accounts are coproduced with international organizations (Samuel 2011, 2013). Member states are obliged to provide the IMF with economic figures for international surveillance and for the monitoring of its financial assistance programs. Macroeconomic data are thus produced under the guidance and scrutiny of international financial institutions (IFI) and with the help of experts. Following Martha Lampland's (2010) suggestion that the production of *false numbers* is mundane, occurring when formal requirements of quantification surpass the importance of veracity, I argue that the IMF's practices led to what can be called *false accounting*. In particular, the so-called *financial programming* method, which has guided IMF missions' work since the 1980s and 1990s, has favored conceptions of *consistency* that seem to neglect basic requirements of macroeconomic analysis. To prepare *consistent* scenarios and programs, IMF economists seek to fill in standard tables with comprehensive sets of estimates and forecasts, provide timely information, and ensure the coherence of scenarios with the economic views of the IMF. Yet IMF approaches to macroeconomic quantification are centered on monetary, fiscal, and external accounts, and they disregard the synthetic national accounting framework, preferring simpler approaches to calculate the gross domestic product (GDP) to more demanding and accurate methods. I show that this approach to inference leads to negotiated and inaccurate aggregates and to erroneous indicators of economic fluctuations. The IMF's audit and surveillance procedures have thus led to the production of national accounts that, while formally respecting institutional requirements and international statistical standards, can be considered *false*.

This article is based on my extensive research undertaken after being involved as an economist and statistician in African countries particularly in Mauritania from 2003 to 2007. After briefly describing the history of Mauritania's *statistical lie*, I analyze the formalities of quantification that African administrations carry out with IMF mission teams. I then study the empirical techniques used in Mauritania to compute the GDP in the period of the denounced *statistical lie*.

1. The Overflow of Mauritania's Macroeconomic Framework in 2004

In 2003, while the IFIs were vocally supporting Mauritania's economic policies, the country's economic and social dynamics seemed to go unnoticed by the IFIs' tools of economic and statistical analysis. The gap between the national currency's black market and official exchange rates with the euro and the US dollar had sharply increased, reaching 20 percent in July 2003. This should have signaled a foreign reserves shortage, but according to the official macroeconomic indicators, this was not the case: the central bank (Banque centrale de Mauritanie) was allegedly holding sufficient reserves to convert the equivalent of twelve months of imports. These exchange rate tensions in turn provoked price hikes on imported products. Along with the consequences of several successive bad agricultural seasons, these exchange rate tensions touched off dramatic price increases at the end of 2003, particularly on food products. But while the media discussed the inflationary pressure and its social consequences (e.g., Bakari 2004), the price index published by the national statistical office (Office National de la Statistique, ONS) remained flat until the end of 2003. Finally, after President Maaouya Ould Sid'Ahmed Taya's regime faced an attempted coup d'état in June 2003, the government reacted by freezing all public expenditures except military spending—deemed necessary to face the security situation—and a costly food emergency plan. The November 2003 presidential election took place in this context, involving large expenditures for the benefit of the presidential party, ceremonies, and gifts. But again, these dynamics could not be discerned in public finance data.

The controversy around data issues remained limited until mid-2004. In the official reports by the IFIs, the economic and social tensions could hardly be perceived. When they were not ignored, discussion was limited to specific technical issues expressed in the characteristic technocratic language of the IFIs. In 2003, the IMF devoted a study to exchange rate policy, exploring abstract considerations on Mauritania's export competitiveness and optimal exchange rate and hardly mentioning the black market issue. IMF teams did not publish the data they had compiled on unofficial exchange rates in their reports, although at that time those rates were among the most important variables for understanding the economic situation. "Mauritania has implemented an impressive array of macroeconomic and structural reforms" remained a ritual sentence in IMF and

World Bank documents, while the country remained a good candidate to participate in pilot schemes from debt cancellation to the new types of financial support.[1]

At the end of 2003, within the government of Mauritania, high-level civil servants began to express their disapproval of the ONS numbers and criticize the likely manipulation of the price index. The government also entered into a face-off with IMF teams, who requested in 2003 an audit of the central bank's foreign reserves. The Mauritanian authorities refused this audit for fear of being unmasked. The "black market premium" reached 30 percent in July 2004 (see Ould Ghoulam 2004; IMF 2006), and inflationary pressures continued, so that the refusal of the audit of the central bank sounded like an admission of statistical deceit. If the authorities wanted to stay on good terms with the IMF, whose certification was necessary to access financing from other donors, they had no choice but to proceed with this audit.

In September, Zeine Ould Zeidane, a recently appointed governor of the central bank, flew to Washington, DC, to report on the "statistical deceit" he had discovered. According to him, high unrecorded expenses occurred in 2003 and 2004 because of the security situation and poor agricultural performance: the level of public expenditures reached more than 60 percent of GDP in 2003 and 48 percent in 2004—twice the initially reported level—and foreign currency reserves were used for imports of military material and food. The ongoing financial programs with the IMF were suspended, and a procedure denouncing Mauritanian "misreporting" was launched. Before the IMF's executive board could declare them irregular, the central bank also decided to repay the current withdrawal and to reveal that the level of foreign reserves covered only two weeks of imports and not twelve months as previously indicated. Yet the rewriting of the macroeconomic story had just begun: IMF teams were aware that the new numbers presented by Zeidane were highly implausible and that the misreporting started well before 2003. The whole affair was embarrassing for IMF officials, who had been very casual in their monitoring of Mauritania's economy, and so they preferred to keep a low profile and move on as soon as possible. In the following period, during which the twenty-year-old regime was ousted by a coup d'état in 2005, the IMF and the Mauritanian government researched the country's recent economic and financial history, exploring archives, gathering documents, and com-

1. Like the so-called budget support.

ing up with new numbers. The 2005 broad money aggregates were twice the levels shown in the official statistics, the budget balance for 1995–2004 showed a mean annual deficit of 7.7 percent of GDP and not a surplus of 0.7 percent, and the official data completely omitted the state's huge interior indebtment (République Islamique de Mauritanie 2006). As the IMF mission chief at that time, Jean Le Dem, told me, one could discover a completely new economic history of the country.

2. False Accounting with the IMF as Formalizing Practices

Previous authors have questioned the representation of economic calculation as aiming to achieve the most reliable, accurate, or pertinent descriptions of reality. Quantification practices—putting facts into figures—are social and political processes that may reflect a plurality of logics of actions, and which can bear a social value and be performative even if they are incomplete or insincere descriptions of the world, purposely or not detaching themselves from a search for objectivity.

2.1. Statistical Fictions as Collective Processes

Studying the sociology of the production of economic data in the unstable social and political situation of Mauritania requires one to explore the variety of motivations and logics of action that supported their elaboration, validation, and diffusion (Hibou and Samuel 2011; Samuel 2011). The economists and statisticians who elaborated them had heterogeneous interests and motivations: some hoped to enhance the methods to produce better numbers in the future (Samuel 2013), others accepted that the production of data was enmeshed with political considerations (e.g., Mauritanian civil servants who were also members of the presidential party and helped the regime prepare its economic arguments), others worked to make the technocratic representation of Mauritania internationally acceptable (e.g., IFI employees concerned with preserving their institution's reputation and continuing lending activities), others chose to denounce the statistical trickery, while still others earned their living by preparing figures as consultants. If the pre-2005 Mauritanian economic fiction involved some actors who intentionally hid the real situation, most of the producers were simply doing their regular jobs (Hibou and Samuel 2011; Samuel 2011).

The quantifications of the Mauritanian economy were also inserted into a plurality of political struggles, inside and outside the bureaucracy: for example, among political actors or businessmen and bankers involved in the foreign currencies trafficking, who lobbied in 2005 against the confession of the *statistical lie*, or among social actors protesting price hikes and building alternate economic information (Samuel 2017). The quantitative picture of Mauritania's economy was thus the result of temporary compromises around the production and validation of data. I follow Béatrice Hibou (2011, 2017) in defining statistical fiction as the social and political process consisting of this collective elaboration and use of quantified discourses. Recalling that quantification is not about distinguishing truth from falsehood in the appreciation of economic or social facts, in particular in national contexts where data are particularly untrustworthy, Hibou shows that the production and use of numbers entail power relations among a constellation of heterogeneous actors with diverse understandings and logics of action, and that economic fiction plays a part in the establishment of political domination by putting technocratic skills and rhetoric at the center of the exercise of power, often with the help of international organizations. And as the Mauritanian case confirms, the fiction is at the heart of the establishment of a political order: when the compromises around numbers did not hold anymore and the quantification of the national economy was "overflowed," it contributed to the regime's fall.

2.2. Economic Calculation as Formalizing Practices

Specialists in the sociology and epistemology of data production would say that statistics are always partly fictional because their elaboration implies necessarily subjective processes of valuing, categorizing, or, in accounting, finding ways to balance the identities (Bowker and Star 1999; Thévenot 2016). Following Alain Desrosières (2001), the practices of users and producers of statistics can be described as an "unconscious intermingling" of four types of attitudes to reality, of which two are of interest here. One type involves a "pragmatic" conception of realism: a willingness to admit reliance on subjective or even arbitrary choices— like the way to balance the accounts in double-entry bookkeeping or to use one among many possible forecasting techniques—and the validation and adjustment of their methods occur through the repetition of tests of reality. Those with this attitude are driven by a principle of prudence in their communication with users and seek a stability in their methods. In the

Mauritanian case, before and after the crisis, economists and statisticians of both the IMF and the national government displayed this attitude, trying to preserve the plausibility of their estimates, in order to ensure (or restore) good relations with the IMF board. The second pertinent attitude toward realism Desrosières mentions is typical of users' relation to data: it avoids questioning the reliability of numbers and chooses to trust the numbers found in databases, in order to work with them in economic analysis. Data are, then, "self-sufficient," not needing any "metadata" or "footnote to interfere with the message." Desrosières associates this attitude with the idea that data are "investments in forms," as Laurent Thévenot (1984) named them, aiming at the production of a stable and socially accepted coordination of the many actors involved in the production and use of data. This idea of "self-sufficient" data is a useful one for understanding the Mauritanian situation, first because it underlines the importance of formalism—data inspire trust as soon as they are formally integrated in an official database—and second because it underlines a singularity and ambivalence of the IMF staff's position in international macroeconomic surveillance as both users and producers. Staff members collect data from the auditee, as an auditor usually does, but they also advise the auditee and help with preparing and disseminating the accounts. Referring to Michael Power's (1999) work on the "audit society," my argument thus complicates Desrosières's typology. When the auditor and the auditee try to present a firm's activity as "auditable," they are confronted with the obligation to use predetermined and formalized frameworks, and they try to build and preserve a mutual trust around the use and acceptance of a common language, sometimes with a certain degree of collusion. The formal requirement of data production can therefore surpass the concern with veracity. This is precisely the point Lampland (2010) proposes when considering quantification as a "formalization practice." She highlights two types of formalization practices, *provisional numbers* and *false numbers*, arguing that some of the most common and important quantifications may become misleading descriptions of reality because they are required to satisfy certain requirements in terms of formalism. The actors she studies learn how to fill in empty cells even in the absence of data and sometimes without any initial technical knowledge. Lampland shows that *false numbers* may result from the use of the formal rules of calculation, and not from their circumvention.

In Mauritania, the fiction also resulted from the implementation of norms and "good practices" recommended by normalizing authorities. I argue that the Mauritanian accounts produced with the IMF can be considered *false* because the formal criteria they have to satisfy to reach *consistency* impede a more detailed and better national accounts calculation. In particular, the balancing of accounting identities is guided by principles influenced by the bureaucratic constraints and power relations internal to the IMF. *False accounts* are not a transgression of the norms of the surveillance but a way to conform to them. In this respect, I consider the denunciation of the *statistical lie* in Mauritania as a crisis of an accepted and routinized method that leads to what should be called *false accounting*.

3. The IMF's Approach to Macroeconomic Accounts

Have the Mauritanian fictional aggregates been produced through the use of formal international accounting rules? What role do accounting standards play in the calculation of macroeconomic indicators in countries with sparse and fragmentary raw data? Can international accounting norms be employed to estimate national aggregates that are formally valid but lead to accounts that can also be considered *false*, and in what sense? The next section presents empirical observations on Mauritania to help answer such questions. Beforehand, existing works should be mobilized to help refine those questions and examine what we already know about them.

3.1. Judgment in the Use of Outdated Macroeconomic Models at the IMF

Drawing on various sources, one can come to understand IMF economists' method of *financial programming*, one of the central tools guiding their quantitative work when interacting with the national governments.[2] Financial programming is not a rigorous model but a series of interrelated tables and lists of indicators covering the four "macroeconomic accounts" falling under IMF scrutiny: public finance, balance of payments, financial and monetary sector, and productive sector (or "real sector," in IMF terminology). Standard accounting identities are also used to establish the coherence between the various accounts (e.g., the coherence between the public deficit, appearing in public finance statistics, and the data on the

---

2. This account of the validation criteria and the social norms employed by IMF economists draws on Harper 1998, Mussa and Savastano 1999, and Easterly 2002.

banking sector's net claims on the government, appearing in monetary statistics). A few simple behavioral equations are also used, like the monetarist "quantity equation of money" linking inflation to money creation. Financial programming's accounting backbone helps IMF teams verify the coherence of the macroeconomic data collected from past periods, to recalculate them, and to build forecasts. In practice it serves as the IMFs central analytic tool kit for conducting the "reviews" of ongoing lending agreements, preparing scenarios for new lending agreements, or performing required surveillance activities.[3] The quantitative activities of an IMF economist in charge of a country (and thus part of one of the institution's "area departments") are centered on the management of the country's indicator tables. National civil servants cooperate by gathering data, computing indicators, and presenting both to the IMF teams who will verify, discuss, and amend the calculation methods.

In his ethnography of the IMF, Richard Harper (1998) describes the preparation of official documents by IMF staff. He reveals that the main preoccupation of the area departments' economists is not to achieve a high level of rigor or precision in either their statistical work or their economic analysis but to provide analytic work in support of proposed lending programs that can be considered adequate given the IMF's organization. Their validation criteria find expression in what they call the *consistency* of a program or a scenario, and in the *thoroughness* of an indicator, concepts that substantially differ from notions of scientificity, or rigor. First, IMF staff must gather as much relevant data as possible to build the program scenarios. Programs and indicators must comply with certain formats, nomenclatures, and predefined presentation templates. Second, the policy scenarios should be shown to be in accordance with the IMF's statutory missions and views, that is, they should aim at reducing countries' external disequilibrium and at ensuring financial stability. This will translate into typical policy recommendations for which IMF adjustment policies have become famous: limiting public expenditure levels and money creation (i.e., access to credit) (see also Easterly 2002: 3). To justify proposed policy measures, they refer to certain dominant interpretations of the economy embraced by the IMF. Financial programming relies on the quantity theory of money, as already mentioned, and also on the so-called monetary (fiscal) interpretation of the balance of payments, which links the level of credit (of

3. Article IV of IMF status obliges any member country to provide the IMF with all the information needed to assess its economic and financial situation.

public expenditure) to the level of imports. These simple equations have been at the heart of many controversies, and many academics and former staff of the IFIs have reproached this elite institution's use of outdated textbook economics in its analytic packages (e.g., Easterly 2001; Stiglitz 2003), particularly the IMF monetary model, or Polak model, that formalized the monetary interpretation of the balance of payments, dating back to the 1950s (Polak 1997).[4] The IMF staff interviewed by Harper testified to the fact that they use financial programming as a practical accounting backbone in their mission work, centering the dialogue with governments on concrete policy and data discussions, explaining that the use of financial programming is pragmatic and iterative—inscribed in a series of exchanges with the governments, in order to adjust figures, policy variables, and targets for the future. The model also leaves ample discretionary margins for judgment, with many options for estimating detailed indicators or using more advanced specific modules (e.g., to model monetary dynamics or exchange rate fluctuations [Berg, Karam, and Laxton 2006]). In sum, financial programming enables area departments' economists to express their professional quality by building informed, detailed judgments on the economy they observe while respecting certain formal requirements. This is what the notion of *consistency* refers to. IMF directors thus claim that no model would be adequate to express the fine-grained and concrete approach to policy analysis of its staff, whose flexible approaches to using models prove that they are not dogmatic (Mussa and Savastano 1999).

3.2. Discipline in the Use of Outdated Macroeconomic Models at the IMF

One could argue that trial and error and "cooking" are characteristic of any modeling work (Boumans 1999).[5] So how could we better characterize the singularity of the IMF's use of financial programming? We could go beyond Harper and add that the affinities of IMF economists' economic work with certain interpretive frames can be expressed in very pragmatic terms. For example, the formal monetarist equations have to remain a general reference point in their arguments. Consider their use of the quantity theory of money. It relies on the always verified equation, pT

---

4. Jacques Polak was director of the IMF's research department from 1958 to 1979.

5. For empirical illustrations of the trial and error process in national accounts computation and macro-modeling, see Fourquet 1980 and Kramarz 1988.

$=MV$, where p stands for prices, T for volume of transactions, M for money in circulation, and V for velocity of money. According to monetarist theories, the velocity of money should be constant, yielding a permanent link between prices and money creation. In IMF programs, the value of the velocity of money will be checked *ex post*, but its assumed stability will be seen as a sign of *consistency* of the scenario, although empirical economics has cast serious doubt on this assumption (Easterly 2002).

Harper also indicates that the use of models by the IMF is related to hierarchical organization of the IMF's work. IMF economists in charge of a country strive to produce documents that will be as persuasive as possible to the supervising bodies of the IMF, their work being inserted into a top-down bureaucratic authority structure. In particular, staff productions have to be immediately *legible* to their colleagues and by the hierarchy. Documents are subject to a strict peer review before being presented to the IMF's executive board and before any possible validation. For the economists, it is important not to risk presenting documents that will likely be criticized. The peer review procedures take place after each mission, that is, every three months in "program countries." Therefore, the choices of estimating methods, projections, and economic analysis, as well as the presentation of tables, have to conform as much as possible to the board's and reviewers' expectations: they should respect the traditional interpretive frameworks of the IMF, and there should be "no surprise" analyses or methods (Harper 1998: 123). This attitude is guided less by the fear of sanctions—since the review mechanisms ensure that disputable points are dealt with—than by the need to anticipate what will be considered reasonable and to avoid losing time and energy. Conformity with the monetary approach of balance of payments, or with the quantity theory of money, will be taken as signs of consistency; arguments based on any other interpretive framework must be compelling enough to convince the entire hierarchy and will appear risky. In the same vein, indicator tables have to be complete and standardized. Those are the conventions regulating IMF economists' work.

Despite the flexible use they make of it, financial programming makes the obligation of formal legibility a pivotal element in economic and statistical works inside the IMF. The links between an IMF country economist and government officials are therefore quite strong and complex: they share a common cause when facing the board; but economists are also accountable for the rigor of their surveillance and must put pressure on a country's government when needed. The quantification thus occurs in a context in accordance with what Power (1999) described about the audits taking place in a company, yielding to ambivalent and close relationships between the auditor and the auditee. This surveillance is exerted by very formal means, which opens the way to overvaluing formal conformity over the pertinence of economic description and advice.

3.3. Problematic Uses of Accounting Identities

William Easterly's account of the quantitative estimation procedures occasioned by financial programming also helps to explain why its methodological choices appear to be disputable in terms of economic pertinence and precision. Financial programming is centered on various balance-sheet identities that link monetary and fiscal variables to the balance of payments to ensure the consistency of estimates. But IMF economists exploit the central accounting identities in disputable ways to do their estimation job. For example, in using the classical identity $Y = C_h + C_g + I_h + I_g + X - M$, they decide on an ad hoc basis which variable should be labeled "exogenous" (typically Y [the GDP], about which economists generally have information or make hypotheses, or X [exports], generally calculated by simple hypotheses on the future production levels of export sectors); which variable is a policy variable, on which the government is supposed to act (e.g., the level of public expenditures C_g and I_g); and which one will be calculated as a residual, by applying the accounting identity. In the example, imports (M) and household consumption and investment (C_h and I_h) remain to be inferred by trial and error. M can be projected exogenously using simple methods suggested in one of the ready-to-use financial programming manuals, and I_h will typically be set to zero, leaving household consumption C_h to be calculated as the residual. Easterly shows how in each of the accounting identities, this process creates a mechanical link between the endogenous variable and the policy variable, a "one-to-one" relationship, which, he shows, has no theoretical basis (here between household consumption C_h and public expenditures, $C_g + I_g$). He also shows that the estimation procedures used in financial programming not only fare poorly empirically but do worse than very simple procedures would, for example, adding a simple random variable to a linear historical tendency. Further, for many of those accounting identities, all the terms of the equation are in fact interrelated and thus "endogenous," and contemporary macroeconomics provides more-refined models to make sense of their evolutions. The IMF does not integrate such knowledge into its standard packages, even though some of the models have been explored by the IMF research department (Berg, Karam, and Laxton 2006). The financial-planning approach discourages IMF economists from building more-refined and pertinent models for their work, as this would be both time consuming and less legible than the process just described.

In the remainder of this article, I show empirically why those IMF "accounting inferences" can be considered *false accounting* practices that can be added to Lampland's typology of formalizing practices (*provisional numbers* and *false numbers*). By *false accounting*, I mean an inferential practice validated by formal compliance with accounting identities, in which estimation choices and judgments in the quantification process are guided by institutional relations and yield nonpertinent results in terms of economic analysis (because they fare badly empirically and analytically). The discovery and resolution of data discrepancies is at the heart of the national accountants' science, whose judgments are dedicated to artfully balancing necessary identities. Historically, several methods have been applied. The lack of data and weakness of statistical services has sometimes justified a partial and simplified use of national accounts identities, notably in the "developing world" where, according to historians like André Vanoli (2002: 260) or Paul Studenski (1958: 256), some variables like household revenues have often been calculated as residuals, opening the way to Desrosières's (2001) pragmatic accounting position. However, as I show, IMF economists use such simplistic estimation procedures even when better solutions are available, for reasons that appear linked to the IMF's economic work organization. I have identified three pillars that guide the economist's work at the IMF: the reference to the search for artful judgments in IMF economic analysis and modeling, the need to build scenarios in accordance with a rigid set of consistency criteria, and finally the necessary compliance with accounting identities and standardized templates. My argument, which neither Harper nor Easterly makes, is that the formal compliance of economic work with these criteria surpasses the objective of veracity in the computation of the accounts. *False accounting* occurs as IMF economists strive to comply with accepted social norms inside the IMF and in their work with national economists. I thus contradict Harper's optimism with regard to the IMF's analytic work and complete Easterly's argument by explaining the social practices that legitimate problematic accounting inferences.

4. The Formal Requirements of GDP
Calculation in Mauritania

I now offer an empirical examination of the estimation procedures used to create national accounts in Mauritania, especially the calculation of the GDP. My aim is not to provide a detailed explanation of the constitution of Mauritania's statistical fiction over the years.[6] Rather, by focusing on a fragment of the macroeconomic puzzle at the very moment when the omissions were the largest (2003–4), I illustrate how macroeconomic aggregates could be produced, unchallenged by a more detailed analysis, simply to fuel the formal procedures of macroeconomic management of the IMF.

In addition, the replacement of the old and basic series of national accounts by a much more sophisticated set of accounts was underway in 2004–6, during the revision of the macroeconomic data. Comparing the two series offers the opportunity to underline the characteristics of the national accounting practices employed by the IMF for the surveillance of the country, illustrates other functions these accounts can perform, and explains how *false accounting* was encouraged.

National accounts play a role in IMF surveillance activities, the GDP being a central indicator of economic activity in program countries. The GDP also serves as a denominator in calculating economic performance ratios, like those included in the most commonly "selected macroeconomic indicators" that serve in the evaluation of financial programs (e.g., the public expenditure to GDP ratio, or the current account balance as a percentage of GDP).[7] Other IMF departments also deal with national accounts data, as the promotion and monitoring of international standards and codes is one of the IMF's missions (see IMF 2001). Finally, the IMF also has technical assistance units that include national accountants, some of which are in Africa. Even so, national accounts are not the heart of IMF's quantitative work. The institution is merely a user of the systems of national accounts historically produced under the auspices of the United Nations Statistical Division. In surveillance work, financial programming does not use the national accounts as the integrative statistical framework it is conceived to be, with the balance of payments and monetary and fiscal issues being given much more attention (Easterly 2002).

---

6. For a comprehensive examination of the construction of GDP figures over the years in several African countries, see Jerven 2014.

7. On the resilience of the use of GDP, see Fioramonti 2013 and Hirschman 2016.

4.1. Calculating the GDP with IMF Missions:
Filling the Cells with Numbers

Detailed Discussions of GDP Figures but with Superficial Use of Accounting Identities.   Apart from the mission chief, IMF mission teams generally include specialists in public finance, external payments, monetary accounts, and the "real economy"; the economists (called desk officers) may remain assigned to a country for several years. In African "program countries" (i.e., those having a lending program with the IMF), the missions take place every three months, enabling one or two weeks of joint work with national administrations. IMF staff thus have the opportunity to build a deep knowledge of a country's economy and to link up with its administration. For IMF mission teams, there is one obligation: should the national administrations be faring poorly in their analytic jobs, should the national data be trustable or not, they have to come up with an image as complete as possible of the country's economy in order for the IMF to complete its surveillance mission and monitor its financial assistance programs. National administrations of member countries are obliged to provide IMF economists with all available and necessary data to do so. So when a mission to Mauritania arrives in Nouakchott, these delegations of economists go to long rounds of meetings with the economic and financial administrations to collect data, interviewing large and strategic companies and leading businesspeople, banks, and industries, and foreign cooperation or diplomatic corps in search of information. The essence of their task is to fill in the blanks in the numerous financial programming tables with the bits of information they gather, simple recipes being included in the financial programming manual to suggest estimation methods and cope with data limitations. For example, accessing the production and export quantities of cement enables one to estimate the activity of the construction sector (IMF 1996; Daumont et al. 1999: 127; Barth and Hemphill 2000).

It is through such tasks that the qualities of economists are supposed to find their expression: intuition, good judgment, and the ability to come up with artfully created documents and figures, adequately formalized, and consistent with the IMF's expectations. Such work may seem reminiscent of activities of the so-called pioneers of development economics, like Stolper, who, after contributing to the elaboration of Nigeria's first plan, produced the classic account of the construction of statistics and economic policies in contexts with limited data (Stolper 1966; Morgan 2008). Stolper would travel the country, keeping records of all the information parcels he

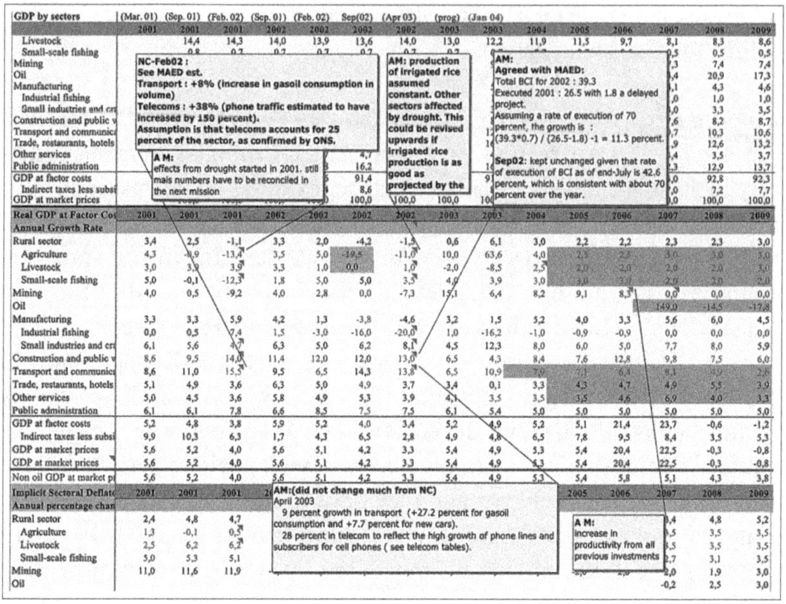

Figure 1 IMF financial programming worksheet on GDP for Mauritania (Feb. 2004).

could gather, and integrate these fragments into a global representation of the economy. The similarity with my description of IMF economists is striking. On paper, the IMF economist's ethos seems to embody an empirical approach very much in accordance with Stolper's attention to details. But is the comparison pertinent?

The examination of an IMF file on Mauritanian GDP dating back to the beginning of 2004 (figure 1) may give some clues to the IMF economist's effective practices. The table presents the detailed calculation of GDP growth and its decomposition by sectors. In almost every cell, staff members placed comments to explain calculation choices, revealing the type of reasoning used for estimation or projection work.[8] Each cell indicates how the collected information is used to estimate sectoral growth in recent periods or to project it in the near future. The first striking element to appear is the relational dimension of this estimation work, the comments suggesting a lively discussion between economists and statisticians from

8. These comments do not appear unless the user places his or her mouse on the cell; I activated an option to make some of them visible.

various institutions over the calculation choices. These institutions include Mauritanian administrations, like the ministry of economic affairs and development (MAED), the ONS, the ministry of finance, or the World Bank. In the absence of perfectly matching indicators, the comments explain the subjective judgments and hypotheses made to estimate the sectoral growth figures. The confrontations and exchanges between economists of different institutions show that the macroeconomic quantification of the economy is a coproduction.

They also refer to earlier periods, either to compare the observed results to the projections made earlier or to find inspirations in the tricks used in the past, sometimes years before and by a predecessor ("AM" and "NC"). They show the reproduction from year to year, with minor changes, of the same techniques without much debate, and the search for alternate variables when the usual indicators are not available. In addition, records of the successive estimates corresponding to each mission of the year are kept in the file several years later. They recall the permanent data revision work and point to the importance of keeping track of the justification of past choices, which may engage governments and IMF staff. The presence of the economists' names, institutions, and positions personalizes these exchanges, ensuring a kind of traceability of calculation choices— maybe in relation to their personal responsibility in the calculation.[9]

Also striking is that IMF economists interact with the government on an equal basis. They not only verify the national civil servants' effort, by discussing their hypotheses and methods, contradicting them or suggesting alternatives; the statistical work conducted by IMF economists is a complete recalculation of the GDP by sector. As I show, their calculations may become the official figures, endorsed by the government. The roles of the auditor and the auditee may thus somehow be inverted. This is all the more problematic in that the method remains very simple, almost simplistic. GDP is only estimated by combining sectoral growth figures, a method considered insufficient when judged by the generally accepted standards of national accounting.

The verification and triangulation lying at the heart of the national accounting job, ensuring the aggregate's accuracy, consists in confronting the supply side (production and imports) and demand (consumption, export, and investment), and making sure that they balance. Financial programming procedures balance this equation by calculating household

9. The file was anonymized to be presented here.

consumption as a residual. This may be necessary in countries with sparse data on households (Studenski 1958; Vanoli 2002). But as I show below, by comparing the IMF numbers with much more detailed series published by the ONS a year and half later, the resulting data on household consumption appear to be inaccurate and economically incoherent. The IMF could employ more refined calculation procedures but does not: in 2006, when the improved series of national accounts became available, IMF teams chose to accept the new data but to keep their own calculation procedures for future mission work.

The time frame of the data revisions also proves the low interest of IMF teams in accepted international standards for national accounting. No revisions are entered after the first trimester following a given year (first trimester of year $N + 1$ for year N accounts), although the recommended time frame for the revision of provisional figures and the publication of definitive national accounts is in mid $N + 2$ for year N figures.

Coming back to the comparison between IMF missions and Stolper's approach, some major differences appear. If following Harper's (1998: 198) expression, calculating an indicator is for IMF teams like "peeling an onion" (because each component needs verification), a main difference with Stolper is that the onion already exists. IMF economists reconduct a routinized and unsatisfactory set of techniques of inference to calculate the indicators in cooperation with the government. Keeping in mind the objective to "provide no surprise" to the hierarchy, their method gathers secondary data to use with previously established and routinized methods (Harper 1998: 123). By doing so, they not only neglect the most basic tools of national accounting but also risk reproducing mechanically the same macroeconomic fiction from year to year. Stolper's relation to the data is entirely different: it is centered on using every bit of information to document and quantify social processes. The paradox is that their ethos refers to a Stolper style, portraying their information gathering in an adverse environment as heroic and representing their analysis as the result of artful judgments. IMF economists are proud of the fact that they can reveal to a minister what he or she ignores about his or her own economy (Harper 1998). But in national situations where administrations are fragmented and where information hardly circulates, this capacity to centralize information is a source of power. IMF teams can gather the information because of the dominant position they occupy due to their international role in certifying the macroeconomic situation of a country, the Article IV obligation being their main tool. Contrary to their account, their authority may result in elaborating *false accounts* of the economy, although one considered *consistent* by IMF standards (Harper 1998; Samuel 2011, 2014).

Finally, the ambivalence of the relation described by Power (1999) between the auditor and the auditee, made by a mix of collusion and control through the use of formal obligation, is perfectly illustrated by the preceding material. Much more than providing a pertinent diagnosis of a firm's situation (here a country), an audit sets the condition for reconducting the audit relationship. It permanently aims at enhancing the auditability while never achieving it. The cycle of estimates and revisions can be considered an illustration of this process; neither the level of aggregation, the methods, nor the variables are ever called into question, despite being unsatisfactory; they define the boundary of the auditing norms, of the thinkable, and set the condition to continuously reproduce the relation between the auditor and the auditee. *False national accounting* works here as a formalizing practice enabling a reconducting of the IMF-country relationship.

Rigidity versus Rigor in Estimation Work.   According to Harper (1998: 137), when numbers produced for mission work lack rigor and pertinence, because they conform to the timeliness and institutional requirements of "consistency," they end up being replaced by more robust data in the IMF's databases. But is this really the case? Does time really enable the validation and production of national country figures, freed from the constraints of the audit relation in which they were initially produced? Given the time frame of data revisions mentioned in the previous section, we may doubt it. Indeed, the revision of data, although it belongs to the normal process of statistical production, has proved to be difficult over the history of IMF intervention in African countries.

The IMF may indeed impose some decisions in the validation of long-term series, rightfully or not. An example from Burkina Faso is noteworthy. The 1997–98 agricultural season had been particularly bad in Burkina, and the estimates of agricultural production had been revised several times after the end of the season—a normal phenomenon when large changes occur, requiring the compilation of robust, definitive information from the ground. The drop in the production level was revealed to be more dramatic as data were refined: the definitive figures showed a yearly decline of 20 percent, while the first figures showed a 10 percent drop. These new figures required an alteration of assumptions in the national Burkinabè model that administrations were using to calculate growth. This model was more sophisticated than the IMF's calculation method, and a change in the agricultural sector would yield to a change in the economic equilibrium because the model could take into account the lower exports, lower household incomes, lower consumption levels, and so forth. The IMF, however, refused to modify the figures it had established the year before, insisting that those numbers had to be considered official. The country's economists, and those managing the model within the General Directorate of Economic Planning, engaged in a tug-of-war because their work was threatened by this institutional rigidity. The refusal of IMF teams indeed placed them in a difficult situation: they would either ignore the IMF's reaction and compute new and rigorous estimates that differed from all the indicators that international organizations and economists were using, which aligned with the IMF numbers, or they could keep the *false number*, only mitigating the effects of this number on the estimation of the rest of the national data by using tricks to disconnect it in the model. And this is what they did, choosing the *false accounting* solution.

Such examples of rigidity of IMF teams are actually frequent when dealing with the IMF's work. In Mauritania, at the end of the 1990s, the IMF did not agree on certain estimates for fisheries and agriculture, but the ONS never consented to align with the IMF's estimates. For this reason, the GDP data published by the IMF and the ONS differed until the post-2004 data revision. However, this decision was costly for ONS: in the first half of the 2000s, the IMF judged its contact with the ONS to be problematic and not useful enough for the IMF's short-term imperatives. Instead, IMF missions discussed their national accounts estimates and projections with the ministry of economy and decided on a discretionary basis when to take the ONS figures into account to revise their past data. ONS had lost the status of an official source on national accounts, and the IMF had also forsaken its contact with the country's only experts in national accounting.

Struggles occurred again in 2006 around the fisheries sector. As a result of the intervention of national accounts experts, and of the use of the 1993 System of National Accounts, the added value of the fisheries had to be substantially revised: quantities caught in Mauritanian waters and directly exported without being landed had to be considered production. IMF teams remained reluctant to apply this norm, which would raise the level of the GDP, although the recommendations were clear, but they finally accepted. The relation between the IMF and Mauritania, both directed by surveillance (auditor to auditee) and by the contractual relation (lender to creditor), places a burden on the formalization of the economy. In such conditions, the very notion of *consistency* of data over time may reflect not the usual conception where homogeneity refers to a stable statistical definition and to comparable sources but the respect of past definitions, when they were considered official, taking a contractual value.[10] Rigidity may be opposed to rigor in the quantification of African economies.

4.2. When a Mauritanian Statistical Innovation
Uncovers the False GDP Accounting

The Mauritanian macroeconomic data just presented, used in the 2000s, are part of a series started in 1983. But twenty years without a new base year make a series comparable to a distorting mirror for a national economy, and the 1983 series followed an outdated standard. Modernization projects thus emerged at the end of 1990, with the support of Afristat, a subregional francophone statistical organization.[11] Started in 1999, the production of the new series progressed very slowly, requiring a stable team of national accountants to gather exhaustive sources on the economy and aggregate them. The project eventually took twelve years, leading to the publication in 2011 of a complete and definitive series of accounts for 1998–2007 (Office National de la Statistique 2011). However, in 2006 some of the estimates emerging from the project were used to correct macroeconomic data after the misreporting scandal. Comparing the two series helps formulate a number of hypotheses on the type of inference involved in GDP and growth calculations prior to 2006.

The qualitative differences between the old and the improved data series were indeed important. The improved national accounts were built with attention to reconciling supply and demand, both inside each economic branch and for the economy as a whole. The consumption of households, of the administration, the investment of firms and the capital formation, considered completely impossible to document in former IMF-led practices, were calculated using existing sources (e.g., household surveys, or accounting documents of the firms). Following the macroeconomic data scandal, the IMF sent a mission to Nouakchott to determine the most suitable revision method for national accounts—but not until the end of the revision process, a year and a half after the denunciation of the Mauritanian "misreporting."[12] The mission was led by a French national accountant from the

10. On the tables and series as heterogeneous patchworks, see Samuel 2013: 108.
11. Observatoire économique et statistique d'Afrique Sub-sahariennes.
12. Three years—1998, 1999, and 2000—had already been produced.

IMF regional center for technical assistance (Afritac) based in Bamako, who had previously worked for Afristat. He understood the methodology that the national office had adopted to produce better data. His mission proposed a compromise that involved putting up the available years of the new data series, taking advantage of the work done with Afristat and of the existing years of accounts (Métreau 2006). However, he did not propose to abandon the financial-programming-compatible supply-side approach of GDP, which contributed to the *false accounting* practice. At that time, he could have done so by recommending the use of a similar technique as employed in Burkina, based on an input-output table, even for rapid estimates. One must believe that it was not IMF economists' priority.

The comparison between the revised series and the old one is particularly revealing. First, consider the most problematic variable of the old series, the data on household consumption, calculated as a residual. The original series, which the IMF continued to publish in its official reports until 2003 despite its evident statistical problems, was subjected to variations that cannot be linked to any important economic events and that unrealistically exceed 10 percent of GDP for a single year. The revised series gives a completely different picture, based on detailed calculations using household survey data. Over the same years, between 1998 and 2002, final household consumption shows regular variations, consistent with known events of the period.[13]

Figure 2 shows a chart that compares aggregate economic growth derived from the two series, for the same years, 1999 to 2004. The initial growth level of the series endorsed and published by the IMF has a much higher mean and a much more restrained variability: growth is never below 3 percent, let alone showing a recession. Variations are smooth, between 3 and 6.5 percent. The revised series, however, shows years of recession or slow growth, with strong variability, not surprising for a small economy subjected to many external shocks, in agriculture, mining, and fisheries in particular. The steady growth record portrayed in the old series is likely linked to the "no surprise" imperative that guides IMF economists, and their preoccupation with the *consistency* of the macro-

13. The IMF consumption series, labeled "non-government consumption," is itself highly hybrid, since it includes public enterprises and households. Its values as a percentage of GDP from 1998 to 2002 were as follows: 1998, 79.1; 1999, 78.1; 2000, 66.1; 2001, 71.1; 2002, 76.9 (IMF 2003: 4). Compare this to the ratio of "final household consumption" to "total resources" calculated from the revised estimates over the same period: 1998, 54.7; 1999, 53.3; 2000, 51.3; 2001, 50.3; 2002, 51.6 (Office National de la Statistique 2011: 39).

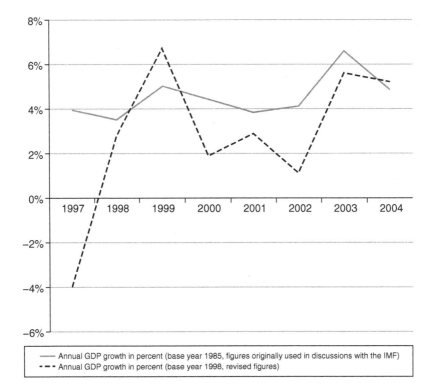

Figure 2 Mauritanian growth calculated with the IMF (base year 1985) versus growth calculated with ONS's definitive figures (new series of national accounts, base year 1998): aggregate growth.
Source: Data from ONS and IMF, author's calculations.

economic scenario (IMF 2004). The IMF's excessive optimism in its programs (overestimates of growth and underestimates of inflation) has been documented, even by the IMF's Internal Evaluation Office. In the Mauritanian case, I have seen diplomatic documents showing that international donors wanted to make the country a "good pupil" and a "success story." For example, despite the macroeconomic scandal of 2004–6, Mauritania was among the first countries to benefit from the new multilateral debt cancellation mechanisms launched in the mid-2000s.

Figure 3 enables one to be more precise about the calculation tactics used to make the data appear more *thorough* and *consistent*. The graph allows one to analyze the fluctuations of the national economy by grouping the contribution to growth of stable versus unstable sectors: sectors highly subject to external shocks, like agriculture, mining, and fisheries

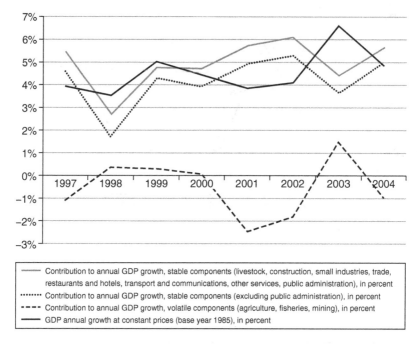

Figure legend:
——— Contribution to annual GDP growth, stable components (livestock, construction, small industries, trade, restaurants and hotels, transport and communications, other services, public administration), in percent
········ Contribution to annual GDP growth, stable components (excluding public administration), in percent
---- Contribution to annual GDP growth, volatile components (agriculture, fisheries, mining), in percent
——— GDP annual growth at constant prices (base year 1985), in percent

Figure 3 Mauritanian growth calculated with the IMF (base year 1985) versus growth calculated with ONS's definitive figures (new series of national accounts, base year 1998): stable versus volatile components of growth.

Source: Data from ONS and IMF, author's calculations.

were grouped, and their consolidated contribution to growth was then contrasted with that of the more stable sectors (construction and public works, trade, small industries, services, etc.). Aggregate fluctuations of growth are largely determined by the unstable sectors. The stable sectors have a regular and strong contribution to growth, between three and six points a year. But the graph also shows a curious pattern: since 1999, the unstable sectors' and stable sectors' contributions to growth vary in opposite directions, as if their respective fluctuations were compensating each other. The pattern suggests a negative correlation between these two sources of aggregate growth. There is, however, no reason to expect such a negative statistical relation. The most logical explanation is given by the growth computation procedure resulting from the negotiation of programs and surveillance by the IMF, under the supervision of the board, in the search for "consistency." Economists look for an "acceptable" record of growth. When unstable sectors tend to collapse, the economists will, of course, let it appear in the calculation—a severe drop in the mining sector or in agriculture is widely discussed in the press and cannot be ignored. But overall growth should never appear too high or too low, which would seem unlikely and risky. It is easy, however, to adjust aggregate growth by manipulating some calculation mechanism for the stable sectors: choosing one price deflator instead of another, or changing the methodology used to calculate a sector's growth. This is precisely the judgment work of economists. But with such judgment, 2004's Mauritania is a country that, despite flourishing mineral prices, has no sign of higher growth or recessions or low-growth years. What this graph most probably reveals is the objective of teams of Mauritanian and IMF economists and statisticians to display an acceptable growth story with no surprises, reproducing the well-known through standardized calculation methods. And one can say without a doubt, using the IMF's ethereal language, that Mauritania's growth is sustained but still insufficient and that the country is subjected to regular external shocks.

When confronted with more robust data, these old series reveal their creators' lack of concern for realism. They use accounting equations and methods to calculate numbers, without making use of the available data that would contribute to a better representation of the economy, and orient the results to conform to institutional considerations that are external to their main inferential goal. This exemplifies what I have called false accounting practices.

Conclusion

This article has studied the inference procedures used to estimate macroeconomic indicators used in the IMF's monitoring of country financial assistance programs and international surveillance tasks.

It was motivated by a puzzle: in 2005 the IMF launched a procedure to denounce a Mauritanian "misreporting," leading to a revision of the country's macroeconomic indicators over a twelve-year period and revealing statistical omissions of a very large magnitude. The omissions and the economic tensions that accompanied them, like price hikes, interior indebtment, or the currency's external value erosion on the black market, had remained largely unnoticed in official statistics and publications of the IFIs. The fragmentary and diverse nature of the activities dedicated to computing macroeconomic statistics makes it possible to consider that the production of this statistical fiction was a collective social process and unintentional for many of the actors involved—although it had of course large political and social effects. In its "Report on the Revision of Economic Data, 1992–2004," the Mauritanian government stated that "macroeconomic management became increasingly inappropriate to the real situation, often with the advice of partners who had been misled, leading to the taking of measures that fostered imbalances instead of combating them" (République Islamique de Mauritanie 2006). Policies were elaborated, formally discussed, and implemented on the basis of this fiction. If statistics and accounting figures are always fictional in the sense that they integrate partial subjectivity in the calculation, statisticians and accountants generally look for a pragmatic validation of their estimates, using tests of reality. How could this statistical fiction be validated over the years by the IMF in spite of its continuous detailed economic and financial surveillance, data collection and verification, and advisory activities? What part did IMF teams and methods take in the elaboration of Mauritania's statistical fiction?

The work of Power (1999) showed that the auditor-auditee relation between IMF teams and governments may place less importance on veracity and pertinence than on the formal conformity of data and policy scenarios with various formal expectations inside the IMF. As Harper (1998) demonstrated, IMF economists' collaboration with national civil servants subjects the production of data and policy scenarios to IMF internal validation criteria and cycles. In particular, for programs and scenarios to be considered "consistent," tables of estimates must be comprehensive, even when basic data are sparse, and the economic diagnosis must comply with the IMF's economic preconceptions. Conformity of economic analysis with economic frameworks like the so-called monetary interpretation of the balance of payments ensures the legibility of documents and programs presented to the board. Unlike Harper, who argued that the deployment of artful economic judgments by IMF staff enabled high-quality statistical work and policy advice, I acknowledge the position of authors like Easterly, for whom the IMF's quantitative techniques entail the misuse of accounting identities for the production of macroeconomic estimates. However, while affirming that IMF economists use empirically disproved relations and estimation procedures, Easterly does not explain why they may do so.

This is what I do by analyzing the financial programming tables used in Mauritania in the early 2000s. I focus on national accounting in Mauritania and show that the treatment of basic accounting identities like the supply-demand equilibrium neglect the importance of fundamental economic variables like household consumption or investment. In addition, the techniques used to estimate and build short-term GDP forecasts combine sectoral figures, so that the use of interchangeable proxies is at the heart of negotiations with government agencies. According to their internal comments, the reconducting of the same calculation techniques over the years is taken as a validation criteria by IMF economists, ensuring both the stability of relations between the auditor (IMF) and the auditee (government) and the legibility of the calculation to internal reviewers. However, these estimation techniques exclude the accurate apprehension of important variables, and they do not capture emerging economic tensions. Such methodological choices are made even when alternative methods could be used, for example, after the new and more robust series of national accounts was produced by the government in 2006. I also show that there has long been a rigidity in IMF calculation methods. I therefore argue that national accounting data coproduced by the IMF and national economists can be called *false accounting*, with reference to Lampland, where formal conformity with IMF consistency criteria surpasses the importance of veracity. This interpretation offers a solution to the puzzle posed by the coexistence of arguments testifying to the problematic character of the IMF analytic tool kit and the observations that IMF economists are building their professional recognition on the quality of their judgment and analysis. I show that, given the criteria used to define consistency inside the IMF, some judgments that can be considered artful actually neglect the importance of veracity to favor conformity with the formalism and expectations of the IMF board.

References

Bakari, G. 2004. "Flambée des prix, le panier de la ménagère soumis à rude épreuve." *Nouakchott Info* (February 23): 1, 3.

Barth, Richard, and William Hemphill. 2000. *Financial Programming and Policy: The Case of Turkey*. Washington, DC: International Monetary Fund.

Berg, A., P. Karam, and D. Laxton. 2006. *A Practical Model-Based Approach to Monetary Policy Analysis—Overview*. Working Paper WP/06/80. Washington, DC: IMF.

Bonnecase, V. 2014. "Des revenus nationaux pour l'Afrique? La mesure du développement en Afrique Occidentale française dans les années 1950." *Canadian Journal of Development Studies* 35, no. 1: 28–43.

Boumans, Marcel. 1999. "Built-in Justification." In *Models as Mediators*, edited by M. Morgan and M. Morrisson, 66–96. Cambridge: Cambridge University Press.

Bowker, G. C., and Susan Leigh Star. 1999. *Sorting Things Out: Classification and Its Consequences*. Cambridge, MA: MIT Press.

Daumont, R., M. de Zamaróczy, P. Callier, and B. Ziller. 1999. *Programmation financière: Méthodes et application à la Tunisie*. Washington, DC: IMF.

Davie, G. 2015. *Poverty Knowledge in South Africa: A Social History of Human Science, 1855–2005*. Cambridge: Cambridge University Press.

Desrosières, Alain. 2001. "How Real Are Statistics? Four Possible Attitudes." *Social Research* 68, no. 2: 339–55.

Easterly, William. 2001. *The Elusive Quest for Growth: Economists' Adventures and Misadventures in the Tropics*. Cambridge, MA: MIT Press.

Easterly, William. 2002. "An Identity Crises? Testing IMF Financial Programming." Working Paper Number 9, August. Center for Global Development, Washington, DC.

Fioramonti, L. 2013. *Gross Domestic Problem: The Politics behind the World's Most Powerful Number*. London: Zed Books.

Fourquet, F. 1980. *Les comptes de la puissance: Histoire de la comptabilité nationale et du plan*. Paris: Encres, Éditions Recherches.

Harper, R. H. R. 1998. *Inside the IMF: An Ethnography of Documents, Technology, and Organizational Action*. San Diego: Academic.

Hibou, Béatrice. 2000. "The Political Economy of the World Bank's Discourse: From Economic Catechism to Missionary Deeds (and Misdeeds)." Translated by Janet Roitman. *Les Études du CERI*, no. 39

Hibou, Béatrice. 2011. "Macroéconomie et domination politique en Tunisie : du 'miracle économique' benaliste aux enjeux socio-économiques du moment révolutionnaire." *Politique africaine*, no. 124: 127–54.

Hibou, Béatrice. 2017. *The Political Anatomy of Domination*. The Sciences Po Series in International Relations and Political Economy. Basingstoke UK: Palgrave Macmillan.

Hibou, Béatrice, and Boris Samuel. 2011. "Macroéconomie et politique en Afrique." *Politique Africaine*, no. 124: 5–27.

Hirschman, D. A. 2016. "Inventing the Economy. Or: How We Learned to Stop Worrying and Love the GDP." PhD diss., University of Michigan.

IMF (International Monetary Fund). 1996. *Financial Programming and Policy: The Case of Sri Lanka*. Washington, DC: IMF.

IMF (International Monetary Fund). 2001. "Standards and Codes: The IMF's Role." *IMF Factsheet*. Washington, DC: IMF.

IMF (International Monetary Fund). 2003. *Islamic Republic of Mauritania: Statistical Appendix*. Country report no. 03/315. Washington, DC: IMF.

IMF (International Monetary Fund). 2004. *Policy Formulation, Analytical Frameworks, and Program Design*. Washington, DC: IMF.

IMF (International Monetary Fund). 2006. *Islamic Republic of Mauritania: 2005 Article IV Consultation—Staff Report*. Country report no. 06/247. Washington, DC: IMF.

Jerven, M. 2013. *Poor Numbers: How We Are Misled by African Development Statistics and What to Do about It*. Ithaca, NY: Cornell University Press.

Jerven, M. 2014. *Economic Growth and Measurement Reconsidered in Botswana, Kenya, Tanzania, and Zambia, 1965–1995*. Oxford: Oxford University Press.

Kramarz, F. 1988. "La comptabilité nationale à la maison." Paper presented at "Colloque International Logiques d'Entreprise et Formes de Légitimité," Paris, January 20–22.

Lampland, Martha. 2010. "False Numbers as Formalizing Practices." *Social Studies of Science* 40, no. 3: 377–404.

Métreau, E. 2006. *Compte-rendu de mission, révision de la série de comptes nationaux sur la période 1992–2005, Mauritanie, 5 au 15 Avril 2006*. Bamako: Afritac Ouest.

Morgan, Mary S. 2008. "'On a Mission' with Mutable Mobiles." Working Papers on the Nature of Evidence: How Well Do "Facts" Travel No. 34/08. Department of Economic History, London School of Economics.

Morgan, Mary S. 2011. "Seeking Parts, Looking for Wholes." In *Histories of Scientific Observation*, edited by L. Daston and E. Lunbeck, 303–25. Chicago: University of Chicago Press.

Mussa, M., and M. Savastano. 1999. "The IMF Approach to Economic Stabilization." Working Paper No. 99/104. International Monetary Fund.

Office National de la Statistique. 2011. "Le rapport 'provisoire' des comptes nationaux consolidés (1998–2007)." Nouakchott, July.

Ould Ghoulam, B. 2004. "La dévaluation a-t-elle eu lieu?" *Nouakchott Info*, May 6.

Polak, Jacques. 1997. "The IMF Monetary Model: A Hardy Perennial." *Finance and Development* 34, no. 4: 16–19.

Power, Michael. 1999. *The Audit Society: Rituals of Verification*. Oxford: Oxford University Press.

République Islamique de Mauritanie. 2006. "Rapport sur la Révision des Données Macroéconomiques, 1992–2004." Nouakchott, June.

Samuel, Boris. 2011. "Calcul macroéconomique et modes de gouvernement: Les cas du Burkina Faso et de la Mauritanie." *Politique Africaine*, no. 124: 101–26.

Samuel, Boris. 2013. "La production macroéconomique du réel: Formalités et pouvoir au Burkina Faso, en Mauritanie et en Guadeloupe." PhD diss., Institut d'Études Politiques, Paris.

Samuel, Boris. 2014. "Economic Calculations, Instability, and (In)formalization of the State in Mauritania, 2003–2011." *Canadian Journal of Development Studies* 35, no. 1: 77–96.

Samuel, Boris. 2016. "Studying Africa's Large Numbers." *Annales: Histoire, Sciences Sociales* 71, no. 4: 897–922.

Samuel, Boris. 2017. "Illegal Prices: The Social Contestation of High Living Costs in Guadeloupe and Mauritania." In *The Architecture of Illegal Markets*, edited by J. Beckert and M. Dewey, 268–85. Oxford: Oxford University Press.

Serra, G. 2015. "From Scattered Data to Ideological Education: Economics, Statistics, and the State in Ghana, 1948–1966." PhD diss., London School of Economics and Political Science.

Speich, D. 2011. "The Use of Global Abstractions: National Income Accounting in the Period of Imperial Decline." *Journal of Global History* 6, no. 1: 7–28.

Stiglitz, J. 2003. *Globalization and Its Discontents.* New York: Norton.

Stolper, Wolfgang F. 1966. *Planning without Facts.* Cambridge, MA: Harvard University Press.

Studenski, Paul. 1958. *The Income of Nations: Theory, Measurement, and Analysis, Past and Present: A Study in Applied Economics and Statistics.* New York: New York University Press.

Thévenot, L. 1984. "Rules and Implements: Investment in Forms." *Social Science Information* 23, no. 1: 1–45.

Thévenot, L. 2016. "From Social Coding to Economics of Convention: A Thirty-Year Perspective on the Analysis of Qualification and Quantification Investments." *Historical Social Research* 41, no. 2: 96–117.

Vanoli, André. 2002. *Une histoire de la comptabilité nationale.* Paris: La Découverte, Repères.

Inference in Time

Narrative Inference with and without Statistics: Making Sense of Economic Cycles with Malthus and Kondratiev

Mary S. Morgan

1. Drawing Inferences from Statistics: A Very Brief History

Statistical inference of the "classical" kind is bound by strict rules. It relies not just on numerical information but also on the fact that the set of observations is known to follow certain kinds of rules in terms of "sampling" and that the observations have come from a specific type of "population." Having such knowledge, or reason to believe it, was taken to support inferences to answer *what* questions in the nineteenth century, such as to provide the true measure of the path of a heavenly body (Carl Friedrich Gauss's question and the development of the law of error and least squares measure) or to find the average and distribution of deviancy in a population (Adolphe Quetelet's questions and the transfer of the error law from natural to human and social sciences). Thenceforth, such statistical thinking reframed the natural and human/social error curve into the biological "normal distribution" and measures of "co-relation" (to answer Francis

I thank the editors of this volume, Jeff Biddle and Marcel Boumans, the referees of the article, and the participants at the preliminary workshop, particularly Tom Stapleford and Aashish Velkar, for their really helpful comments and critiques, which pushed me to clarify the ideas in the article. I also thank my colleagues in the Narrative Science project (www.narrative-science. org/) in helping me think through these issues. This project has received funding from the European Research Council under the European Union's Horizon 2020 research and innovation program (grant agreement No. 694732).

History of Political Economy 53 (annual suppl.) DOI 10.1215/00182702-9414803

Galton's / Karl Pearson's biometric questions with a measure of covariance).[1] The development, in the twentieth century, of statistical inference rules of hypothesis testing involved formalizing scientific questions in ways that extended the inference domain to go one step beyond correlation to imply (possibly) causal relationships, and so potentially to answer *why* questions about the relationships between things.

These final moves to probability-based inference were understood in the early twentieth century to be fraught with difficulties for the social sciences, particularly economics, given both the nonsample nature of much economic data and the peculiar difficulties of time-series data. For economics, Trygve Haavelmo is credited as the source of a probability revolution prompting the gradual introduction of formal statistical inference methods and rules into economics.[2]

This short account raises the question: what was inference like before the rule-bound, probability-based, statistical inference of the twentieth century? One relevant element that has been well researched in the history of science is the attention paid in the early modern period to careful observation, often in extended scales over time, space, or institutions, in order to collect information en masse (see Pomata 2011). These observational activities in medicine, meteorology, commercial currents, and other phenomena of the natural and human worlds created pages, folios, and archives of "evidence." While recording such "observations" was often thought sufficient in itself, speculation about their meaning was not always considered proper until the eighteenth century, when observation and conjecture became viable partners in the tool box of natural philosophers (see Daston 2011).

There remained the problem of how such an observer/collector might figure out ways to abstract, generalize, or extract knowledge from such a mass of observations, that is, how to learn from, or draw inferences from, those observations. In one of the few explicit historical treatments of this question for economics, Harro Maas (2011) outlines how political economists of the late eighteenth to the late nineteenth century made arguments from observations. I take his account to suggest three modes: *generalizing*

1. These developments are broadly interrogated in two separate monographs (Porter 1986; Stigler 1986) and in the two volumes that came out of "the Probabilistic Revolution project" (see Krüger, Daston, and Heidelberger 1987; Krüger, Gigerenzer, and Morgan 1987). These writings offered new starting points following a more dispersed earlier literature on the history of statistics. This short survey history of the problem leaves aside issues of classical probability vs. Bayes's alternative, the history of the latter going back into the eighteenth century (see Daston 1988).

2. See MacKenzie 1981 on social science vs. biometrics and Morgan 1997 on correlation; on the introduction of probability thinking into economics, see Morgan 1987, 1990; Biddle 2017; and the editors' introduction to this volume.

from many observations (William Stanley Jevons following John Stuart Mill's argument about induction); *synthesizing* heterogeneous observations (taking John Elliott Cairnes as the exemplar); or *picking out particulars* for individual attention (with Richard Whately as a relevant figure). These three modes of learning from observations suggest that the nineteenth-century inference menu offered a variety of flexible practices according to the questions and materials at issue.[3] This article suggests a fourth mode of inferential reasoning from observations based on *narrative making*.

2. Narrative Inference?

I use the term *narrative inference* to label an inference from some empirical materials that involves the construction of a narrative to fit the observations together *and/or* an inferential statement that draws on narrative. First, it is important that the word *narrative* here does not refer just to the use of words but involves a much stronger claim. There are many definitions of narrative available, and some of them focus on its structure, such as a narrative account involves a "beginning-middle-end" or a "change of state between beginning and end." It is difficult to pin down a well-honed definition of narrative that works for all sites of inferential argument in the sciences. But there is an umbrella notion that works across a range of scientific contexts in which narrative is used in scientific argument, reasoning, inference claims, descriptions of relationships, and so forth. This is that: narrative functions to order and relate materials together, possibly very heterogeneous materials (rather than the similar ones of statistical inference). Narrative accounts, in both deductive and inductive modes, are particularly found in scientists' account of relations and events that occur through time. My use of the label points to a wider and generic reliance on, and usage of, narrative, not just in economics but in many fields of science, and where connections are spatial or causal, as well as those made across time.[4]

3. Maas in a number of papers (e.g., 2021) also implies that this nineteenth-century flexibility also exhibited a mash-up of deductive and inductive reasoning—a point that comes back later in my considerations of Malthus's reasoning.
4. Time sequencing of the elements is not necessary for an encompassing definition of narrative for the sciences: the events could be spatially or conceptually sequenced. The critical difference is that a *narrative* is about the connections in the sequence, in contrast to a *chronicle*—whose events are sequenced in time but are otherwise unconnected. Cycle and developmental accounts are only two kinds of typical circumstances in the sciences where narrative thrives, and this is not a claim that narrative will thrive in all sites in all sciences (see Morgan 2017; Morgan and Wise 2017; and Morgan, Hayek, and Berry forthcoming).

Nevertheless, it is evident that narratives often do play an important role in two domains of inferential reasoning in sciences precisely where the nature of the subjects under study involved changes over time and where the kind of time-connected evidence they produce both lend themselves to narrative modes of reasoning. One is the natural historical sciences, and the other is sciences that study the development of phenomena. The former—geology, paleontology, evolutionary biology, and so forth—are sciences that depend on traces of evidence that need to be time ordered and put into relation with each other to provide explanatory accounts. Narrative functions almost "naturally" in these contexts, just as for the historical phenomena of social sciences (including development economics). Narrative also functions in the same self-evident way when scientists are dealing with dynamic phenomena where the events (such as, development stages) follow one another in regular sequences; where the causal links between events may be ambiguous or irregular as well as clear and regular; where the time-dynamic relation between the elements of the sequence are difficult to discern; or where those relations may be complex or interactive. Thus the circadian rhythm, the developmental cycles found in the animal kingdom, the circulation of blood, the seasonal patterns of life, and so forth—just as cycles in economic life—all rely on dynamic processes that can well be narrated and might even be best explained in a narrative account of the internal relations of a phenomenon to suggest why and how it appears repetitive, rather than because it is a simple pattern of output response that can be matched to an input.

Narrative forms used at such sites provide not just a means or method of communication like a piece of rhetoric, any more than the use of metaphors or analogies in the sciences are just rhetorical in function. Just as analogical reasoning in sciences has proved critical to scientists' understanding of a phenomenon, so narrative reasoning and narrative inference have proved important to explanatory accounts of certain kinds of phenomena (see Morgan forthcoming; Morgan and Wise 2017). Both forms of argument, analogy and narrative, may be deeply associated with the scientific accounts of the identity and behavior of phenomena, rather than simply glosses on their expression. But to argue that these means of expression are not merely rhetorical does not interrogate what epistemic work they do in the sciences and how they do that work. For the use of narratives in economics, this work is not self-evident.

It may help to unpack the history of economists' use of narrative in their arguments in order to understand what is involved at different sites and see how the narrative form has fulfilled different roles. Narrative arguments in twentieth-century economics are sometimes quasi-theoretical or deductive arguments.[5] One kind of example is found in the imagined scenarios that accompany particular games in game theory, such as the narrative that defines the rules of the game for the two prisoners in their dilemma game—where, without the narrative element, the rules remain unspecified, and so the relative numbers in the game matrix remain unexplained and unconstrained. These narratives are important inputs into setting up the problem, without which the deductive apparatus cannot work. Another kind of deductive usage is found in the narratives that accompany model simulations, epitomized in Paul Samuelson's (1938) first ever numerical simulation of a Keynesian macro-model. Choosing different parameter values in the model created different outcome cycles (explosive or damped) over the simulated time horizon. Each of these provided a narrative of what would happen in this little model world, and Samuelson used these to explore the possible event sequences that might come from government actions in such a model. In both cases, but in different ways, the narratives formed part of the identity of the model—the kind of Keynesian stories consistent with Samuelson's model and the kinds of outcomes consistent with the narrativized rules of the game situation.

The term *narrative inference*, however, points to economists' empirical arguments. It is in relation to empirical elements, not just data series, but numerical or qualitative characteristics more generally, where the terminology of *narrative inference* may prove apt. And we might expect such usage to be most evident in dealing with cyclical and developmental phenomena. Exploring this usage lies behind the choice for this article of two key cases where economists used statistics in accounts of cyclical phenomena in the economy before statistical inference became formalized: Thomas Robert Malthus (1766–1834), writing at the turn of the eighteenth and nineteenth centuries; and the Russian economist Nikolai Kondratiev (also Kondratieff, Kondrat'ev; 1892–1938), working in the early twentieth century. These exemplary cases both employed narratives but in very different ways.

Setting the narrower historical agenda is important. Malthus and Kondratiev both sit within the mainstream history of economists' efforts to understand economic cycles, in which statistical inference has appeared in a variety of forms, only some of which have needed, or used, narrative.[6] Thus, Jevons's late nineteenth-century sunspot theory was initially supported

---

5. Morgan 2012 (chaps. 9 and 6, respectively) explores the following two examples mentioned in the text here.

6. The following examples all come from an earlier study, Morgan 1990.

by a numerical inference based on matching the periodicity of the two statistical series on trade and sunspots. It was only subsequently filled in (because of the shakiness of numerical matches in cycle lengths) with his narrative inferential account that linked data on sunspots, via agricultural output in India, with data on India's trade with England, to indicate a causal mechanism behind the trade cycle. Warren M. Persons (1919: 8) had seen the statistics of business cycles that he developed at Harvard as representing a "confused conglomerate growing out of numerous causes which overlie and obscure one another," and so forbore to explain or narrate them. In the interwar period, Ernst Wagemann at the Berlin business-cycle institute—as others at other national institutes such as Jan Tinbergen at the Dutch institute—developed Persons's methods to create appropriate national "barometers." These nation-based statistical packets of information were designed to give relational content to predictive inferences through specifying—in narrative terms rather than in formal inference terms—the causal connections to be made between the sectors of the economy.[7] Tinbergen (1939) used both theorizing narratives and empirical narratives in the first macroeconometric modeling; significantly, both of these were represented not in words but in visual form. For the theory narratives, he used small, time-labeled, causal-arrow diagrams (visual narratives indicating the dynamic structure of the theoretical model); for the empirical narratives, he used graphic techniques of regression that pinpointed critical causal factors (in a visual narrative account of the empirical record of the 1920s through to the Great Crash). Even when these economists used formal numerical or statistical inference procedures, they often relied on narrative forms of reasoning in pinpointing causal connections between the data series under discussion. Here, narrative reasoning was not just a substitute for lack of technical apparatus but a necessary complement, for the simple correlation or periodic-based analysis of these days from Jevons to Tinbergen did not offer insight into the causal interconnections between elements in the economy (see Morgan 1997).

This all changed after the 1940s probabilistic revolution, and the establishment of clear criteria to ensure the reliability and integrity of the statistical inference process was associated with that change. And, then, from the late twentieth century, inference became mechanized, that is, inference statements about the value of a parameter and the statistical test of its significance typically became the output of a computerized statisti-

---

7. See Lenel, this volume.

cal package. And when data came ready-prepared (downloaded from some source or other), this smoothed over, indeed often hid, important questions about the observations (the difficult practices of collecting, collating, cleaning, and abstracting data). All this reduced the need to tease out the relevant inferential questions (about what was to be aligned with what, and how, in statistical models). Modern practices often lose these significant parts of the sequence of drawing inferences from evidence.[8] In addition, as Deirdre McCloskey warned long ago, such inferential output statements report only statistical significance, not economic significance. Narrative, usually only present in the seminar room and not in journal publications, came to play only a post hoc role in exploring the economic significance of that statistical inference statement with respect to questions of interest about the phenomena. This narrative moment became a narrative exploring what the statistical inference answer meant, not a narrative of how that answer had been gained; it became a narrative about the possible ontology of the world, not a narrative engagement in the epistemology of investigation.

This foray into historical and current practices of economists points to the problematic at issue in this article: What was involved in the earlier informal processes of inference that economists relied on? How were inferences drawn from a mass of empirical materials? As noted earlier, Maas suggested three modes of working from observations: by generalizing, synthesizing, and picking out particular cases. These processes did not need to involve narrative or that the final outcome statement provide a narrative, though narrative elements might accompany any of those three modes. But (as suggested above), for any phenomenon involving a time process such as cyclical and developmental processes, the narrative form has obvious benefits for expressing and for explaining the outcome and so may well play a dominant role in inference. And while narrative as a noun may work well as the format for an outcome account (i.e., expressing the cyclical pattern, or giving an account of the development process), narrative needs to take on verblike qualities to play a role in the activity of making the inference, that is, in the process of drawing an inference. Thus I propose we need something like *narrative making* to express the way a

---

8. Of course, there are always matters of judgment, alignment, and so forth where subject matter expertise is critical to drawing a statistical inference: our two special issue editors, Jeff Biddle and Marcel Boumans, have opened up this agenda in their past writings (see their introduction, this volume, for references).

scientist pulls together and combines the elements involved to make sense of and construct an account of their phenomena.[9]

Once we recognize that this narrative-making process occurs, we also see why it has not just been associated with time-based phenomena. We can see this narrative making in habitual form in, for example, the way economists use the terms *principles* or *laws* of supply and demand in their empirical work, where those laws are made relevant for, or *applied to*, different kinds of markets with different interactive processes or different degrees of competition in order to give adequate accounts of the phenomena. We see such narrative making both in Alfred Marshall's arguments about supply and demand in interaction with his observations about specific or particular markets and in late nineteenth-century attempts by US economists to make sensible analyses of railways and other natural monopolies and so design their regulation. We can also see narrative making in the slightly later (but still prestatistical inference) econometric work of the 1920s on agricultural markets, where econometricians used narrative forms to make sensible inferences from the empirical cobweb diagrams found for specific markets. But caution is needed: narratives at such sites may not all be cases of *narrative inference*. In some cases narrative making involves reasoning that enables inferences for specific empirical sites about the actions of the laws—thus *narrative inference*. Other times, the narrative element serves as something more like an illustration—critical in making the point but not an inference from statistical observations, as seems to be so in the case of Adam Smith's many well-known micronarratives that attend his account of the division of labor.

There is one other important historical point about inferences from *statistics* that is relevant for economics from at least the eighteenth century into the mid-nineteenth century—that the original root notion of the label *statistics* is information on the *state*, not necessarily quantified.[10] Two elements are important here. First, the cut between numerical information and other observable or well-attested information held less power in the late eighteenth century, in the time of Malthus, than it came to in the early twentieth century, the time of Kondratiev. Thus for economists of the past such as Malthus, state information in both modes—numerical and qualitative—offered equal grist for their inferential mill. Second, the

9. See Morgan 2017, and forthcoming, for my account of what is involved in this process, which I express as one of *colligation*.

10. With particular relevance for the history of economics, see Nikolow 2001.

state refers not to the government but to the kingdom and its many descriptions and characterizations.

Given this broad terrain of what constitutes statistics, and so statistical inference, how do both these economists' reasonings look in hindsight? For both Malthus and Kondratiev, statistics mattered to establish the phenomena of oscillations. Both used narrative reasoning in their studies of cycles, but as I show, at different points and in different ways. This article thus expands Maas's already generous account of the preformal epistemological practices of arguing from observations to include narrative resources and narrative reasoning.

3. Malthus on Economic-Demographic Oscillations

Malthus's writings on population have proved to be some of the most broadly influential works in the history of political economy. His argument that populations will always grow faster than the supply of food over the long term, exposing humanity to the dual "checks of misery and vice," led Thomas Carlyle to label Malthus's account "the dismal science," a moniker that attached itself to classical economics through the nineteenth century. The epithet referred not only to the grip that Malthus's predictions gained over the popular imagination (prompting nineteenth-century cartoons of a Malthusian monster devouring children) but also to the miserable prognostications of later classical economics, especially the gloom of "the stationary state"—when economic growth ran dry.

Though Malthus lived well into that period, his tract "An Essay on the Principle of Population" (1798) was written in the late eighteenth century, at a time recognized by fellow intellectuals as one of scientific discovery, utopian dreams about the social system, and romantic ideas about the future of humanity. He argued against these roseate views of the future, not because he wanted to be gloomy, or because he was not forward-looking, but because he just could not see a way out of the population problem revealed by his knowledge of the statistics of the day and of his analysis. He shared, however, the vigorous mode of argument of that late eighteenth century and purposefully used it not just to celebrate "the blazing comet" of the French revolution but to make fun of, and undermine, the speculative reasoning of his day. By contrast to those revolutionary and utopian writings, his own political economy was couched in the language of "disinterestedness" (Keynes 1933), surely designed to provide credibility to his account. Here is how Malthus ([1798] 1976: 15–16) posed his question of interest and his commitment to reason with evidence:

> It is an obvious truth, which has been taken notice of by many writers, that population must always be kept down to the level of the means of subsistence; but no writer that the Author recollects has inquired particularly into the means by which this level is effected: and it is the view of these means which forms, to his mind, the strongest obstacle in the way to any great future improvement of society. . . . He professes to have read some of the speculations on the future improvement of society in a temper very different from a wish to find them visionary, but he had not acquired that command over his understanding which would enable him to believe what he wishes, without evidence, or to refuse his assent to what might be unpleasing, when accompanied by evidence.

It is worth pausing on this issue of speculation and the rhetorical contrast that Malthus uses, for rhetoric is never *mere*, as he well recognized.[11] Malthus wanted to distance his own scientific arguments—reasoning with evidence—from the characteristics of argument made by those "speculative philosophers . . . who preach up ardent benevolence and draw captivating pictures of a happier state of society . . . or as wild and madheaded enthusiasts whose silly speculations and absurd paradoxes are not worth the attention of any reasonable man" (17). Here is Malthus, the reasoning scientist, complaining about such speculative philosophers:

> A writer may tell me that he thinks man will ultimately become an ostrich. I cannot properly contradict him. But before he can expect to bring any reasonable person over to his opinion, he ought to shew that the necks of mankind have been gradually elongating, that the lips have grown harder and more prominent, that the legs and feet are daily altering their shape, and that the hair is beginning to change into stubs of feathers. And till the probability of so wonderful a conversion can be shewn, it is surely lost time and lost eloquence to expatiate on the happiness of man in such a state; to describe his powers, both of running and flying, to paint him in a condition where all narrow luxuries would be contemned, where he would be employed only in collecting the necessaries of life, and where, consequently, each man's share of labour would be light, and his portion of leisure ample. (19)

---

11. Malthus's words become a salient resource for later evolutionary theorists, with Darwin picking up his phrase "the struggle for existence."

This passage against speculation immediately preceded his own population account, which served to show by contrast what a carefully reasoned and reasonable account based on evidence (as he sought to provide) should be.

Malthus is well aware of the difficulties in making a good scientific argument, and there are two elements in his argument: laws and evidence. The laws, he understood, must be reasonable conjectures about the world as it is—not utopian speculations about progress or utopias. He believed his two laws could hardly be argued with:

> I think I may fairly make two postulata.
> First, That food is necessary to the existence of man.
> Secondly, That the passion between the sexes is necessary and will remain nearly in its present state. (19–20)

But he then continues with two further *factual* or *empirical* laws that he later sought to justify with evidential claims and by careful reasoning that explored the implications of these two in creating checks to population growth:

> Assuming then, my postulata as granted, I say that the power of population is indefinitely greater than the power in the earth to produce subsistence for man.
> Population, when unchecked, increases in a geometrical ratio. Subsistence increases only in an arithmetical ratio. A slight acquaintance with numbers will shew the immensity of the first power in comparison of the second.
> By that law of our nature which makes food necessary to the life of man, the effects of these two unequal powers must be kept equal.
> This implies a strong and constantly operating check on population from the difficulty of subsistence. This difficulty must fall somewhere and must necessarily be severely felt by a large portion of mankind.

While the two earlier laws of nature seemed unassailable, Malthus sought to support the two latter ones of the inequality in population growth and the power of the earth to feed them by "experience, the true source and foundation of all knowledge, invariably confirms its truth" (21).[12] Malthus thus turned his account away from the deductive mode toward a more

12. The terminology of experience becomes closely aligned with that of experiment and features strongly in the empirical and inductive work of gathering information from observations in the early modern period into the eighteenth century (see introductory essays by Pomata and Daston in Daston and Lunbeck 2011).

inductive mode in his chapter 2, and here is where we find his arguments meeting up with evidential claims in statistics as information about the state of the kingdom, rather than statistics as numbers. And "the test of experience" (16), which he relies on, is shorthand for *evidence*: knowledge of particulars from varied sources, which are relevant for understanding the demography and economy of his day and their histories.

It may be thought that Malthus picked out of thin air his claim that population—unchecked—grows in geometric ratio. But he justifies this by referring to the experiences of a population least checked by means of subsistence, that is, to certain contemporary populations in the United States. Such evidence suggested that population can double every fifteen years, but he takes a somewhat milder rate (and thus more conservative outcome) of doubling in twenty-five years, that is, a "geometric ratio." On the other side, the arithmetic growth of food output is less obviously sourced, but Malthus was living through the agricultural revolution in Britain, with experimental farming investigating the efficacy of fertilizer application, and "spade husbandry" to increase output per acre, as well as extending cultivation into unused lands. Some of these changes reduced usable food supply (e.g., when enclosure replaced arable-crop lands with animal pastures). More important, he understood that these changes had limits. These changes, and their effects, were hotly debated in the political arithmetic discussions of the day, not least in the letters between David Ricardo and Malthus.[13]

Such attested knowledge buttressed a nicely framed arithmetic argument to prove the greatness of the problem, and thus how the *law of necessity* (the requirement for food) is found reflected in an *empirical law* or knowledge from "experience," which reflects these checks to population growth. Even though Malthus and his work are well known to historians of economics, I quote his discussion at length, both so that we can see the reasonableness of his argument chain, and how his competent use of numbers fed into what might be counted as factual, and what inferences followed from his numerical arguments and evidence. The reasoning or argument takes a narrative form that traces out, from the combined assumptions and evidence, the implied sequence of events over future years:

13. See chapter 2 in Morgan 2012, both for the narrower discussions between the two and the wider discussions and evidence used in political economy of the time.

In the United States of America, where the means of subsistence have been more ample, the manners of the people more pure, and consequently the checks to early marriages fewer than in any of the modern states of Europe, the population has been found to double itself in twenty-five years. . . . a geometrical ratio.

. . . Let us now take any spot of earth, this Island for instance, and see in what ratio the subsistence it affords can be supposed to increase. We will begin with it under its present state of cultivation.

If I allow that by the best possible policy, by breaking up more land and by great encouragements to agriculture, the produce of this Island may be doubled in the first twenty-five years, I think it will be allowing as much as any person can well demand.

In the next twenty-five years, it is impossible to suppose that the produce could be quadrupled. It would be contrary to all our knowledge of the qualities of land. The very utmost that we can conceive is that the increase in the second twenty-five years might equal the present produce. Let us then take this for our rule. . . . The most enthusiastic speculator cannot suppose a greater increase than this. In a few centuries it would make every acre of land in the Island like a garden.

Yet this ratio of increase is evidently arithmetical.

Let us now bring the effects of these two ratios together.

The population of the Island is computed to be about seven millions, and we will suppose the present produce equal to the support of such a number. In the first twenty-five years the population would be fourteen millions, and the food being also doubled, the means of subsistence would be equal to this increase. In the next twenty-five years the population would be twenty-eight millions, and the means of subsistence only equal to the support of twenty-one millions. In the next period the population would be fifty-six millions, and the means of subsistence just sufficient for half that number. And at the conclusion of the first century the population would be one hundred and twelve millions and the means of subsistence only equal to the support of thirty-five millions, which would leave a population of seventy-seven millions totally unprovided for. (Malthus [1798] 1976: 22–23)

Clearly such a future outcome is not possible; it is no more credible than that man should turn into an ostrich. But this is indeed his point—he does not claim the incredible outcome as a realistic possibility; rather, he uses a narrative to follow the inference chain step by step to show how you get to such an impossible outcome. In later chapters, Malthus uses similar modes of narrative reasoning to pinpoint the problems in other incredible argu-ments of his day, particularly by William Godwin, that humankind would become ever more perfect and society attain a state of utopian bliss!

For Malthus, something must be happening that stops the population growing beyond the means of subsistence. And indeed, for Malthus the economist, as opposed to demographer, the clever part is still to come: namely, his explanation of the processes by which the checks to popula-tion occur. Again, his explanation takes a narrative form, following the interactions of demographic processes with economic ones. In Malthus's account, the actions of the two empirical laws (population growth and food supply) working together create oscillations between experiences of "severe distress" and "tolerable comfort," as the actual population grows first more, then less, than the output of food:

> We will suppose the means of subsistence in any country just equal to the easy support of its inhabitants. The constant effort towards popula-tion, which is found to act even in the most vicious societies, increases the number of people before the means of subsistence are increased. The food therefore which before supported seven millions must now be divided among seven millions and a half or eight millions. The poor consequently must live worse, and many of them be reduced to severe distress. The number of labourers also being above the proportion of the work in the market, the price of labour must tend toward a decrease, while the price of provisions would at the same time tend to rise. The labourer must therefore work harder to earn the same as he did before. During this season of distress, the discouragements to marriage and the difficulty of rearing a family are so great that population is at a stand. In the mean time the cheapness of labour, the plenty of labourers, and the necessity of an increased industry amongst them, encourage cultivators to employ more labour upon their land, to turn up fresh soil, and to manure and improve more completely what is already in tillage, till ulti-mately the means of subsistence become in the same proportion to the population as at the period from which we set out. The situation of the labourer being then again tolerably comfortable, the restraints to popula-tion are in some degree loosened, and the same retrograde and progres-sive movements with respect to happiness are repeated. (24–25)[14]

14. Malthus concedes that the Marquis de Condorcet has foreseen such oscillations between "good and evil," but Condorcet was convinced such an outcome was so far in the future it was not of serious concern; he did not, however, fill in the details of the demographic-economic interactions in the way Malthus was able to do.

Revealing the interactive sequences between demographic and economic processes required Malthus to make a *narrative argument* of the kind that economists love to make, just as much then at the turn of the nineteenth century as they do now in the early twenty-first century. Such arguments were used then to show how their laws work out in the activities of the world just as economists now use narrative arguments with their models to explore how that mini economic world might work. And these narrative economic arguments—then as now—may be applied to the real world in the current time, to the counterfactual world for the past, or the imagined world for the future just as Malthus did.[15]

It is especially worth noting that Malthus's narrative was—in a particular sense—not about the observed world but about the nature and processes of economic life that sat behind the observations, a narrative about what was really happening, not what was on the surface, creating a mode of argument that we can recognize as habitual in the way economists still grapple with the empirics of our aggregate world. As Malthus remarked: "This sort of oscillation will not be remarked by superficial observers, and it may be difficult even for the most penetrating mind to calculate its periods" (25). We do not *see* these oscillations directly in our histories, he argued, first because our histories are histories of the rich, not the poor where these checks will be at work, and extremely patient observation would be needed to discern them. Second, the oscillations would be irregular because of many other relevant but "interrupting causes" (such as new manufactures, agricultural improvements, wars, plagues, institutional changes) and "so much friction, and minute circumstances occur in practice" that it is impossible to see even what has stood "the test of experience" (18). (This argument parallels Mill's later claims about our histories not revealing our economic realities because of disturbing causes at work.) Malthus's third reason, and his most important economic insight, relied on recognizing "particularly, the difference between nominal and real prices of labour, a circumstance which has perhaps more than any other contributed to conceal this oscillation from common view" (25). For "common view," we can understand that this hides the oscillations not only for experienced observers but even to those laborers in the economy whose experiences this account narrates.

We might see and assess more clearly what narrative is doing in Malthus's reasoning by drawing the contrast between his treatment and

15. I analyze the way economists use model narratives in counterfactual and imagined world cases and in historical/empirical cases in Morgan 2014 and 2017.

discussion of the same problem by Adam Smith. Rather than advance any explicit "laws" of demography (in *Wealth of Nations*, bk. 1, chap. 8), Smith draws on anecdotal kinds of evidence ("I have frequently been told") and generality claims, whose observational status is unknown ("barrenness, so frequent among ladies of fashion, is very rare among those of inferior station"). In contrast, Malthus referred to the facts reported from specific times and places. On the basis of his more cursory observations, Smith advances an explanation of the checks to population based on a class division. In his demographic account, the rich who have the means but have small families experience no checks, while the poor produce large numbers of children but the check of poverty keeps their families small. His subsequent economic argument is not an inferential process based on evidence but a simple deductive one using the laws of supply and demand: labor is in a market, just like "any other commodity," with periods of over- (and under-) supply. And the possibility of oscillations in the demography is not explicitly discussed as a phenomenon of this market, while any more serious interaction of the demographics and the labor market are hardly explicated. Smith's text lacks both the analytic subtlety of Malthus's reasoning and the observational credibility the latter brought to bear on the topic. Smith's text cannot be analyzed so easily into evidence claims and law claims and thus not easily open to argument either!

This very brief comparison of Malthus with Smith suggests that the credibility of Malthus's arguments rests not just on matters of rhetoric but on a much closer and clever argument that brings inductive statistical (broad notion) and deductive modes of reasoning together into a narrative that traces the dynamic interaction between demography and economy and, from that, of what we should reasonably expect to see and equally reasonably why we cannot do so. It is evidently difficult to make any clear distinctions between induction and deduction in the economic argumentation of Malthus. Smith and Malthus argued about the topic in very different ways: whereas casual observation and short deductive sequences are clear in Smith, what is happening in Malthus is much less clear, for his inferences based on his empirical claims and his arguments from laws are not so much integrated but bleed like textile dyes into each other. While it would be awkward to claim Malthus's argument from evidence as *statistical inference* in our formal modernist terms, the way he dealt with the problem, and the way he used narrative in drawing inferences from empirical evidence, shows a considerable degree of sophistication, which prompts further analysis.

As we see with Malthus's arguments: his imperative is for careful reasoning in process and a reasonableness of outcome. The latter is defined as consistent with our knowledge, thus his appeal to, and then contrast, throughout his arguments in his book, between the knowledge from *experience* and the utopian outcomes found from *speculation*. These give him criteria for his inferential accounts but provide neither recipes nor rules for drawing inferences. Narrative making provides these means: *narrative making takes him from the evidence to the expression*.[16] What this entails is a bit tricky, but it is important to keep in mind the difference between the inferential process and inference outcome.

Malthus's account of the interaction between demography and economy with respect to labor and poverty has a narrative form—events follow one another in interaction, and the account is explanatory, for it joins up the elements rather than just recognizing a sequence, and it melds them into an account of an oscillatory phenomenon. It is necessarily complicated because the elements interact with each other: the sequence is neither linear nor simple. It relies also on the evidence of activities we could not easily see, hidden, but revealed by economists' superior analytic insight (for example, into the difference between the nominal and the real wage rate), to discern the causal chain in events, and their implications wrapped into the narrative account. Much is involved here. First, the narrative Malthus tells does more work than just expressing the evidence in a narrative in the sense that Malthus must first construct his narrative in such a way that it gives a joined-up account of the evidence; this narrative making marks the process of making his inference. Second, the narrative he tells is not just an outcome expression of the evidence. Rather, in his narrative-making process, Malthus has integrated the lawlike postulates along with the statistical evidence to give an account of the interactive process between demography and economy. This is perhaps a true form of inference—inference is drawing an outcome from the evidence with respect to a claim, lawlike or one-off, about something. It not just that the claim and evidence are not separated out—as later rules require—into a hypothesis about the claim and an inference outcome.[17]

16. Thanks to Tom Stapleford, who suggested at the workshop that "narrative takes us from evidence to expression"—but note that in my rendering of this, the important words are verbs so that my preferred version of the maxim is "making the narrative takes us from evidence to expression," i.e., the process takes us to the outcome, where that process involves narrative making.

17. The more recent version of statistical inference might be well be expressed using the metaphor that Aashish Velkar suggested at the workshop, namely, "that narrative functions as a bridge that takes you from evidence to outcome." If the process of making the narrative is a process of linking theories and empirics, then it does provide a means of bridging, but since in Malthus's work, the narrative also operates as a process *integrating* the two sides, the bridge analogy remains a little problematic. However, it may well be that for other economists, who keep their empirics and theories/laws/models rather separate, narrative does work as a bridge.

Rather, Malthus's narrative making does take us from evidence to expression, but what is expressed is not a simple outcome statement but an integrated process account showing how the world works.

This account of Malthus's inference process may make more sense when contrasted with Kondratiev's use of narrative in conjunction with long-wave cycle accounts, for there we are unambiguously into inductions based on numerical evidence. And when induction refers to inference from observable information (on the state), such statistical inference can quickly find its place on a continuum from older forms of informal inference from evidence as in Malthus, to numerical claims in Kondratiev, and later to formal statistical inference. At the same time, the Kondratiev case makes the problem more complicated because of the need to pin down claims with respect to numerical observations in a way that Malthus, with his limited numerical evidence, avoided.

4. Kondratiev on Long Waves

It is well recognized that economists across the international community became obsessed with the study of economic cycles in the late nineteenth and early twentieth centuries—short ones for stock market activity ("Kitchins"), middle-length ones for the "business cycle" (associated particularly with W. C. Mitchell),[18] the investment cycle ("Kuznets"), and "long waves" ("Kondratievs"). These studies were instrumental in developing generic methods of studying time series statistical data in order to *pin down* these phenomena. Compared with the late eighteenth-century account Malthus gave of his demographic-economic oscillations, this was extremely numerically data-heavy work. For some of those involved, this was an entirely empiricist project, inference from statistical data to establish patterns, but not formal statistical inference according to rules. For others, such as Kondratiev, it involved arguments about the dynamic mechanisms involved in long waves, though he stopped short of claiming "a theory of long cycles."

Kondratiev has his name attached to these long fifty-year cycles, for though there were others speculating about their existence before him, he was the first to conduct sustained empirical data collection, data preparation, and data analysis in order to establish them as a valid phenomenon of the economy. Kondratiev was the first director of the Conjuncture Insti-

18. See Stapleford, this volume.

tute in Moscow, one of a group of international cycle research institutes in the 1920s. These economists followed one another's work closely, their papers were quickly "abstracted" into other language publications across the community, and they, including Kondratiev, traveled abroad and met each other. Kondratiev's findings were published first in Russian in 1924, prompting detailed discussions among his Russian contemporaries (see Makasheva, Samuels, and Barnett 1998), and thence translated into German in 1926, and selected parts into English in 1935.[19]

Kondratiev's two main problems were, first, establishing the economic phenomenon, that is, that long waves existed; and second, giving an account of the phenomenon, which he presumed was one element in the complicated "dynamics of economic life" (made up of all these different kinds of cycles). Here is how he introduced his study in the first English translation:

> The idea that the dynamics of economic life in the capitalistic social order is not of a simple and linear but rather of a complex and cyclical character is nowadays generally recognized. Science, however, has fallen far short of clarifying the nature and the types of these cyclical, wave-like movements.
>
> When in economics we speak of cycles, we generally mean seven to eleven year business cycles. But these seven to eleven year movements are obviously not the only type of economic cycles. The dynamics of economic life is in reality more complicated. In addition to the above-mentioned cycles, which we shall agree to call "intermediate," the existence of still shorter waves of about three and one-half years' length has recently been shown to be probable.
>
> But that is not all. There is, indeed, reason to assume the existence of long waves of an average length of about 50 years in the capitalistic economy, a fact which still further complicates the problem of economic dynamics. (Kondratiev 1935: 105)

As might be expected, establishing that long waves occurred in the economy was not so easy. The availability of data was relatively more restricted than it is now, and Kondratiev had to rely on the kinds of public data created by markets or governments (financial, foreign trade, output

19. There are several contemporary versions of Kondratiev's long waves (see Makasheva, Samuels, and Barnett 1998). The quotations here come from a 1935 partial translation by Wolfgang Stolper of Kondratiev's 1926 German paper. On Kondratiev, see Barnett 1995, 1998.

figures) and by some economists who were by then collecting long-period data and creating index numbers for certain economic characteristics (such as wages and prices). The second problem was that these data had limited past existence, and if long waves were a phenomenon characteristic of capitalism as he thought, then there was hardly, or perhaps just enough—as he showed—for 2.5 waves in full. He relied on data on France and England (as they were the most complete), and the United States, and made claims that similar timed waves were evident in other "European capitalist countries" (111).

A comparison with Malthus's situation is useful here. First, Malthus's arguments were about some variables that had clear economic content and meaning, even though the data were not available (his demographic ones would have been available by Kondratiev's time, but the economic labor market ones only by the mid-twentieth century). So while Malthus could conceptualize the problem he examined, he did not have raw data, just some statistical (i.e., of the state) characteristics that he believed to be true: the arithmetic versus geometric growth rates. But it was less clear what Kondratiev was trying to get at with his data sets: what was *the economy* that was being represented in the long wave? The economy was not yet conceptualized as a macroeconomy. But the many different cycles that were being characterized and labeled in contemporary statistical work with time-series data might now be best understood under the term *economic activity*, or as Kondratiev said, "economic and social life as a whole" (111). Such life had its own multiple kinds of dynamics, and it was one of these dynamics (or cycles) that he sought. He had data on lots of different economic series, presented in graphs and tables, and they were prepared to represent the dynamics of his cycles. That is, they were turned from raw numbers into data series relevant to represent the phenomena using the by then standard Persons/Harvard techniques of secular trend removal, normalizing on population size where needed, and using moving averages.[20] Some of the data series can be understood as direct measurements of economic activity, or to use Kondratiev's language, "natural elements" (production, consumption). Others that he labeled "financial" (interest rates, wages, bank deposits) we might better understand as indirect "indicators" of economic activity, using a label that was just then coming into widespread usage among those economists studying cycles. Still others he regarded as mixtures of the "natural" and "financial" (e.g., foreign trade). These different kinds of variables were used in his many tables and charts

---

20. Again, see Lenel, this volume.

to establish his long waves: this was statistical inference—without probability reasoning and without narrative.

Establishing the long waves was, for Kondratiev, rather separate from characterizing them, but here, too, his focus was on the empirical. Here is how he introduced and summarized the "Empirical Characteristics" of his long waves on the basis of his statistical work:

(1) The long waves belong really to the same complex dynamic process in which the intermediate cycles of the capitalistic economy with their principal phases of upswing and depression run their course.

(2) During the recession of the long waves, agriculture, as a rule, suffers an especially pronounced and long depression. This was what happened after the Napoleonic Wars; it happened again from the beginning of the 1870's onward; and the same can be observed in the years after the World War.

(3) During the recession of the long waves, an especially large number of important discoveries and inventions in the technique of production and communication are made, which, however, are usually applied on a large scale only at the beginning of the next long upswing.

(4) At the beginning of a long upswing, gold production increases as a rule, and the world market [for goods] is generally enlarged by the assimilation of new and especially of colonial countries.

(5) It is during the period of the rise of the long waves, i.e., during the period of high tension in the expansion of economic forces, that, as a rule, the most disastrous and extensive wars and revolutions occur. (Kondratiev 1935: 111)

It is to be emphasized that we attribute to these recurring relationships an empirical character only, and that we do not by any means hold that they contain the explanation of the long waves.

As with Malthus, it is in wrestling with this second problem—giving an account of the dynamic elements in his long waves—that we find narrative at work. Kondratiev's text positioned the latter four empirical characteristics (2–5)—treated generically—into particular phases within the long waves. Thus, the timing with which these types of events occur is associated with particular phases of the long waves. So, as we can see in the quoted passage, this is a commentary on the timing of such events within the long cycles: the inference is about *what* happens, and *when*—not about *why*.

In further discussing their place in the dynamics of long waves, Kondratiev rejects each of the characteristics (2–5) as causes of his waves. Indeed, he is convinced that this has the argument backward: these factors are *consequences*, not *causes*. They are factors that occur in a particular historical time but whose effects only come into play when the long wave brings them in, so he tells a *consequential* narrative for each factor to bring them into his account of long waves. Thus the inventions of the scientific revolution are not accidental, but they come into widespread economic activity only during the long wave of the industrial revolution; new countries or new gold fields are discovered but are pulled into the international trade and economic monetary system in a major way only because of the long wave; wars and revolutions occur because of the pressure of long-wave activities. In effect, each generic factor has its own generic narrative that knits the factor into the long-wave pattern at a particular generic phase of the wave, not as a cause of the wave but as gaining power as a consequence of the dynamics within the wave. They are part of the dynamics of the long waves but not the source of the long waves. Kondratiev's view of these empirical characteristic elements places them into his narratives as add-ons—they do not explain the long waves, they are not needed to make sense of the long waves, but they are salient characteristics of economic life that need to be connected into this major dynamic of the capitalist system.

It is perhaps unexpected that these narratives of empirical characteristics are treated generically—that is to say, he does not pinpoint particular gold discoveries, or particular wars, and attach them to particular historical points in his graphs of the 2.5 long waves. This would have seemed the obvious way to go, then as it is now, for we regularly see time-series charts with specific events (the global financial crisis of 2008–9 or the great crash of 1929–32) written on the charts. Yet each of these generic consequences had its own historically specific events that Kondratiev discussed in the text and that could have been pinned on particular time moments in his graphs. Indeed, the 1926 discussion by his Russian colleagues of his original 1924 long-wave research (as reported in Barnett 1995: 431–36) showed much willingness to affix the timing of particular examples of the various historical factors into their relevant long wave.

Kondratiev's overall text narrative did, however, claim that long waves are inherent in the capitalist system. He took seriously, as the likely endogenous cause, the long-run "replacement and increase in the stock of basic capital goods" which "occurs in spurts, and this rhythm is reflected in the long waves of economic life" (Barnett 1995: 435). As Vincent Barnett reports, this critical endogenous cause in the system came from Mikhail Tugan-Baranovsky's (Kondratiev's teacher) theorizing on the matter. Given the context of postrevolutionary Russia, this careful equivocation about causes might have been politically astute, for it keeps the capitalist dynamics free of these kinds of historical factors as main causes, leaving the waves as endogenous to that system. However, it seems that these consequential narratives about long waves were not so politically problematic as his analysis and advice on how to stimulate economic growth and the role of agriculture in the new plan for the economy. In 1928 he was dismissed, the institute was shut down, and in 1932 he was sent to prison, where he continued with his economics writing until 1938, when he was executed.

Just as Malthus's numerical claims and associated narratives put demographic-economic oscillations into economists' agendas, Kondratiev's statistical work put long waves into the list of empirical economic cycles, and the phenomenon has been a topic for economic research ever since.[21] Just as attention to Malthusian population crises wax and wane, Kondratiev's questions have continued to reverberate through the decades: Do these long waves exist? And if so, are the specific cycles correctly identified in time? These worries were raised by his Russian colleagues in their 1926 discussions, when they complained about errors in dating the long waves and, at the same time, doubted their existence. Over the last century, economists have focused on similar worries: correcting Kondratiev's timing of the waves; analyzing his claims about their regularity; collecting further data; developing smarter statistical techniques; and so forth. It seems that the jury is still out on their *statistical* existence: they are not yet proved either in an irregular form or as a regular periodic cycle. Equally, economists have been arguing ever since about the dynamics of the causal account—either as causes or as consequences of the inherent system of capitalism, and it has been equally problematic to tell a good generic narrative account that makes sense of the timing of such factors for both Marxist and non-Marxist economists alike. Following Kondratiev's thesis about the overall endogenous dynamics of long waves, much of the discussion has focused on the timing implications of long-term capital replacement and innovations of multipurpose (or general-purpose) technologies (i.e., steam, steel, railways, electricity, computers). In so doing, these arguments essentially turn factor 3, which Kondratiev argued was a *consequence*, into the main *cause* of the phenomenon. Significantly, and perhaps because of the difficulties in reducing these wide and deep innovations into well-defined variables with matching statistical measurements, these explanatory accounts have more often been dominated by "analytic

---

21. This is a very considerable literature, exemplified in Rosenberg and Frischtak 1984, and surveyed (but only up to 1979) in a "selective annotated bibliography" of nearly forty pages (Barr 1979)!

narratives," economic explanatory narratives more closely knitted to inference from economic historical evidence than to the more rule-bound regimes of formal statistical inference.[22]

5. Conclusion

Using narrative in inference relies, as do other modes of inductive scientific investigation, on beginning with questions about phenomena. Malthus and Kondratiev shared much the same question. Both were interested in probing the relational dynamics of the economic system as it manifested in cycles. For Malthus, these dynamics were given an account in his narrative reasoning; he had not the means to see the arithmetic and geometric laws directly in his evidence and, as I have shown, argued that evidence of their interactions would not be seen. In contrast, Kondratiev could display the long waves in his data graphs yet did not weave the consequences of the system into its causal dynamics, although, just like Malthus, this did not stop him arguing about those elements. Both Malthus and Kondratiev had good questions about economic cycles, and used statistical knowledge, but this proved not enough—narratives were needed to make economic sense out of that statistical information. Whereas Kondratiev added a narrative on top of the statistics to put sense on the numbers, Malthus practiced narrative inference to explain his cycles. For Malthus, the statistical information/claims were an integral part of his narrative, and the narrative was an integral part of his making sense of the numbers.

At the beginning of this article, I remarked that narrative statements serve to relate (possibly disparate) elements, event, and factors together; narrative making offers a way for scientists to explore and explain how such elements might be related together, especially where those events are already time-sequenced. So narrative making is a site where scientists can probe and fashion answers to their questions about the relational nature of events through time: are those events somehow causally related and if so, how? Making sense of statistical evidence by constructing narratives about them offers a way to draw inferences about the relations embedded in such statistical information. Narrative making in this sense offers a kind of mechanism, even an engine, for drawing inferences. Narrative statements may also serve as the mode of expression for an inference outcome statement (in contrast to an outcome expressed as the value of

---

22. This phrase has a particular meaning in economic history and refers to narrative accounts that meld together both theoretical and historical empirical materials (see Bates et al. 1998).

parameters and their *t*-statistics from a statistical program). *Narrative inference* thus refers to these situations, namely, where narrative making is a major part of the inferential process and in which narratives are used to explain and justify the inference, not just to state the outcome.[23] Since narratives are fundamentally expressions about the relationships between things, they are associated with economic explanations, rather than economic descriptions, namely, about answering questions about *why* things are the way they are rather than *what* they are: about *why* population does not grow beyond the means of description rather than *what* kinds of waves are found in capitalist economies.

References

Barnett, Vincent. 1995. "A Long Wave Goodbye: Kondrat'ev and the Conjuncture Institute, 1920–28." *Europe-Asia Studies* 47, no. 3: 413–41.

Barnett, Vincent. 199. *Kondratiev and the Dynamics of Economic Development: Long Cycles and Industrial Growth in Historical Context*. Basingstoke, UK: Macmillan.

Barr, K. 1979. "Long Waves: A Selective, Annotated Bibliography." Review (Fernand Braudel Center) 2, no. 4: 675–718.

Bates, Robert H., Avner Greif, Margaret Levi, Jean-Laurent Rosenthal, and Barry R. Weingast. 1998. *Analytic Narratives*. Princeton, NJ: Princeton University Press.

Biddle, J. 2017. "Statistical Inference in Economics, 1920–1965: Changes in Meaning and Practice." *Journal of the History of Economic Thought* 39, no. 2: 149–73.

Daston, L. 1988. *Classical Probability in the Enlightenment*. Princeton, NJ: Princeton University Press.

Daston, L. 2011. "The Empire of Observation, 1600–1800." In Daston and Lunbeck 2011: 81–113.

Daston, L., and E. Lunbeck, eds. 2011. *Histories of Scientific Observation*. Chicago: University of Chicago Press.

Keynes, J. M. 1933. *Essays in Biography*. New York: Norton.

Kondratiev, N. D. (1924) 1998. "The Concepts of Economic Statics, Dynamics, and Conjuncture" (includes the 1926 critical discussions of the paper). In Makasheva, Samuels, and Barnett 1998: 1–255.

Kondratiev, N. D. 1935. "The Long Waves in Economic Life," translated by W. F. Stolper. *Review of Economic Statistics* 17, no. 6: 105–15.

Krüger, Lorenz, Lorraine J. Daston, and Michael Heidelberger, eds. 1987. *The Probabilistic Revolution, Vol. 1: Ideas in History*. Cambridge, MA: MIT Press.

Krüger, Lorenz, Gerd Gigerenzer, and Mary S. Morgan, eds. 1987. *The Probabilistic Revolution, Vol. 2: Ideas in the Sciences*. Cambridge, MA: MIT Press.

Maas, Harro. 2011. "Sorting Things Out: The Economist as Armchair Observer." In Daston and Lunbeck 2011: 206–29.

23. I thank Tom Stapleford for discussions that clarified my claims.

Maas, Harro. 2021. "Jevons and Marshall as Humboldtian Scientists." In *Marshall and the Marshallian Heritage: Essays in Honour of Tiziano Rafaelli*, edited by K. Caldari, M. Daldi, and S. G. Medema, 121–45. Cham, Switzerland: Palgrave Macmillan.

MacKenzie, D. A. 1981. *Statistics in Britain: 1865–1930*. Edinburgh: Edinburgh University Press.

Makasheva, Natalia, Warren J. Samuels, and Vincent Barnett. 1998. *Economic Statics, Dynamics, and Conjuncture*. Vol. 1 of *The Works of Nikolai D. Kondratiev*, translated by S. S. Wilson. London: Pickering and Chatto.

Malthus, T. R. (1798) 1976. *An Essay on the Principle of Population*. Edited by Philip Appleman. New York: Norton.

Morgan, M. S. (1987) 1990. "Statistics without Probability and Haavelmo's Revolution in Econometrics." In *The Probabilistic Revolution*, vol. 2 of *Ideas in the Sciences*, edited by L. Krüger, G. Gigerenzer, and M. S. Morgan, 171–97. Cambridge, MA: MIT Press.

Morgan, M. S. 1990. *The History of Econometric Ideas*. Cambridge: Cambridge University Press.

Morgan, M. S. 1997. "Searching for Causal Relations in Economic Statistics: Reflections from History." In *Causality in Crisis?*, edited by V. McKim and S. Turner, 47–80. Notre Dame, IN: University of Notre Dame Press.

Morgan, M. S. 2012. *The World in the Model*. Cambridge: Cambridge University Press.

Morgan, M. S. 2014. "What If? Models, Fact, and Fiction in Economics." *Journal of the British Academy* 2: 231–68.

Morgan, M. S. 2017. "Narrative Ordering and Explanation." *Studies in History and Philosophy of Science* 62: 86–97.

Morgan, M. S., and M. Norton Wise. 2017. "Narrative Science and Narrative Knowing: Introduction to Special Issue on Narrative Science." *Studies in History and Philosophy of Science* 62: 1–5 (open access).

Nikolow, S. 2001. "A. F. W. Crome's Measurements of the 'Strength of the State': Statistical Representations in Central Europe around 1800." In *The Age of Economic Measurement*, edited by J. Klein and M. S. Morgan. *History of Political Economy* 33 (supplement): 23–56.

Persons, W. M. 1919. "Indices of Business Conditions." *Review of Economic Statistics* 1: 5–110.

Pomata, Gianna. 2011. "Observation Rising: Birth of an Epistemic Genre." In Daston and Lunbeck 2011: 45–80.

Porter, T. M. 1986. *The Rise of Statistical Thinking, 1820–1900*. Princeton, NJ: Princeton University Press.

Rosenberg, N., and C. R. Frischtak. 1984. "Technological Innovation and Long-Waves." *Cambridge Journal of Economics* 8: 7–24.

Samuelson, P. A. 1938. "Interactions between the Multiplier Analysis and the Principle of Acceleration." *Review of Economics and Statistics* 21: 75–78.

Smith, Adam. (1776) 1991. *The Wealth of Nations*. New York: Everyman's Library.

Stigler, S. M. 1986. *The History of Statistics: The Measurement of Uncertainty before 1900*. Cambridge, MA: Belknap Press of Harvard University Press.

Tinbergen, J. 1939. *Statistical Testing of Business-Cycle Theories*. 2 vols. Geneva: League of Nations.

Searching for a Tide Table for Business: Interwar Conceptions of Statistical Inference in Business Forecasting

Laetitia Lenel

By the early twentieth century, the existence of a so-called trade or business cycle had become commonplace. The idea of crises as "abnormal" phenomena had given way to the concept of crises as some inherent trait of capitalism, alternating with periods of prosperity. As economists began to search for uniformities in the past, hopes sprang up that they could "figure out a tide table for business" and thus give business forecasting a scientific basis (Collins 1923: 8). Meteorologists had led the way. In the late nineteenth century, the introduction of new methods and networks had allowed meteorologists to overcome weather forecasting's dubious status and successfully transform its reputation from "prophecy" to science (Anderson 2005; Pietruska 2011, 2018). Economists hoped that they could achieve the same for economic forecasting. Of course, their tools and techniques should equal their counterparts in the natural sciences. Economists aimed to create forecasting tools that allowed for objective, reproducible knowledge practices and thus for a shared language between economic forecasters on different continents.

I thank participants at the *HOPE* conference "Statistical Inference in Twentieth-Century Economics" (April 23–26, 2020) for their comments and feedback on the first version of this article. There are six readers to whom I owe special thanks: Jeff Biddle, Marcel Boumans, Mary Morgan, and an anonymous referee provided helpful criticisms and suggestions on the final version. The article has also greatly benefited from the continuous discussion and support provided by Aline Lenel and Marcus Mikulcak.

History of Political Economy 53 (annual suppl.) DOI 10.1215/00182702-9414817
Copyright 2021 by Duke University Press

The recent expansion of economic statistics seemed to offer promising opportunities for impartial investigation and inference. Statistics, contemporaries hoped, could help them replace mercury with figures and the glass tube and brass case with mathematical paper to set up economic "barometers" that were by no means inferior to their meteorological counterparts (*Oakland Tribune* 1915). Like them, they would be based on measurement and prove their practical efficiency by helping business executives navigate the stormy waters of capitalism. As such, they seemed to present promising avenues for turning economics from "childish" metaphysics into "robust manhood" (Mitchell 1919b: 230; Mitchell 1927: 189).

One of the most successful and influential groups in communicating these aspirations was the Harvard Committee on Economic Research, established in 1917 at Harvard University. Hoping to prove the scientific validity of its young field, the committee developed the so-called Harvard Index of General Business Conditions, which aimed to meet the highest scientific standards. The index and its history bear witness to the goal of developing—and distributing—an instrument that yields objective knowledge about the future, independent from personal judgment and untainted by subjectivity. Its simple application as a forecasting tool was intended to allow its users to capture the future with as little human intervention as possible (Daston and Galison 2010: 20, 123). By this means, the Harvard "barometer," as contemporaries called the index, became a powerful instrument in the boundary work that statisticians and economists in the early twentieth undertook to distinguish "scientific" forecasting from quackery (Gieryn 1983, 1999). Similarly, its founders, most of all the economist and statistician Warren M. Persons (1878–1937), became prominent advocates of an economic science that vanquished economic uncertainty by processing and using economic statistics in a "mechanical" and objective fashion (Daston and Galison 2010: 115–90). In his first publications on the Harvard index, and as part of his efforts to model economics on the natural sciences, Persons (1919a: 125–26) urged economists to employ the mathematical theory of probability, whose application, according to him, promised the most objective and reliable results.

Yet the Harvard index did not manage to forecast the future correctly. Less than three years after its introduction, it started to make predictions that proved wrong by subsequent economic data. As a result, the members of the Harvard Committee not only performed a remarkable change in methods but also revoked their former statements on the opportunities and limitations of economic statistics and the importance of inferential procedures based in probability theory. In the summer of 1922, they began an extensive correspondence with economic and political decision-makers that allowed them to base their forecasts on "inside information." This change in methods went largely unseen by the public and has remained largely undiscovered until today. Research has focused entirely on the official method of investigation (Armatte 2003: 63–65; Fayolle 2003: 12–17; Morgan 2003: 56–63; Friedman 2009; Friedman 2014: 128–65; Boumans 2016). Persons's new stance on statistical inference, namely, his dismissal of the use of inferential measures based in probability theory, by contrast, became as influential as his older one (see Biddle 2017).

My article tells the history of the index and the methodical debates that accompanied its introduction, its widespread adoption, and its failure on both sides of the Atlantic. The story I tell complicates the history of probability in economics, as it illustrates the manifold changes and quarrels that took place before statistical inference based in probability theory came to take the central place it inhabits in economics until today (on its current contestations and, perhaps, erosion, see Stapleford, this volume). Statistical inference with probability, from that perspective, was not the long-sought solution for the problem of objectivity but a long-contested, and repeatedly discarded, approach. This makes the almost unanimous embrace of methods of inference derived from probability theory in the early 1960s all the more noteworthy.

While changes in methodology in economics have usually been explained by disciplinary changes, my article argues for the importance of the broader historical context. I understand forecasting tools as representations of specific worldviews. These are not necessarily based on description but often pursue constitutive purposes. This utopian refrain is especially relevant in the case of economic forecasting, which often aimed at stabilizing or engineering the future. Changes in methods and convictions, then, indicate changes in worldview. In economic forecasting, these were often triggered by deviations between forecasts and the conditions actually observed (see also Biddle, this volume). In tracing the history of the Harvard index, its adoption, modifications, and failure over the 1920s, I seek to make visible the contestations and replacements of worldviews of which the changes in methods bear witness.

1. The Harvard Index of General Business Conditions

1.1. Looking for Stable Conditions in an Unstable World

In the summer of 1915, one year after the outbreak of the war in Europe, which disrupted not only global trade but also American financial and commodity markets, Persons presented a "business barometer" to the American Statistical Society. Persons explicitly situated his own research in the line of the work of the commercial forecasters Roger Babson (1909) and James Brookmire (1910), who had started to forecast business conditions after the Panic of 1907. "The basis of the Babson and Brookm[ire] forecasts is the assumption that the law of action and reaction applies to business conditions as well as to physics and chemistry," explained Persons in August 1915. "This is undoubtedly true, and my criticism of their methods is aimed at their selection of statistics. A heterogeneous collection of figures, taken in an unscientific way and handled in a naive and rule of thumb manner" (*Oakland Tribune* 1915; see also Persons 1916: 746–47). While picking up on his predecessors' analogy to the natural sciences, their indicator technique and their metaphorical reference to meteorology, Persons strove for a different approach to economic statistics. According to Persons, for economic forecasting to become a science, economists had to employ uniform, replicable procedures for compiling forecasts from economic data. As Persons (1919b: 7) explained later, "No method is thought worth while testing that cannot be made entirely objective, that cannot be reproduced exactly by an individual working according to the directions laid down."

In the years that followed, Persons laid out his methods to a wider public. In 1916, he presented his methods in the *American Economic Review*. One year later, Persons was appointed professor of economics at Harvard University and leading statistician of the newly founded Harvard Committee on Economic Research, which was established by the Harvard economist Charles Bullock (1869–1941) in 1917 to analyze and improve the scientific quality of economic statistics, "with a view to making them more valuable for both business and scientific purposes."[1] In this position,

---

1. Charles J. Bullock, Committee on Economic Research, December 1, 1919, box 156, folder 310, UAI.5.160, Records of President Abbott Lawrence Lowell, Harvard University Archives. Hereafter cited as Lowell Records.

Persons devised the Harvard Index of General Business Conditions, which became one of the most popular and most influential economic forecasting tools of the twentieth century. As a member of the Harvard Committee and as president of the American Statistical Association (1923), Persons gained worldwide fame. His statistical methods were copied and criticized throughout the United States, Australia, Europe, South America, and the Soviet Union, and spurred the foundation of institutes of business-cycle research on four continents. Persons helped turn economic forecasting from a commercial enterprise into a respected field of economic science, and the leading indicator approach popularized by him became one of the most influential forecasting techniques up until today.

What, then, were Persons's views on the "proper" handling of economic statistics? Which data did he analyze and why, and why did he believe that he could base his forecasts on these data? In the following, I explain his methods of time series selection and decomposition, his methods of aggregating different time series into a single indicator, and the reasoning that led him and his colleagues to believe that they could forecast the future on the basis of different indicators.

As the leading statistician of the Harvard Committee on Economic Research, Persons analyzed, corrected, and compared about fifty series regularly published by trade papers, financial journals, and government agencies. He noted that these series were problematic not only because of frequent errors and discrepancies due to misprints, revisions, and lack of continuity in method but also because of their necessarily selective nature. The *Commercial and Financial Chronicle*, for example, which Persons and his colleagues consulted frequently, published preliminary figures for gross earnings of railroads around the fifteenth of each month, which were sometimes based on as few as nineteen roads and at other dates on around two hundred roads. Similarly, information on bank clearings, as published by Bradstreet's, covered only a select group of cities (Persons 1919b: 6). Noting that there "is need of a division of function," Persons nevertheless decided to work with those series that he found "most reliable and significant among those available" and to focus on methods of handling them (7). Reliability and significance, according to Persons, depended, first, on the size of samples and on the time period covered by the data. Second, Persons deemed those series significant that other researchers had found important. In this manner, of the fifty series considered, Persons decided to analyze, correct, and compare only twenty-three series. His selection rested on the notion that these series "ordinarily serve as the basis for judgments concerning fundamental business conditions" (Persons 1919a: 114).

Among the twenty-three series analyzed, Persons found twenty series to possess "well marked cyclical fluctuations or wave movements, connected with the ebb and flow of business activity" (111). To employ these twenty series as indices of business conditions, Persons sought to compare them over time and to each other. To secure their comparability over time, Persons "corrected" the data for secular trend and seasonal variation. Only thus, explained Persons (1919b: 35, 33), could secular trend and seasonal variations be isolated from cyclical and irregular fluctuations. To eliminate the influence of the war, Persons decided to focus on data from 1903–14. As Persons explained, forecasts had to be based on analogy. To interpret the present in peace times, therefore, the statistician had to consult the data of past "ordinary peace times" (Persons 1919a: 116–17). Persons's goal, then, was to derive an ideal type of the structure of the business cycle from historical records (see Löwe 1925: 373).

To measure the degree of correlation between the cyclical fluctuations of the various series, Persons (1919a: 121) plotted the graphs of the different series on translucent tracing cloth and placed one chart on another on the glass top of an illuminated box. Together with two other "observers," Persons compared the correspondence and lag between the twenty series. When the three men compared their results—twenty graphs made for 190 possible pairing combinations—disagreement arose over the nature and degree of correlation (127–28). For instance, one observer would describe the correlation between two graphs as "high," while the other observers would call it "moderate" (128). As Persons later explained, "personal equation, preconceived notions, or theoretical bias" might have influenced the conclusions of the all-too-human scientists (121; on personal equation, see Schaffer 1988). While Persons (1919a: 120–21) had believed that he had devised a "mechanical contrivance," the appraisal of the degree of correlation turned out to depend on visual judgment.

Looking for "a more objective method," Persons computed coefficients of correlation between those pairings of items that, from the preliminary comparison, appeared likely to result in maximum correlation (121–22; on the difference between the graphic method and the coefficient of correlation, see also Persons 1910). To accomplish this, he assumed an underlying normal distribution of the samples of economic data and, thus, a normally distributed error in the examination of the correlation of pairs of time series. This allowed him to calculate the margin of error of the determined correlation coefficients, that is, the "probable error" from the number of pairs from which the correlation coefficient was determined as well as the correlation coefficient itself (on the statistical background of his work, see Persons 1919a: 126).

On the basis of this two-step process of a preliminary graphic analysis and subsequent correlation measures, Persons sorted the series into five groups according to the similarity and simultaneity of their fluctuations (on the combination of graphic and correlation methods in Persons's work, see Morgan 1997: 69–73). Out of these groups, Persons chose those series that he deemed most representative and that he called the "standard" for the respective group. Subsequently, he compared the selected "standard" series to Bradstreet's index of commodity prices, assuming that, in line with "the consensus of opinion of writers on business cycles," business cycles are "preeminently characterized by price movements" (Persons 1919a: 129; Persons 1916: 750–51; Williams 1919). Bradstreet's index of commodity prices, which Brookmire had used as representative of general business as well, presented a composite of ninety-six wholesale prices of raw materials and manufactured goods (Persons 1919a: 139–41). To give what Persons called "a clearer picture of the time relationship of the cyclical movements," he rearranged the series into three groups containing bimonthly instead of monthly data. To do so, he selected only thirteen of the twenty series, explaining that six of the twenty series fluctuated "more erratically than others" and that one was not available on a bimonthly basis (Persons 1919a: 114). Group A consisted of series covering the average price of ten railroad bonds, the average price of industrial stocks, the price of twenty railroad stocks, the volume of sales on the New York Stock Exchange, and New York clearings, and was supposed to afford an index of speculation. Group B, which combined series on pig-iron production, bank clearings outside New York City, Bradstreet's indices of commodity prices, and the index of commodity prices of the Bureau of Labor Statistics, was described as relating to "business." Group C, relating to "money," presented series on the rates on commercial paper as well as on loans, deposits, and reserves of New York banks (Persons 1920: 41).

To determine the temporal relation between the fluctuations of the different series, Persons initially performed a visual comparison of the standard series and Bradstreet's index of prices. As a 1924 article reveals, Persons and his colleagues additionally employed correlation measurements to investigate further the relationships between the timing of the

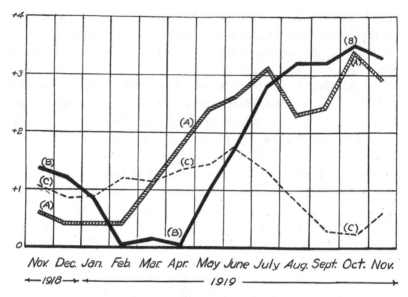

Figure 1 The Index of General Business Conditions.
Source: Harvard Committee on Economic Research 1919: 2.

fluctuations of the three groups. To assess the exact timing or lag of one curve with respect to another, they compared the coefficients of correlation for different lags observed in the past (see the explanation in Crum 1924: 19). On this basis, Persons (1919a: 114) explained that the cyclical fluctuations of group A have "systematically precede[d] in time" those of group B, while the movements of group B "systematically precede[d]" those of group C during the prewar period. Their approach made Persons (1919a: 126) and his colleagues confident enough to project these findings into the future.

Persons presented the curves of the three groups in one chart that he called "The Index of General Business Conditions" and constructed a similar index for the postwar period (see figure 1). Explaining that some series "have permanently lost their significance as indices of business conditions because of a change in economic organization and for other reasons," Persons (1920: 48) discarded some of the series previously used. The postwar index, then, was based on only seven series. While Persons believed that allowance had to be made for changes in the economic structure or underlying conditions, he nevertheless explained that the fluctuations of the three curves were to be interpreted "according to the rules drawn from the analysis of the period 1903–1914" (48). After all, the current index had shown "that the normal pre-war sequences between speculation, business, and banking have been resumed" (Persons 1922: 7).

In July 1919, eight months after the end of the Great War, Persons and his colleagues started to present their index of business conditions in a monthly bulletin. In 1922, they launched a so-called *Weekly Letter*, now under the name "Harvard Economic Service." A subscription to the service, which included the quarterly *Review of Economic Statistics*, cost $100 per year (about $1,500 today) and was advertised throughout the country.[2]

Persons (1919a: 117) believed that the index offered a "guide to the fundamental economic movements of the years that lie ahead." As he explained, "It may be expected . . . that, as conditions return to normal, the relations that existed between most, if not all, of our series of economic and business statistics will tend to be reestablished upon the basis which obtained from 1903 to 1914" (117). While he confessed that "a supplementary economic analysis is necessary," he explained that this analysis was only necessary to include possible changes due to so-called irregular causes like the war (Persons 1920: 40). Believing in the existence of an "ordinary universe" with "normal" conditions, Persons expected that the assumed relations between the different series remained stable. He therefore generalized the results obtained from the study of past data to forecast future conditions.

The economist's task, Persons (1919a: 134) believed, was to "discover system in the midst of variation." To this end, the economist had to employ the mathematical theory of probability. For the "probability that a discovered sequence will be repeated depends, obviously, upon the breadth of the sample or the number of times the sequence has been observed and upon the variability of the sequence" (134). Researchers therefore had to find a

---

2. This amount put it out of reach of individuals and small businesses (Mason and Lamont 1982: 415). Bullock himself noted that "study of the results of the circularizing campaign shows that large concerns are our best prospects, and that our present Service does not appeal to small concerns having a capital of less than $500,000" (Bullock, *Report of the Work of the Committee on Economic Research for the Year 1921–1922*, June 20, 1922, p. 8, box 156, folder 310, UAI.5.160, Lowell Records). The committee spent $35,174 in newspaper, magazine, and direct mail advertising in 1921–22. Bullock estimated that the committee had circularized around 110,000 individuals, firms, and corporations and sent out about 440,000 letters. In June 1922, the campaign was estimated to have yielded $62,395 of new business (p. 8). As Bullock noted, besides academics, who would focus on the *Review of Economic Statistics*, the majority of subscribers were presidents and treasurers (p. 9).

"functional expression of average experience" by fitting a curve to the economic data, measure the amount of variation in experience by examining the calculated coefficient of correlation, and determine the probable error of experience based on the size of the sample. Only then, argued Persons (1919a: 134), was it possible to utilize "experience as a basis of action." It was this belief in the validity of the theory of probability that encouraged the members of the Harvard Committee to rejoice that they had demonstrated a "definite relationship in the speculative, commodity, and money market" (*Chicago Tribune* 1923; see also Harvard Economic Service 1922g: 3). And why would that not be the case? As Persons (1919a: 133) explained with extended reference to the writings on biological evolution by Karl Pearson and Francis Galton, "The rationale we have used differs in no way from that of any other scientific investigation." Like them, he had submitted knowledge to measurement and number and thus bestowed economic forecasting with the status and dignity of science (130).

In 1919, the Great War was over, but "normal conditions," whatever they are, were far from being restored. European countries struggled with unrest and revolutions and dramatic economic instability. The international gold standard, which economists back then regarded as essential, had not yet been reestablished. The United States was the only major country that had not suspended the gold standard during the war. But the American economy, too, although less disrupted by the war than the European economies, struggled with the adjustment from wartime to peacetime. Persons's claim of the return of "ordinary peace times" that equaled the years before 1914 must therefore be understood as a utopian vision aiming to render economic activities coherent and predictable just as everything seemed fluid and contingent. His argument that economists could determine an "objective probability" of the occurrence of future economic events from available statistics seems like a reaction to the chaos and disorder that the world was left in after the war (Persons 1919a: 125).

1.2. Unstable Conditions Exact Their Toll: Changes in Methods and Convictions

Actual economic conditions, however, soon cast doubt on the existence of stable patterns. In December 1919, the members of the Harvard Committee had successfully "forecast" the recession of 1920–21. They had informed their readers that their "forecaster"—curve A—had showed a decline from October 1818 on, which "indicates that we may expect a check to the upward movement of commodity prices and business activity" (Harvard Committee on Economic Research 1919: 2). This forecast, which Persons and his colleagues had renewed in the following weeks, had been confirmed by the conditions realized over the summer of 1920, which proved to be a considerable success to the Harvard Committee. From January 1922 on, however, the index showed unsettling signs of failure (see Lenel 2018). In early January 1922, the Harvard Economic Service alluded to the upward move of curve A, representing speculation, which, according to the service, forecast a "rise of curve B, reflecting increased commodity prices and business activity, in the spring of 1922" (Harvard Economic Service 1922b: 1). In February, and despite a recent decline of curve A, the service renewed its forecast, pointing out that curve C had moved down sharply from June to December 1921, and that a "decline of curve C usually precedes, and hence forecasts, an upward movement of curve A, representing speculation, and then of curve B, representing business" (Harvard Economic Service 1922c: 45). The recovery, the members of the service promised, was imminent. Yet, in the weeks that followed, curve B moved farther down (45). Apparently, the "established sequences of movements of speculation, business and money," which Persons (1922: 9) and his colleagues had previously identified, had dissolved. The depth of the 1920–21 recession had not been forecast by the Harvard index.

As the curves did not behave according to protocol anymore, Persons and his colleagues gradually lost faith in the forecasting value of their index. They almost entirely ceased to use the curves for predictive purposes and instead referred to them only when explaining the curves' movements retrospectively. In May of that year, they explained the decline of curve B by the coal strike and the "generally unfavorable weather conditions" (Harvard Economic Service 1922f: 122). In early September 1922, readers learned that curve A had only moved down because the number of shares traded had decreased in June and July 1922. This, however, was of no predictive value: "Since the volume of trading fluctuates irregularly, and is frequently small during these two months, the decline which occurred this year is not to be regarded as significant" (Harvard Economic Service 1922d: 215). A few weeks later, the researchers informed their readers that "while we have no sources of information which are not open to all our subscribers, we believe that when the present episode is over it will be found that European conditions were responsible in no small measure for the movement of our money curve during the month of September" (Harvard Economic Service 1922e: 240). While the members of the Harvard Committee continued to print the index in the *Weekly Letters* and to revise the index as they saw fit (see Bullock, Persons, and Crum 1927: 75), the comparison of the movements of the curves for predictive purposes increasingly declined in importance.

In the meantime, the members of the Harvard group initiated a dramatic change in methods. Increasingly, they started to complement their "mechanical" forecasting procedures, which purported to display the future on the graph almost automatically, by trained judgment (Daston and Galison 2010: 309–61). From June 1922 on, discussions of the probable course of policies and their effects became of crucial importance. Repeatedly, the researchers assured their readers that they did not possess any "inside knowledge" and that their forecasts were "premised only upon such facts as are familiar to competent observers" (Harvard Economic Service 1922a: 140). These, however, were false promises. As Bullock's papers reveal, he started an extensive correspondence with economic and political decision-makers in the United States and abroad—and correspondents repeatedly accused him of having passed on confidential information in the *Weekly Letters*.[3] From the summer of 1922 on, Bullock regularly consulted with members of the Federal Reserve banks to inquire about their plans.[4] Benjamin Strong, the influential governor of the Federal Reserve Bank of New York, became a close acquaintance of Bullock, regularly sending him "confidential" information, which Bullock shared with Persons and other members of the Harvard Economic Service.[5] To find out about the probable behavior of other banks, Bullock asked bank officials in the New York and Chicago area about their beliefs and expectations regarding the behavior of Federal Reserve members and their views on the consequences for the credit situation.[6] To induce them to reveal their estimations of the current business situation, Bullock told them about his own views and sent them comments on the business situa-

3. Charles J. Bullock to Benjamin Strong, December 27, 1923, Correspondence L-Z, box 6, HUG 4245, Charles J. Bullock Papers, Harvard University Archives (hereafter cited as Bullock Papers); Charles J. Bullock to Benjamin Strong, January 10, 1924, Correspondence L-Z, box 6, HUG 4245, Bullock Papers.

4. Charles J. Bullock to Benjamin Strong, July 25, 1923, Correspondence L-Z, box 6, HUG 4245, Bullock Papers.

5. Charles J. Bullock to Benjamin Strong, November 29, 1922, p. 2, Correspondence L-Z, box 6, HUG 4245, Bullock Papers; Charles J. Bullock to Benjamin Strong, September 24, 1923, p. 1, Correspondence L-Z, box 6, HUG 4245, Bullock Papers; Charles J. Bullock to Benjamin Strong, June 2, 1924, Correspondence L-Z, box 6, HUG 4245, Bullock Papers.

6. Leonard P. Ayres to Charles J. Bullock, July 24, 1923, Correspondence A-K, box 5, HUG 4245, Bullock Papers.

tion by "friends" of his.[7] Instead of statistics, his correspondents answered by elaborating on their "impression" or "belief" about the stance of Federal Reserve officials and any possible effects.[8] They reported on meetings with other bankers and the impressions they gained during these meetings.[9] Bullock also met in person with bank officials to find out about their mood. After a trip to New York in November 1923, he noted, "I visited most of the large banks there, and found them feeling cheerful and confident about the outlook. If a business depression is coming, there is certainly nothing in the large New York banks to indicate it."[10] As Bullock once described the Harvard Economic Service's forecasting procedure in a letter to Keynes, "We are feeling our way along."[11]

As a professor at Harvard since 1903, Bullock had easy access to American bankers and business leaders, manifested in physical facilities like the Harvard Club in New York, which Bullock frequently visited. Bullock took great pains to maintain and expand his network. Besides conducting an extensive correspondence via letters and telephone, Bullock regularly visited bank officials in Chicago and New York, sent them artworks, self-composed verses, and connected them with other acquaintances of his.[12] With economic and political conditions in Europe affecting gold movements to and from the United States, Bullock's network was not confined to American bankers and business leaders but also included European economists and bankers. In March 1928, for example, Bullock reported

7. Warren Randolph Burgess to Charles J. Bullock, August 20, 1928, Correspondence A-K, box 5, HUG 4245, Bullock Papers.

8. Burgess to Bullock, August 20, 1928; Warren Randolph Burgess to Charles J. Bullock, May 5, 1928, Correspondence A-K, box 5, HUG 4245, Bullock Papers; Ayres to Bullock, July 24, 1923.

9. Warren Randolph Burgess to Charles J. Bullock, October 9, 1928, Correspondence A-K, box 5, HUG 4245, Bullock Papers.

10. Charles J. Bullock to Walter Lichtenstein, November 7, 1923, p. 1, Correspondence L-Z, box 6, HUG 4245, Bullock Papers.

11. Charles J. Bullock to John M. Keynes, March 4, 1925, Correspondence A-K, box 5, HUG 4245, Bullock Papers.

12. T. S. Estrem to Charles J. Bullock, March 11, 1935, Correspondence A-K, box 5, HUG 4245, Bullock Papers; Bullock to Strong, September 24, 1923, p. 4; Charles J. Bullock to Benjamin Strong, October 28, 1923, Correspondence L-Z, box 6, HUG 4245, Bullock Papers; Charles J. Bullock to Benjamin Strong, March 26, 1924, Papers of Benjamin Strong Jr., Federal Reserve Bank of New York Archives; Benjamin Strong to Charles J. Bullock, February 27, 1925, Correspondence L-Z, box 6, HUG 4245, Bullock Papers; Benjamin Strong to Charles J. Bullock, October 19, 1927, Correspondence L-Z, box 6, HUG 4245, Bullock Papers; Benjamin Strong to Charles J. Bullock, February 27, 1925, Correspondence L-Z, box 6, HUG 4245, Bullock Papers; Charles J. Bullock to Benjamin Strong, March 26, 1924, Papers of Benjamin Strong Jr., Federal Reserve Bank of New York Archives.

that he intended "to spend a week or two in London, trying to learn some things there about the London money market that can't be picked up out of books or even learned from American bankers."[13] Soon, Bullock had built a vast network of informants and described the maintenance of correspondences as a mandatory task of the Harvard Economic Service.[14]

Bullock and his colleagues used their inside knowledge in their *Weekly Letters*.[15] As Bullock put it, they prepared their *Letters* "after extended conference with all the concerns in New York and elsewhere that had information about the subject."[16] The correspondence shows that bank officials, members of the business community, and economists engaged thoroughly with the *Weekly Letters*, voicing agreement or disagreement with the outlooks given. Disagreeing with the statement in a *Weekly Letter* on the effects of an increase in the rediscount rate, for example, the president of the National Bank of Commerce in New York pointed Bullock in May 1923 to the psychological effects that an increase in the rediscount rate might have, as it "would probably be interpreted as justifying lack of confidence in the general situation."[17] Keynes, too, regularly engaged with the views voiced in the *Weekly Letters*.[18] The *Weekly Letters* thus had a vital function in coordinating expectations on the course of economic development. In autumn each year, at the annual Harvard Economic Conference, representatives of various companies and officials of several Federal Reserve Banks met in person with members of the Harvard Committee to exchange their outlooks for the next year.[19] Conferences also took

13. Charles J. Bullock to John M. Keynes, March 5, 1928, p. 1, Correspondence A-K, box 5, HUG 4245, Bullock Papers; Charles J. Bullock to Ernst Wagemann, February 9, 1935, p. 1, Correspondence L-Z, box 5, HUG 4245, Bullock Papers.

14. Charles J. Bullock to Chingtao T. Chu, November 23, 1926, p. 2, Correspondence A-K, box 5, HUG 4245, Bullock Papers; Bullock to Strong, January 10, 1924, p. 1.

15. Charles J. Bullock to A. Lawrence Lowell, October 25, 1923, p. 1, folder 211, box 190, UAI.5.160, Lowell Records.

16. Charles J. Bullock to Thomas W. Lamont, October 2, 1923, p. 3, Correspondence L-Z, box 6, HUG 4245, Bullock Papers.

17. J. L. Alexander to Charles J. Bullock, May 10, 1923, Correspondence A-K, box 5, HUG 4245, Bullock Papers.

18. John M. Keynes to Charles J. Bullock, December 15, 1924, Correspondence A-K, box 5, HUG 4245, Bullock Papers; John M. Keynes to Charles J. Bullock, October 4, 1928, Correspondence A-K, box 5, HUG 4245, Bullock Papers; John M. Keynes to Charles J. Bullock, November 13, 1928, Correspondence A-K, box 5, HUG 4245, Bullock Papers.

19. William Justus Boies to Carl Snyder, November 22, 1924, Papers of Benjamin Strong Jr., Federal Reserve Bank of New York Archives; Gilbert King, *Summary of Papers Read at Harvard Economic Conference, 13 and 14 November, 1925*, box 36, folder 25, Wallace Brett Donham Papers, Harvard Business School Archives, Baker Library; Estrem to Bullock, March 11, 1935.

place in Philadelphia, Chicago, and New York, sometimes up to three times a year. Here, Bullock met with representatives of various banks to discuss money and credit conditions in the United States and abroad.[20]

The growing emphasis on the importance of personal networks was in line with the realization of the human influence on business cycles. The increasingly proactive policy of the Federal Reserve after 1921 challenged the idea of the existence of stable patterns inscribed in the Harvard index. Realizing that the purchase and sale of government securities in the open market influenced market interest rates and credit conditions, Reserve Bank governors in the early 1920s increasingly coordinated their operations in government securities to proactively lessen economic fluctuations (for different evaluations of the success of these attempts, see Friedman and Schwartz 1963: chap. 6; Meltzer 2003). Already in 1923, Strong warned Bullock that "a change has taken place in the control of credit— which makes prognostication of the future of prices when based upon the gyrations of past curves—extremely dangerous."[21] Two years later, in a letter to Bullock, Keynes explained that the business cycle could "be largely eliminated and . . . certainly depends on such things as the policy of the Federal Reserve Board more than on anything else." This view, noted Keynes, was incompatible with the approach of the members of the Harvard Economic Service, which seemed to liken the shape of the curve "to a natural phenomenon such as the tide."[22] Bullock was well aware of this.[23] As he explained in 1924, "I think that probably I am in substantial, and perhaps complete, agreement with you with reference to the degree of power which Federal Reserve authorities have over price movements."[24] Rather than give up on the attempt to forecast business conditions, however, Bullock and his colleagues modified their forecasting approach accordingly. They ceased their search for stable patterns and instead adopted an interactive, collaborative approach, enabling political and economic decision-makers "to participate in the epistemic process of forecasting" (Reichmann 2013: 858). Increasingly, the Harvard group's forecasts relied not on statistics but on "foretalk" (on this term, see Gibson 2011: 504; Gibson 2012; Reichmann 2013).

20. Charles J. Bullock, *Third Annual Report of the President of the Harvard Economic Society*, 1930, p. 7, box 292, folder 265, UAI.5.160, Lowell Records.

21. Bullock to Strong, December 27, 1923.

22. John M. Keynes to Charles J. Bullock, February 11, 1925, pp. 1–2, Correspondence A-K, box 5, HUG 4245, Bullock Papers.

23. Bullock to Strong, July 25, 1923, p. 1.

24. Bullock to Strong, March 26, 1924. Papers of Benjamin Strong, Jr., Federal Reserve Bank of New York Archives.

In October 1923, Bullock explained that the service's announcement that they had demonstrated a "definite relationship in the speculative, commodity, and money market" had been a mistake. Although "perfectly true so far as we know when understood in a scientific sense," it "would not be understood by people who do not know the difference between a scientific demonstration and what popularly passes for demonstration," explained Bullock in private letters.[25] With this, Bullock probably referred to the differences in a demonstration under controlled laboratory conditions and those occurring in the "real" world. Forecasting failures and a new understanding of economic change forced the members of the committee to revoke their previous stance on forecasting and instead accept the uncertainty of economic life. A few years later, in what seemed like a recantation of their earlier views, they explained that "a mechanical application of the sequence doctrine may not give satisfactory results," as there were no "fixed mechanical, or exact mathematical, relationships in the economic world" (Crum 1925: 218; Bullock, Persons, and Crum 1927: 79). Since business conditions were understood to depend on human behavior, the researchers gave up on the idea of the existence of universal patterns.

Some economists were outraged about the change in methods. Wesley Mitchell (1919a: 872; 1924: 1), for example, who had praised the approach of the Harvard Committee as "ultra-scientific" in 1919, noted with irritation that the members of the Harvard group had begun "to modify or supplement the forecast given in a more or less mechanical way by their statistical series." "Of course," explained Mitchell, "just so far as the Harvard Group is relying on general information or broad observations or tips or 'hunches' they are precisely in the same position as many another group which makes no pretensions to scientific method." Mitchell thought "most emphatically that the two types of forecasts"—the "mechanical," "scientific" one based on statistics and the "unscientific" second one based on inside information—ought to be kept separate, and demanded that "all future forecasts make clear, definite and unmistakable precisely what forecast, if any, the statistical series as analyzed by Persons justify."[26]

Persons, however, simply distanced himself from the old emphasis on the importance of inferential procedures that were objective and reproducible. In his 1923 presidential address at the annual meeting of the

25. Bullock to Lowell, October 25, 1923; Charles J. Bullock to Thomas W. Lamont, October 25, 1923, Correspondence L-Z, box 6, HUG 4245, Bullock Papers.
26. Wesley C. Mitchell to Henry S. Dennison, February 5, 1924, p. 1, box 8, Wesley C. Mitchell Papers, University Archives, Rare Book and Manuscript Library, Columbia University, New York.

American Statistical Association, Persons rejected the use of inferential measures based in probability theory in the statistical analysis of economic data. Citing Keynes's *Treatise on Probability*, Persons (1924: 3–4) explained that statistical devices such as charts or coefficients of correlation were never arguments in themselves. Instead, they presented mere descriptions of a past period. This period was never "random" with respect to the present, but necessarily presented "a special period with characteristics distinguishing it" from later periods (6–7; on the history of this argument, see Morgan 1997). To draw an inference, therefore, the technique of statistical probability was entirely useless. Statistical data could never be considered a random sample "except in an unreal, hypothetical sense," Persons (1924: 6) insisted. To draw inferences from economic statistics and make forecasts of economic developments, therefore, economists had to employ "the usual methods of argument" like analysis, comparison, and differentiation (8).

With his address, Persons provided a "scientific" justification for the change in methods employed from 1922 on. American economists embraced his view (Biddle 2017: 153–54). As Edmund E. Day (1925: 380) explained with extensive reference to Persons's 1923 address, "The theory of probability is hardly applicable to most economic data." Statistical results may "serve to simplify the situation; possibly to remove from the range of reasonable expectation certain factors previously regarded as important. But statistical analysis rarely, if ever, entirely eliminates uncertainty as to the factors involved in any situation" (381). Other economists agreed. "In business, conditions are not opportune for a general application of the theory of mathematical probability," explained the economist David Jordan two years later. "Its domain includes only those cases where all possible happenings are known in advance" (Jordan 1927: 5). This was a new perspective on economic change, one that accepted the openness and uncertainty of the future.

In 1922, Persons had withdrawn from editorial work on the *Weekly Letters*, which had, as Bullock explained, "interfer[ed] with his scientific activities."[27] A few years later, Persons completely resigned his position on the Harvard Committee to become vice president of the National Investors Corporation and establish his own consulting agency.[28] Here, Persons advised companies on a case-by-case basis. Unlike his former colleagues

27. Bullock, *Report of the Work*, June 20, 1922, pp. 1–2.
28. Charles J. Bullock, *First Annual Report of the President of the Harvard Economic Society*, 1928, p. 3, box 258, folder 148, UAI.5.160, Lowell Records; Warren M. Persons to Charles J. Bullock, July 5, 1934, Correspondence L-Z, box 6, HUG 4245, Bullock Papers.

on the Harvard Committee, who seem to have based their forecasts entirely on information exchange with economic and political decision-makers, Persons continued to rely on an index of industrial production and trade in his own forecasting efforts. His concept and use of the index, however, had altered fundamentally. Persons (1931: 43) now condemned all "mechanistic systems and generalizations concerning the permanency of statistical relations." In line with his 1923 address, he understood the index not as an automatic guide to the future but as "the living record of business experience" (Persons 1931: 40). Taken alone, it was of no forecasting value, for "this is not a world of economic forces operating in a vacuum" (39–40). The index's "meaning," claimed Persons, therefore remained opaque to "the mechanistic chart reader" (40). Only if interpreted in the light of the economic and political chronology of the time and "rationalized by economic analysis" could the index shed light on the future (40).

In newspaper articles and a 1931 monograph, Persons continued to issue forecasts of business conditions in the United States that were based on statistical analysis and trained judgment. He did not try to quantify the probability of his forecasts and used the term *probability* only to distinguish his forecasts, understood as "elastic realistic concept[s] of probable future developments," from statements of certainty (33). Like the forecasts of his colleagues on the Harvard Committee, Persons's forecasts failed spectacularly. He did not foresee the Great Crash and mistakenly predicted an imminent recovery in 1931. The combination of statistical analysis and the exercise of trained judgment, it seemed, was no sure formula either.

Wrong forecasts, a continued depression in industry, and, maybe most important, the formal separation of the Harvard Economic Service and Harvard University in 1928 led to a decline in subscription numbers. As one business executive explained in 1931, "I imagine if subscribers were given a notice that the Harvard Economic Society was not connected with Harvard University in any way, shape or manner, that their subscriptions would materially fall off."[29] In a reaction to their forecasting failures and to dwindling subscription numbers, the members of the Harvard Committee explained in 1932 that "a mechanical reading of the chart in June 1929 clearly foretold the coming of a major cyclical decline. . . . If we had read the Index mechanically in the summer of 1928, we should have forecast a

---

29. Edward H. Angier to A. Lawrence Lowell, January 13, 1931, box 292, folder 265, UAI.5.160, Lowell Records.

serious recession, and possibly a business depression" (Bullock and Crum 1932: 137, 142). From now on, Bullock promised, they would "make no forecasts except such as result from a mechanical reading of our index."[30] This was a last desperate attempt to restore the Harvard group's scientific standing and secure its survival. These efforts, however, were in vain. In 1935, the group had to cease operation.

Conceptions of statistical inference seem to have changed with every unpredicted turn of events. They seem to have fluctuated as violently as economic life itself. It is perhaps no coincidence that Persons's colleagues proclaimed a congruency of past and future patterns just as the world seemed to fall apart. Amid all the uncertainty, and faced with the loss of academic status, the hope that there existed something like stable patterns— and hence the opportunity for mechanical means of forecasting—was greater than ever.

2. The Adoption of the Harvard Index in Europe

2.1. Trying to Stabilize European Economies Using the Index

In the early 1920s, international economists were well impressed by the index and its seemingly mechanical working. At the instigation of the Italian economist Costantino Ottolenghi (1874–1947), who suggested establishing a European statistical "observatory" with headquarters in London and "observers" in various countries, Keynes reached out to Bullock, proposing a cooperation between the Harvard Committee and a group of British economists (Bowley 1922a: 145). Keen to put business forecasting "upon a truly international basis" and to spread the influence of their work,[31] Bullock and his colleagues accepted enthusiastically and offered to underwrite, up to the sum of five thousand dollars, the expenses of the British group.[32] In February 1922 Bullock traveled to London to meet with the group. Four months later, the London and Cambridge Economic Service was officially established "on the lines of the Harvard

---

30. Charles J. Bullock to Charles F. Adams, September 15, 1931, pp. 1–2, box 37, folder 1, Wallace Brett Donham Papers, Harvard Business School Archives, Baker Library.

31. Bullock, *Report of the Work*, June 20, 1922, p. 5.

32. Bullock, *Report of the Work*, June 20, 1922, pp. 3–4. In 1928, a second donation was offered by the Harvard Economic Society and accepted by John Maynard Keynes, *Minutes of the Eighteenth Meeting of the Executive Committee*, December 18, 1928, box 2, Minute Book, London and Cambridge Economic Service, London School of Economics and Political Science Archives).

Economic Service."[33] The British economists arranged with the *Manchester Guardian* to publish their results as well as the Harvard index for six months in its monthly supplement "Reconstruction in Europe," which was published in English, French, Italian, German, and Spanish (Bowley 1922a: 145; "Harvard Economic Service for Business Conditions in the United States" 1922). From January 1923 on, the Harvard index and the British index as well as about sixty statistical series on finance, trade and output, transport, and employment were published in a monthly bulletin edited by the executive committee of the London and Cambridge Economic Service.[34] The British index, in turn, was published in the Harvard Committee's *Weekly Letter.*

"It is at once evident that we have been greatly influenced by the work of the Harvard Committee," claimed the economist and statistician Arthur Bowley (1869–1957), member of the London group (Bowley 1922a: 145). Indeed, the British index seemed to closely resemble the Harvard index at first sight. Four curves were plotted in one chart. Bowley and his colleagues substituted the Harvard group "speculation" by the price of twenty industrial stocks (A), the Harvard group "business" by wholesale prices of commodities (B^1) and the volume of exported manufactures (B^2), and the Harvard curve "money" by the short money index (C) (see figure 2). Yet a closer look reveals stark differences. While the members of the British group adopted the methods of time series decomposition employed by the Harvard group (see Keynes 1922: 54, 57), they deemed it problematic to average different series to present them in one curve. As Bowley (1922a: 146) explained, they did not consider any series "sufficiently homogeneous to make the process legitimate, or sufficiently numerous to result in a useful elimination of the unessential." Hence, only the short money index, which comprised the Bank of England rate of discount, other banks' rate of interest on deposits, and the market rates for day-by-day money and for three months' bank bills, presented an average of "unlike things" (148). In the other cases, the members decided for individual series, which they, together with a group of prominent business executives, had selected as "specially symptomatic and representative" ("Barometer of Economic Conditions" 1922: 54). Also, the members of the British

33. Bullock, *Report of the Work*, June 20, 1922, p. 4; William H. Beveridge, July 5, 1922, p. 1, *Minutes of the First Meeting of the Executive Committee*, box 2, Minute Book, London and Cambridge Economic Service, London School of Economics and Political Science Archives. For a short history of the London and Cambridge Economic Service, see Cord 2017.

34. Bullock, *Report of the Work*, June 20, 1922, p. 4; Beveridge 1923.

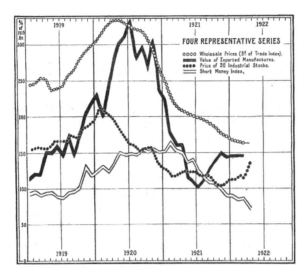

Figure 2 The United Kingdom barometer.
Source: Bowley 1922b: 116.

group were much more reluctant to base any forecasts on the index. While they did hope that the curves of their index possessed a temporal relation that would allow them to forecast future business conditions (see Beveridge 1923: 3), they admitted that the "barometer" could not replace but only assist individual judgment (7; on the term *barometer*, see, e.g., "Barometer of Economic Conditions" 1922). As William Beveridge (1879–1963), director of the London School of Economics, explained, the British service should not be expected "to sell for a few pounds a magic formula for coining wealth" (Beveridge 1923: 7).

Nevertheless, Beveridge insisted that there was something like a "calculable element in the trade cycle" and that the Harvard Committee had helped discover the "laws" of the trade cycle (5, 6, 2). These, explained Beveridge, were valid for the United States and Great Britain alike. While Beveridge and Bowley alluded to the fact that the breakdown of the currency system and the shift of the channels of trade made it difficult to use experience as a guide to the future, Beveridge still deemed the study of the indices of business conditions in Britain and the United States most helpful in assessing the probable future course of the economy (Bowley 1922a: 146; Beveridge 1923: 5, 6). At a gathering of business executives in Manchester in November 1922, Beveridge even argued that a business executive might study the British index "with the same confidence with which he now consulted the indications of the thermometer or the barometer," the *Times* (1922) reported.

Other economists were equally eager to adopt the Harvard approach in their country. From 1922 to 1935, the London and Cambridge Economic Service used parts of the payments by the Harvard Committee to finance foreign correspondents. German, Belgian, French, and Italian economists were asked for monthly contributions of current statistics and comments, which were published in "Reconstruction in Europe" and, later, in the monthly bulletin. The cooperation between the Harvard and London group and their various European and Canadian correspondents proved extremely fruitful, initiating the formation of similar economic services in various countries. In 1923, and in cooperation with the Harvard and the British groups, the newly founded Institut de Statistique of the University of Paris started to publish a quarterly journal, which contained a graphical reproduction of eighty-three statistical series as well as four indices that were chosen as "particularly significant of the general economic situation" in France (Huber 1933: 272–73; March 1923: 275; International Labour Office 1924: 54). These indices—the index of the price of 194 stocks of various yields (curve A), the index of wholesale prices (curve B), the index of British wholesale prices, expressed in francs (curve B_2), and the index of discount rate of the Bank of France (curve C)—were plotted in one chart and published alongside the British and American indices (March 1923: 276). As Lucien March (1859–1933), founding member and honorary director of the institute, explained, the postwar curves followed each other in the same succession as in the prewar period from 1903 to 1914. March believed, however, that the succession in the movements of the curves in France was not as pronounced as in other countries due to the special role of the depreciation of the currency and the sharp discontinuation of the discount rate in France (276–77).

At the instigation and with the financial support of the members of the Harvard group, who described the formation of the French connection as "very advantageous," 1926 saw the establishment of an economic service in Italy.[35] Under the auspices of the University of Padua and the University of Rome and in collaboration with various industry and banking bodies, the Italian committee regularly published 166 time series, which were

35. Charles J. Bullock, Report of the Work of the Harvard University Committee on Economic Research for the Year 1923–1924, June 2, 1924, p. 12, box 190, folder 211, UAI.5.160, Lowell Records.

believed to be "the most likely ones to give the safest expression of the rhythm of the Italian economic life" (Pietra 1926b: 7). Like their French colleagues, the Italian group around the statistician Corrado Gini (1884–1965) believed that Italy's current economic situation impeded the derivation of reliable forecasts. As Gini and his colleague, the Italian statistician Gaetano Pietra (1879–1961), argued, the war debts hampered Italy's stability and autonomy and had therefore "interrupted the regularity of the rhythm" of the Italian economy (Gini 1926: 4; Pietra 1926b: 39). The members of the Italian committee therefore postponed the construction of synthetic curves until a stable economic rhythm had been established, restricting themselves to the presentation of the American, British, and French synthetic curves (Pietra 1926b: 39; Comitato per gli Indici del Movimento Economico Italiano 1926). However, when Pietra (1926a: 38) undertook a first attempt to construct an index along the lines of the Harvard Committee, he found that the "laws" of temporal interrelation observed in the United States and in Great Britain were valid also for the Italian case.

Economists in other countries followed suit. Together with the League of Nations and the Rockefeller Foundation, which supported these attempts in the hope that objective information on business conditions might serve economic and political stabilization, the Harvard group fostered these efforts. After all, Bullock and his colleagues had an early interest in the development and extension "of our chain of 'economic observatories'" throughout the world.[36] From its foundation in 1919 on, the Harvard Economic Service had experienced a meteoric rise. This rise, however, had not been unproblematic. As Bullock started to speak of forecasting services as "concerns" or "enterprises," the yearlong struggle between the Harvard Committee and Harvard University about "the connection of so large a money-making undertaking with the University" deepened.[37] For President Abbott Lawrence Lowell, the financial success of the Harvard Economic Service could cast doubt on the academic status of the Harvard Economic Service and Harvard University more generally.[38] After all, the increasing commercialization of their forecasting service seemed to stand in stark contrast to an ethos of disinterestedness and communalism, which many saw as pivotal for a truly scientific endeavor (Merton 1942; see also Margócsy 2014).

36. Bullock, *Report of the Work*, June 2, 1924, p. 12.

37. Lowell and Bullock 1924; Bullock to Lowell, October 20, 1925, box 225, folder 147, UAI.5.160, Lowell Records; Bullock, *Report of the Work*, June 20, 1922, p. 5.

38. See Bullock to Lowell, October 25, 1923.

The cooperation with international services, which had been established under the auspices of distinguished universities, must therefore also be understood as an attempt to justify the committee's own affiliation with Harvard University and its right to use "the name Harvard" to maintain and enhance the prestige and scientific standing of the organization.[39] As Bullock explained in 1925, "these connections will be very advantageous in giving our work not only an international status but also a definite university status in the leading universities of the leading countries of the world."[40] Not surprisingly, the members of the committee considered university affiliation of the international economic services an important funding criterion.[41] Of course, to their international colleagues, too, cooperation with one of the most prestigious universities in the world must have seemed advantageous. The scientific status of business forecasting was, after all, still highly contested. Additionally, European researchers had a financial interest in cooperating with the Harvard Committee. With European countries beset with reparations and war debts, cooperation with the Harvard Committee was attractive, as it promised access to American money. The Austrian economist Friedrich Hayek (1899–1992), who was hoping for American funds to "encourage" business-cycle research in Austria, remarked in a private letter in 1926, "With relatively little dollar amounts one could achieve quite something here."[42] British, French, German, Italian, and Austrian economists all tried to raise American funds for their ventures. In many cases, the Harvard group was happy to give.[43] After all, the international circulation and adoption of the index promised to demonstrate its universality (O'Connell 1993; Bourguet, Licoppe, and Sibum 2002).

And yet, while most European researchers endorsed the methods of time series decomposition, the adoption of the Harvard methods of aggregating different time series into single indicators and of basing forecasts on their temporal interrelation proved difficult. European economists

39. Charles J. Bullock to subscribers, January 13, 1928, 2–3, Correspondence L–Z, box 5, HUG 4245, Bullock Papers.

40. Bullock to Lowell, October 20, 1925, box 225, folder 147, UAI.5.160, Lowell Records; Bullock, *Report of the Work*, June 20, 1922, p. 5

41. Charles J. Bullock, *Report of the Work of the Harvard University Committee on Economic Research for the Year 1924–1925*, June 5, 1925, pp. 7–9, box 190, folder 211, UAI.5.160, Lowell Records; Bullock, *Report of the Work*, June 2, 1924, p. 12.

42 Friedrich A. von Hayek to Oskar Morgenstern, December 11, 1926, box 2, Correspondence 1925–1936: H–K, Oskar Morgenstern Papers, Duke University Archives, Durham, NC.

43. See, e.g., Bullock, *Report of the Work*, June 2, 1924, pp. 11–12.

ascribed their failure to adopt the Harvard index as a forecasting tool to the exceptional economic and political conditions and to the poorer statistical situation prevailing in their country. In the early 1920s, none of them called into question the value of the Harvard index. On the contrary, they explained their difficulties by the fact that their country had "not yet" reached the advanced stage of the United States, postponing the construction of an equivalent index until a later date. All of them expressed the hope that, once the "normal" course of business had been resumed, economic barometers could help forecast the future. Beveridge deemed the study of the general indices of business conditions in Britain and the United States "the first and most obvious guide to the future course of trade" (Bowley 1922a: 146; Beveridge 1923: 5, 6). March expressed the hope that economic barometers could someday be as precise as instruments of measures in the physical sciences and maybe even more successful in forecasting the future than meteorological instruments (March 1923: 281; March 1924: 356; see also March 1926: 4, 28). For economic barometers to become precise instruments of measure, however, economists had to apply the same procedures as employed in the physical sciences, March (1923: 277–78) insisted. A "methodical, meticulous observation by disinterested organizations" was necessary, covering a great number of phenomena for as long a period as possible (March 1926: 28; March 1923: 277; Pietra 1926a: 35; Gini 1926: 4). Economists and statisticians had to refrain from personal judgment, which was always subjective and thus deemed not scientific (March 1926: 4; see also Jovanovic and Le Gall 2001: 91–92). Instead, European statisticians argued, their task was to issue "objective indications," which could assist the individual judgment of their subscribers (Gini 1926: 3; Beveridge 1923: 6–7).

In the early 1920s, most European business-cycle researchers adhered to the ideal of mechanical objectivity (Daston and Galison 2010; Porter 1995). Like Persons in his early publications on forecasting, they strove for rule-based, replicable procedures that yielded impersonal and thus objective results. All of them borrowed the *barometer* term of Persons's 1916 article—even though Persons had not used it since. And they made extensive use of the atmospheric semantics that the *barometer* term evoked. They dreamed of forecasting "the business weather" by employing the same techniques of observation, measurement, classification, and comparison as did meteorologists and compared the movements of the business cycle to the unmistakable regularity of the tides (cf. Bowley 1922b: 115; on the "ebb and flow of economic life," see Beveridge 1923: 1;

on the "Gezeiten der Wirtschaft," see Mises and Hayek 2003: 109). This is especially noteworthy, as European business forecasters were faced with a stronger opposition toward "mechanistic" conceptions of the economy than their American colleagues in the 1920s (see, e.g., Sorer 1914: 194). In line with this, some European researchers explained that the business cycle depended on human actions and was therefore alterable. This, however, did not seem to deter them from looking for stable patterns with predictive power. Indeed, March (1923: 281; 1926: 28) believed that the fact that economic fluctuations "depend to a great degree on human will" could even render these patterns more stable, as mutual observation might help coordinate and harmonize economic activities.

While European countries were still struggling with economic turmoil, the United States had experienced a spectacular upswing and return to economic stability from 1922 on. Some European economists believed that this was also due to the introduction of the Harvard index (Löwe 1925: 376–77; Mises and Hayek 2003: 112–13; van Zeeland 1929: 3–4). Adopting the index, then, was an attempt to trigger economic stability and progress by replacing emotions by numbers. The index acted at once as a utopian vision and an instrument, designed to actualize the order it described.

2.2. New Techniques to Grasp a Future That Was Different from the Past

Beginning in 1923, and repeatedly so since the mid-1920s, the members of the Harvard Committee began to subject their index to a number of revisions, which cast doubt on the universality of the index and the existence of stable patterns (see Persons 1923; "Review of the Year 1924" 1925: 18; Bullock, Persons, and Crum 1927; Crum 1928; Persons, Crum, and Frickey 1926). As a reaction, the tone in Europe changed. At an international conference on economic barometers, which was organized by the League of Nations and took place in Paris in December 1926, European economists called into question the validity of the Harvard index as a forecasting tool. The attendees alluded to the fact that indices that had successfully forecast economic activity in the past did not necessarily continue to do so in the future.[44] As Bowley explained, it was "quite unsafe to apply any inference

44. Committee of Experts on Economic Barometers, *Report*, December 15, 1926, p. 6, Registry Document No. 56297, Dossier No. 51866, League of Nations Archives, Geneva. Hereafter cited as LNA.

drawn from conditions before the war to conditions after the war."[45] The Harvard methods, at least, had not appeared to be valid for the past five years. Indices that had been most sensitive in one decade proved insensitive in another, Bowley had found. Neither prices nor stock exchange indices, it seemed, could be used "in order to draw any valid inference for the future."[46] Bowley therefore encouraged statisticians to just continue their studies and use "common sense."[47] In the same spirit, the German economist Ernst Wagemann (1884–1956) argued for a "prudent use of the deductive method."[48] Economists could benefit from inquiring about which indices were "logically likely to precede economic movements."[49] The volume of orders placed, for example, which was a good indicator of businesspeople's expectations, usually anticipated the volume of business well in advance. In the search for suitable indices, the economists therefore agreed, theoretical methods were as valid as empirical ones.[50]

Rather than recommending a strict empirical approach, they argued that the "right of investigators remained absolute and [that] experience would show the method which must succeed."[51] At the end of the three-day conference, a consensus solidified that the Harvard approach was not yet at a stage that made it seem desirable to recommend its adoption in other countries.[52] For a number of economists, the search for time-invariant patterns did not seem promising at all anymore. As the British economist and statistician Alfred William Flux (1867–1942), chairman of the committee of experts on economic barometers, put it, "Acute business men ha[ve] means of appreciating the immediate future which [a]re not at the disposal of statisticians." Therefore "statisticians c[an] never hope to

45. Committee of Experts on Economic Barometers, *Provisional Minutes of the Third Meeting, Held at 10 a.m. on December 14th, 1926*, December 14, 1926, p. 6, Registry 451, Document No. 56940, Dossier No. 51866, LNA.

46. Committee of Experts on Economic Barometers, *Provisional Minutes of the Third Meeting*, p. 6.

47. Committee of Experts on Economic Barometers, *Provisional Minutes of the Third Meeting*, p. 7.

48. Committee of Experts on Economic Barometers, *Provisional Minutes of the Third Meeting*, p. 7.

49. Committee of Experts on Economic Barometers, *Provisional Minutes of the Third Meeting*, p. 7.

50. Committee of Experts on Economic Barometers, *Provisional Minutes of the Third Meeting*, p. 3; see also Committee of Experts on Economic Barometers, *Provisional Minutes of the Fourth Meeting*, p. 12.

51. Committee of Experts on Economic Barometers, *Provisional Minutes of the Fourth Meeting*, p. 1.

52. Committee of Experts on Economic Barometers, *Report*, December 15, 1926, p. 6.

see further ahead than the business experts. All that the statisticians c[an] do [i]s to infer the intentions of the business men by means of the statistics in which his activities [a]re expressed."[53] This came up to a capitulation. Not even the best statistics based on the largest possible set of data, analyzed with the most advanced methods, from that point of view, possessed the forecasting value that entrepreneurial experience and expectation showed. At the end of the three-day conference, Alexander Loveday (1888–1962), in charge of the League's Economic Intelligence Service, noted that the conference had not left him "at all optimistic" that countries like Italy might come up with "a really barometric index," concluding that "in view of all this, . . . it will not be desirable to hold another meeting of these barometricians for some considerable time to come"[54]

Indeed, European business-cycle researchers had not managed to lay the basis for a world barometer or observatory, as they had hoped beforehand. What is more, the conference had revealed a general distrust of the significance and predictive power of statistics. In the months that followed, Russian and European economists published a number of articles in which they queried the existence of regularities or "laws" in economic life (Lansburgh 1926: 574; Kondratiev 1927: 59; Sommer 1929: 268; Löwe 1929: 419–20). This, European economists argued, made forecasts that were based on the observation of time lags in the past, as in the case of the Harvard index, worthless (Löwe 1929: 420; see also Lansburgh 1926). Economists like Oskar Morgenstern and Adolf Löwe also rejected the application of probability theory in business forecasting, as the data covered by time series were never independent of one another but causally interrelated in time (Löwe 1929: 419).[55] In line with this, the Austrian Institut für Konjunkturforschung explained in 1927 that there was nothing like "normal times" in business and that "the only rule in economic life seems to be the continuous change . . . and the irregularity with which these changes come about" ("Die Methoden der Konjunkturforschung" 1927: 2). Statistics could therefore never, in themselves, yield reliable forecasts but had to be interpreted by theory and trained judgment (10–11). Like their American colleagues, European forecasters understood their experience with different indices as showing that statistics, in themselves, never allowed for

53. Committee of Experts on Economic Barometers, *Provisional Minutes of the Third Meeting*, pp. 8–9.

54. Alexander Loveday to Henri Heer, December 30, 1926, p. 2, Registry 476, Document No. 56473x, Dossier No. 56473, LNA.

55. Several European economists explicitly referred to Persons's 1923 address in their critique, see, e.g., Sommer 1929: 272.

inferences about the future. This parallels the story told by Jeff Biddle (this volume) about agricultural forecasters in the early twentieth century. In all three cases deviations between forecasts and reality prompted forecasters to supplement their statistical analysis by the exercise of trained judgment.

What may have sounded like an admission of defeat opened up new avenues of research. Doubts in the predictive value of purely statistical methods enabled business-cycle researchers to pursue different paths of investigation. In the years that followed, European economists developed a number of distinct but sometimes complementary approaches to business forecasting. The adoption of techniques like polling and modeling, which became prominent tools of economic forecasting in the 1930s, was also a reaction to the perceived shortcomings of the Harvard approach. Also, the discussions about the Harvard index prompted a redesign of the empirical approach. In 1926, discussions in Paris had centered on the question of which index might best represent the idea of "the general economy of a country."[56] Economists were in complete dissent. The disagreements voiced in Paris lay bare the fact that economists had not yet found a shared convention to measure "the economy." Consequently, in the aftermath of the 1926 conference, European economists began to expand their search for adequate measures of national economic activity.[57] This was a reaction not only to the failure to gauge the cycle by the fluctuations of so-called sensitive indices but also to the idea that a shared convention would facilitate international comparisons.[58] This idea, of course, was yet another consequence of the widespread adoption of the Harvard index, which had prompted economists to search for adequate representations of "the economy" and to position their endeavors as national arms of an international movement.

56. Committee of Experts on Economic Barometers. Provisional Minutes of the Fourth Meeting, Held at 3:45 p.m. on December 14, 1926, p. 9.

57. On the empirical macroeconomics developed at the Berlin-based Institut für Konjunkturforschung, see Tooze 2001: 103–48. Adam Tooze argues that the contrast between the Harvard approach and Wagemann's innovations "could hardly have been more stark" (125). As I argue here, the former fueled the latter. The introduction and widespread adoption of the Harvard methods prompted a concerted search for adequate measures of national economic activity and means of international comparison, which, in turn, provided the decisive stimulation for the measurement of national income initiated by the Berlin Institute. On the importance that Wagemann attached to the search for means of international comparison, see *Zum Problem der Bewegungsformen der Wirtschaft (Strukturveränderung und Konjunktur; Dominanten und sekundäre Reihen)*, November 26, 1926, 6–7, Registry 408, Document No. 55837, Dossier No. 30796, LNA.

58. Committee of Experts on Economic Barometers, *Provisional Minutes of the Third Meeting*, pp. 5, 9; on hopes for a world barometer, see also Ernst Wagemann to Alexander Loveday, November 17, 1926, p. 1, Registry 451, Document No. 52192, Dossier No. 51866, LNA; on the advantages of international comparisons of economic observations more general, see March 1926: 11.

Despite their doubts of the predictive value of the Harvard index, most European economists continued to place their research in the Harvard tradition in the 1920s. This might have had financial reasons. Most important, however, the continued references to the Harvard approach by European economists seem to have been a "concession" to the public, as Hayek once put it.[59] In this manner, March expressed fears that the public would not "accept any test of economic prosperity unless it was possible to discover some economic instrument, such as a barometer, which would serve as a precise and scientific indication."[60] The Harvard tradition, from that point of view, formed a kind of cover for a field whose scientific status was still contested.[61] Protected by this cover, a pluralism of methods and a novel role of the economist as expert emerged, whose forecasts were not only based on numbers, crunched by statistical rigor, but also on experience, "feeling," and interpretation.

3. Conclusion

Between 1915, when Warren Persons first presented his "barometer" to the public, and 1926, when European business-cycle researchers met in Paris to discuss the adoption of the Harvard approach in Europe, a significant change in method and presentation took place. In a number of articles published between 1916 and 1922, Persons had argued that statistical analysis and probability-based inference could yield reliable, objective forecasts of the economic future. His elaborate articles on the methods by which he had inferred a temporal sequence between the movements of different time series that was valid for both the pre- and the postwar period prompted economists in Australia and Europe to search for a similar sequence among economic data in their respective country. Indeed, European economists' faith in Persons's methods was so strong that they ascribed their failure to adopt the Harvard approach to the unusual conditions in their country—and not to the approach itself. However, as the Harvard index began to fail to forecast the future in 1922, a consensus crystallized in both Europe and the United States that statistical analysis

59. Hayek to Morgenstern, December 11, 1926, p. 2.

60. Committee of Experts on Economic Barometers, *Provisional Minutes of the Third Meeting*, p. 7.

61. However, European and American economists did adopt Persons's methods of time series decomposition and continued to rely on them over the decades that followed. See, e.g., Shiskin 1957: 223.

could never, in itself, generate reliable forecasts. Instead, economists had to apply trained judgment to interpret the data and factor in information that was not part of their data set.

As I have argued in the introduction, economic forecasting was still a contested venture in the early twentieth century. It began to be viewed as a legitimate field of scientific investigation only during the 1920s. This was to no small degree a consequence of the research of the Harvard Committee and its widespread adoption throughout Europe and other parts of the world. As institutes of business-cycle research sprang up in European metropoles, which published so-called bulletins that presented an array of different national barometers to their readers, business forecasting slowly began to cast off its reputation as prophecy. The search for mechanical procedures and their widespread adoption, from that perspective, was also a means to render economics more like the natural sciences. This might explain why European and American economists alike continued to publish indices of general business conditions in the late 1920s and often tried to keep secret certain practices that were not deemed replicable. The rejection of any probabilistic theory of inference from 1923 on would then have been no more than a reaction to the researchers' experience that mechanical procedures alone could not produce reliable forecasts. This is in line with Persons and his colleagues' own explanation. As they noted in 1927, "If there is anything which we have learned from experience since 1919, it is the necessity of considering the whole situation revealed by our index chart" (Bullock, Persons, and Crum 1927: 79).

I believe, however, that there is more to the story. The changes in methods and convictions that I have traced in this article are indicative of changes in the conception of the economy more generally. Forecasting tools encapsulate specific views on the economy and suggest different temporal frames. They are, however, constantly contested. The future only needs to evolve differently than predicted to discredit forecasting tools and the specific worldviews they present. From this perspective, forecasting tools, and more specifically their failures, can trigger changes in worldview. In this manner, the Harvard index was also a factor in the shift that took place from the mid-1920s on. By issuing predictions that proved inaccurate, it helped bring into being the idea of the business cycle as the result of human transactions that did not develop according to some natural laws but depended on individual expectations that were influenced by emotions, instincts, and proclivities. Or, as Persons put it in 1931, "The world of affairs in which we live is not a mechanistic world; it is a bewildering world of multiplicities, complexities, interactions, repercussions, and the vagaries of human wants, fears and hopes" (3–4).

The realization of the uncertainty of the future brought about new responsibilities for economists in the years that followed. Increasingly, economists were consulted to advise politicians on a case-by-case basis. The new demand for "objective" policy advice in the 1930s, again, promoted the application of mathematics and statistics, which seemed to warrant unbiased interpretations (Morgan and Rutherford 1998: 9). Only if we map changes in economic methods and methodical convictions in this broader context can we understand their reasons but also their wide-ranging implications.

References

Anderson, Katharine. 2005. *Predicting the Weather: Victorians and the Science of Meteorology*. Chicago: University of Chicago Press.

Armatte, Michel. 2003. "Cycles and Barometers: Historical Insights into the Relationship between an Object and Its Measurement." In *Monographs of Official Statistics: Papers and Proceedings of the Colloquium on the History of Business-Cycle Analysis*, edited by European Commission and Dominique Ladiray, 45–74. Luxembourg: Office for Official Publications of the European Communities.

Babson, Roger Ward. 1909. *Business Barometers Used in the Accumulation of Money: A Text Book on Fundamental Statistics for Investors and Merchants*. Wellesley Hills, MA: Office of R. W. Babson.

"Barometer of Economic Conditions Issued Monthly by the London School of Economics, University of London." 1922. "Reconstruction in Europe." Supplement to the *Manchester Guardian Commercial*, April 20, 54–57.

Beveridge, William H. 1923. "Business Cycles and Their Study." *London and Cambridge Economic Service: Issued in Co-operation with the Harvard University Committee on Economic Research* 1 (January, introductory number): 1–7.

Biddle, Jeff. 2017. "Statistical Inference in Economics, 1920–1965: Changes in Meaning and Practice." *Journal of the History of Economic Thought* 39, no. 2: 149–73.

Boumans, Marcel. 2016. "Graph-Based Inductive Reasoning." *Studies in History and Philosophy of Science Part A* 59: 1–10.

Bourguet, Marie-Noëlle, Christian Licoppe, and H. Otto Sibum. 2002. Introduction to *Instruments, Travel, and Science: Itineraries of Precision from the Seventeenth to the Twentieth Century*, edited by Marie-Noëlle Bourguet, Christian Licoppe, and H. Otto Sibum, 1–19. London: Routledge.

Bowley, Arthur L. 1922a. "An Index of British Economic Conditions." *Review of Economic Statistics* 4 (supplement 2): 145–56.

Bowley, Arthur L. 1922b. "The General Purpose and Method." "Reconstruction in Europe" (supplement). *Manchester Guardian Commercial*, May 18, 115–19.

Brookmire, James H. 1910. *The Brookmire Economic Charts: A Graphic Record of Fundamental, Political, and Industrial Conditions as a Barometer to the Financial and Business Situation for a Period Beginning 1885 and the Science of the New York Stock Market*. St. Louis, MO: James H. Brookmire.

Bullock, Charles J., and William L. Crum. 1932. "The Harvard Index of Economic Conditions: Interpretation and Performance, 1919–31." *Review of Economic Statistics* 14, no. 3: 132–48.

Bullock, Charles J., Warren M. Persons, and William L. Crum. 1927. "The Construction and Interpretation of the Harvard Index of Business Conditions." *Review of Economics and Statistics* 9, no. 2: 74–92.

Chicago Tribune. 1923. "Harvard Business Forecasts as a Help to You." September 28, 25.

Collins, James H. 1923. "Casting Your Business Horoscope." *Business Magazine* 4, no. 11: 7–9, 42–43.

Comitato per gli Indici del Movimento Economico Italiano. 1926. "Tavola XI." *Indici del Movimento Economico Italiano.*

Cord, Robert A. Jan. 2017. "The London and Cambridge Economic Service: History and Contributions." *Cambridge Journal of Economics* 41, no. 1: 307–26.

Crum, William L. 1924. "The Pre-War Indexes of General Business Conditions." *Review of Economic Statistics* 6, no. 1: 16–21.

Crum, William L. 1925. "The Interpretation of the Index of General Business Conditions." *Review of Economics and Statistics* 7: 217–35.

Crum, William L. 1928. "Revision of the Index of General Business Conditions." *Review of Economics and Statistics* 10, no. 4: 202–12.

Daston, Lorraine, and Peter Galison. 2010. *Objectivity.* New York: Zone Books.

Day, Edmund E. 1925. *Statistical Analysis.* New York: Macmillan.

"Die Methoden der Konjunkturforschung und ihre Anwendung in Österreich." 1927. *Monatsberichte des* Österreichischen *Institutes für Konjunkturforschung* 1, no. 1: 2–17.

Fayolle, Jacky. 2003. "The Study of Cycles and Business Analysis in the History of Economic Thought." In *Monographs of Official Statistics: Papers and Proceedings of the Colloquium on the History of Business-Cycle Analysis,* edited by European Commission and Dominique Ladiray, 9–44. Luxembourg: Office for Official Publications of the European Communities.

Friedman, Walter A. 2009. "The Harvard Economic Service and the Problems of Forecasting." *History of Political Economy* 41, no. 1: 57–88.

Friedman, Walter A. 2014. *Fortune Tellers: The Story of America's First Economic Forecasters.* Princeton, NJ: Princeton University Press.

Friedman, Milton, and Anna Jacobson Schwartz. 1963. *A Monetary History of the United States: 1867–1960.* Princeton, NJ: Princeton University Press.

Gibson, David R. 2011. "Speaking of the Future: Contentious Narration during the Cuban Missile Crisis." *Qualitative Sociology* 34, no. 4: 503–22.

Gibson, David R. 2012. *Talk at the Brink: Deliberation and Decision during the Cuban Missile Crisis.* Princeton, NJ: Princeton University Press.

Gieryn, Thomas F. 1983. "Boundary-Work and the Demarcation of Science from Non-Science: Strains and Interests in Professional Ideologies of Scientists." *American Sociological Review* 48, no. 6: 781–95.

Gieryn, Thomas F. 1999. *Cultural Boundaries of Science: Credibility on the Line.* Chicago: University of Chicago Press.

Gini, Corrado. 1926. "Prefazione." *Indici del Movimento Economico Italiano*: 3–4.

Harvard Committee on Economic Research. 1919. "General Business Conditions." *Review of Economic Statistics* 1 (December): 2–9.

Harvard Economic Service. 1922a. "Commodity Prices during the Present Decade." *Weekly Letter* 1, no. 24: 133–40.

Harvard Economic Service. 1922b. "General Business Conditions." *Weekly Letter* 1, no. 1: 1–4.

Harvard Economic Service. 1922c. "General Business Conditions." *Weekly Letter* 1, no. 8: 45–47.

Harvard Economic Service. 1922d. "General Business Conditions." *Weekly Letter* 1, no. 36: 215–18.

Harvard Economic Service. 1922e. "General Business Conditions." *Weekly Letter* 1, no. 40: 239–44.

Harvard Economic Service. 1922f. "General Business Conditions." *Weekly Letters* 1, no. 21: 121–24.

Harvard Economic Service. 1922g. "The Harvard Index of General Business Conditions: Its Interpretation." *Weekly Letters*, 3–8.

"Harvard Economic Service for Business Conditions in the United States." 1922. "Reconstruction in Europe" (supplement). *Manchester Guardian Commercial*, April 20, 52–53.

Huber, Michel. 1933. "Nécrologie. Desroys du Roure (1852–1933). Lucien March, 1859–1933." *Journal de la société statistique de Paris* 74: 266–80.

International Labour Office. 1924. *Economic Barometers: Report Submitted to the Economic Committee of the League of Nations*. Geneva: B.I.T.

Jordan, David F. 1927. *Practical Business Forecasting*. New York: Prentice-Hall.

Jovanovic, Franck, and Philippe Le Gall. 2001. "March to Numbers: The Statistical Style of Lucien March." In *The Age of Economic Measurement*, edited by July L. Klein and Mary S. Morgan. *History of Political Economy* 33 (supplement): 86–110.

Kondratiev, Nikolai D. 1927. "Das Problem der Prognose, in Sonderheit der sozialwirtschaftlichen." *Annalen der Betriebswirtschaft* 1: 41–64, 221–52.

Lansburgh, Alfred. 1926. "Logische Konjunkturforschung." *Die Bank: Wochenhefte für Finanz-, Kredit- und Versicherungswesen* 10: 571–94.

Lenel, Laetitia. 2018. "Mapping the Future: Business Forecasting and the Dynamics of Capitalism in the Interwar Period." *Jahrbuch für Wirtschaftsgeschichte / Economic History Yearbook* 59, no. 2: 377–413.

Löwe, Adolf. 1925. "Der gegenwärtige Stand der Konjunkturforschung in Deutschland." In *Die Wirtschaftswissenschaft nach dem Kriege: Festgabe für Lujo Brentano zum 80. Geburtstag*, edited by Moritz J. Bonn and Melchior Palyi, 2:329–77. Munich: Duncker & Humblot.

Löwe, Adolf. 1929. Review of *Wirtschaftsprognose*, by Oskar Morgenstern. *Zeitschrift für die gesamte Staatswissenschaft / Journal of Institutional and Theoretical Economics* 87, no. 2: 419–23.

March, Lucien. 1923. "L'étude statistique du mouvement général des affaires." *Journal de la société statistique de Paris* 64: 251–81.

March, Lucien. 1924. "Les indices économique." *Metron* 3, nos. 3–4: 334–36.

March, Lucien. 1926. "L'étude des cycles économiques: Son utilité dans les entreprises de toute nature." *Indices du mouvement général des affaires*, January (supplement), 3–29.

Margócsy, Dániel. 2014. *Commercial Visions: Science, Trade, and Visual Culture in the Dutch Golden Age*. Chicago: University of Chicago Press.

Mason, Edward S., and Thomas S. Lamont. 1982. "The Harvard Department of Economics from the Beginning to World War II." *Quarterly Journal of Economics* 97, no. 3: 383–433.

Meltzer, Allan H. 2003. *A History of the Federal Reserve. Volume 1: 1913–1951.* Chicago: University of Chicago Press.

Merton, Robert K. 1942. "Science and Technology in a Democratic Order." *Journal of Legal and Political Sociology* 1: 115–26.

Mises, Ludwig von, and Friedrich A. von Hayek. 2003. "Denkschrift betreffend der Einrichtung eines österreichischen Konjunkturbeobachtungsdienstes." In *Der unbekannte Mises: Reden und Aufsätze zur* österreichischen *Wirtschaftspolitik der Zwischenkriegszeit*, edited by Kurt R. Leube, 109–17. Frankfurt am Main: Frankfurter Allgemeine Buch.

Mitchell, Wesley C. 1919a. Review of *The Review of Economic Statistics*. *American Economic Review* 9, no. 4: 872–76.

Mitchell, Wesley C. 1919b. "Statistics and Government." *Publications of the American Statistical Association* 16, no. 125: 223–35.

Mitchell, Wesley C. 1927. *Business Cycles: The Problem and Its Setting*. New York: NBER.

Morgan, Mary S. 1997. "Searching for Causal Relations in Economic Statistics." In *Causality in Crisis? Statistical Methods and the Search for Causal Knowledge in the Social Sciences*, edited by Vaughn R. McKim and Stephen P. Turner, 47–80. Notre Dame, IN: University of Notre Dame Press.

Morgan, Mary S. 2003. *The History of Econometric Ideas*. Cambridge: Cambridge University Press.

Morgan, Mary S. and Malcolm C. Rutherford. 1998. "American Economics: The Character of the Transformation." *From Interwar Pluralism to Postwar Neoclassicism*, edited by Mary S. Morgan and Malcolm C. Rutherford. *History of Political Economy* 30 (supplement): 1–26.

Oakland Tribune. 1915. "New Barometer, This Records Trend of Business." August 13, 13.

O'Connell, Joseph. 1993. "Metrology: The Creation of Universality by the Circulation of Particulars." *Social Studies of Science* 23, no. 1: 129–73.

Persons, Warren M. 1910. "The Correlation of Economic Statistics." *Publications of the American Statistical Association* 12, no. 92: 287–322.

Persons, Warren M. 1916. "Construction of a Business Barometer based upon Annual Data." *American Economic Review* 6, no. 4: 739–69.

Persons, Warren M. 1919a. "An Index of General Business Conditions." *Review of Economic Statistics* 1, no. 2: 110–205.

Persons, Warren M. 1919b. "Indices of Business Conditions." *Review of Economic Statistics* 1, no. 1: 5–48.

Persons, Warren M. 1920. "A Non-Technical Explanation of the Index of General Business Conditions." *Review of Economic Statistics* 2, no. 2: 39–48.

Persons, Warren M. 1922. *Interpretation of the Index of General Business Conditions.* Cambridge, MA: Harvard Economic Service.

Persons, Warren M. 1923. "The Revised Index of General Business Conditions." *Review of Economic Statistics* 5, no. 3: 187–95.

Persons, Warren M. 1924. "Some Fundamental Concepts of Statistics." *Journal of the American Statistical Association* 19, no. 145: 1–8.

Persons, Warren M. 1931. *Forecasting Business Conditions.* New York: John Wiley.

Persons, Warren M., William L. Crum, and Edwin Frickey. 1926. "Revision of the Index of General Business Conditions." *Review of Economics and Statistics* 8, no. 2: 64–68.

Pietra, Gaetano. 1926a. "Gli indici del movimento economico in Italia." *Economia: Rivista Mensile di Politica Economica e di Scienze Sociali* (January): 23–42.

Pietra, Gaetano. 1926b. "I numeri indici del movimento economico in Italia nel settennio post-bellico 1919–1925." *Indici del Movimento Economico Italiano,* 1926: 5–39.

Pietruska, Jamie. 2011. "US Weather Bureau Chief Willis Moore and the Reimagination of Uncertainty in Long-Range Forecasting." *Environment and History* 17, no. 1: 79–105.

Pietruska, Jamie. 2018. *Looking Forward: Prediction and Uncertainty in Modern America.* Chicago: University of Chicago Press.

Porter, Theodore M. 1995. *Trust in Numbers: The Pursuit of Objectivity in Science and Public Life.* Princeton, NJ: Princeton University Press.

Reichmann, Werner. 2013. "Epistemic Participation: How to Produce Knowledge about the Economic Future." *Social Studies of Science* 43, no. 6: 852–77.

"Review of the Year 1924." 1925. *Review of Economics and Statistics* 7, no. 1: 1–18.

Schaffer, Simon. 1988. "Astronomers Mark Time: Discipline and the Personal Equation." *Science in Context* 2, no. 1: 115–45.

Shiskin, Julius. 1957. "Electronic Computers and Business Indicators." *Journal of Business* 30, no. 4: 219–67.

Sommer, Albrecht. 1929. "Die Konjunkturprognose: Zur Möglichkeit der Wirtschaftsvoraussage." *Allgemeines Statistisches Archiv* 18, no. 2: 260–78.

Sorer, Richard. 1914. "Über die Berechnung von Korrelationskoeffizienten zwischen den Symptomen der wirtschaftlichen Entwicklung in Österreich." *Allgemeines Statistisches Archiv* 8, no. 2: 193–209.

Times. 1922. "A Trade Barometer. Scientific Guide for Business Men." November 21, 9.

Tooze, J. Adam. 2001. *Statistics and the German State, 1900–1945: The Making of Modern Economic Knowledge.* Cambridge: Cambridge University Press.

Van Zeeland, Paul. 1929. "Editorial." *Bulletin de l'Institut des Sciences* Économiques 1, no. 1: 3–7.

Williams, John H. 1919. "Memoranda: The Role of Prices in the Business Cycle." *Review of Economic Statistics* 1, no. 2: 206–10.

Revisiting the Past?
Big Data, Interwar Statistical
Economics, and the Long History
of Statistical Inference
in the United States

Thomas A. Stapleford

In December 1924, Wesley C. Mitchell used his presidential address to the American Economic Association to assess the place of "quantitative analysis in economic theory." Linking his project to Alfred Marshall's 1907 prediction that the most promising space for future economic research lay not in "qualitative analysis" but in "the higher and more difficult task" of quantitative analysis, Mitchell insisted that he had no desire to oppose the two or even to suggest "that one type should predominate over the other" (Marshall 1907: 7, 8; Mitchell 1925: 1). Yet though Mitchell concurred that qualitative and quantitative analysis necessarily moved hand in hand, he was much less sanguine about the fruits of past qualitative work, namely, existing economic theory. That was not because he expected future quantitative analysis to contradict prominent theories; instead, it would simply ignore them (cf. Mitchell 1925: 5). Making use of "the accumulating masses of data" would require "recasting old problems into new forms amenable to statistical attack," and as a result, "economic theory will change not merely its complexion but also its content" (Mitchell 1925: 2, 3). The rise of statistical inference, Mitchell insisted, would fundamentally transform the practice of economics.

I am very grateful for the comments and suggestions of all participants in the 2020 *HOPE* workshop on the history of statistical inference and especially grateful for detailed comments from Laetitia Lenel, Béatrice Cherrier, and the volume editors.

History of Political Economy 53 (annual suppl.) DOI 10.1215/00182702-9414832

Four decades later, many of Mitchell's predictions about the rise of quantitative analysis had come true. In a 1968 survey article, for example, Robert Strotz (1968: 352) declared that econometrics, the use of mathematical models and statistics in economics, was "becoming now nearly coterminous with the entire field of economics." Strotz was surely overstating the case, but dominant forms of economics indeed looked radically different by 1968. Yet that transformation had not always followed the path that Mitchell predicted. First, as Jeff Biddle (2017) has shown, the broader notion of statistical inference that Mitchell had touted had been eclipsed by a narrower, more formal, probability-based analysis that had played almost no role in Mitchell's vision. Second, whereas Mitchell had predicted that the data and tools of statistical inference would drive the construction of a new form of economic theory, the "measurement without theory" debate (Koopmans 1947) had pushed econometrics in a very different direction. Certainly, Marshallian microeconomic theory had not been abandoned in the way Mitchell had anticipated.

But perhaps Mitchell's vision had only been delayed. Starting in 2014, a number of articles began to explore the effects of "big data" on economics (e.g., Einav and Levin 2014b; Varian 2014; Phillips 2014; Taylor, Schroeder, and Meyer 2014). More accurately, we might say that these essays were examining the intersection of economics with what Robert Kitchin (2014) has called the "data revolution." That phrase encompasses the massive quantity of data available but also the overwhelming volume of data production, the burgeoning capacity for data storage, and the ever-growing speed with which data can be analyzed, condensed, and visualized through algorithms. The data revolution rests on a technical foundation—advances in digital storage, transmission, computing power, and software techniques—but it is equally a product of new business practices, government practices, and social behavior (Kitchin 2014; Schneier 2015). Much of our daily life generates extensive digital traces that can be readily archived (courtesy of cheap storage) and efficiently culled and analyzed (courtesy of computer algorithms). At the same time, large swathes of administrative data that were once accessible only on paper at government offices have now been digitized and made available, such as license records, property tax records, and so forth. Within the framework of big data, the main challenge is not creating data but accessing them, "cleaning" them (ridding them of errors, omissions, and extraneous material), and combining them. Indeed, that very abundance has created its own novel research problem: how to analyze massive quantities of data, much of which may be unstructured, have high dimensionality (i.e., a large number of associated variables), or frequent inaccuracies or missing data points. The rise of big data has thus been accompanied by a new professional field—data science—focused on overcoming those challenges.

Contemporary historians of science are skittish about the term *revolution*, wary that it implies radical reversal or uniform homogeneity broken by a sudden shift. Certainly, histories of the assemblage of practices, artifacts, and institutions that Kitchin places at the heart of the data revolution reveal heterogeneous timelines and evolutions that defy a simple chronological binarism (Aronova, Oertzen, and Sepkoski 2017). Yet at the level of discourse, Kitchin is certainly correct: from the modest origins of the phrase "Big Data" at an electrical engineering conference in 1997, talk about its prospects and dangers had become commonplace by the early 2010s across a host of disciplines: computer science, engineering, physics, biology, social sciences, medicine, and even the humanities (Lemov 2017: 21–23). As scholars such as Kitchin recognized, much of this discussion went well beyond the size of data sets per se to encompass issues such as machine learning, the speed of collection and transmission, ubiquitous monitoring of persons and phenomena, privacy concerns, and many others (Boyd and Crawford 2012). The host of commentaries on these topics illustrates that practitioners across multiple fields saw themselves at the nexus of new practices and technological capabilities that demanded sustained reflection. Since 2014, for example, leading economists have published several major papers on these topics, such as "The Data Revolution and Economic Analysis" (Einav and Levin 2014a), "Big Data: New Tricks for Econometrics" (Varian 2014), or "The Impact of Machine Learning on Economics" (Athey 2019), along with numerous other accounts from other scholars (e.g., Harding and Hersh 2018; Silvia, Iqbal, and Pugliese 2017). For the present article, I am adopting Kitchin's (2014) phrase "data revolution" to refer to the assemblages of practices (e.g., machine learning techniques, ubiquitous data collection and storage, widespread digitization) and technologies (cell phones, computer and network hardware, database protocols, etc.) that have led some economists to see themselves on the cusp of transformations in their field. As the Stanford economist Susan Athey (2019: 508) recently proclaimed, "The combination of ML [machine learning] and newly available data sets will change economics in fairly fundamental ways."

Perhaps surprisingly, there are multiple parallels between these commentaries on the data revolution and the vision for quantitative analysis in economics that Mitchell articulated nearly a century before. For example, economists immersed in the data revolution have given much less attention to the formal probabilistic forms of inference that have characterized econometrics since the 1960s, returning instead to the broader view of the 1920s–1950s. As Liran Einav and Jonathan Levin (2014b: 1243089–5) explain, researchers from a data science background

> put more emphasis on predictive fit, especially out-of-sample fit, and on the use of data-driven model selection to identify the most meaningful predictive variables. There often is less attention paid to statistical uncertainty and standard errors and considerably more to model uncertainty. The common techniques in this sort of data mining—classification and regression trees, lasso and methods to estimate sparse models, boosting, model averaging, and cross-validation—have not seen much use in economics.

The economists of the data revolution have not abandoned probability theory. But, reversing the historical trend documented by Biddle (2017), they also no longer identify statistical inference exclusively with probabilistic analysis.

The relationship between existing economic theory and the inferential tools of the data revolution has also become fraught. Some observers have declared that the data revolution has brought us to the cusp of a new scientific revolution predicated on black-box algorithms that yield successful predictions without causal understanding, traditional models, or discipline-specific theories (Anderson 2008). Prominent economists promoting the data revolution have pushed back against that view, insisting that traditional economic theory and tools for causal analysis can complement the analysis of big data, with each enriching the other (e.g., Einav and Levin 2014b; Varian 2014; Athey and Imbens 2017: esp. 22–27). Even here, however, there are strong hints of Mitchell's view that quantitative analysis would invert the relationship between empiricism and deductive reasoning: rather than just testing or refining existing theory, Mitchell (1925: 3–5) argued that quantitative analysis would yield new and better ways to generate theories and would study new kinds of relationships. In a similar vein, Einav and Levin have contrasted the new approaches of the data revolution with "traditional econometric techniques." Rather than beginning with a priori models and using data to estimate parameters, data scientists may use algorithms to generate models or to determine key variables in a large, high-dimensional data set (Einav and Levin 2014b, 1243089–5; cf. Harding and Hersh 2018: 4–6).

In the remainder of this article, I examine a number of parallels between the approaches to economics that have accompanied the data revolution and the vision for statistical economics outlined by Mitchell in 1924 and that was at least partially instantiated by both Mitchell and those interwar American economists who shared his outlook. In doing so, I hope to shed new light on the long history of statistical inference in economics. The comparison rests on four shared traits:

1. A deemphasis on probability-based assessments of sampling error in favor of other concerns
2. Prioritizing building theories from data rather than applying or refining existing theoretical models
3. Strong interdisciplinary connections built on shared methodology for data analysis
4. Reshaping the world to facilitate data collection and prediction

These four traits, of course, are not exclusive to either interwar statistical economics in the United States or to the economics of the data revolution. Arguably, items 2–4, for example, are often equally characteristic of experimental economics—especially in some forms. (Indeed, as I show, an emphasis on experimentation was part of Mitchell's 1924 prediction for the future of economics, and some of the most prominent economists of the data revolution have also pursued experimental work.) But taken together, these four traits help to differentiate Mitchell and the economists of the data revolution from competing views of how to integrate statistical data into economics that rose to prominence in the mid-twentieth century.

By making this comparison, I am not claiming that Mitchell or his 1924 presidential address has inspired contemporary economists (to my knowledge, none has ever cited him) or that there are subterranean historical lines of influence connecting Mitchell to the data revolution. My point is much more prosaic: that the existence of these parallels complicates any simple, linear narrative about the history of statistical inference in economics. As Biddle (2017) argues, by the 1960s, the concept of statistical inference in economics had largely collapsed into what we might call classical econometrics: estimating parameters in a prespecified, linear regression model, with justifications and error estimates grounded in probability theory. Mitchell's work had little direct connection to that classical approach, and hence Mitchell's research program at the National Bureau of Economic Research is typically a foil to the main narrative in histories of econometrics.[1] From the perspective of the 1960s, in which econometrics is nearly coextensive with statistical inference, Mitchell and his interwar compatriots are relegated to being noble but ultimately unproductive pioneers who saw the promise of uniting statistical analysis with economics but were unable to hit on the proper conceptual framework (probability theory) or to grasp the central role of deductive economic reasoning in establishing structural models.

If we pull our lens forward to the data revolution, however, the situation looks rather different. Mitchell did not anticipate or cause the new assessments of statistical inference we are now seeing, and of course his research methods per se look very different than the machine learning algorithms or massive databases analyzed by economists in the data revolution. But the parallels between his outlook and those of more recent economists suggest a more fractured, nonlinear history of statistical inference in economics. We might characterize the general similarity between Mitchell and the economists of the data revolution as arising from a broad orientation to inference that is fascinated by the complexities and promise of data: eschewing the simplifying assumptions required to apply probability theory (trait 1), building theories from data rather than testing a priori theories on data (trait 2), collaborating across disciplines with those facing similar data problems (trait 3), and intervening in the world to improve data and facilitate inference (trait 4). In the conclusion, I share some speculations as to why this orientation might have been more prominent in both the interwar period and today.

Revisiting the Past in Four Movements

1. The Diminishment of Mathematical Probability

Mitchell's 1924 address said very little about the role of probability in inference, and when Mitchell (1927) took up the topic at greater length in his survey of business cycles, he emphasized its limits for economics. Time series data could not be treated as repeated observations of the same entity (203–5), and correlations of time series were subject to many hazards,

---

1. E.g., Mitchell is barely mentioned in Epstein 1987, and both Mary S. Morgan (1991) and Duo Qin (1997) distinguish Mitchell and his business-cycle research at the National Bureau of Economic Research from classical econometrics.

notably the ease with which economists could adjust the data to produce high but spurious correlations that might not hold true for future observations (262–70). Such doubts did not prevent Mitchell from making use of probability theory and its many derivative inferential techniques; his comprehensive treatise on business cycles with Arthur Burns, for example, employed correlations and variance ratios (F-tests). But here, as always, Mitchell continued to stress the importance of "judgment" when drawing conclusions, informed by "economic analysis and historical knowledge" (e.g., Burns and Mitchell 1946: 389–401, esp. 400).

Mitchell's attitude was not unusual. As Biddle (2017) argues, up until the 1940s almost all American economists found only limited value in probabilistic theories of inference. Drawing inspiration from Keynes (1921) and his American advocates such as Warren Persons, economists felt that the strong assumptions needed to utilize probabilistic theories of inference were rarely met in standard economic analyses. As Biddle shows in detail, Persons's interpretation of Keynes became a common reference for American economists as they thought about statistical inference, a reach that included Mitchell's statistical expert at the National Bureau of Economic Research (Frederick C. Mills) and some of the most expansive and creative users of statistical inference, namely, agricultural economists such as Elmer Working.

In Persons's (1924: 6) opinion, "The view that the mathematical theory of probability provides a method of statistical induction or aids in the specific problem of forecasting economics . . . is wholly untenable." The trouble, Persons insisted, was that the time series data typically used in economic analysis represented not a truly random sample but "a special period with characteristics distinguishing it from other periods"; moreover, the sequential data were not independent from one another (6, 7). Accordingly, standard error estimates for correlations based on time series data were invalid.

In place of probability theory, Persons offered three criteria for judging the reliability of inferences: "first, if similar or consistent statistical results obtain for sub-periods; second, if similar or consistent statistical results obtain for other periods and under different circumstances; and third, if all of the statistical results agree with, are supported by, or can be set in the framework of, related knowledge of a statistical or non-statistical nature" (5; see also Lenel, this volume). In Biddle's (2017: 153–58) view, Persons's skepticism toward probabilistic inference heavily shaped American empirical economics through the 1930s, despite the development of statistical hypothesis testing and its incorporation by economists such as Frederick Mills and Henry Schultz. Trygve Haavelmo's (1944) reconceptualization of time series data as random draws from an underlying, stable economic mechanism allowed Cowles econometricians to deploy sophisticated, probability-based analyses. Yet, as Biddle describes at length, they did not fundamentally address the core objections raised by Keynes or his American supporters, such as the sequential independence of data, effects of unobserved variables, or the stability of the underlying structural relationships over time. In turn, the probabilistic methods did not fully predominate in economics until the mid-1960s (Biddle 2017: 159–61).

Histories of econometrics often present Haavelmo (1944) as a critical turning point (a "probabilistic revolution" in Mary S. Morgan's [1991: 229] terms), even if it took fifteen years to consolidate, as Biddle suggests. The data revolution has complicated that narrative, however, returning to something much closer to the interwar view. The statistician Leo Breiman's (2001) influential assessment of the "two cultures" of statistical modeling captures this well. Breiman begins by describing the traditional approach, "data modeling," which follows the logic of post-1960s econometrics. The empirical data under consideration are assumed to represent independent draws from an underlying function (typically linear and including an error or noise generator) specified in advance by the analyst. Regression techniques are used to estimate parameters in this underlying function, and statistical probability theory permits the analyst to calculate confidence intervals or significance levels for coefficients (Breiman 2001: 199, 202). Yet, sounding much like the interwar American economists, Breiman emphasizes that the validity of these probabilistic tests rests on a series of questionable assumptions, for example, that all key variables are known and prespecified, that they are independent, and that they combine in a linear way. Not only are such assumptions often unjustified, but following this process in practice can generate multiple models that have quite different structures yet yield similar confidence intervals for their parameters. Decrying the "fairy-tale aspect of the procedure," Breiman approvingly cites Frederick Mosteller and John Wilder Tukey's (1977) observation that "the whole area of guided regression is fraught with intellectual, statistical, computational, and subject matter difficulties" (quoted in Breiman 2001: 203).

In its place, Breiman proposes "algorithmic modeling," in which the analyst uses machine learning tools to generate a set of models (a process I consider in the next section) and then tests them against a separate data sample. Rather than worry about error estimates for model parameters, the analyst focuses on predictive accuracy (204). Given a set of inputs, how well does each model predict the relevant outcomes in question? Evaluating that performance requires testing models on different subsets of data, just as Persons had argued back in 1924. Typically, one portion of the data is used for training models (constructing and tuning them to maximize predictive accuracy) and a second for validating them (evaluating their performance). The training data can be further subdivided, such as in *k-fold cross-validation*. Here, the training data are split into *k* subsets. One subset is reserved, and the model is trained on the rest. The model is then tested on the reserved subset, and the entire process is repeated with a slightly different training algorithm. The version of the model that best matches its reserved test sample is taken as the most robust iteration. In short, prediction across multiple data sets is the key criterion for algorithmic modeling, not calculations of standard errors from regression on a single sample.

Like Mitchell before them, the economists most involved in the data revolution have not given up probabilistic inference entirely. For example, Athey and Guido Imbens (2016) have adapted machine learning techniques to focus on causal analysis rather than just prediction in out-of-sample data, with Athey (2017) arguing that the former is essential for many policy applications where we wish to know how an intervention might affect an outcome. Such modifications to standard data science techniques require stronger assumptions but allow the use of probability theory to assign confidence intervals to expected outcomes for specific interventions. Athey and Imbens continue to rely on cross-validation and out-of-sample testing, however, thereby creating a hybrid with traditional econometric practices.

As I have shown, both interwar economists and later critics doubted that the assumptions needed to properly employ probabilistic inference were actually sustained in many real-world applications. That suggests, therefore, that the diminishment of probability theory in data science derived in no small part from having the resources—notably the data—to take an alternate approach. In Breiman's (2001: 200) account, his turn away from being an "academic probabilist" was connected to his departure from the university in the late 1960s to become a consultant for various government agencies. Yet it was also clearly connected to the sheer scale of data collected by those same agencies, which then became available to him for analysis (a point I take up in section 4). Having lots of data meant that those data could be subdivided into multiple sets for training and testing, thereby eliminating the need for probabilistic inference and its related tools. Hal Varian (2014: 7) makes a similar point about how big data has given new life to nonprobabilistic methods:

> For many years, economists have reported in-sample [probability-based] goodness-of-fit measures using the excuse that we had small datasets. But now that larger datasets have become available, there is no reason not to use separate training and testing sets. Cross-validation also turns out to be a very useful technique, particularly when working with reasonably large data. It is also a much more realistic measure of prediction performance than measures commonly used in economics.

Though the lack of big data is not sufficient to explain economists' turn toward probability theory (see Biddle 2017: 167–71), its emergence has at the very least eased the return to broader notions of statistical inference.

2. Theory Building from Data

In his 1924 address, Mitchell insisted that the expansion of statistical data would do more than provide material for testing existing economic theory. Instead, it would entail "a recasting of the old problems into new forms amenable to statistical attack" and thereby "change not merely [economic theory's] complexion but also its content" (Mitchell 1925: 3). In particular, Mitchell believed that the theoretical neoclassical analysis of individual behavior had no concrete or testable connection to the data from "real markets" available to economists, namely, records of "mass phenomena" such as time series or cross-sectional data on prices, wages, production, financial transactions, and so forth. As Mitchell drily commented, it "seems unlikely that the quantitative workers will retain a keen interest in imaginary individuals coming to imaginary markets with ready-made scales of bid and offer prices. Their theories will probably be theories about the relationships which measure objective processes" (5). These theories might be informed by an economist's intuitions or general economic knowledge. But they would not be created a priori; they would be constructed through long interaction with the data themselves, arising from inductive analysis informed by more theoretical reflection.

Nothing exemplifies this process better than Mitchell's decades-long battle to bring order to the study of business cycles, the centerpiece of his involvement with the National Bureau of Economic Research. As Mitchell and his coauthor and successor, Arthur Burns, explained in the introduction to the culmination of his work, *Measuring Business Cycles* (1946), "systematic factual research" was often considered part of "inductive verification," something that occurred after the serious theoretical work had been conducted. But anyone who followed this path either stopped at the construction of theory or quickly found that it "rest[ed] on assumptions purposively chosen to simplify the situation that is analyzed" (8–9). Moreover, the complexity of the phenomena the constituted business cycles belied any attempt to isolate a single aspect or cause. Rather than try to verify a single hypothesis, the researcher would have to proceed holistically, dealing with large numbers of variables, and using that study to inform the selection or construction of relevant hypotheses that might be operating synchronously:

> An investigator who seeks earnestly to discover the cause or causes of business cycles should not restrict himself to testing any single hypothesis. If he concludes that the facts of experience are consistent with one hypothesis, he should make sure that they are not equally consistent with other hypotheses. In the measure that he is thorough, his effort will broaden into an attempt to test many hypotheses and determine how they fit together. (9)

Constructing a theoretical understanding required immersing oneself in the data and discovering the actual patterns within them: "Only by analyzing numerous time series, each of restricted significance, can business cycles be made to reveal themselves definitely enough to permit close observation. If we wish to know what the wholes are like, we must study the parts and then see what sort of wholes they make up" (11). Theories would be built slowly from repeated interaction with masses of empirical data; they would not be imposed a priori.

That outlook, however, did not match what would become the classical approach to econometrics, closely associated with the Cowles Commission and Haavelmo (1944), which used economic theory to create a structural model whose parameters would be further specified and evaluated against a data set using probability theory. Not surprisingly, then, in a famous 1947 review of the Burns and Mitchell volume, Tjalling Koopmans, a Cowles's economist, chastised the authors for failing to make use of existing neoclassical microeconomic theory. Indeed, Koopmans's argument was almost the inverse of Mitchell's 1924 mockery of "imaginary individuals," with Koopmans (1947: 164) critiquing Burns and Mitchell for refusing to build a "theoretical analysis of the aggregate effects of assumed patterns of economic behavior of groups of individuals" and instead studying "the 'behavior' . . . of certain measurable joint effects of those actions and responses." In other words, Koopmans complained that Burns and Mitchell had done precisely what Mitchell had advocated over two decades earlier: construct theories about the relationships between measurable data. Though Rutledge Vining (1949) mounted a robust defense of Mitchell and Burns, and though the Cowles Commission economists themselves subsequently realized the challenges confronting their research program (Morgan 1991: 251–53; Qin 1997: 149, 177–80), the 1950s marked a shift in emphasis for American economics. As Morgan (1991: 263–64) describes, "Data were taken less seriously as a source of ideas and information for econometric models, and the theory-development role of applied econometrics was downgraded relative to the theory-testing role. . . . Econometric models came to be regarded as the passive extensions of economic theory into the real world."

Mitchell's emphasis on building theory from data, however, resonates strongly with the extensive use of machine learning as part of the data revolution, including in economics. Rather than start with a model and use the data to adjust its parameters (the standard econometric technique), machine learning applies an algorithm to the data (or, rather, a subset of the data) in order to generate a model. A common strategy used in economics is to generate a "regression tree," a type of decision tree (now generally known as "classification and regression trees," or CARTs) that can be used to assign an output value to a data point consisting of multiple input variables. For example, given a data set with information on height, sex, age, and foot size of various people, an analyst could use an algorithm to construct a regression tree that would report a predicted foot size for a thirty-year-old, six-foot-tall female.

As Varian (2014: 10) notes, regression trees "tend to work well for problems where there are important nonlinearities and interactions"—in other words, for problems with the characteristics that troubled interwar American economists. Moreover, while economists do use single regression trees, many data scientists have found better results by taking advantage of modern computing power to construct "random forests": large collections of individual CARTs, each generated automatically by an algorithm with a random tuning parameter. The average prediction across the "forest" becomes the final output variable. In effect, the "model" here is actually a cluster of individual models, all built through algorithms with a certain level of random variability.

CARTs and similar model-building algorithms presume that the analyst has already defined the outcomes that he or she wants to predict. But the scope and high dimensionality of big data have also raised the prospect of discovering new, unforeseen relationships within the data. Using algorithms to discover such relationships is commonly known as "data mining" or "unsupervised learning" and typically takes the form of subdividing a data set into various clusters that share common properties. The most well-known applications for data mining include text analysis, which is only beginning to draw attention within economics (see, e.g., Gentzkow, Kelly, and Taddy 2019). Yet a good deal of informal data mining often takes place before moving into model building, typically through an iterative process that involves playing with the data using various algorithms. For example, here is Einav, in 2013, describing his initial work on auction and search data from eBay with Levin:

> We kind of came to it not having a particular idea of what exactly we want to do. We just wanted to formulate reasonable questions that could kind of leverage the idea that you have the Big Data rather than some sort of a smallish portion of it. So initially we were basically for six months just playing with the data, trying to understand, you know, what we could do with it and what could be interesting. (quoted in Taylor, Schroeder, and Meyer 2014: 7)

Einav and Levin (2014a: 21) have seen a similar pattern with their own graduate students at Stanford who work on big data projects:

> In working with very large, rich data sets, it can be nontrivial just to figure out what questions the data might be able to answer convincingly. While in the past a researcher could simply open up her data on the screen and visually get a sense of the key features, large data sets require time and effort for conceptually trivial tasks, such as extracting and summarizing different variables, and exploring relationships between them. Just looking within the last several years at our own program at Stanford, we see dissertations that use [big data from various sources]. Many of these projects have turned out very successfully, but almost all of them started with a long and slow process of just figuring out what exactly was in the data and how to manage it.

It is not difficult to see parallels in these quotations to Mitchell's insistence on immersing oneself within business-cycle data before attempting to formulate hypotheses. Yet the process that took Mitchell close to three decades has now been made vastly more efficient through twenty-first-century computing power.

Theory has not disappeared any more than it did for Mitchell, and few economists seem ready to join the business journalist and entrepreneur Chris Anderson (2008) in proclaiming the "end of theory" (cf. Taylor, Schroeder, and Meyer 2014: 5–6). Indeed, one of the major proponents of machine learning in economics, Athey, has been equally vociferous about using those tools to build causal theories, not merely predictive models (e.g., Athey and Imbens 2017; Athey 2017). But Athey (2019: 512) has praised machine learning for facilitating "data-driven model selection" in which "the functional form is at least in part determined as a function of the data," with an algorithm generating multiple models from data and then "select[ing] among them to maximize a criterion." When the economist Sascha Becker declared in 2013 that "I think theories [in light of Big Data] . . . don't have the same value," his remarks should be understood in those terms: with big data and machine learning, theories are the output of the inferential process, not an input (quoted in Taylor, Schroeder, and Meyer 2014: 6). Amid the data revolution, statistical inference is less about testing a priori hypotheses and more about the "hypothesis-seeking" that Vining (1949: 78) identified as the goal of Burns and Mitchell.

3. Interdisciplinary Connections Built on Shared Methods

Building models from data (rather than applying existing models to data) does not allow an analyst to dispense with what we might consider discipline-based knowledge. Indeed, such knowledge might shape the model-building process in subtle but significant ways. But that reorientation does have important consequences for how we understand the nature of that discipline, its pedagogy, and its relationship to other fields.

As a helpful contrast, consider the pedagogical structure of the postwar Chicago school of economics, explored in detail by Ross Emmett. By the late 1950s, graduate students entering Chicago were required to take two "core courses in price theory and money." The economic theory introduced in these courses provided "tools for analysis" (in Theodore Schultz's terminology) that the budding student then learned to use in preparation for the core exams and finally began to apply in a sustained way to a particular problem (the eventual dissertation) in an apprenticeship conducted through the Chicago workshop system (Emmett 2011: esp. 148–

50). The Chicago approach maps onto a common understanding of the relationship between theory and application: first the student learns a theory and then learns how to apply it. The theory forms the intellectual core of the discipline; the application process demonstrates the practical value of the theory and hence helps to justify the value of the discipline. Theory is, as the Chicago courses rightly described it, the "core" of the field. Despite the rupture between the Chicago school and the Cowles Commission (whose approach to econometrics had been championed by Koopmans in his review of Burns and Mitchell), they were nonetheless united in the primacy of a discipline-specific theory for defining economics.

Mitchell had a quite different view. In his 1924 lecture, Mitchell predicted the dispersion of economics, not that it would fragment into incompatible or isolated subfields but that it would no longer be defined by a set of overarching theories: "The literature which the quantitative workers are due to produce will be characterized not by general treatises, but by numberless papers and monographs. . . . Books will pass out of date more rapidly. The history of economic theory will receive less attention. . . . It will be harder for anyone to cover the whole field, perhaps quite impossible." The primacy of theory would give way to strategies for statistical inference: "Economists will be valued less on their erudition and more on their creative capacity. The advances will be achieved not only by conceiving new hypotheses, but also by compiling statistics from fresh fields, by inventing new technical methods, by refining upon old measures, and perhaps by devising experiments upon certain types of behavior" (Mitchell 1925: 6–7).

As theories ceased to define and unify disciplines, Mitchell foresaw an increasing blending of the social sciences built around the primacy of building knowledge of human behavior from quantitative data rather than applying disciplinary theory to data. Under this conception, "All of the social sciences have a common aim—the understanding of human behavior; a common method—the quantitative analysis of behavior records; and a common aspiration—to devise ways of experimenting upon behavior." As a result, it would be increasingly difficult to draw clear disciplinary boundaries: "The problems of each of these groups are significant for all the others, their technical methods are suggestive, their results pertinent" (Mitchell 1925: 6). Economists might confine themselves to particular topics or questions that had a historical connection to their field, but their methods would not look fundamentally different than those of parallel practitioners in other disciplines, and they would need to draw on results from across the social sciences.

Mitchell's prophecies have come true in many respects. Certainly, books pass out of date more rapidly (or are simply never written); the "history of economic theory" undoubtedly receives less attention; devising experiments and "new technical methods" are valued contributions; and a host of methods and practices central to economics are shared with other fields: regression analysis, the use of probabilistic inference, the techniques of game theory (shared with political science), or notions of bounded rationality (shared with psychology). Yet at least at the level of undergraduate education, Mitchell's expectations for the demotion of discipline-specific theory have not been fulfilled: standard micro, macro, and monetary theory continue to be at the heart of undergraduate economics courses in the United States. However, this prominence may be a residual of an older view of the field, the roughly quarter century after the Second World War in which many American economists saw an overarching, loose form of neoclassical economic theory as the core of their field, namely, "formal treatments of rational, or optimizing, economic agents joined together in an abstractly conceived free-market, general equilibrium world" (to borrow the description from Morgan 2003: 279). Roger E. Backhouse and Béatrice Cherrier (2017b: 5) have traced the gradual shift away from that perspective and toward what they label "applied theory," or "theoretical models that are formulated in relation to specific empirical problems," that is, highly local and contextualized models. When one combines these localized models with an emphasis on building theory from data (trait 2), methodology (not theory) becomes the unifying factor among scholars. And insofar as that methodology is shared across multiple fields, disciplinary boundaries begin to lose their status.

Consider the growing salience of the experimental ideal in economics. Although papers on experimental economics formed only 9 percent of papers in 2011 (Hamermesh 2013: 168), proponents won a major symbolic victory in 2019 when the Nobel Prize in economics was awarded to three scholars for their research with randomized controlled trials (RCTs) for development economics. Beyond RCTs per se, Matthew T. Panhans and John D. Singleton (2017) have documented the rise of "quasi-experimental" approaches using "natural experiments" over the last several decades. As they argue, this represents a shift in primacy from "[a priori] models to methods" (130). The familiar trope of economics imperialism has thus taken a new form: "Rather than the application of a behavioral model of purposive goal-seeking, 'economic' analysis is increasingly the empirical investigation of causal effects for which the quasi-experimental toolkit is essential" (152–53). As the quotation marks around "economic" suggest, this "toolkit" is not derived from economic theory per se; rather, these are general-purpose analytic techniques for uncovering causal relationships. For example, Joshua D. Angrist and Alan B. Krueger's (2001) article in the *Journal of Economic Perspectives* on instrumental variables has been cited in journals in epidemiology, psychology, medicine, and criminology (just to name a few)—but that is precisely because it is a tool for causal statistical inference that has no ties to specific theories about human behavior.

Given the empiricism of data science, it should be no surprise to see how many of its advocates are equally enthused about the experimental ideal for the social sciences. We have already noted that even in 1924, Mitchell saw the "common aspiration" of the social sciences as "devis[ing] ways of experimenting on human behavior" (Mitchell 1925: 6). Indeed, one section of his address (8–9) was devoted to considering the prospects of experimentation, and he ventured to hope that "the tentative experimenting of the present may develop into the most absorbing activity of economists in the future" (9). Valorizing experiments flowed naturally from Mitchell's efforts to construct a predictive science of human behavior; after all, experiment formed the backbone of the successful predictions of the natural sciences.

Mitchell recognized that a social scientist pursuing an experimental agenda faced different challenges than his or her peers in the natural sciences, especially physics:

> The experimenter must rely far more upon statistical considerations and precautions. The ideal of a single crucial experiment cannot be followed. The experiments must be repeated upon numerous individuals or groups; the varieties of reactions to the stimuli must be recorded and analyzed; the representative character of the samples must be known before generalizations can be established. (9)

Equally important were the differences in the entities studied (human beings vs. molecules, atoms, or inanimate objects) and the constraints on experimental procedures:

> First, the cases summed up in our statistics seldom if ever approach in number the millions of millions of molecules, or atoms, or electrons of the physicist. Second, the units in economic aggregates are less similar than the molecules or atoms of a given element. Third, we cannot approach closely the isolation practices of the laboratory. (11)

Broadly speaking, a "science of human behavior" was hampered by the lack of sufficient observations, the complexity of underlying mechanisms and environment, and the difficulty of isolating simpler components.

Mitchell was right, of course, to see these distinctions between the natural sciences and social sciences of his era. But some of those divisions are beginning to break down amid the data revolution. Millions of data points are now accessible, high-dimensional microdata can permit the analysis of specific subgroups, extensive administrative data have expanded the scope for so-called natural experiments, and economists' roles in government agencies and businesses (see section 4 below) have even permitted large-scale controlled experiments using big data. As Einav and Levin (2014a: 15) point out, "Highly granular [administrative] data can be particularly useful for finding natural experiments," and "as companies rely more heavily on data for their day-to-day operations, it has become easier and more cost effective . . . to experiment" (16). Rather than aim for general theories, the granularity and scale of big data can permit an extreme version of the "applied theory" discussed by Backhouse and Cherrier (2017b): "One can imagine," Einav and Levin (2014a: 18) report, "that [with granular big data] some research might shift from measuring and reporting average estimates, toward 'tool building,' where the purpose of an econometric model would be to capture treatment effects or make policy predictions for a large number of different subpopulations." Athey (2019: 528–29, 539–40) has predicted that the data revolution will spark a surge of dynamic, adaptive experimentation, especially in online environments where algorithms can learn on the fly and shift "treatment" allocations based on prior results.

Just as the valorization of experimentation in general has led to a focus on methods that are shared across disciplines, proponents of the data revolution in economics stress the need to develop new skills and to reconsider how students are trained (e.g., Einav and Levin 2014b: 715; Varian 2014: 3, 24–25; Harding and Hersh 2018; Athey and Luca 2019: 227–28). The basic techniques and tools of the data revolution—new forms of databases, machine learning algorithms, strategies for boosting the out-of-sample stability for trained models, and so forth—are shared and discussed independently of particular applications. In this respect, they function much like the familiar tool kits of mathematical probability or regression analysis. But there is a catch—precisely because traditional econometrics started with specifying a model, teaching methodology was closely tied to teaching subject matter. That was why economics departments taught econometrics themselves rather than having students just take general courses on statistics. Now, however, methods and disciplinary theory can increasingly be divorced: "My standard advice to graduate students these days," Varian (2014: 3) reports, "is go to the computer science department and take a class in machine learning."

Even those, like Athey, who have argued that standard machine learning approaches need to be modified to handle the causal analysis and policy aims of economics see the "economics" contribution coming from inferential techniques, not micro- or macroeconomic theory. Naturally, such techniques will be of interest across the social sciences. Thus Athey (2019: 538) foresees a "substantial increase in interdisciplinary work," where "computer scientists and engineers" focus on algorithm design, computational efficiency, and related concerns" while "academics of all disciplines" shape these tools to "facilitate measurement and causal inference." Looking at the rise of joint degree programs in computer science and economics, Athey suggests that "economic education" will focus on teaching students "how to use data to answer questions" (and not, notably, general theories of human behavior). Though data science writ large currently draws mainly from computer science and engineering, she "predict[s] that these programs will over time *incorporate more social science*, or else adopt and teach *social science empirical methods* themselves" (541; emphasis added). Note that rather than economic theory, it is "social science empirical methods" (namely, a concern for causal prediction) that Athey sees as being integrated into data science. Under the data revolution and the experimental ideal, methodology is becoming the stable core, and it is shared across multiple fields, becoming the kind of general science of human behavior Mitchell had envisioned.

4. Reshaping the World to Facilitate Data
Collection and Prediction

In December 1918, just after the end of the First World War, Mitchell delivered a presidential address to another major American academic society: the American Statistical Association (ASA). Reflecting on how ASA members (including Mitchell himself) had helped the war effort by joining federal agencies to expand and improve official statistics, Mitchell (1919: 223) could not help but be proud: "Probably there are few professional societies which have had so considerable a proportion of their membership engaged in war work as this Association." Yet it was not the past that concerned Mitchell but the future. The prospects for "social reform," he argued, rested on the possibility of securing an improved "knowledge of human behavior," which in turn demanded extensive "social statistics" (229, 230, 231). To secure such statistics, however, would require "participating aggressively in the rough and tumble of statistical practice"—that is, participating in the construction and collection of quantitative data (232). And since the federal government was the most promising sponsor for such large-scale data collection, Mitchell urged the ASA to "seek a more active share in the work of federal statistics in the future than it has ever taken in the past" (223).

Many of the interwar economists most interested in statistics took up this charge. Young economists captivated by the promise of statistics moved into the Departments of Commerce and Agriculture in the 1920s and the Department of Labor in the 1930s, with Agriculture in particular becoming a site for cutting-edge statistical research (Fox 1989; Hawley 1990; Banzhaf 2006; Stapleford 2009: 145–83; Rutherford 2011a). Beyond pushing new conceptual frameworks for federal economic statistics, they transformed administrative structures and processes for data collection and tabulation (Leach 1993: 349–78; Stapleford 2007, 2012). Morris Copeland, for example, who considered himself "something of a disciple of Mitchell," was instrumental in working with a group of government economists to overhaul the federal statistical system during the New Deal (Rutherford 2011b: 112, 106–9). Such actions followed logically from how Mitchell and like-minded statistical economists prioritized data as the foundation for the future of economics: if theory is to be built from data (trait 2), then securing more and higher quality data is an essential step.

By joining major institutions involved in constructing economic data, a scholar also gains access to details that might not be apparent to those relying only on published tables and indeed can potentially direct collection in ways that facilitate further research. No agency illustrated that promise more during the interwar period than the Bureau of Agricultural Economics (BAE), where, as Biddle (this volume) describes, BAE statisticians could combine analysis of survey results with their knowledge of survey procedures to reshape the latter (e.g., in the pig surveys and crop yield estimates) and to develop inferential strategies. Close involvement with data collection allows for a dialectic between data collection and inference in which the two processes become closely entangled rather than rigidly separated. Generally speaking, however, that also requires economists to move outside the academy to join or collaborate with institutions that generate substantial data. During the interwar period, that meant the federal government, especially during the statistical explosion that occurred during the New Deal and the Second World War. Today, despite the ongoing value and use of government administrative data, the most promising collaborations are happening with businesses.

One of the more striking features of the data revolution in economics is how it is turning businesses, especially in the tech and financial industries, into sites for scholarly economic research, not merely places to apply existing knowledge. Some top economists, such as Hal Varian, an emeritus professor at Berkeley who is now chief economist at Google, have left academe entirely even as they continue to publish major research. More remarkable have been the rising number of economists who maintain dual ties, either as consultants, direct employees, or entrepreneurs. Patrick Bajari is chief economist at Amazon.com and a professor at the University of Washington; Steven Tadelis, distinguished economist at eBay, is a professor at Berkeley; Levin (the 2011 John Bates Clark Medal winner) has consulted with "a number of Fortune 500 companies, as well as the Federal Communications Commission and the U.S. Treasury";[2] Athey (the 2007 Clark Medal winner) was a "consulting chief economist at Microsoft" for six years and is currently on the board of five corporations.[3]

Meanwhile, the job market for economists is shifting. Athey and Michael Luca (Harvard Business School) have both documented and heralded the rise of tech companies' interest in economists ("tech economists," in Athey's term). Such interest is both broad (essentially all major tech companies with data mining or analysis as a core part of their business) and deep: Amazon has hired 150 economists in the last five years and now employs "several times more full-time economists than the largest academic economics department" (Athey and Luca 2019: 209–10, esp. 209). Athey and Luca describe how their own graduate students have taken positions "at companies ranging from Facebook, Microsoft, and Amazon to Wealthfront, Uber, and Airbnb," and they envision a future in which economists routinely shift back and forth between academe and tech companies, whether through joint appointments, temporary positions, or career moves (212, 228).

Such fluidity is both a product of, and a requirement for, the data revolution in economics. Much of the promise of that revolution requires access to sequestered data, either proprietary data from firms or micro-level

2. Jonathan Levin, accessed March 26, 2020, www.gsb.stanford.edu/faculty-research/faculty/jonathan-levin.

3. Susan Athey, accessed March 26, 2020, www.gsb.stanford.edu/faculty-research/faculty/susan-athey.

administrative data that cannot be publicly disclosed because of privacy concerns. Gaining access to such data requires building trust, collaborative relationships, or even being embedded in a company or government unit (Taylor, Schroeder, and Meyer 2014: 7–8). In the financial industry, for example, JPMorgan Chase has drawn talented economists by establishing an in-house, quasi-public research team. Founded in 2015, the JPMorgan Chase Institute is "a think tank dedicated to delivering data-rich analyses and expert insights for the public good" by using the company's "unique proprietary data, expertise, and market access." The institute is led by Diana Farrell, who joined the institute from McKinsey & Company, previously served on the US National Economic Council, and is on the board of directors for the National Bureau of Economic Research, the Urban Institute, and eBay. The institute's director of business research, Chris Wheat, held junior faculty positions at MIT and Rutgers.

Beyond access to data per se, collaborating with private firms can help economists run experiments (Einav and Levin 2014b: 1243089–4). Michael Ostrovsky and Michael Schwarz's (2009) experiment with Yahoo!'s reserve prices for advertising auctions, for example, was facilitated by Schwarz's leadership of an economics research group at Yahoo! (Schwarz is now chief economist at Microsoft while Ostrovsky is at Stanford.) Athey (2019) predicts that "as digitization spreads across application areas and sectors of the economy," economists with access to the right businesses or government agencies will become involved in dynamic experimentation, using "bandit" techniques in which machine learning algorithms adapt to interactions with users in real time. Such adaptive experimentation "requires the statistical analysis to be embedded in the system that delivers the treatments" (i.e., an automated inferential analysis through machine learning must be embedded in the experimental process itself): "For example, a user might arrive at a web site. Based on the user's characteristics, a contextual bandit might randomize among treatment arms in proportion to the current best estimate of the probability that each arm is optimal for that user. The randomization would occur 'on the fly' and thus the software for the bandit needs to be integrated with the software for delivering the treatments" (Athey 2019: 540).

This tight integration "requires a deeper relationship between the analyst and the technology" than when a scholar "analyzes historical data 'offline'" (539, 540). For these reasons, Athey and Lucy (2019) suggest that the boundaries between academe and business will become increasingly blurred as research and intervention are intertwined:

Microsoft, Google, Yahoo!, Facebook, Amazon, eBay, Yelp, Uber, and other companies have all hosted faculty during sabbaticals. Tenured faculty members have left academia for positions at Amazon, Google, and elsewhere. Practitioners have also transitioned into academia—for example, leaving Facebook and Microsoft for MIT and Stanford. We believe this is the beginning of a larger movement in which a greater share of academic economists spend time in practice, acquiring a deeper understanding of what issues are most important for efficiency and profitability in technology firms, as well as getting exposure to unsolved business problems that may highlight fruitful academic research questions. As more PhD economists accept positions at tech companies, clearer paths for spending time (or re-entering) academia will likely appear. (228)

As inference becomes more dependent on access to data and control of data collection, the limits of universities as sites for economics research are also becoming more apparent.

The entanglement between analysis and experiment that Athey describes also has consequences for what we understand as the object of statistical inference in economics. Historians and philosophers of science have long understood that observation requires intervention (e.g., Hacking 1983), a recognition that includes the construction of statistical data as well (Gitelman 2013). And as Morgan (2003: 275) rightly notes, economics has increasingly been "an engineering science" since the turn of the twentieth century (Duarte and Giraud 2020). Yet that should not blind us to differences in the scale or mode of intervention. As described by Edward Nik-Khah and Philip Mirowski (2019: 275–78), many economists have de facto abandoned the idea that a generic, timeless "market" exists whose properties can be studied and assumed to have some meaningful application to real-world situations. Instead, these economists tout their ability to design markets with different properties whose parameters can be adjusted to be the most "efficient" for whatever priorities their clients identify. Athey explicitly links her vision for adaptive experimentation to the conception of "economist as engineer" that has animated market design. But she sees a radical expansion in the scope of applications as the digital traces of our lives are linked together and analyzed by machine algorithms that can feed back into the automated systems that shape our environment and the options available to us. Outside of obvious sites such as online retail and finance, "farming advice, online education, health information . . . , government-service provision, government collections, and personalized resource allocation"—all will become fodder for endless cycles of data collection, inference, and experimentation, much of which will be automated (Athey 2019: 539).

This utopia (dystopia?) of the data revolution recalls one of Mitchell's reflections in his 1924 presidential address, namely, how the centrality of human institutions (laws, customs, organizations) in shaping human behavior allows those very institutions to aid the statistician:

> If our present beliefs are confirmed, that the human nature which men inherit remains substantially the same over milleniums, and that the changes in human life are due mainly to the evolution of culture, economists will concentrate their studies to an increasing degree upon economic institutions—the aspect of culture which concerns them. For whatever hopes we may cherish for the future of our race are bound up with the fortunes of the factor which certainly admits of change and perhaps admits of control. The quantitative workers will have a special predilection for institutional problems, *because institutions standardize behavior, and thereby facilitate statistical procedure.* (Mitchell 1925: 8; emphasis added)

As inference and intervention become bound together, the latter can aid the former by making behavior more legible and more regular. The data revolution permits such intertwining on a scale and degree that Mitchell could never have envisioned.

The Long History of Statistical Inference

Reflecting on the recent history of the "applied economist," Backhouse and Cherrier (2017b) suggest that the dominance of high theory from the 1950s into the 1970s may have been a short interlude rather than the inevitable telos for economics that it was once thought to be. Likewise, just as Biddle (2017) has shown that the narrowing of statistical inference in economics to mathematical probability theory occurred much later than previously thought (not fully until the mid-1960s), perhaps its triumph was equally short-lived. The combination of those two shifts is seen quite dramatically in the practice of statistical inference amid the data revolution in economics, wherein economic theory is built from data (not just tested on them) and probability theory plays a diminished role. That transformation in turn has further consequences. As data analysis becomes the foundation for economics, and not merely a testing ground to verify theory, methods for producing and analyzing data take center stage, eroding disciplinary boundaries built on the primacy of theory. Moreover, access to data becomes a leading concern, drawing economists outside the academy and encouraging them to participate in reshaping the world through constant data collection, experimentation, and intervention.

These traits, I have suggested, have parallels to the vision for quantitative economics espoused by Mitchell in the 1920s. Of course, the economics of the data revolution is not identical to Mitchell's. Most notably, for example, the focus on modeling at the heart of the data revolution has no direct parallel for Mitchell (who spoke of "theories," but not "models"); modeling entered economics through a different path (Boumans 2005: 21–50). The data revolution is thus not a reversion to the past but a reemergence of previous themes, now in a different context and modulated in new ways. Yet the comparison with the interwar period suggests a more fragmented and heterogeneous history to statistical inference in economics than we might otherwise expect.

How can we account for these parallels? Mitchell's work was not the inspiration or source for the practices of the data revolution in economics. Nor were these parallels to the past caused solely by the emergence of big data and machine learning. The shift toward empiricism over deductivism in economics predates the data revolution (witness the rise of experimental economics), and the weaknesses of classical econometrics were already attracting significant attention by the 1980s (e.g., Hendry 1980; Sims 1980; Black 1982; Leamer 1983). Economists were in certain respects primed for the data revolution; moreover, we cannot treat computing technologies as an exogenous cause given how closely the development of econometrics has been intertwined with those technologies (Renfro 2011; Backhouse and Cherrier 2017a).

Yet I think it would be a mistake to overlook the "revolutionary" character of the data revolution—that is, the perception that an emergent assembly of technologies and practices is quickly opening a vast new frontier for empirical work. In his own day, Mitchell (1925: 2) perceived an "accelerated" growth in statistics, a "steady improvement in the technical methods of statistical analysis," and a new consolidation of resources that could equip some analysts with "a statistical laboratory, a corps of [human] computers, and sometimes a staff of field workers." Small wonder that he found hope in the potential of a new, data-driven economics to overcome what he saw as the all-too-evident limits of deductive theorizing. Small wonder, too, that in the 2010s, those economists closest to the data revolution might be enthralled by the prospect of bypassing the well-known limits of traditional econometrics through a new empiricism—an approach to inference that relishes the complexity of data, eschews simplifying assumptions, embraces heterogeneity, and dreams of a profusion of predictive models built from ever-expanding cascades of information.

References

Anderson, Chris. 2008. "The End of Theory: The Data Deluge Makes the Scientific Method Obsolete." *Wired*, June 23. www.wired.com/2008/06/pb-theory/.

Angrist, Joshua D., and Alan B. Krueger. 2001. "Instrumental Variables and the Search for Identification: From Supply and Demand to Natural Experiments." *Journal of Economic Perspectives* 15, no. 4: 69–85.

Aronova, Elena, Christine von Oertzen, and David Sepkoski. 2017. "Introduction: Historicizing Big Data." *Osiris* 32, no. 1: 1–17.

Athey, Susan. 2017. "Beyond Prediction: Using Big Data for Policy Problems." *Science* 355 (6324): 483–85. doi.org/10.1126/science.aal4321.

Athey, Susan. 2019. "The Impact of Machine Learning on Economics." In *The Economics of Artificial Intelligence: An Agenda*, edited by Ajay Agrawal, Joshua Gans, and Avi Goldfarb, 507–47. Chicago: University of Chicago Press.

Athey, Susan, and Guido Imbens. 2016. "Recursive Partitioning for Heterogeneous Causal Effects." *Proceedings of the National Academy of Sciences* 113, no. 27: 7353–60.

Athey, Susan, and Guido W. Imbens. 2017. "The State of Applied Econometrics: Causality and Policy Evaluation." *Journal of Economic Perspectives* 31, no. 2: 3–32.

Athey, Susan, and Michael Luca. 2019. "Economists (and Economics) in Tech Companies." *Journal of Economic Perspectives* 33, no. 1: 209–30.

Backhouse, Roger E., and Béatrice Cherrier. 2017a. "'It's Computers, Stupid!' The Spread of Computers and the Changing Roles of Theoretical and Applied Economics." In *The Age of the Applied Economist: The Transformation of Economics since the 1970s*, edited by Roger E. Backhouse and Béatrice Cherrier. *History of Political Economy* 49 (supplement): 103–26. doi.org/10.1215/00182702-4166239.

Backhouse, Roger E., and Béatrice Cherrier. 2017b. "The Age of the Applied Economist: The Transformation of Economics since the 1970s." In *The Age of the Applied Economist: The Transformation of Economics since the 1970s*, edited by Roger E. Backhouse and Béatrice Cherrier. *History of Political Economy* 49 (supplement): 1–33.

Banzhaf, H. Spencer. 2006. "The Other Economics Department: Demand and Value Theory in Early Agricultural Economics." In *Agreement on Demand: Consumer Theory in the Twentieth Century*, edited by Philip Mirowski and D. Wade Hands. *History of Political Economy* 38 (supplement): 9–31.

Biddle, Jeff. 2017. "2016 HES Presidential Address: Statistical Inference in Economics, 1920–1965: Changes in Meaning and Practice." *Journal of the History of Economic Thought* 39, no. 2: 149–73.

Black, Fischer. 1982. "The Trouble with Econometric Models." *Financial Analysts Journal* 38, no. 2: 29–37.

Boumans, Marcel. 2005. *How Economists Model the World into Numbers.* New York: Routledge.

boyd, danah, and Kate Crawford. 2012. "Critical Questions for Big Data." *Information, Communication & Society* 15, no. 5: 662–79.

Breiman, Leo. 2001. "Statistical Modeling: The Two Cultures (with Comments and a Rejoinder by the Author)." *Statistical Science* 16, no. 3: 199–231.

Burns, Arthur F., and Wesley Clair Mitchell. 1946. *Measuring Business Cycles.* New York: National Bureau of Economic Research.

Duarte, Pedro Garcia, and Yann Giraud, eds. 2020. *Economics and Engineering: Institutions, Practices, and Cultures.* Supplemental issue to volume 51 of *History of Political Economy.* Durham, NC: Duke University Press.

Einav, Liran, and Jonathan Levin. 2014a. "The Data Revolution and Economic Analysis." *Innovation Policy and the Economy* 14 (January): 1–24.

Einav, Liran, and Jonathan Levin. 2014b. "Economics in the Age of Big Data." *Science* 346 (6210): 1243089-1–1243089-6.

Emmett, Ross B. 2011. "Sharpening Tools in the Workshop: The Workshop System and the Chicago School's Success." In *Building Chicago Economics: New Perspectives on the History of America's Most Powerful Economics Program*, edited by Robert Van Horn, Philip Mirowski, and Thomas A. Stapleford, 93–115. New York: Cambridge University Press.

Epstein, Roy J. 1987. *A History of Econometrics.* New York: Elsevier.

Fox, Karl A. 1989. "Agricultural Economists in the Econometric Revolution: Institutional Background, Literature, and Leading Figures." *Oxford Economic Papers* 41: 53–70.

Gentzkow, Matthew, Bryan Kelly, and Matt Taddy. 2019. "Text as Data." *Journal of Economic Literature* 57, no. 3: 535–74.

Gitelman, Lisa, ed. 2013. *"Raw Data" Is an Oxymoron.* Cambridge, MA: MIT Press.

Haavelmo, Trygve. 1944. "The Probability Approach in Econometrics." *Econometrica* 12: iii–115.

Hacking, Ian. 1983. *Representing and Intervening: Introductory Topics in the Philosophy of Natural Science.* Cambridge: Cambridge University Press.

Hamermesh, Daniel S. 2013. "Six Decades of Top Economics Publishing: Who and How?" *Journal of Economic Literature* 51, no. 1: 162–72.

Harding, Matthew, and Jonathan Hersh. 2018. "Big Data in Economics." *IZA World of Labor*, September.

Hawley, Ellis W. 1990. "Economic Inquiry and the State in New Era America: Antistatist Corporatism and Positive Statism in Uneasy Coexistence." In *The State and Economic Knowledge: The American and British Experiences*, 287–324. Cambridge: Cambridge University Press.

Hendry, David F. 1980. "Econometrics-Alchemy or Science?" *Economica* 47: 387–406.

Keynes, John M. 1921. *A Treatise on Probability.* London: Macmillan.

Kitchin, Rob. 2014. *The Data Revolution: Big Data, Open Data, Data Infrastructures, and Their Consequences.* London: Sage.

Koopmans, T. C. 1947. "Measurement without Theory." *Review of Economics and Statistics* 19: 161–72.

Leach, William. 1993. *Land of Desire: Merchants, Power, and the Rise of a New American Culture.* New York: Pantheon Books.

Leamer, Edward E. 1983. "Let's Take the Con out of Econometrics." *American Economic Review* 73: 31–43.

Lemov, Rebecca. 2017. "Anthropology's Most Documented Man, Ca. 1947: A Prefiguration of Big Data from the Big Social Science Era." *Osiris* 32, no. 1: 21–42.

Marshall, Alfred. 1907. "The Social Possibilities of Economic Chivalry." *Economic Journal* 17, no. 65: 7–29.

Mitchell, Wesley C. 1919. "Statistics and Government." *Publications of the American Statistical Association* 16: 223–35.

Mitchell, Wesley C. 1925. "Quantitative Analysis in Economic Theory." *American Economic Review* 15: 1–12.

Mitchell, Wesley C. 1927. *Business Cycles: The Problem and Its Setting.* New York: National Bureau of Economic Research.

Morgan, Mary S. 1991. *The History of Econometric Ideas.* New York: Cambridge University Press.

Morgan, Mary S. 2003. "Economics." In *The Modern Social Sciences*, vol. 7 of *The Cambridge History of Science*, edited by Dorothy Ross and Theodore M. Porter, 275–305. Cambridge: Cambridge University Press.

Mosteller, Frederick, and John Wilder Tukey. 1977. *Data Analysis and Regression: A Second Course in Statistics.* Reading, MA: Addison-Wesley.

Nik-Khah, Edward, and Philip Mirowski. 2019. "On Going the Market One Better: Economic Market Design and the Contradictions of Building Markets for Public Purposes." *Economy and Society* 48, no. 2: 268–94.

Ostrovsky, Michael, and Michael Schwarz. 2009. "Reserve Prices in Internet Advertising Auctions: A Field Experiment." SSRN Scholarly Paper ID 1573947. Rochester, NY: Social Science Research Network.

Panhans, Matthew T., and John D. Singleton. 2017. "The Empirical Economist's Toolkit: From Models to Methods." In *The Age of the Applied Economist: The Transformation of Economics since the 1970s*, edited by Roger E. Backhouse and Béatrice Cherrier. *History of Political Economy* 49 (supplement): 127–57.

Persons, Warren M. 1924. "Some Fundamental Concepts of Statistics." *Journal of the American Statistical Association* 19, no. 145: 1–8. doi.org/10.2307/2277253.

Phillips, Matt. 2014. "The Remarkable Rise of Big Data Economics." Quartz. November 18. qz.com/297790/the-remarkable-rise-of-big-data-economics/.

Qin, Duo. 1997. *The Formation of Econometrics. A Historical Perspective.* Oxford: Oxford University Press.

Renfro, Charles G. 2011. "Econometrics and the Computer: Love or a Marriage of Convenience?" In *Histories on Econometrics*, edited by Marcel Boumans, Ariane Dupont-Kieffer, and Duo Qin. *History of Political Economy* 43 (supplement): 86–105.

Rutherford, Malcolm. 2011a. "The USDA Graduate School: Government Training in Statistics and Economics, 1921–1945." *Journal of the History of Economic Thought* 33, no. 4: 419–47.

Rutherford, Malcolm. 2011b. *The Institutionalist Movement in American Economics, 1918–1947: Science and Social Control.* New York: Cambridge University Press.

Schneier, Bruce. 2015. *Data and Goliath: The Hidden Battles to Collect Your Data and Control Your World.* New York: W. W. Norton.

Silvia, John E, Azhar Iqbal, and Michael Pugliese. 2017. "Big Data Applications in the Economics/Financial World Part I: Opportunities and Challenges." Special Commentary. Wells Fargo Securities Economics Group. www.fxstreet.com/analysis/big-data-applications-in-the-economics-financial-world-part-i-opportunities-and-challenges-201704061326.

Sims, Christopher A. 1980. "Macroeconomics and Reality." *Econometrica* 48, no. 1: 1–48.

Stapleford, Thomas A. 2007. "Market Visions: Expenditure Surveys, Market Research, and Economic Planning in the New Deal." *Journal of American History* 94: 418–44.

Stapleford, Thomas A. 2009. *The Cost of Living in America: A Political History of Economic Statistics, 1880–2000.* New York: Cambridge University Press.

Stapleford, Thomas A. 2012. "Navigating the Shoals of Self-Reporting: Data Collection and US Expenditure Surveys since 1920." In *Observing the Economy: Historical Perspectives,* edited by Harro Maas and Mary S. Morgan. *History of Political Economy* 44 (supplement): 160–82.

Strotz, Robert H. 1968. "Econometrics." In *International Encyclopedia of the Social Sciences,* edited by David L. Sills and Robert King Merton, 350–59. New York: Macmillan.

Taylor, Linnet, Ralph Schroeder, and Eric Meyer. 2014. "Emerging Practices and Perspectives on Big Data Analysis in Economics: Bigger and Better or More of the Same?" *Big Data & Society* 1, no. 2: 1–10. doi: 2053951714536877.

Varian, Hal R. 2014. "Big Data: New Tricks for Econometrics." *Journal of Economic Perspectives* 28, no. 2: 3–28.

Vining, Rutledge. 1949. "Koopmans on the Choice of Variables to Be Studies and the Methods of Measurement." *Review of Economics and Statistics* 31, no. 2: 77.

Inference without a Cause

Pictorial Statistics

Marcel Boumans

This article discusses Francis Galton's method of inductive inference where the data are photographs. Although Galton used photographs of all kinds of objects, such as human faces, human skulls, medallions, and animals, in particular racehorses, this discussion focuses on the portraits of people. His aim of induction was to determine the *typical* characteristics of the *natural class* to which the individuals belong. The populations he studied, among others, were Jews, criminals, and people suffering the same illness, such as consumption. The aim of this method was to make the main characteristics of the natural class in question visible by composing the relevant photographs in a specific photographic way. The idea was that this composite photograph is the portrait of the "typical" member of the natural class concerned. The method and technique of this photographic composition was Galton's own design. He called this process of induction that led to a "composite," "pictorial statistics" (Galton 1879: 162).

The advantage of pictorial statistics is that it enables the determination of the *average* of nonmetric objects. The composition is based on the exposure of the photographs of the individuals to a photographic plate, each during a same specified time interval. As such, this procedure was considered *mechanical*, leading to an *objective* representation of a class.

I would like to thank all participants of the *HOPE* conference on the history of statistical inference for their great inputs, and Theodore Porter for his constructive suggestions. In particular, I am grateful to Chiara Ambrosio for having shared her expertise on Galton's pictorial statistics.

History of Political Economy 53 (annual suppl.) DOI 10.1215/00182702-9414846

Lorraine Daston and Peter Galison (2007) have shown that the rise in dominance of the epistemological virtue of mechanical objectivity can be understood as an insistent drive to reduce subjective bias. This article, however, argues that despite the fact that Galton aimed at this kind of objectivity, subjective judgments nevertheless appear to be a necessary part of this kind of inductive inference to achieve purity. At first sight, this seems very much in the line of Daston and Galison's account. They argue that in the twentieth century the awareness arose that mechanical-objective pictures still could contain errors that should be erased by *trained judgment*. Galton's case of inductive reasoning, however, departs from Daston and Galison's account by showing that the correct composites were achieved by a combination of mechanical procedures and *un*trained judgments. To find the most appropriate balance between fit to the data and purity, fit was dealt with by objective procedures but impurity reduced by *familiarization* with the data.

To support this claim, I first discuss the design and applications of the method of composite photographs by Galton and the "typical pictures" of Henry Pickering Bowditch. Then I unpack this method to see what else other than mechanical objectivity is involved, and what the specific role of familiarized judgment is.

1. Composite Portraits

In a series of publications, appearing between 1878 and 1906, Galton explained his own developed method of "composite portraits" and discussed some of his results in detail.[1] The year before the first publication on composite portraits, in a presidential address to the Anthropological Department of the British Association at Plymouth, Galton already proposed to study the external physical characteristics of a group of persons resembling one another in some "mental quality," not by anthropometric measurements but by photographs. According to Galton (1878: 97), the photographic process

> enables us to obtain with mechanical precision a generalised picture; one representing no man in particular, but portrays an imaginary figure, possessing the average features of any given group of men. These

---

1. These publications may be found on a website, galton.org, dedicated to Galton, and edited and maintained by Gavan Tredoux. A special section of this website, galton.org/composite.htm, contains all publications on composite portraits.

ideal faces have a surprising air of reality. Nobody who glanced at one of them for the first time, would doubt its being the likeness of a living person. Yet, as I said, it is no such thing; it is the portrait of a type, and not of an individual.

Galton implicitly assumed that the outlines of each individual component are distributed according a Normal (Gaussian) distribution:

> Those of its outlines are sharpest and darkest that are common to the largest number of the components; the purely individual peculiarities leave little or no visible trace. The latter being necessarily disposed equally on both sides of the average, the outline of the composite is the average of all the components. It is a band, and not a fine line, because the outlines of components are seldom exactly superimposed. The band will be darkest in its middle whenever the component portraits have the same general type of features, and its breadth or amount of blur will measure the tendency of the components to deviate from the common type. (97)

He compared this process of photographic composition with "shot-marks" on a target, where these marks are more thickly clustered near the bull's-eye than away from it (97). This kind of metaphorical reasoning on the likes of marksmen and target practices is explored extensively in Judy Klein's (1997) *Statistical Visions in Time*, starting with a discussion of Lambert Adolphe Jacques Quetelet's comparison of his "l'homme moyen" with the bull's-eye of a target. Galton (1877a: 493) himself was clear about the source of this idea of variation: "It was to Quetelet that we were first indebted for a knowledge of the fact that the amount and frequency of deviation from the average among members of the same race, in respect to each and every characteristic, tends to conform to the mathematical law of deviation." The adequacy of this kind of metaphorical reasoning is discussed in section 2.

An important advantage of this method, according to Galton (1878: 97), is that the results are neither biased nor subjective: "The merit of the photographic composite is its mechanical precision, being subject to no errors beyond those incidental to all photographic productions," thereby in his view meeting the epistemic virtue of mechanical objectivity. This claim is questioned after I explore the details of the production of a composite photograph.

The method of composition was explained in his article on "composite portraits" (Galton 1878; see figure 1). The first step is to collect photographs of the persons belonging to a category one would like to study.

Figure 1 Setup for making a composite photograph.
Source: Galton 1878: 97.

"They must be similar in attitude and size, but no exactness is necessary in either of these respects" (97). They, then, should be hanged in such a way that the pupils of the eyes of each portrait have the exact same position when exposed to the camera. Each photograph is exposed for the same amount of seconds, for example, ten seconds, to the same part of the sensitized plate. If we are dealing with eight photographs, then the plate has a total exposure of eighty seconds. After being exposed to these photographs, the plate is developed, and the print taken from it is the resulting composite portrait. In two 1881 articles, published in *Photographic News* and *Photographic Journal*, Galton presented a technically more advanced method that was easier to manage, but the underlying principle was the same: the composite portrait is a superimposition of several photographs.

Figure 2 Composite portraits showing "features common among men convicted of crimes of violence," ca. 1885.
Source: University College London.

Galton's (1877b: 11) first composite portrait was that of the "ideal criminal" (see figure 2), which he described as follows: "His conscience is almost deficient, his instincts are vicious, and his power of self-control is very weak." The question was how these peculiarities correlated with physical characteristics and features. To approach this question, he could use a large collection ("many thousands") of photographs of criminals, provided by Edmund Du Cane, director general of prisons in England. In the aforementioned presidential address, Galton (1877b: 12) explained how he sorted the photographs before exposing them to the camera:

> I may as well say, that I begged that the photographs should be furnished me without any names attached to them, but simply classified in three groups according to the nature of the crime. The first group included murder, manslaughter, and burglary; the second group included felony and forgery; and the third group referred to sexual crimes. The photographs were of criminals who had been sentenced to long terms of penal servitude. By familiarizing myself with the collection, and continually sorting the photographs in tentative ways, certain natural classes began to appear, some of which are exceedingly well marked. It was also very evident that the three groups of criminals contributed in very different proportions to the different physiognomic classes.

The second major study in pictorial statistics dealt with the question of how one "might be able to ascertain whether there are any facial characteristics common to any large proportion of cases of phthisis" (Galton and Mahomed 1882: 476). This study was carried out with Frederick Akbar Mahomed.[2] For this study, there were no photographs yet available, and therefore they had to photograph the patients themselves. They started with the phthisical patients of Guy's Hospital in London, in January 1881, but because this did not accumulate enough photographs, they also included the patients of the Brompton and Victoria Park Hospitals for Diseases of the Chest in London.

"To protect ourselves from any charge of a prejudiced selection of cases or distortion of facts" (Galton and Mahomed 1882: 477), the selection of the patients to be photographed was based on cards with fixed categories on which the chief details of the cases were recorded by making a tick in the appropriate space (see figure 3).

The first selection was "all cases of well ascertained phthisis occurring in either sex within the limits of fifteen and forty years of age" (Galton and Mahomed 1882: 477–78). The limits of age were chosen to further comparability and to exclude "the more evidently acquired phthisis of

---

2. Mahomed (1849–1884) "must be regarded as one of the most important pioneers in the field of arterial hypertension" (O'Rourke 1992: 212) and developed the first quantitative sphygmogram (a mechanical device used to measure blood pressure). He contracted typhoid fever in 1884, probably from one of his patients at Guy's or the London Fever Hospital, where he still held a visiting appointment, and died in the same year.

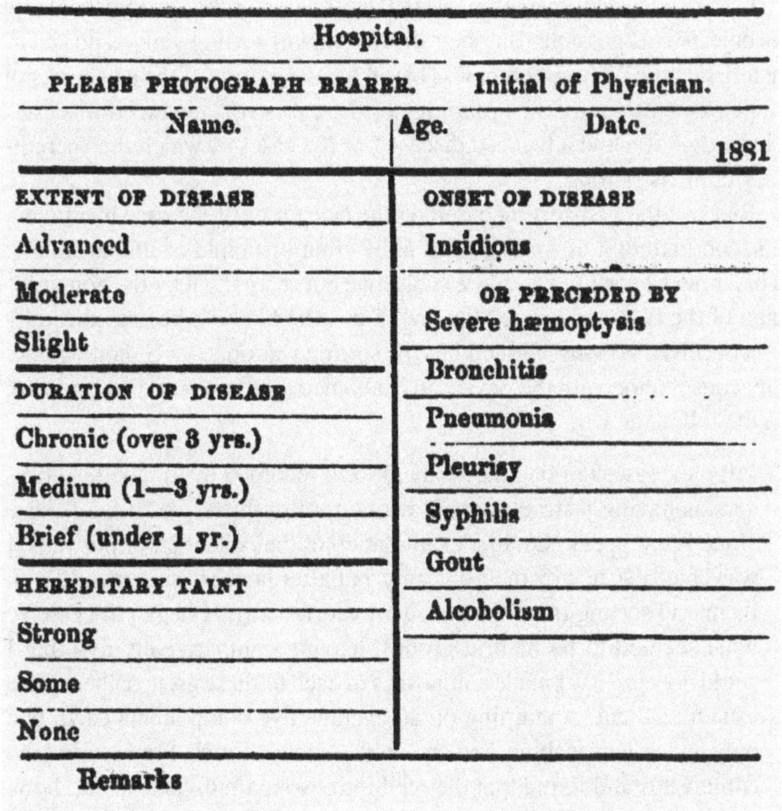

Hospital.	
PLEASE PHOTOGRAPH BEARER.	Initial of Physician.
Name.	Age.	Date.

1891

EXTENT OF DISEASE	ONSET OF DISEASE
Advanced	Insidious
Moderate	OR PRECEDED BY
Slight	Severe hæmoptysis
DURATION OF DISEASE	Bronchitis
Chronic (over 3 yrs.)	Pneumonia
Medium (1—3 yrs.)	Pleurisy
Brief (under 1 yr.)	Syphilis
HEREDITARY TAINT	Gout
Strong	Alcoholism
Some	
None	

Remarks

Figure 3 Card on which the chief details of the cases could be recorded.
Source: Galton and Mahomed 1882: 477.

advanced age" (478). This selection process resulted in 442 portraits of patients suffering from phthisis, of whom 261 were males and 181 females.

The next step was to make composite portraits of subsets of these photographs. These "composites" were then used to make "co-composites," that is compositions of composites. And these co-composites were in turn used to make a "co-co-composite." But before Galton and Mahomed made these composites, they first viewed the individual portraits and were "struck with the absence of those characteristic faces which we expected to find among them" (481). One could even question whether there is a tubercular diathesis. It appeared that only by "much sorting and arranging into groups, and after combining the individuals, so as to test the similarity of their features" (481), the characteristics of phthisis became visible.

Galton and Mahomed emphasized, however, that the sorting should be as objective as possible. But their first attempt of sorting yielded no "characteristic type." This attempt was based on using some of the categories of the cards (see figure 3): groupings of the cases of "advanced disease," "brief duration and advanced disease," or the cases of which the "hereditary taint" is "strong."

Because the first sorting based on the categories of the card had failed, a second attempt at sorting used a different principle of unbiasedness. This time the sorting was more subjective but carried out by the nonphysician of the two, and hence "the one of us least likely to be prejudiced by preconceived notions" (481). Thus the sorting was done by Galton without any consultation with the physician Mahomed (who was away to London), in the following way:

> Fifty-six cases (among the women) were recorded by the medical officers as having a strong hereditary taint of phthisis, and it is of these alone I now speak. On first examination of the collection of portraits, I was chiefly struck by their diversity, but after familiarising myself with them and sorting them tentatively in various ways, I began to perceive what seemed to be natural groups, leaving comparatively few that I could not classify. I made composites of each of these groups; there were eleven of them, containing on an average five components each, one only had as few as three, and one only as many as nine. I then sorted the composites and found that they fell into two main divisions, not, however, separated by any abrupt line of demarcation. In the one division there were six composites of, on the whole, thirty-six portraits, and in the other there were five composites of twenty portraits in all. The first division had blunted and thickened features, the second had thin and softened features. I then made a compound composite of each of the two divisions . . . , and finally I threw both divisions into a doubly compound composite (co-co-composite, . . .) to form the general average. (482)

When Mahomed returned from London, he concluded that the first type with the blunted and thickened features coincides with what physicians described as the "strumous" and the second type with the thin and softened features as the "tubercular" (see figure 4). Galton and Mahomed then proceeded with sorting out the patients with these two types and putting these selections to the test by making composite portraits of them, with the result of obtaining "very striking and highly characteristic faces" (483).

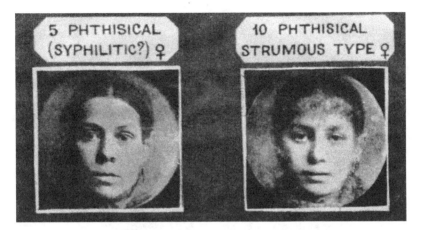

Figure 4 Composite portraits showing two types of phthisical, 1882.
Source: galton.org/composite.htm.

Reviewing these results, Galton and Mahomed came to the following conclusions. If the composites are made without any selection of "natural classes," the "average" "presents no features or expressions characteristic of what may be called secondary types" (483). But by taking "very carefully selected faces," it is possible to form a composite portrait having certain characteristic features. This method of evaluating composite portraits of specially selected faces was considered "an excellent test of the correctness of the selections made. If the result obtained has lost the special characteristics sought for, we may be sure that the faces selected were ill assorted" (484).

The third major study with the use of photographic composites was on the "race characteristics of Jews." This had resulted in a few composites that Galton (1885: 243) considered "the best specimens of composites I have ever produced." Although not explicitly noted, the reason why he considered them the best composites is probably because he had advanced the procedures to get the individual photographs on the same scale and position, which made adjustment of the camera much easier and therefore the results more "beautiful." The description of these advanced procedures takes up the largest part of the publication (Galton 1885) in which he discusses this study. Unfortunately, however, Galton did not say much about how he selected the photographs. The only thing he wrote about it is to mention that "the individual photographs were taken with hardly any

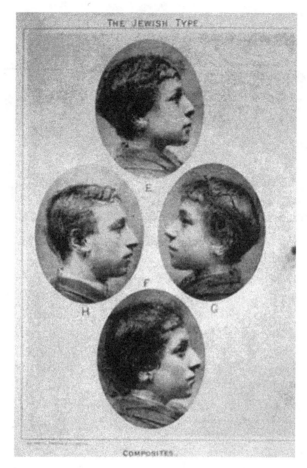

Figure 5 Composite portraits showing the Jewish
type, 1885.
Source: University College London.

selection from among Jewish boys in the Jew's Free School, Bell Lane"
(243). He made eight composites, labeled A to H. A, B, E, and F were each
based on five individual portraits of these Jewish boys (see figure 5).
C was the co-composite of A and B, with the addition of three other
individual portraits "to increase its sharpness" (243). D was a composite
of five adult faces; G, a co-composite of E and F; and H, a composite of
five "older faces."

2. The Determination of Types

In 1894, *McClure's Magazine* published an article by Bowditch titled "Are Composite Photographs Typical Pictures?" Influenced by Galton's composite photography, Bowditch had made eight composite portraits: one composition of twelve Boston physicians, another with the same physicians but five years later, two of twelve horse-car conductors each, two of twelve Saxon soldiers each, and two of twelve Wend soldiers each, with the aim of the determination of "types" or "typical forms."

To Bowditch, the method of composite portraits had several advantages over other methods. It gives "the typical form a truly objective character" and removes the "subjective source of error" (Bowditch 1894: 331). He admits, then, that as far as size and proportions of the body are concerned, by measuring and weighting large numbers of individuals belonging to a certain group, and from these figures thus obtained calculating the mean and variation of the dimensions selected for study, the "typical form," the "truly representative of the group," may be deduced. However, there are "certain anatomical peculiarities of too subtle a character to be expressed in figures, but producing results which reveal themselves with unerring certainty to the trained eye" (334). In particular, according to Bowditch, "for the recognition of racial peculiarities the unmeasurable seem to be more important than the measurable differences" (335). Despite the fact that we have to deal with the unmeasurable, the method of composite portraits enables a "scientific discussion" of the conception of racial physiognomy and "shows clearly the importance of devising some method by which mean and average values may be determined for those unmeasurable anatomical peculiarities" (336). His own study of the faces of the physicians, horse-car conductors, and soldiers "certainly suggests the conclusion that there must be some racial peculiarities showing themselves in the composite portraits" (340–41).

According to Bowditch, the method of composite photography enabled the objective determination of a typical form of unmeasurable features. Both Galton and Bowditch placed this method on an equal footing as statistics in which the "average" was supposed to represent the typical, hence the name "pictorial statistics" Galton gave to this method. Following Quetelet and Galton, Bowditch (1894: 333–34) also compared the "ideal forms round which individuals group themselves in accordance with the law of accidental variation, as shots group themselves round the bull's-eye of a target" (see figure 6). To reinforce this image of the target, in his eight

Figure 6 "Plate I Twelve Boston physicians and their composite portrait—the composite in the center."

Source: Bowditch 1894: 332.

plates the twelve individual portraits were arranged around the bull's-eye of the composite photograph, as noted by Klein (1997: 128).

Before we can discuss whether statistical analysis and pictorial statistics are really the same kinds of target practices, we first have to discuss what the target of pictorial statistics actually represents, the claimed typical form or something else. To Galton, in contrast to Bowditch, the composite portraits, particularly when the whole set of photographs was used, were problematic. It appeared that for the cases where no preselection has been carried out, the typical characteristics had disappeared in the average.

In the first case, the composite portrait of criminals (see figure 2), Galton (1878: 97–98) observed that

> the features of the composites are much better looking than those of the components. The special villainous irregularities in the latter have disappeared and the common humanity that underlies them has prevailed. They represent, not the criminal, but the man who is liable to fall into crime. All composites are better looking than their components, because the averaged portrait of many persons is free from irregularities that variously blemish the looks of each of them.

Contrary to what he hoped would happen, it appeared that "the special expressions of different criminals do not reinforce one another in the composite, but disappear" (Galton 1879: 162).

Also, in the case of the composite portrait of the patients suffering consumption, Galton (1881a: 144) seemed surprised by the beauty of the resulting portrait: "a very striking face, thoroughly ideal and artistic, and singularly beautiful. It is, indeed, most notable how beautiful all composites are. Individual peculiarities are all irregularities, and the composite is always regular." This case, however, was more problematic. Unlike the case of the criminals, the individual photographs did not show the characteristics of the "type," but he hoped that these characteristics would nevertheless become apparent in the process of composition:

> On looking over the individual portraits of the patients suffering from phthisis, one is first struck with the absence of those characteristic faces which we expect to find among them. With the exception of a few who were very severely ill, the faces did not seem to differ much from those of any group of ordinary patients, indeed there seemed nothing characteristic about them. (Galton and Mahomed 1882: 481)

By taking all photographs without any selection, the co-co-composite "presents no features or expressions characteristic of what may be called secondary types" (483). These secondary types were the "strumous" and the "tubercular" and could only be found when based on a preselection that resulted in these two co-composites. In this sense, the method had failed, according to Galton and Mahomed, "to obtain for us so typical a face" (484): "There is no foundation for the belief that persons possessing certain physical characteristics are especially liable to tubercular disease" (492).

And again in the case of the Jewish schoolboys, Galton (1885: 243) came to a similar observation. While driving through the Jewish quarter near the Jew's Free school, the feature that "struck" him most was the "the cold scanning gaze of man, woman, and child, and this was no less conspicuous among the schoolboys." But these "dirty little fellows individually" appeared to be "wonderfully beautiful" in the composites.

As Elizabeth Stephens (2013) shows, Galton's composite portraiture was a failure as a scientific project for several reasons, but the reason here of most relevance is that it undermined rather than substantiated the anthropometric and physiognomic theories Galton intended to illustrate. While Galton's work in composite portraiture was motivated by eugenicists' concerns, in which some types were understood as superior to others, the composites seem to prove that all types are "beautiful." Rather than enforcing the signs of the prisoners' villainy or racial inferiority, the composite portraits erased them. Or as Gavan Tredoux (2020) phrased it aptly: "The portraits of criminals tended to blend away into normality." While to Galton, Quetelet's average was the "type of the race" (Gigerenzer et al. 1989: 58), the portrait of the average did not look like that.

3. The Familiarized Eye

The characteristics of the type in question did not became visible when the composition was based on mechanical-objective procedures alone, for example, by using the categories of the patient card (figure 3). They only became visible because a part of the procedure was a sorting of the photographs in "natural classes" based on a judgment of the eye. For Galton, it was, however, important that the eye be untrained, to avoid prejudice by preconceived notions. The sorting was done after having "familiarized" the untrained eye with the materials. And subsequently, the correctness of this selection was tested by a visual assessment of the composite photograph.

As was quoted above, in section 1, by continually sorting the prisoners' photographs, "certain natural classes began to appear" (Galton 1877b: 12). The "assurance of the truth" of the "pictorial deductions" was to be found in the "substantial agreement" of the different batches of components, "this being a perfect test of truth in all statistical conclusions" (Galton 1878: 99). To achieve an accurate portrait of the "genus" of the "criminal,"

the objects to be portrayed must all have many points of likeness in common, and it is of especial importance that characteristics of a medium quality should be much more common among them than those that deviate widely. No statistician dreams of grouping heterogeneous facts in the same table; no more do I propose to group heterogeneous forms in the same picture. Statistical averages, and the like, are nonsensical productions unless they apply to objects that cluster towards a common centre; and composite pictures are equally monstrous or meaningless unless they are compounded of objects that have a common similarity to a central ideal type. (Galton 1879: 160–61)

The clustering of the components was, like in numerical statistics, seen as an indication of the truth.[3]

It might be thought that blended portraits would form mere smudges, and so they would if only a few specimens of extremely different casts of features were combined, but in all groups that may be called generic the common points of resemblance are so numerous, and medium characteristics are so much the most frequent, that they predominate in the result. All that is common to the group remains; all that is individual disappears. (Galton 1879: 161)

A composite that showed the most common outlines and least "smudges" was seen to be "generic" for the "natural group" at hand. These natural classes were based on familiarization and subsequent sorting of the photographs available of that population. The sorting was based on looking for visual "likenesses" by an eye that is supposed to be unbiased.

Daston and Galison (2007) describe the history of objectivity as a move from the dominance of the epistemic virtue of "truth-to-nature" to the dominance of "mechanical objectivity." Galton's work on pictorial statistics can be considered a part of, or even a contributor to, this move, but

Galton's method is a perfect instance of an image-making routine poised between our two ordinarily disjunct modes of observation: on the one side, it aimed for an ideal type that lay "behind" any single individual. On the other side, Galton's face-machine proceeded toward that ideal not with what he and others had come to see as subjective idealization (stemming from "biases," "fancies," and "judgment") but with the quasi-automated procedures of mechanical objectivity. (Daston and Galison 2007: 169)

3. Clustering is usually seen as an indication of accuracy, which is closeness to truth. This is, however, a common misconception. Clustering is actually an indication of precision, which should be distinguished from accuracy. When there is a systematic bias, the data will not cluster around the truth. For a more detailed discussion of this distinction between precision and accuracy, see Boumans 2020.

Truth-to-nature is the aim to portray the underlying type of a species, rather than any individual specimen. "It is an image of the characteristic, the essential, the universal, the typical" (Daston and Galison 2007: 20). The image of the typical was usually made by a specially gifted observer with artistic talents. At several places Galton made clear that he wished to go beyond this too-subjective portrayal of a type.

> A composite portrait represents the picture that would rise before the mind's eye of a man who had the gift of pictorial imagination in an exalted degree. But the imaginative power even of the highest artists is far from precise, and is so apt to be biased by special cases that may have struck their fancies, that no two artists agree in any of their typical forms. The merit of the photographic composite is its mechanical precision, being subject to no errors beyond those incidental to all photographic productions. (Galton 1878: 97)

Although admitting that "many poets and painters have had the visualising faculty in an extraordinary degree, while it is in the brains of poets and painters generally that we find the artistic power to reside of producing pictures that are not copies of any individual, but represent the characteristics of larger classes" (Galton 1879: 160), when the phenomena are submitted to measurement, "very many of the notions that were derived from general impression are discovered to be wrong, even absurdly so" (157), and "it is only by the strict methods of scientific inquiry, namely by measurement and number, that these fallacies can be cleared away and the truth discovered" (158). According to Chiara Ambrosio (2016: 556), photography was an "indispensable aid to the kind of ideal empiricism Galton aspired to."

> By blurring the idiosyncratic and retaining in view only the typical, composite photography not only lends visual evidence to the material content of our generalizations, it also shows that "pure" generalizations, independent of the differences and peculiarities of particular individuals arriving at those generalizations, are a desirable empirical aspiration in the first place. (556)

Daston and Galison (2007: 169) describe Galton's view on objectivity as follows: "The device would remove the process of abstraction from the artist's pen," which was indeed Galton's intention. But a closer look at the way Galton arrived at what he considered pure generalizations shows that the aim at complete mechanical objectivity was not reached. In a sense, Galton's approach, which was partly based on the epistemic virtue of mechanical objectivity and partly on a visual judgment to sort the photos, fits Daston and Galison's account that in the history of objectivity one can observe a subsequent move from mechanical objectivity to what they call *trained judgment*: the acknowledgment that the images produced by mechanical-objective procedures contain instrumental artifacts. These should be removed by trained judgment. The removal of these artifacts requires expertise, not only theoretical but also of the instruments. But the case of the image of the phthisical patient shows that Galton did not want to have the *trained* eye correct for the inaccuracies of a purely mechanical approach. His nonphysician's eye was preferred to do the sorting above the trained judgment of Mahomed. It was the untrained eye that should be part of this process of inference. Untrained here means that the analyst is not educated in the medical or psychological studies of the population in question. The eye was supposed to be "trained" in another sense, namely, that it had familiarized itself with the materials.

This part of statistical inference, the necessary familiarization with the data, here photos, appears not to be particular for Galton's pictorial statistical inference but is a "normal problem of inductive science," according to John Maynard Keynes ([1921] 1973). When discussing the "nature of statistical inference" in his *Treatise on Probability*, Keynes emphasizes that in determining the accuracy of the statistical characteristics of a certain "mass of individual records," the statistician "must pay attention to a new class of considerations and must display a different kind of capacity" (360). The statistician "must take into account of whatever extraneous knowledge may be available regarding the sample of population which came under observation, and of the mode and conditions of the observations themselves. Much of this may be of a vague kind, and most of it will be necessarily incapable of exact, numerical, or statistical treatment" (360).

For Galton, to avoid arriving at "nonsensical productions," the photos needed to be sorted on likeness before a composition could be made. A meaningful inference was looking for the homogeneous facts that were supposed to be grouped in "natural classes." This homogeneity of a class, the "common similarity to a central ideal type" could be seen only by the eye that had familiarized itself with the material. Therefore Galton had to assume that natural classes he studied with the photographic techniques are real, in other words, that group of criminals, phthisical, and Jews each belong to a *natural* class and that the familiarized eye can pick them up.[4]

---

4. I would like to thank Chiara Ambrosia for emphasizing this point.

The fewer the smudges, then, a composite of a natural class showed, the better the sorting was done, confirmed by the fact that "the ideal faces have a surprising air of reality" (Galton 1878: 97). Thus, as a matter of fact, the photographic procedure that results in a composite is not where the inference takes place: it is the process of the sorting that is the inference. The composition functions, then, only as the test whether the inference is done accurately.

4. Conclusions

Despite Galton's hope of achieving objective generalizations through photography, composite photography did not give him what he had hoped for. Mechanical generalizations did not show the "typical," "generic" characteristics of a specific population; they showed the "beautiful" face of common humanity. The characteristics of a type became visible only after having sorted visually the photographs into "natural classes." The more "beautiful" the composites were, the less they show the characteristics of a type.

Because the concept of beauty played such a significant role in Galton's method of inference to the characteristics of a type, it must briefly be demonstrated why it could be used in this way without Galton feeling the need for further justification. A detailed historical-cultural contextualization of beauty goes beyond the main topic of this article; Mary Shelley's *Frankenstein* suffices to illustrate that at Galton's time humanity and beauty were closely linked. In this famous work, Shelley relates ugliness with the inhuman nature of Frankenstein's creature. Because of his "miserable deformity," he is considered a "monster," despite the fact that the behavior of the creature at the beginning showed all the features of Victorian virtues: gentle demeanor, inquisitiveness, and refinement. "God, in pity, made man beautiful and alluring, after his own image; but my form is a filthy type of yours, more horrid even from the very resemblance" (Shelley [1818] 2018: 127).

Galton indebted the principles of his target practice from Quetelet. The average person was considered representative of true human nature. But all the qualities of the *average man* "represent all which is grand, beautiful and excellent" (Quetelet 1842: 100); the face of *l'homme moyen* is beautiful. This face of the average therefore conflicted with Galton's aim to portrait the criminal, the sick, and the Jew; they were not supposed to look "grand beautiful and excellent," but "ugly."

Quetelet (1849: 102) suggested the introduction of "limits" to deal with the "extraordinary" cases. The limits are distances to the mean that can be used to define several nonordinary categories. In terms of the "height of man" he defined distances to the mean with which he established the following categories: "giants," "large men," "the ordinary size," "small men," "dwarfs," and "monstrosities," the latter to be found beyond the most distant limits at both sides of the mean. But this more mechanical kind of categorization based on preset limits is not applicable to the nonmetric features of a face. To arrive at categories to be found beside the "ordinary," Galton had to develop a different method. The camera was used not as a tool of inference but as a tool of testing the inference based on the familiarized eye.

References

Ambrosio, Chiara. 2016. "Composite Photographs and the Quest for Generality: Themes from Peirce and Galton." *Critical Inquiry* 42: 547–79.

Boumans, Marcel. 2020. "Visualizing Ignorance." *East Asian Science, Technology and Society: An International Journal* 14, no. 2: 331–45.

Bowditch, Hendry Pickering. 1894. "Are Composite Photographs Typical Pictures?" *McClure's Magazine*, September, 331–42.

Daston, Lorraine, and Peter Galison. 2007. *Objectivity*. New York: Zone Books.

Galton, Francis. 1877a. "Typical Laws of Heredity." *Nature* 15 (April 5): 492–95, 512–14, 532–33.

Galton, F. 1877b. *Address to the Anthropological Department of the British Association*. London: Clowes and Sons.

Galton, F. 1878. "Composite Portraits." *Nature* 18 (May 23): 97–100.

Galton, F. 1879. "Generic Images." *Nineteenth Century* 6 (July): 157–69.

Galton, F. 1881a. "Composite Portraiture." *Photographic Journal* 5: 140–46.

Galton, F. 1881b. "Composite Portraiture." *Photographic News* 25: 316–17, 332–33.

Galton, F. 1885. "Photographic Composites." *Photographic News* 29: 243–45.

Galton, Francis, and Frederick Akbar Mahomed. 1882. "An Inquiry into the Physiognomy of Phthisis by the Method of 'Composite Portraiture.'" *Guy's Hospital Reports* 25 (February): 475–93.

Gigerenzer, Gerd, Zeno Swijtink, Theodore Porter, Lorraine Daston, John Beatty, and Lorenz Krüger. 1989. *The Empire of Chance: How Probability Changed Science and Everyday Life*. Cambridge: Cambridge University Press.

Keynes, John Maynard. (1921) 1973. *A Treatise on Probability*. Vol. 8 of *The Collected Writings of John Maynard Keynes*. London: Macmillan.

Klein, Judy L. 1997. *Statistical Visions in Time*. Cambridge: Cambridge University Press.

O'Rourke, Michael F. 1992. "Frederick Akbar Mahomed." *Hypertension* 19, no. 2: 212–17.

Quetelet, L. A. 1849. *Letters Addressed to H.R.H. the Grand Duke of Saxe Coburg and Gotha, on the Theory of Probabilities, as Applied to the Moral and Political Sciences*. London: Charles and Edwin Layton.

Quetelet, Lambert Adolphe Jacques. 1842. *A Treatise on Man and the Developments of his Faculties*. Edinburgh: William and Robert Chambers.

Shelley, Mary. (1818) 2018. *Frankenstein*. London: VIVI.

Stephens, Elizabeth. 2013. "Francis Galton's Composite Portraits: The Productive Failure of a Scientific Experiment." Working paper. www.researchgate.net/publication /323275029_Francis_Galton%27s_Composite_Portraits_The_Productive_Failure _of_a_Scientific_Experiment.

Tredoux, Gavan. 2020. Francis Galton and Composite Portraiture. galton.org.

Making Inferences from Index Numbers (1860–1914)

Aashish Velkar

> The laws of inference are the laws of probability,
> and the former is a particular case of the latter.
> —John Maynard Keynes, *A Treatise on Probability* (1921)

> If one explanation is much more plausible than any other, it is an *inference to the best explanation*. Many pieces of reasoning in science are like that.
> —Ian Hacking, *An Introduction to Probability and Inductive Logic* (2001)

If making an inference is an act of reasoning, with or without using the laws of probability, then economic measurements provide a fecund basis for a historical examination of inference. This article uses the case of index number measurements to study how economists made inferences about economic phenomena and makes observations about the multiple inferential gaps they encountered. By examining the early history of index numbers, it becomes clear that the particular context—who made the inference and for what purpose—is especially pertinent, and that inference is a cognitive and not just a heuristic process of reasoning. The article further examines how contemporaries challenged the economists' inferences and what these reactions tell us about the broader ecology in which economists made inferences.

I am grateful to Mary Morgan, Harro Maas, Marcel Boumans, Jeff Biddle, and an anonymous referee for invaluable comments on earlier drafts of this article. Comments by the participants of the Duke workshop were also extremely helpful in revising this article.

History of Political Economy 53 (annual suppl.) DOI 10.1215/00182702-9414860

Toward the end of the nineteenth century, British economists increasingly began to use index numbers to study a range of economic phenomena, such as price trends, depreciating value of the monetary standard, or the cost of living of the working classes (Fisher 1922; Edgeworth 1925). Later in the interwar years, index numbers were used to make inferences about levels of economic activity and estimations of national income (Rowe 1927; Tolles and Douglas 1930; Crowther 1934; Flux 1927; Bowley and Stamp 1927). Such inferences were based on apparently more precise measurements than had been possible in the nineteenth century. Nonetheless, the index numbers themselves remained indirect measurements of an "elusive quantity" (Rhodes 1936).[1] The two case studies examined in the article, Stanley Jevons's price index and the Board of Trade's cost-of-living index, show some similar challenges that economists encountered as they tried to make index numbers more precise. Simultaneously, the cases also sharpen the focus on the problems of making index numbers more *accurate*, not just precise.[2]

F. Y. Edgeworth (1925: 379) had claimed that index numbers were especially useful in those instances where changes in magnitude are not susceptible to direct measurement. Jevons 1863 had articulated this problem earlier, which was also observed by Arthur Bowley and John Maynard

1. Edmund Cecil Rhodes (1936: 142) considers index numbers to mean a particular estimation, such as a "Wholesale Price Index [which] various authorities in a particular country are all attempting in their various ways to measure." The precision he discusses is governed by "the possibility of wrong estimation of the index" on successive occasions. Thus, with greater precision the various estimations of the index begin to resemble one another, somewhat like Theodore M. Porter's (2007: 343) analogy of the "tight clustering" of bullet holes made by a marksman with a rifle. Rhodes's "elusive quantity," on the other hand, alludes to the purpose for which that index number was constructed or used, or the question that the measurer is attempting to answer. This purpose may be harder to pin down or objectively establish in any quantitative sense, and where some degree of reasoning or inference is required.

In this article, increased "precision" of index numbers refers to the elimination of the possibility of wrong estimations of the index. The elusiveness—or whether the index number estimation is "fit for purpose"—is the extent to which the index number estimation enables the measurer to capture the socioeconomic reality being examined. Thus the measurer could be similar to Porter's marksman with a rifle (index number) with a tight clustering (right estimation) but may be left with precise estimations that are not fit for purpose. In this article, the latter problem is understood to be a problem of "accuracy" rather than lack of "precision."

2. For this article, precision is understood to be a problem of estimation, whereas accuracy is understood to be a problem of the index being "fit for purpose"; see note 1 above. As Marcel Boumans (2007: 15) observes, the problem of accuracy is sociological and depends much more on qualitative knowledge rather than quantitative techniques.

Keynes.[3] British economists never really accepted that there was an "ideal formula" for index number calculation or that a single method of designing index numbers could be applicable for all purposes. Correspondingly, Alfred Marshall recommended caution about what index numbers could really reveal: "They do not lie badly, but we must analyze how badly they lie," to paraphrase Marshall.[4] He especially warned against the "mechanical interpretation" of index numbers. Thus, there was considerable concern among British economists about how to interpret the index numbers, what exactly they revealed, and how to make inferences from them.

This historiography of index number measurements reflects what Marcel Boumans (2001: 316) terms the "instrumental approach" to making rigorous measurements to achieve the "best balance between theoretical and empirical requirements." The sources examined here also demonstrate the various strategies adopted such that, as measuring instruments, index numbers "embodied the frameworks and techniques to turn the observations into measurements" (Morgan 2001: 236). While index numbers could theoretically assist in making observations of an economic phenomenon, such as the rise or fall in commodity prices or workers' wages and expenditures, making measurements from such observations (e.g., changes to the value of the monetary standard or to the cost of living of the working classes) required employing strategies such as assigning weights to aggregated elements, accounting for "the whole" by observing "the parts," and making theoretical claims about causal relationships. Bowley had compared the problem of inference to that of "describing the entire animal from a single bone."[5] Index numbers constructed from data

---

3. Bowley (1901: 217) wrote, "Index-numbers are used to measure the change in some quantity which we cannot observe directly, which we know to have a definite influence on many other quantities which we can so observe." Similarly, Keynes (1921: 212) wrote, "It has not been clear whether index numbers really represent measures of a composite quantity or whether they are probable estimates of the value of a single quantity formed by combining a number of independent approximations towards the value of this quantity."

4. Marshall's original statement is "I think that in fact [index numbers] do not lie very badly, but in order to know how badly they lie we must analyse" (Marshall 1996: 734; Marshall to Pierson, January 20, 1903, in Marshall 1996).

5. Bowley's (1906: 541) entire statement read as follows: "Purely arithmetical work is limited to the tabulation of exact records, [where] no approximation or interpolation is necessary, and where statistics becomes only another name for accountancy; whereas the application of mathematical principles makes it possible to measure the inaccessible, to describe the animal from the single bone, to make firm observations from a shifting base, to dispense with the fixed meridian which the base practice of industrial and official needs obscures." J. E. Cairnes (1862: chap. 3) had made a similar observation earlier in the context of economic reasoning.

such as wages, consumer expenditure, or commodity prices were not based on direct observations by those constructing the index. As Thomas Stapleford (2012) suggests, many of these "observations" are derived from self-reported data by businesses or households over which the economists and statisticians themselves had little control. This posed challenges to economists, who had to account for observational vagaries when making inferences from index numbers. Particular measurement strategies could therefore potentially amplify or dampen the "inferential distance," as Kevin D. Hoover and Michael E. Dowell (2001: 139) term it, that is, the gap between some sort of a phenomenon being measured (if it existed) and its measurement.

But, as this article argues, economists grappled with multiple inferential gaps simultaneously in order to make inferences from index numbers. Some of these gaps were due to the theoretical frameworks that economists used to set up the hypothesis about the phenomena, others stemmed from the specific measurement strategies they employed. Here, the choice of theory or measurement strategy may have a bearing on the precision of the index number, that is, the right estimation given the data and causal assumptions. For instance, Jevons's price index was based on the causal link between the value of gold and the commodity prices as specified by the quantity theory of money. The cost-of-living index, on the other hand, was based on the purchasing power of money theory. Both indices used a selection of commodities whose prices were used to make up the index, leaving out other commodities from the basket. In the case of the cost-of-living index, weights were assigned to the data in a manner that was reasoned to reflect how they were consumed. These decisions about the theoretical frameworks and measurement strategies set up a series of inferential gaps that the economists had to bridge in the process of reasoning (sections 1 and 2).

However, in the manner in which their contemporaries reacted to their measurements, economists also had to contend with inferential gaps that were ideological or political in nature. Economists operated within an ecology composed of individuals and institutions interested in their measurements and what the measurements revealed about a social condition or economic phenomenon. In the case of the cost-of-living index, a fairly heterogeneous group of people, including politicians and trade unions in addition to economists working within state bureaucracies, were interested in the measurements of prices, wages, and expenditures. These groups introduced their own political and ideological persuasions into the interpreta tion of the measurements and the inferences that could be made as a consequence. In the example discussed here (section 3), some groups simply ignored the index numbers of the economists and made alternative inferences using individual commodity prices that suited their political propaganda. We can see how the act of making inferences was entangled with the political economy of the period. Operating within such an ecology, the economists encountered inferential gaps that were vastly different from those stemming from the choice of theory or measurement strategy. Such gaps sharpen the focus on the problem of accuracy: what did the index number really capture about, say, the deterioration of the monetary standard or the living conditions of the working classes?

Bridging all these inferential gaps meant reconciling these simultaneous cognitive influences, whether theoretical, ideological, or experiential. Inferential gaps need not be limited to the "distance" between the measurement and the phenomenon that Hoover and Dowell (2001) described, especially if it is not really clear what the "phenomenon" actually is. There was no general "the price level" or "the cost of living" that was out there to be measured. These quantities were purely instrumental in that sense; the measurement instrument defined the "cost of living" in a particular way. Ultimately, the problem of inference could be specified in terms of the extent to which the index numbers were fit for purpose, distinct from how precisely they measured economic quantities such as changes in prices, wages, or expenditure. Did the index numbers help answer the questions that had prompted the measurements to be made in the first place? Could they meet the institutional objectives underlying the measurements? Such questions, in addition to particular measurement strategies, determined the closeness of the inferential distances, in terms of how well index numbers achieved their ultimate purpose. In sum, making inferences was not just a heuristic process (one that eliminated gaps by getting the estimations right) but a cognitive one as well (one that constituents of the broader ecology could accept as being "fit for purpose").

1. Jevons and the Price Index

The case of Jevons's price index of 1863 serves as an entry point to consider the relationship between theoretical frameworks, measurements, and inferences. The manner in which Jevons constructed his index numbers illustrates at least two distinct inferential gaps. The first is the theoretical basis for using commodity prices to measure the depreciation of gold (as specified by the quantity theory of money); the second was the use of a measuring instrument that could reliably isolate the relative changes in price levels (as specified by his theory of index number measurements). Both elements were important to Jevons in terms of making inferences. Here the manner in which he framed the two questions—or specified his hypotheses—was crucially important. As the following narrative shows, his use of the quantity theory to measure the commodity prices to infer changes in the value of gold was not disputed by his contemporaries. However, his use of index number measurements to infer that gold had depreciated by a measurable amount did come under some criticism. Making reliable inferences—or inferences that were fit for purpose— therefore involved addressing multiple inferential gaps.

As an assayer at the Royal Mint in Sydney, Australia (1854–59), Jevons had developed a keen interest in gold and its function as a monetary standard. Consequently, he observed the increases in the overall amount of gold available as a result of new discoveries and began to study its effect on the political economy of the British Empire (Steer 2016). Jevons followed the debates about the probable link between gold discoveries and the value of gold, especially in Michel Chevalier's (1859) writings about this issue. On his return to Britain, he compiled tables of monthly prices and was "struck by the enormous rise in prices" of commodities in 1853 and the possibility of "permanent rise in prices" as a consequence of the increased amount of gold available (Jevons 1863: 1–2). This convinced him that there was a link between new discoveries of gold in Australia and North America, the resultant fall in the value of gold, and the corresponding rise in commodity prices. He remained unconvinced by the conclusions of his contemporaries such as William Newmarch and John Ramsay MacCulloch that "rapid extension of trade and wealth" might lead to the "absorption of new supplies of gold without the depreciation in its value" (Jevons 1863: 1).[6]

Jevons reasoned that making reliable inferences about the depreciating value of gold depended on precise measurements of the changes in commodity prices and argued that a price index was capable of isolating the relative changes in their price levels. He could then use these measurements to make inferences about gold depreciation. As Sandra Peart (1996:

---

6. William Newmarch (1820–1882) was an economist who compiled the *Economist* price index first published in 1863. James Ramsay McCulloch (1789–1864) was a political economist who lobbied for regular publication of economic statistics.

176) argues, Jevons sought to establish the "fact" of depreciation of gold (the inferential question) using a "spectacular array of data" (prices). Jevons (1863) set out the "enormous, general and permanent" rise of commodity prices caused by the fall in the "standard of value," that is, the value of gold. To do this, he isolated the changes in comparative values to ascertain which side of the exchange value had changed. He invoked the analogy of the balance in ascertaining the circumstances affecting the demand and supply just as "a balance may be disturbed by an upward or downward force applied to either arm" (Jevons 1863: 3).[7] Thus on one arm of Jevon's balance is the price of gold (the monetary standard) and on the other arm are arrayed the prices of individual commodities that gold could be exchanged for. He explained that the fall in the price of gold signifies that there is a higher probability it was due to the changes in the supply of gold rather than the "separate and concurring causes" affecting the demand and supply of commodities (4). Jevons referred to "probabilities" in order to discriminate between the "permanent and temporary" fluctuations of prices.[8] He used the wholesale price statistics reported in the *Economist* to develop his ideas about secular price trends. His method of comparing the ratio of price in a given year was highly sensitive to the selection of a "datum line" (or base year). Jevons acknowledged that his method (using geometric means) was "partly the same as previously used by Mr. Newmarch" (using arithmetic means) and based on the prices of thirty-nine commodities published by the *Economist* between 1845 and 1862. He also explained that index numbers differed from calculating percentage changes in prices by discriminating between "temporary fluctuations" (inflation) and more "permanent fluctuations" (trends).

Jevons's (1865: 308) inferences about the depreciation of gold were unequivocal: "Gold discoveries caused [the secular] rise of prices," he claimed at the meeting of the Royal Statistical Society in May 1865. The discovery of gold deposits, according to him, also "neutralized [any] fall in prices which may have been expected from the continuous progress of invention and production" (309). However, he was cagey about the extent of depreciation he observed: "The real permanent rise due to the gold

7. For other applications of Jevons's balance, see Maas 2001.

8. Jevons explains how "probabilities" show that it is "more likely" that price change should have been on the "side of gold" rather than on the "side" of commodities because one cause affecting gold would suffice to explain the change; it would require several separate but concurring causes to explain commodity price changes. The odds of the single cause are higher than the alternative (Jevons 1863: 3).

discoveries is doubtless something between 11 percent or probably nearer the higher limit of 21 [percent]" (309). This was a considerable range of values, which Jevons later revised in 1869. In his letter to the *Economist*, he reasserted "with utmost confidence that a real rise of prices, to the extent of 18 per cent as measured by 50 commodities has been established since the year 1849. This is an undoubted depreciation of gold because it represents a real diminution in the general purchasing power of gold" (Jevons 1869: 531).

Jevons's inferences need to be considered within the broader discussions about depreciating gold values and index number measurements. Walter Bagehot, who was Jevons's contemporary and became the *Economist*'s chief editor in 1861, understood the analytic value of numerical information but also its limitations. It was Bagehot more than James Wilson, the newspaper's founder, who was able to work toward realizing Wilson's (1843: 15) vision of using numbers to form the groundwork of "reasonings, opinions and actions of the economist, the legislator, the merchant, or the trader." This aspect is certainly visible in the publication of the *Economist* price index from 1863 on. The price index published by the newspaper was aimed at all their different groups of readers who were interested in the changes in commodity prices in conjunction with the changes to the monetary standard. Initially, the *Economist*, using Newmarch's methods, published individual price indices for each of twenty-two separate commodities, rather than a composite index for a basket of commodities. When the newspaper did publish a "Total Index Number" for a basket of commodities in its March 13, 1869, issue, this composite number was an arithmetic sum of the price indices of the twenty-two commodities for a given year. The *Economist* (1869: 44) claimed that by combining the price indices of commodities in this fashion, it "eliminated the special influence" on each of the individual commodities and instead reflected the "influence of the general causes to have affected all commodities." Alongside this price index was the table showing an index of "Total Note Circulation" in Britain. Only very approximate inferences could be drawn from this data, if at all, about the relative changes between the commodity prices listed and the value of the monetary standard (gold).

To many of Jevons's other contemporaries, the question of determining the probable fall in the value of gold and the related rise in commodity prices was equally important given that gold was the monetary standard for all practical purposes. In Richard Cobden's preface to his translation of Chevalier's thesis, he outlined the concern for the changes in value of gold, which were related to the consequent "amount of currency" in circulation and the erosion in the underlying basis for contracts of exchange, including the determination of "commercial profits, wages, domestic relations of society, payment of national debt and provision of national expenditure" (Cobden 1859: 3–4).[9] He was also greatly concerned that the fall in the value of gold and the consequent rise in commodity prices would lead to an "expansion of credit, increase in speculation," and the shortening of trade cycles; "instead of a crisis visiting the commercial world once in each decade, its return might be expected every five years" (7–8). Cobden, like Jevons, was also unpersuaded by the conclusions of Newmarch that new gold discoveries did not cause a rise in commodity prices.

Reactions to Jevons's inferences illustrate the problem of multiple inferential gaps mentioned earlier. As Peart (2001: 261) observed, "Jevons' contemporaries for the most part accepted the causal [quantity theory] framework" that he used for this project. In this context, and to paraphrase Peart, where Jevons operated within an "established" theoretical framework like quantity theory, his inferences met with relative success. But where the inferences were based on a theoretically less familiar framework, such as his use of index numbers to isolate the effect of price levels, his inferences were met with greater resistance. In other words, many contemporaries did not challenge his inference that the rise in commodity prices was the result of the depreciation of gold (first inferential gap). But many economists such as J. E. Cairnes, Étienne Laspeyres, and Edgeworth criticized his price index using a "method of means" to establish the extent of depreciation in any reliable manner (Edgeworth 1883; Peart 2001: 261–63). Others such as T. C. Leslie "threw doubt upon all [Jevons's] conclusions" (Jevons 1869: 531), criticizing his entire approach as a "chimerical exercise" (Peart 2001: 261). Using index numbers to get at the extent of depreciation is an example of another inferential gap that Jevons faced.

Notwithstanding the criticism he received from Leslie or Cairnes, many others did not challenge Jevons's method of index number measurements or their usefulness in allowing an observer to make inferences about the depreciation of gold. "Therefore, a depreciation of gold [can be] made out, but there are [important] objections to the conclusions from the figures," claimed the *Economist* (1872: 1580) while discussing Jevons's

9. Richard Cobden (1804–1865) was a manufacturer, a politician, and a tireless promoter of free trade ideas. He worked with Michel Chevalier (1806–1879), the French engineer, statesman, economist, and free market liberal, to negotiate the 1860 bilateral free trade treaty between Britain and France.

measurements. These "objections" concerned the extent of depreciation measured by the index numbers and the use of wholesale rather than retail prices (problem of precision). The availability of relevant price data to make more precise measurements was an institutional issue, one that was only addressed once the Board of Trade put into place an infrastructure to conduct surveys of retail prices in the early 1900s. Both Augustus Sauerbeck (1893), whose method of constructing price indices was used later by the Board of Trade, and a committee of economists working within the British Association for the Advancement of Science (BAAS), who sought to refine the theoretical foundations in order to increase the precision of measurements of the value of the monetary standard, continued to promote the use of index numbers in the 1880s and 1890s (Edgeworth et al. 1888). Meanwhile, Bagehot cautioned economists against using numbers (or "statistics") as a substitute for distinct arguments or inferences: "Political economy is in danger of dissolving into statistics" (quoted in Edwards 1993).[10]

Jevons's strategy of using index numbers to address the question of depreciating gold thus eventually gained greater traction despite early criticism. Following Jevons, economists and statisticians continued to wrestle with the theoretical and practical issues around constructing index numbers to measure changes in the value of the monetary standard. Despite his criticism of Jevons's method of using "means," Edgeworth chaired the BAAS committee of economists and statisticians that investigated ways to make index numbers more suitable in measuring the variations in the value of the monetary standard.[11] This committee, which included Alfred Marshall, Robert Giffen, and Henry Sidgwick among others, made important observations about the theoretical and practical issues involved in constructing index numbers. Chiefly, their report observed that the ideal theoretical approach would be to "distinguish analytically the different purposes which may be subserved by constructing a measure of the change in the value of money and then to show what formula, what particular mode of combining the statistical data is appropriate for each purpose" (Edgeworth et al. 1888: 247). In practice though, the report stated, it seemed "useless to [specify] distinct formulae if in the present state of statistics the numerical data [available] to fill in these for-

10. "Statistics" here refers to numerical data.

11. The committee's first report was published in 1888 and was followed by a series of papers written by Edgeworth, Robert Giffen, and others. An important discussion included selecting an appropriate basket of commodities selected whose prices were used in the construction of the index (Edgeworth et al. 1888).

mulae are deficient" (249). A broad consensus among these economists was that if index numbers were to be used to study an economic phenomenon such as depreciation in the monetary standard, they would need to take into account the "requirements of those for whose use the apparatus is principally designed." In other words, they concluded that index numbers needed to be fit for purpose, not necessarily to approach a theoretical ideal but to be of practical value to those who actually used them. When the Board of Trade constructed its own price index in 1903, it repurposed some of these methods to suit its own specific requirements. Along the way, the board also addressed the issue of paucity of information that had bothered the BAAS committee.

Jevons introduced a new way of reasoning into economics, a "British style of science" for unraveling laws by building mechanical analogies, as Harro Maas (2005: 22) has argued. The use of mechanical analogies (the balancing arm) as tools for reasoning is evident in his work on index numbers. Jevons's work in formal logic, his insistence on using mathematics to make economics a science, is what made his use of index numbers an important tool and method to address the multiple inferential gaps mentioned at the beginning of this section. Jevons's "material mechanism" set the tone for successive generations of work on index numbers by the BAAS and within the Board of Trade. The inferential gap sought to be bridged by measurements (e.g., index numbers to reveal the extent of price change) was distinct from the inferential gap resulting from the specification of the economic phenomenon (e.g., commodity prices could reveal the depreciation of the monetary standard). The bridging of such gaps depended on the mathematical logic underlying the index numbers, as Jevons successfully demonstrated. But was this new mathematical approach to economic data sufficient in making purposeful inferences using other index numbers? The following case of the cost-of-living index examines this question by considering the effect that politics had on making inferences from economic measurements.

2. Board of Trade and the Cost-of-Living Index

Between ca. 1880 and 1920 British government departments, such as the Board of Trade, made significant advances in establishing the infrastructure for data collection on economic and social activity, alongside continual theoretical improvements to constructing index numbers. This process is visible in the case of the cost-of-living indices (COLI) that were constructed to address the cost-of-living problem at the forefront of public debate in late Victorian and Edwardian Britain.[12] The case of the COLI illustrates the problem of multiple inferential gaps from a different perspective compared to Jevons's price index. In this section and the next, I show how economists and statisticians had to contend with inferential issues that were also ideological and political in nature. The theoretical frameworks and measurement strategies adopted by economists collided with the political ideologies shaping competing inferences using Board of Trade statistics.

The construction of the COLI was a joint product of theoretical developments in the construction and application of index numbers and the manner in which the British state took responsibility for the collection and publication of economic statistics. The Board of Trade economists repurposed the index number method used by Jevons and Sauerbeck to address a rather different question about cost of living. Although the COLI retained a significant proportion of the framework of the earlier price indices, different theoretical elements (e.g., purchasing power theory) were introduced into the framework to make these measurements more relevant for the government's purpose. Further, there was a broader ecology of interested groups seeking to use the official data to frame their own inferences about the cost of living. These interested groups included government ministers, politicians representing large working-class constituencies, trade unions and labor associations, economists, public intellectuals, and so forth. The inferential challenges and gaps in this broader political and social context were thus different in the context of COLI compared to those that Jevons had faced.

The statistical data that made up the COLI became rhetorical devices for framing a political debate inasmuch as they formed part of the mea-

---

12. The term *cost-of-living problem* is used in this section to refer to a particular issue of the gap between income and expenditure experienced by a specific section of the population that had access to wage income. It does not refer to the broader political debates on the condition of the poor or unemployed, or to the condition of those with precarious incomes such as in the "sweated" trades. Although Davidson 1985 includes the cost-of-living index issue within his broader definition of the "labour problem," the income-expenditure gap was initially narrowly framed in 1889 in the context of "working men's expenditure"; see "Returns of Expenditure by Working Men," 1889, Cmd 5861, *British Parliamentary Papers* (hereafter cited as *BPP*). To contemporaries like Charles Booth interested in issues of poverty, the problem of labor included broader conditions of employment including both the organization and the remuneration of work, which were not addressed by these income-expenditure debates. In this section, therefore, the cost-of-living problem is understood to be narrower in scope than the broader "labour problem" and refers only to the specific quantities of "wage rates," "household expenditure," and "prices" as studied by the successive Board of Trade reports cited here.

surements available to the state. Further, the construction of the COLI involved the participation of economists and statisticians working within the state bureaucracy, each adding their own political flavor into the mix. Giffen, who was in charge of the Board of Trade statistics throughout 1876–97, wrote that political discussions were increasingly centered on the question of changes in the rate of "material progress." His assessment was that there was "much *prima facie* evidence material prosperity may not have been so great" in the 1870s and 1880s compared with earlier periods (Giffen 1888: 806). However, the statistical tools to go beyond prima facie analysis were not available to successive governments, who found themselves increasingly under pressure to establish what was actually going on. "Statistics" at the time were what Bowley termed "arithmetical statistics," being tabulations from records. By the early twentieth century, Bowley (1906: 548) would claim that the use of index numbers had become one of the most important developments in official statistics, which sought to apply mathematical rigor to arithmetical data. However, he also advised caution when using "mathematical statistics" to make inferences, as he reckoned them to "furnish us with [nothing more than] a microscope to observe differences blurred to the naked eye of arithmetic" (541). This mathematical or "technical" approach in official statistics became especially visible after the arrival of Hubert Llewelyn-Smith in the Labour Department of the Board of Trade. Davidson (1985) has categorized Llewelyn-Smith as "progressive," in contrast to Giffen, whom he categorized as "conservative."

Thus, the growing consciousness of the concept of the cost of living, and a social obligation to maintain some minimum standard of living for the working classes, resulted in a tangible response in the form of a state "machinery" to gather social intelligence and statistics (Wright 1984: 158; Davidson 1985: 79; Agar 2003: 85–87). This is visible in the establishment of the Labour Statistical Bureau in 1886 within the Board of Trade. The board recruited statisticians and economists, including Bowley and Henry Fountain (a career bureaucrat who at the time worked as a statistician in the Labour Department). Llewelyn-Smith, Bowley, and Fountain were responsible for embedding the use of index numbers specifically to examine the question of cost of living by the early 1900s. The bureau, which later became the Labour Department in 1893, thus saw an influx of a "new class" of workers in the form of labor investigators and statisticians at junior levels, who were deployed for the accumulation, collation, and other purely "mechanical" work of producing statistical information

(Davidson 1985: 104–8). The bureau's activities resulted in considerable expansion of its output, with nearly half of its investigative resources devoted to two areas relevant here: estimating wage rates and earnings, and expenditure and cost of living (131).[13]

Government economists were keenly aware that establishing any meaningful relationship between the cost of living and wages[14] was not possible until a reasonably precise measure of retail prices and consumption expenditure was available (Giffen 1903: 593–96; Bowley 1919). In the decade before the First World War there were important developments made in this direction, culminating with the construction of the first official cost-of-living index for the UK. Economic historians have seen this as an "incomplete" development due to the various conceptual, logistical, and measurement problems involved (Wright 1984: 155; Searle 2015). Bowley himself considered the term *cost of living* to be "indefinite" or imprecisely expressing what it actually measured. He reckoned that referring to it as "cost of maintaining a defined standard by a defined family" to be more explicit instead (Bowley 1919: 343). In many ways, Bowley's comment underscores the notion that the cost-of-living index is "instrumental" in the sense that the thing you measure only comes into existence because of the measurement procedure.[15]

Between 1903 and 1914 the Board of Trade, with Bowley's involvement as a "statistical investigator" (Davidson 1985: 121), developed methods to establish the relationship between wages and expenditure in the form of COLI. The board's 1903 *Memoranda, Statistical Tables, and Charts* and the *Report on Wholesale and Retail Prices* (both containing a new price index) were followed by successive surveys of household food budgets, rents, and prices in 1904–5. An initial report, the 1908 *Cost of Living of*

13. This proportion varies substantially between 1886 and 1914. The rest of the bureau's resources were spread across other areas of investigations, including trade unionism, industrial unrest, unemployment, and overseas labor statistics.

14. The term *wages* is used in several ways in the source material consulted here. Various Board of Trade reports use "wage rates" from select occupations, whereas economic historians writing about COLI, such as Rebecca Searle (2015), refer to "real wages." Others such as J. F. Wright (1984), when discussing wages, also refer to household budgets, which were recorded by government surveys. Occasionally, Board of Trade reports mention "working-class incomes" but nonetheless make it clear that board surveys did not "give results of an enquiry into earnings, simply comparisons of standard rates of wages" ("Cost of Living of the Working Classes: Report of an Enquiry by the Board of Trade," 1908, Cmd 3864, 323, *BPP*). The generic term *wages* used in the section includes all these different meanings; where possible, the original term in the source material is retained.

15. I am indebted to Harro Maas for pointing this out to me.

the Working Class, was followed by another cost-of-living report in 1913. This latter report formed the basis of the COLI that the board continued to publish virtually unaltered between 1914 and 1947 (Wright 1984: 155; Searle 2015: 148). With the COLI, index numbers had become institutionalized within the British state bureaucracy.

The Labour Department statisticians sought to make its first price index published in 1903 theoretically distinct to the price indices of Jevons, Sauerbeck, and the BAAS committee. Explaining this difference, Fountain pointed out that the earlier price indices were based on the quantity theory of money. In contrast, the Board of Trade price index was to be based on the theory of the purchasing power of money. In the note, Fountain sets out the fundamental measurement and inferential problems in some detail. According to him, the Labour Department sought to establish the extent to which consumers "pay" for changes in the monetary standard by changing their consumption habits (first inferential gap). This meant establishing a "consumption standard," which could be measurable, was applicable to all consumers, and capable of being measured at regular intervals (second inferential gap).[16] These multiple inferential gaps stemming from various theoretical and empirical issues—in terms of the cause of the phenomenon and how its measurement could be made—were similar to the inferential issues that Jevons dealt with.

Between the two inferential gaps, the second more "practical" issue of measurement was recognized as a more intractable problem: how to obtain a measure of the "considerable difference in the amount of the commodities purchased for a given amount of gold (the monetary standard)."[17] Fountain outlined this issue as follows:

> The theoretical basis of the consumption standard is the proposition that the true measure in the change of the value of money is the change in the amount of gold that must be paid by consumers throughout the country for all commodities in their finished state consumed by them per unit of time. In practice, of course, the only method of approximating to this ideal measure is the method of sample. No trustworthy figures being available for the retail prices of the commodities actually consumed, it is usual to take certain raw materials as typical of these

16. Board of Trade, "Report on Wholesale and Retail Prices in the United Kingdom in 1902," 1903, No. 321, Appendix II, 431–2, *BPP*. This second inferential gap refers to the problem of direct observation that Stapleford 2012 has described.

17. The measurement problems are explained with some detail in Board of Trade, "Report on Wholesale and Retail Prices in the United Kingdom in 1902," Appendix II, 430.

commodities and to assume that, roughly speaking, the changes in the prices of these raw materials . . . over relatively long periods of time, afford a fair measure of these changes.[18]

There were thus multiple inferential gaps that needed bridging, such as relating price changes to consumption habits and making measurements of a defined consumption standard such that changes to that standard reliably indicated changes in consumption habits. The price index could provide a measure of changes in prices, but its "practical" effect on consumption could be discerned only through a composite index number (incorporating both consumption and prices) rather than just a price index that did not necessarily account for changes in consumption.[19] Both components (prices and consumption) were critical in addressing the bigger cost-of-living problem, which at the time was framed as working-class households facing an increasing gulf between their wages and expenditure. There was also a general claim made in public debates that this gulf had widened since the 1870s. This last point led to yet another inferential issue, which was to measure the changes in wages to compare against the expenditure or consumption standard. The measurement solution was to use an index of "wage rates" in select occupations that would provide some estimates of the income-expenditure gap at the heart of the cost-of-living problem.

While all these theoretical and empirical challenges were complex, the practical problems of collecting the necessary data were equally knotty. Under Giffen's direction the Labour Bureau had, in the late nineteenth century, attempted to "procure statistics of the distribution of the expenditure of working class incomes."[20] This first survey of household expenditure in 1887 saw 730 schedules sent out to "selected workmen, trade union officials and [local and regional co-operatives]" seeking information on household incomes and expenditure. The response was a dismal thirty-six replies, making this endeavor "disappointing" and of little practical use

18. Fountain's note appears as a part of appendix 2 of the Board of Trade's 1903 report. His statement is on page 432.

19. Fisher ([1911] 1922: 194–96), alluding to the later versions of the Board of Trade index numbers, included a more generalized discussion of this measurement problem: "Corresponding to changes in individual prices there will be changes in the quantity of the given commodity [which] introduces a new complication [in the construction of an index number of prices]." The reference to Board of Trade index numbers appears on page 204.

20. This attempt at data collection was published as an official report in "Returns of Expenditure by Working Men," 3

(Higgs 1893: 257).[21] The 1903 statistical estimates of working-class expenditure were based on another survey of 286 household budget estimates with a skew toward the London area with 136 households and the balance, 150 households, scattered across other parts of the UK. The board improved this coverage significantly for the 1904–5 household expenditure surveys and reported data for an additional 1,808 households, thereby extending the survey beyond London and the southeast.[22] The board acknowledged that its survey data did not "represent in their exact proportions the different grades of working-class incomes," as the "higher range incomes [were] unduly represented [compared to] those belonging to the unskilled labouring classes."[23]

In 1908, the board sought to "complete and supplement" its cost-of-living inquiry, by adding to the "incomplete information" on expenditure data about accommodation and fuel costs as well as retail prices of food items "most commonly paid for by the working classes."[24] This 1908 survey further sought to make international comparisons about cost of living by incorporating with its domestic data information about working-class conditions in "foreign countries," such as France and Germany. All these series of surveys between 1903 and 1908 set the stage for the board to eventually publish the cost-of-living statistics as index numbers from 1914 on through its publication, the *Labour Gazette* (Searle 2015: 148; Wright 1984: 155; Davidson 1985).[25]

Prior to the 1903 *Report on Wholesale and Retail Prices*, the board had periodically published "Miscellaneous Statistics of the United Kingdom." This contained the (wholesale) prices of various articles traced over a quarter of a century from 1855 on. After the discontinuation of the "Miscellaneous Statistics" series, there had been no official publications of such data on prices, although *Statistical Abstracts of the United Kingdom*

21. The details of the expenditure survey are in "Returns of Expenditure by Working Men," 4.

22. "Second Series of Memoranda, Statistical Tables and Charts prepared in the Board of Trade with reference to various matters bearing on British and Foreign Trade and Industrial Conditions," 1905, Cmd 2337, 19, *BPP*.

23. "Second Series of Memoranda," 20. Bowley's notebook records his comments on such data as he explains that the purpose of the "Index of Average Weekly Wages" was not to measure accurately and completely the changes in average wages or earnings on any particular definition but "to give an indication of the general movement of wage-rates" (COLL MISC 0772/B7, LSE Archives and Special Collections).

24. This was published officially as "Cost of Living of the Working Classes: Report of an Enquiry by the Board of Trade," 1908, Cmd 3864, 323, *BPP*.

25. In practice, the construction of the 1914 COLI was amended somewhat in 1919, and it was this series that continued until 1947.

contained the "average declared values" of individual commodities imported and exported.[26] The price information reported in the 1903 report was compiled from numerous "official reports" supplemented by "direct inquiries" and "unofficial records" to bring them up to date beyond the "Miscellaneous Statistics" series. In addition to the "declared values" of imports and exports, the board also used "contract prices of certain articles" from the records of St. Thomas', Greenwich, and Bethlehem Royal Hospitals as well as other state institutions such as the asylums of the London County Councils.

The board also assembled "market prices," which were just as flimsy as those from the official sources, being based on published "average" prices in the *London Gazette* for commodities such as corn (i.e., wheat, barley, and other grains). The *Gazette* prices incorporated prices of grain sold at certain market towns in England and Wales, and the *Dublin Gazette* became the source for grain sold at the Dublin Corn Exchange. Official prices for "fat cattle" were also available, as recording these data was a statutory requirement under the Markets and Fairs (Weighing of Cattle) Act 1891. Prices of manufactured items involving metals (both ferrous, nonferrous, and precious) as well as prices for textiles (wool and cotton) were obtained through various industry associations, industrial concerns, and chambers of commerce. Prices for coal and iron were "ascertained by accountants in different districts used for the determination of wages." A combination of a variety of sources thus formed the basis for prices of commodities "purchased in bulk," that is, wholesale prices for the 1903 price index. The 1903 prices report had little information about retail prices, and those that were reported were almost entirely for London, with a few examples of prices for bread from Edinburgh, Dublin, or the "other English and Scottish provincial towns."

While much of the price data in the 1903 report was based on historical information already available to the board, later reports contained data that were more purpose-built. The board's 1913 *Cost of Living of the Working Classes Report* extended the surveys conducted since 1903 and proposed a twofold objective. The report compared the "relative levels of rents, retail prices and rates of wages in selective towns" to "ascertain the

26. Board of Trade, "Report on Wholesale and Retail Prices in the United Kingdom in 1902," Appendix II, 426. The "Miscellaneous Statistics" series published since the 1830s was overshadowed with the various Statistical Abstracts that were compiled after 1854, leading Giffen to write about the "inattention" given to the series as a whole (quoted in "Miscellaneous Statistics of the United Kingdom" 1879).

amount of change in rents, prices and wages between 1905 and 1912" (406). This was to be achieved using a composite index number, with London as the base for the indices, and included data on rents and rates for "working class dwellings," prices paid for food and coal (fuel), and "rates of wages" in select occupations (400). The retail price index numbers were obtained by applying to the price data a series of weights based on the surveys of "working class expenditure" in 1904–5 (as outlined above). A similar "index number of rents" was calculated, with the board claiming.to secure data in 1912 "as far as possible from the same sources as in 1905." These data on rents and accommodation, which included information on rates and charges for water, were obtained from "officials of local authorities, surveyors of taxes, house owners, and agents," and by "house to house enquiry." Similarly, retail food prices and the price of coal were collected as far as possible from "retailers who supplied information in 1905." These two indices were combined into a composite index in the ratio of 1:4 each for the rental and price index. There were the same proportions applied when the board had published an earlier iteration of the COLI in 1908.

Price indices could probably be more precisely estimated in 1908 compared with 1888 given the improvements in the quality of the data available to the Board of Trade. Nonetheless, the inferential challenges surrounding COLI transcended the theoretical and practical measurement issues discussed above and became entangled in political rhetoric, as the next section shows.

3. Politics of Inferences

The framers of the COLI sought to establish whether relative changes in wages of the working classes, commodity prices, and their consumption patterns led to a deteriorating standard of living. The working classes, or rather those who claimed to speak on their behalf, were keen to demonstrate that individual lived experiences were encumbered by a widening gap between wages and commodity prices and that this gap was experienced by large sections of the British population. These subtle but crucial differences in aims meant that inferences made by economists using the COLI failed to gather traction with the broader audiences and were generally rejected by others. As shown in this section, individuals arrayed along the political spectrum drew their own inferences using the Board of Trade data to frame their respective political positions. These inferential challenges were substantially different compared with those that arose from the theoretical frameworks and measurement strategies discussed in the previous sections.

Index numbers were relatively uncommon in the public sphere even by the early 1900s, and their use beyond professional economists and statisticians was limited. Therefore, public commentators tended to focus on individual pieces of data (e.g., the prices of single commodities) to challenge the inferences drawn by the Board of Trade economists based on the COLI. Bowley (1920) summed up the problem of how the COLI measurements were seemingly at odds with widely held perceptions about living standards when he observed that a vast majority of adults, who since 1896 had experienced rising prices, were "naturally not impressed by statisticians (including myself) that they were better off than their fathers had been" (20). Such inferences using the COLI measurements, he reckoned, did not reconcile with "superficial observations" that increased commodity prices had made people worse off, never mind the fact that "as money incomes rose, prices rose as much" (Bowley 1937: 94–95, 30). Bowley (1903: 303) despaired that "many writers and speakers are making use of [numerical data] to support inconsistent and confusing conclusions." In other words, he implied that incorrect inferences were being made using only raw data points rather than accepting the correct inferences using the composite index number measurements that statisticians had assembled.

But the so-called superficial observations did matter to the majority of the working-class British whose experience of commodity prices was that they had only risen during their lifetime, and any suggestion that they were "better off" was far-fetched. This issue of rising commodity prices was highly visible in the 1906 and 1910 general elections, where the cost-of-living question featured quite prominently. Political parties made cunning use of "statistics" (i.e., numerical data) to frame the issue in a particular way, as the two political posters shown here demonstrate (see figs. 1 and 2). The posters, each issued by the two largest political parties at the time of the general elections, mention "cost of living" and "cheap food" and present selective information from official data collected as part of the Board of Trade's cost-of-living surveys. Neither poster uses the index numbers, and both of them present prices of commodities loaded with political and cultural symbolism (tea, bread, and meat) and accuse rival political groups of promoting economic policies that result in increased

Figure 1 Liberal Party poster, ca. 1905.

Source: LSE Digital Library: Political and Tariff Reform Posters, COLL MISC 0519/37.

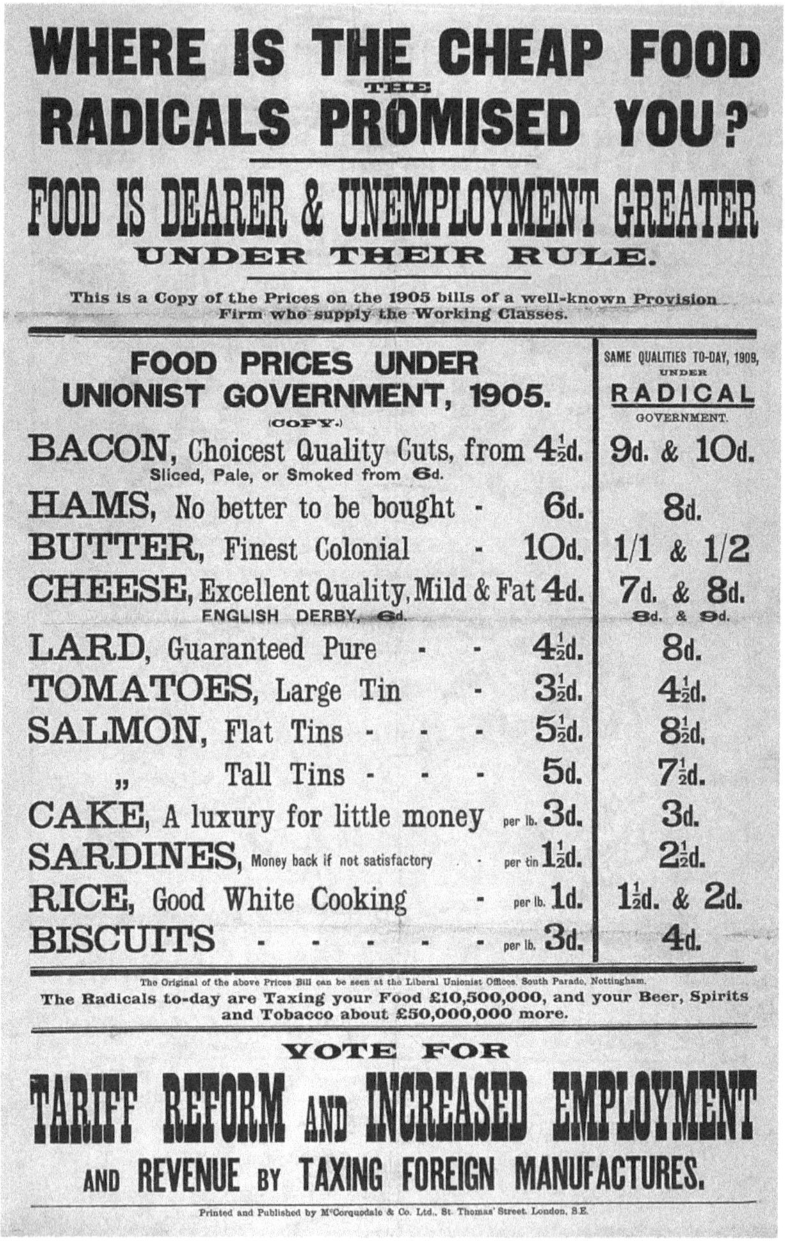

Figure 2 Unionist (Tory) Party poster, ca. 1909.
Source: LSE Digital Library: Political and Tariff Reform Posters, COLL MISC 0519/66.

cost of living, as implied by rising commodity prices.[27] The inference drawn in both posters is that commodity prices increased more than wages, thereby increasing the cost of living. Many such inferences about whether the working classes were actually better or worse off were often made using superficial comparison of commodity prices (as Bowley termed it). While government statisticians used the index numbers to make inferences with statistical techniques, political groups based their inferences on numerical data to promote a specific rhetoric. Both groups were reasoning from data in their own particular way. As James Thompson (2007: 178) suggests, the Edwardian political culture reveals the increasing "visibility, scale and visuality of pictorial propaganda." In addition to this intersection of visual and political cultures, the posters reveal the increasing use of statistics (i.e., numerical data) in shaping public debate. In this context, inferences were shaped by political ideology and lived experience as much as they were based on index numbers. The contrast between Bowley's inferential methods based on index numbers and the political inferences using raw data are palpable.

Such politics of making inferences poses an important issue from the history of inference perspective. Usually, there existed a broad ecology of groups and individuals who were interested in the production of economic measurements and in the inferences made from them. Measurements did not, perforce, lead to uncontested inferences about a social phenomenon, be it the depreciating value of the monetary standard or the deteriorating standard of living. In the case studies examined in this article, although social statistics and index numbers became institutionalized, inferences using these measurements (i.e., reasoning on the basis of measurements) remained a function of who was making the inference and for what purpose. Statistical measurements had to answer specific questions of interest to various groups, not just result in precise measurements. Not only did economic issues become politicized, but the process of inference making itself was mired in the political economy of the period. The inferential gaps resulting from such politics are important in understanding the history of inference just as inferential issues stemming from the theoretical frameworks and measurement strategies. Inference making was only partially conjoined with the theoretical construction of the measuring instrument.

---

27. Although the two posters in figures 1 and 2 do not mention bread, there are other posters that focus on the price of bread; see Political and Tariff Reform Posters, LSE Digital Collection, digital.library.lse.ac.uk/collections/posters/politicalandtariffreform#images. There are several pictures and posters of Joseph Chamberlain holding loaves of bread during political meetings on tariff reform that politicize its price and the issue of cost of living; see Trentmann 2008: 94.

The case of the COLI and institutionalization of index numbers within the British state bureaucracies refracts the broader statisticalization of public life and political debate in the late Victorian and Edwardian period. The use of index numbers by the Board of Trade to frame the cost-of-living debate is an example of the state's attempt to "produce" economic knowledge rather than simply "consume" knowledge generated privately by economists and statisticians. The case of the COLI demonstrates that the economist-statisticians often operated at the intersection of the public and private spheres, in centralized state bureaucracies as well as private institutions.[28] Marshalling the use of index numbers within the Board of Trade resonates with the notion that the state's interest in economic knowledge, at least in this period, stemmed from its motivation to use such knowledge for "practical perception of facts and relationships, discovery and deployment of data concerning the operation of economy and associated social relations, and the articulation of systematic theories that may bear on the state's policies or influence its critics" (Furner and Supple 2002: 4). The state had become a key actor within the broad ecology of index number measurements.

Nonetheless, the state was only one of the actors within this ecology that produced economic measurements and made inferences. Private individuals and organizations also developed their own versions and, more important, debated what exactly the measurements revealed about the economic phenomenon they claimed to measure. This meant some inferential challenges related to the theoretical frameworks on which economic hypotheses were based, such as quantity theory (price index) or purchasing power (COLI). Other challenges related to measurement theories, strategies, and methods on the basis of which index numbers were designed and data gathered. All these challenges presented inferential gaps that needed to be bridged such that people and organizations could make the inferential leaps between information and the likely answer to their question. In addition to these theoretical issues, and especially in the case of COLI, there were other inferential challenges introduced by the political beliefs and ideologies of those who encountered these measurements. These inferential challenges could not be addressed through theoretical refinements, on which the hypotheses and measurements were based, or by gathering more

28. Economists such as Giffen and Bowley straddled multiple spheres, working at the UK Board of Trade as well as occupying prominent positions in professional societies such as the Royal Statistical Society.

robust data. These refinements and data potentially increased the precision with which measurements were made but did not entirely bridge the inferential issues emanating from ideology or belief. A closer look at the broader ecology of COLI beyond the immediate sites of production of these index numbers illustrates these arguments more clearly.

Although the original purpose for assembling data on wages and prices was to address the late Victorian cost-of-living question, measurements of the COLI were also caught up in the tariff reform debates of the early 1900s. Both these political issues were intimately related, and the empirical gap between wages and prices lay at the center of both debates. The COLI was important in addressing the two questions posed since the 1880s, about the "material progress" of the laboring classes and the likely impact of fiscal reforms on living standards. Inferences using the COLI measurements had to potentially satisfy anyone who was interested in either one or both these questions.

Davidson (1985: 137–39) has argued that the COLI was developed to address several imperatives framing what he termed the "labour problem."[29] First, those within the Board of Trade that Davidson classified as holding a "collectivist view" sought to establish that wages, as determined by "market forces," were indeed insufficient to maintain large sections of the workforce at levels consistent with "social justice and economic efficiency" (Davidson 1985: 137; Higgs 1893: 264–65). Simultaneously, those whom Davidson (1985: 137–38) termed "social radicals" wanted the COLI to secure a "scientific and defensible" basis of establishing a need for a shift away from the "market based determinants of wage" and to identify a social criterion to establish a "minimum living wage" that could accommodate the local variations in rents and commodity prices. While these two aims drove the specific manner in which the index was constructed and measured, the data collected to construct the index could also be used to examine the extent to which the participation of female labor (in the industrial workforce) was a reflection of the inadequacies of male wage remuneration, and the extent to which the general industrial discontent was actually due to falling real wages rather than rising social expectations (i.e., changing consumption habits).

While these questions prompted the Board of Trade to set up the infrastructure to systematically gather price information since the late 1880s, it was the tariff reform debate that provided the immediate context to the

29. See also note 12.

board's first attempt at putting together a price index in 1903. The tariff reform issue, or the fiscal controversy as it was known then, had blown into a public spat in 1903 that destabilized Arthur Balfour's government. The board's 1903 *Report on Wholesale and Retail Prices* was hastily assembled to meet Balfour's request for statistical data to address this question of the extent to which working-class consumers had experienced continually rising prices of essential commodities (Wright 1984: 155n14). Gerald Balfour, Arthur's brother, was president of the Board of Trade when the price index and other statistical information was compiled into the "fiscal blue books" during this very public debate. At the time, Bowley (1903: 310) had explained that if the index numbers of prices, consumption expenditure, and wages suggested an improvement, then there was a "strong *a priori* case, though no proof, that the nation is progressing." Cost-of-living statistics were central to both sides of the tariff reform controversy. Joseph Chamberlain (in Balfour's cabinet at the time) and his supporters in the Tariff Reform League wanted to demonstrate how, under free trade, labor wages were depressed and how the resulting cost of living led to deterioration in living standards. On the other hand, free traders sought to convince those who were still undecided that tariff reform would cause food prices to increase, which in turn would lead to further deterioration in living standards. Balfour himself was wavering between the opposing views, although he did believe that preferential tariffs would not lead to price rises. He could not support this publicly, as the prevailing political sentiment would not support a move to introduce such tariffs (Coats 1968; Rogers 2011). These opposing groups looked to the official data that the board published, on the basis of which the COLI measurements were made, to support their own contrasting views. Meanwhile, fourteen economists, including Bowley, Edgeworth, and Marshall, sent a "manifesto" to the *Times* stating that a return to protectionism "would be detrimental to the material prosperity of this country" (Bowley et al. 1903). Even as the tariff reform debate had subsided somewhat by the eve of the war, the question of whether the *real* wages had deteriorated before and during the war lingered on well into the 1920s.

All the noise generated by the political debate tended to overshadow the more theoretical discussions about the causal relations between economic quantities (wages, expenditure, and consumption), purchasing power of money, and the suitability of index numbers in examining these relationships. Often public commentators would use the board's published data to draw their own inferences about wages and prices rather than use the index numbers themselves or the inferences made by the government economists, as the two political posters in figures 1 and 2 show. Official statistics were used by individuals and organizations of different political persuasions to frame their own inferential rhetoric. During a House of Commons debate in March 1913 on the subject of minimum wage legislation, Leo Chiozza Money presented the statistical "facts" that since 1895, wages had increased by 13 percent but that prices increased by nearly 25 percent. According to him, the "statistics" also showed, based on "the authority of the Board of Trade," that between 1900 and 1912 wages increased by 1 percent but that the cost of living went up by 15 percent. Chiozza Money consequently inferred that "it is obvious that the case of the working man has grown worse."[30] Sidney Buxton, who was at the time president of the Board of Trade, countered these claims by pointing out that Chiozza Money's selection of the year 1895 was misleading, since it was the "lowest year from the point of the cost of living" compared with 1882, when "cost of living was forty-one points higher than now and wages were fourteen points lower."[31] Buxton also stated in the parliament that the "*standard* of living increased amongst the working classes during the last thirty or forty years," thereby adding to the rising *cost* of living.[32]

The COLI may well have become a more precise measuring instrument compared with the index numbers that preceded it.[33] However, the major inferential challenges were not only its theoretical construction or the quality of data used but also the manner in which the broader audiences drew their own inferences using publicly available data. This process of inference making, shaped by political landscape, is just as relevant to our purposes here as are inferences made by economists and statisticians using theoretical frameworks to make inferences. Indeed, the posters shown in figures 1 and 2 demonstrate not only the increasing relationship between

30. Leo Chiozza Money (1870–1944) was a politician and journalist writing on economic, social, and political issues, "with a particular penchant for statistical analysis," and favored improvements in the organization of industries and the imposition of minimum wages (Daunton 2004). His comments mentioned here are recorded in House of Commons (HC) Debate, March 13, 1913, vol. 50, cc505.

31. Buxton's replies to Chiozza Money are in HC Debate, March 13, 1913, vol. 50, cc516.

32. HC Debate, March 13, 1913, vol. 50, cc515; emphasis added. It is unclear whether this "standard of living" referred to the "consumption standard" that the Board of Trade's Fountain had described in 1908. See note 18.

33. Some economic historians have dismissed the Board of Trade data used for the COLI as being "of dubious quality" and therefore seriously impairing the reliability of this index; see Gazeley 1989. Nonetheless, these measurements were probably more precise compared with those that Jevons managed with his price index and were not too dissimilar to Sauerbeck's estimation of the price index (Board of Trade, "Report on Wholesale and Retail Prices in the United Kingdom in 1902," Appendix II, 449).

Edwardian visual and political cultures but the increased importance of economic statistics in public debate in this period.[34] Just as the posters reflect the centrality of pictorial propaganda to political conflict, the use of numerical data in these posters reflects the importance of inferences (based on numbers) to consolidate their political message. As Edmund Rogers (2007: 622) observes, the use of statistics (such as in the posters) assisted all sides of the fiscal reform debate to "hold the moral high ground, for proof that [their] desired fiscal policy could materially benefit the working-class consumer." Where their inferences were at odds with that of the state, based on the index numbers, the political groups sought to challenge not only each other's position but also that of economists such as Bowley, who inferred that living conditions had not worsened because money wages rose as prices rose. Notwithstanding the deference with which judgments of more educated people, such as economists and statisticians, were generally held in Edwardian society, the "superficial observations" that so irked Bowley, and the pictorial abstractions of economic conditions in the political posters, proved to be more persuasive than the inferences using the Board of Trade's index numbers in this period.

4. Conclusion

This article has shown how economists grappled with multiple inferential gaps when making inferences using index numbers. The extent to which these gaps could be bridged depended on the theoretical frameworks and measurement strategies that economists used. However, it is also evident that some inferential issues were ideological or political in nature and that economists were confronted with them as they made their inferences. These political issues had little to do with the theoretical construction or the precision with which measurements were made. Nonetheless, the inferences made on the basis of index numbers could, and did, become mired in the politics of the period. If inferences are an act of reasoning—a cognitive process—we need to account for the political context as well. The history of inference in economics needs to incorporate the histories of science, economics, and politics.

Numbers have a rhetorical value of their own and have been used in political propaganda, as shown in the case of COLI here. These numbers may or may not have a theoretical basis. Jevons's price index and the

34. For the relationship between visual and political cultures, see Thompson 2007; for economic statistics in the tariff reform debate, see Rogers 2011.

COLI were based on accepted theoretical formulations, the commodity prices used in the tariff reform posters less so. However, the theoretical basis of the index numbers themselves—a "composite quantity of a number of individual approximations," as Keynes termed it—made it difficult to establish what exactly these measurements captured. In the case of Jevons's index, he was able to show the depreciation in the value of gold, just as economic theory had predicted. But the extent of this depreciation was disputed, especially when compared with other estimates such as those made by the *Economist*. Did this make his index number less precise, but nonetheless accurate? After all, it could be argued that it was "fit for purpose," as his instrument did demonstrate what he set out to do—an inference that was generally accepted by other economists.

The question of precision and accuracy is less clear-cut for the inferences using the COLI. In one sense, the COLI did achieve the state's purpose in establishing the relative changes in income and expenditure. This allowed the economists to infer that even though commodity prices were rising in a given period, the rising money wages meant that living standards did not continue to deteriorate. These inferences were challenged by others, not on the basis of other estimates of the index but based on data that individual prices of essential commodities had increased. In this discourse there were no theoretical challenges or arguments that the construction of the index was flawed in any way. The challenges were based on direct comparison of prices that people were used to making; index numbers were not generally used in public discourse at the time. Why should the index be capturing the "reality" of living standards any better than individual price data? They were both instrumental devices, and as such, the political inferences using rising commodity prices proved to be more compelling compared with inferences using a composite measurement such as the COLI. In this broader sense, the index numbers were not "fit for purpose" or accurate in this period. Consequently, the issue of whether the COLI was precise is, rather, made redundant.

To conclude, index numbers are not only indirect measurements but are also composite quantities that present particular inferential challenges. The early history of the use of index numbers in British economics shows that making inferences using this measuring instrument was rife with problems. The multiple inferential gaps transcended the "difference between the measurement and inference" issue noted by Hoover and Dowell. The gaps could be theoretical or political in nature. Inference making was nevertheless a cognitive process, rather than a heuristic one that could eliminate inferential gaps with better measurements.

References

Agar, John. 2003. *The Government Machine*. Cambridge, MA: MIT Press.

Boumans, Marcel. 2001. "Fisher's Instrumental Approach to Index Numbers." In *The Age of Economic Measurement*, edited by Judy L. Klein and Mary S. Morgan. *History of Political Economy* 33 (supplement): 313–44.

Boumans, Marcel. 2007. "Introduction." In *Measurement in Economics: A Handbook*, edited by Marcel Boumans, 3–18. London: Elsevier.

Bowley, Arthur. 1901. *Elements of Statistics*. London.

Bowley, Arthur. 1903. "Statistical Methods and the Fiscal Controversy." *Economic Journal* 13, no. 51: 303–12.

Bowley, Arthur. 1906. "Address to the Economic Science and Statistics Section of the British Association for the Advancement of Science, York, 1906." *Journal of the Royal Statistical Society* 69, no. 3: 540–58.

Bowley, Arthur L. 1919. "The Measurement of Changes in the Cost of Living." *Journal of the Royal Statistical Society* 82, no. 3: 343–72.

Bowley, Arthur. 1920. *The Change in the Distribution of National Income, 1880–1913*. Oxford: Clarendon Press.

Bowley, Arthur, and Josiah Stamp. 1927. *The National Income, 1924*. Clarendon: Oxford University Press.

Bowley, Arthur. 1937. *Wages and Income in the United Kingdom since 1860*. Cambridge: Cambridge University Press.

Bowley, Arthur, et al. 1903. Letter to the editor, *Times*, August 15.

Cairnes, John Elliott. 1862. *The Slave Power: Its Character, Career, and Probable Designs: Being an Attempt to Explain the Real Issues Involved in the American Conflict*. 2nd ed. New York: Carleton.

Chevalier, Michel. 1859. *On the Probable Fall in the Value of Gold*. Translated by Richard Cobden. New York: D. Appleton.

Coats, A. W. 1968. "Political Economy and the Tariff Reform Campaign of 1903." *Journal of Law and Economics* 11, no. 1: 181–229.

Cobden, Richard. 1859. "Preface." In Chevalier 1859: 3–11.

Crowther, Geoffrey. 1934. "The Economist Index of Business Activity." *Journal of the Royal Statistical Society* 97, no. 2: 241–76.

Daunton, Martin. 2004. "Money, Sir Leo George Chiozza (1870–1944), Politician and Author." *Oxford Dictionary of National Biography*. doi.org/10.1093/ref:odnb/55929.

Davidson, Roger. 1985. *Whitehall and the Labour Problem in Late-Victorian and Edwardian Britain: A Study in Official Statistics and Social Control*. London: Croom Helm.

Economist. 1869. "Commercial Review and History of 1868." March 13, 42–44.

Economist. 1872. "The Depreciation of Gold since 1848." December 28, 1580–82.

Edgeworth, Francis Ysidro. 1883. "On the Method of Ascertaining a Change in the Value of Gold." *Journal of the Statistical Society of London* 46, no. 4: 714–18.

Edgeworth, Francis Ysidro. 1925. "The Plurality of Index-Numbers." *Economic Journal* 35, no. 139: 379–88.

Edgeworth, Francis Ysidro, et al. 1888. "Report of the Committee Investigating the Best Methods of Ascertaining and Measuring Variations in the Value of the Monetary Standard." In *Report of the Fifty-Seventh Meeting of the British Association for the Advancement of Science, Manchester 1887,* 247–301. London: John Murray.

Edwards, Ruth Dudley. 1993. *The Pursuit of Reason, 1843–1993.* Boston: Harvard Business School Press.

Fisher, Irving. (1911) 1922. *The Purchasing Power of Money, Its Determination and Relation to Credit, Interest and Crises, Assisted by Harry G. Brown.* New York: Macmillan.

Fisher, Irving. 1922. *The Making of Index Numbers: A Study of Their Varieties, Tests, and Reliability.* Boston, MA: Houghton Mifflin.

Flux, Arthur. 1927. "Indices of Industrial Productive Activity." *Journal of the Royal Statistical Society* 90, no. 2: 225–71.

Furner, Mary, and Barry Supple. 2002. "Ideas, Institutions, and State in the United States and Britain: An Introduction." In *The State and Economic Knowledge: The American and British Experiences,* edited by Mary Furner and Barry Supple, 3–39. Cambridge, UK: Cambridge University Press.

Gazeley, Ian. 1989. "The Cost of Living for Urban Workers in Late Victorian and Edwardian Britain." *Economic History Review* 42, no. 2: 207–21.

Giffen, Robert. 1888. "The Recent Rate of Material Progress in England." In *Report of the Fifty-Seventh Meeting of the British Association for the Advancement of Science, Manchester 1887,* 806–26. London: John Murray.

Giffen, Robert. 1903. "The Wealth of the Empire, and How It Should Be Used." *Journal of the Royal Statistical Society* 66, no. 3: 582–98.

Higgs, Henry. 1893. "Workmen's Budgets." *Journal of the Royal Statistical Society* 52, no. 2: 255–94.

Hoover, Kevin D., and Michael E. Dowell. 2001. "Measuring Causes: Episodes in the Quantitative Assessment of the Value of Money." In *The Age of Economic Measurement,* edited by Judy L. Klein and Mary S. Morgan. *History of Political Economy* 33 (supplement): 137–61.

Jevons, Stanley. 1863. *A Serious Fall in the Value of Gold Ascertained, and Its Social Effects Set Forth.* London: Edward Stanford.

Jevons, Stanley. 1865. "On the Variation of Prices and the Value of the Currency since 1782." *Journal of the Statistical Society of London* 28, no. 2: 294–320.

Jevons, Stanley. 1869. "The Depreciation of Gold." *Economist,* May 8, 530–32.

Keynes, John Maynard. 1921. *A Treatise on Probability.* London: Macmillan.

Maas, Harro. 2001. "An Instrument Can Make a Science: Jevons's Balancing Acts in Economics." In *The Age of Economic Measurement,* edited by Judy L. Klein and Mary S. Morgan. *History of Political Economy* 33 (supplement): 277–302.

Maas, Harro. 2005. *William Stanley Jevons and the Making of Modern Economics.* Cambridge: Cambridge University Press.

Marshall, Alfred. 1996. *The Correspondence of Alfred Marshall, Economist.* Vol. 3, edited by John King Whitaker. Cambridge: Cambridge University Press for the Royal Economic Society.

"Miscellaneous Statistics of the United Kingdom." 1879. *Journal of the Statistical Society of London* 42, no. 3: 724–27.

Morgan, Mary S. 2001. "Making Measuring Instruments." In *The Age of Economic Measurement*, edited by Judy L. Klein and Mary S. Morgan. *History of Political Economy* 33 (supplement): 235–51.

Peart, Sandra. 1996. *The Economics of W. S. Jevons*. Cambridge: Cambridge University Press.

Peart, Sandra. 2001. "'Facts Carefully Marshalled' in the Empirical Studies of William Stanley Jevons." In *The Age of Economic Measurement*, edited by Judy L. Klein and Mary S. Morgan. *History of Political Economy* 33 (supplement): 252–76.

Porter, Theodore M. 2007. "Precision." In *Measurement in Economics: A Handbook*, edited by Marcel Boumans, 343–56. London: Elsevier.

Rhodes, Edmund Cecil. 1936. "The Precision of Index Numbers." *Journal of the Royal Statistical Society* 99, no. 1: 142–46.

Rogers, Edmund. 2007. "The United States and the Fiscal Debate in Britain, 1873–1913." *Historical Journal* 50, no. 3: 593–622.

Rogers, Edmund. 2011. "A 'Naked Strength and Beauty': Statistics in the British Tariff Debate 1880–1914." In *Statistics and the Public Sphere*, edited by Tom Crook and Glen O'Hara, 224–43. New York: Routledge.

Rowe, J. W. F. 1927. "An Index of the Physical Volume of Production." *Economic Journal* 37, no. 146: 173–87.

Sauerbeck, Augustus. 1893. "Prices of Commodities During the Last Seven Years." *Journal of the Royal Statistical Society* 56, no. 2: 215–54.

Searle, Rebecca. 2015. "Is There Anything Real about Real Wages? A History of the Official British Cost of Living Index, 1914–62." *Economic History Review* 68, no. 1: 145–66.

Stapleford, Thomas A. 2012. "Navigating the Shoals of Self-Reporting: Data Collection in US Expenditure Surveys since 1920." In *Observing the Economy*, edited by Harro Maas and Mary S. Morgan. *History of Political Economy* 44 (supplement): 160–82.

Steer, Philip. 2016. "Gold and Greater Britain: Jevons, Trollope, and Settler Colonialism." *Victorian Studies* 58, no. 3: 436–63.

Thompson, James. 2007. "'Pictorial Lies'? Posters and Politics in Britain c. 1880–1914." *Past & Present* 197, no. 1: 177–210.

Tolles, N. A., and Paul H. Douglas. 1930. "A Measurement of British Industrial Production." *Journal of Political Economy* 38, no. 1: 1–28.

Trentmann, Frank. 2008. *Free Trade Nation: Commerce, Consumption, and Civil Society in Modern Britain*. Oxford: Oxford University Press.

Wilson, James. 1843. "Prospectus." *Economist*, August 1, 14–15.

Wright, J. F. 1984. "Real Wage Resistance: Eighty Years of the British Cost of Living." Supplement: Economic Theory and Hicksian Themes. *Oxford Economic Papers* 36: 152–67.

The Case against "Indirect" Statistical Inference: Wassily Leontief's "Direct Induction" and *The Structure of American Economy, 1919–29*

Amanar Akhabbar

In his 1970 presidential address to the American Economic Association, Wassily Leontief expressed a severe criticism of the "econometric work" of the time and its use of probabilistic inferential tools. According to him, "The validity of these statistical tools depends . . . on the acceptance of certain convenient assumptions pertaining to stochastic properties of the phenomena . . . to explain," assumptions that "can be seldom verified" (Leontief 1971: 2–3). In 1948, Leontief had already stated his case against the probabilistic approach in econometrics in a chapter surveying the recent advances in the field.[1] At the time, he already denied this method the ability to help "bridge" economic theory and "actually observed facts" (Leontief 1948: 394). The approach mobilizing the "indirect methods of probabilistic inference" (407) was called by Leontief (1949, 1952) the method of *indirect statistical inference.* In econometrics, he opposed to it

I am especially grateful to Jeff Biddle and Marcel Boumans for their comments, helpful suggestions, and stimulating discussions. The article has also benefited from the comments of the participants in the *HOPE* conference on the history of statistical inference, as well as those of Matthieu Ballandonne and Carlos Eduardo Suprinyak on earlier drafts. I thank the librarians of the Pusey Library at Harvard University whose help was precious. Sources from the Wassily Leontief Papers at Harvard University are referred to as HUG 4517.

1. Henceforth I rely on Leontief's (1948: 388) definition: "Econometrics as a special type of economic analysis in which the general theoretical approach—often formulated in explicitly mathematical terms—is combined—frequently through the medium of intricate statistical procedures—with empirical measurement of economic phenomena." Thus, here, econometrics does not necessarily entail use of the theory of probability.

History of Political Economy 53 (annual suppl.) DOI 10.1215/00182702-9414874

"less indirect and more reliable inductive procedures" (Leontief 1948: 407) that he called "direct induction" (Leontief 1949: 218). As he discarded the *methods of indirect statistical inference*, Leontief devised "more direct" ways to find estimates that were presumably accurate without mobilizing inferential methods relying on probability theory. In his view, so-called direct induction had to rely more on "direct observation and controlled experiment" (Leontief 1948: 402). Such an alternative approach, Leontief said, was implemented in his econometric method, the interindustry method, as presented in his 1941 book *The Structure of American Economy, 1919–1929* (hereafter cited as *The Structure*). He later coined that approach *direct structural analysis* as opposed to *indirect statistical inference* (Leontief 1954).

This article contributes to the history of statistical inference in economics through a study of Leontief's defense of a nonprobabilistic approach to inference. I examine the statistical method mobilized by Leontief in *The Structure* to draw inferences about the national economy—the economic mechanism *beyond* the data—and how his endeavor contrasted with alternative "indirect" inferential approaches.

As Jeff Biddle and Marcel Boumans (this issue) point out, very little has been written on the history of nonprobabilistic approaches to statistical inference, including on Leontief's interindustry method. This method is almost absent from both the histories of statistical inference in economics and from those on econometrics. As for the former, however, Biddle (2017) stressed the resistance of postwar input-output studies to the development of the probabilistic approach to econometrics. As for the latter, Boumans (2009, 2016) initiated a study of Leontief's alternative view to econometrics and how tensions between "direct observation" and statistical theory led to the development of expert observation. Yet many aspects of the history of Leontief's approach to empirical modeling remain to be examined.[2] My article complements and extends the discussions on econometrics and "direct observation" in relation to the problems raised in economics by statistical inference from passive observations (see Boumans 2015; Biddle 2017).

Furthermore, Leontief's first edition of *The Structure* has received very little attention from economists or historians of economics.[3] It is his post-

---

2. For studies of Leontief's methodology, see Akhabbar 2007, 2019; and Boumans 2012.
3. *The Structure*'s second edition was published in 1951. Here, I am concerned only with the first edition.

war interindustry works that have hitherto attracted most of the attention.[4] One reason is that the field of input-output analysis emerged mostly from Leontief's later works, during World War II, in close collaboration with the Bureau of Labor Statistics (BLS), rather than from his original approach as presented in 1941. Leontief's collaboration with the BLS and the subsequent significant changes introduced in his original interindustry framework have been examined by Martin Kohli (2001). Kohli rightly underlined the specificity of Leontief's methodology and how his interindustry table and model were tightly intertwined, forming a particular "framework for measurement." My study complements and extends Kohli's thesis by focusing on Leontief's earlier researches.

The aim of this article is to show how, in *The Structure*, Leontief conceived his interindustry device as an alternative to the inferential strategies of interwar econometrics and statistical economics. In his book, Leontief gathered a decade of research on "interindustrial relations" studies, from 1931—the year of his move from Germany to the United States—to 1941. He reproduced, with minor changes, already published articles from 1936 and 1937, and added new material from works undertaken in the following years. *The Structure* synthetized and extended his pioneering empirical studies of interindustrial relations. It would soon spread and become known as *input-output analysis*. Nevertheless, I refer to the label of interindustry studies, retaining the expression *input-output analysis* for the post-1941 developments. Although it was called *direct induction* and did not mobilize probabilistic inferential techniques, the use by Leontief of his statistical data to draw conclusions about the economic mechanism *beyond* the data is a problem of statistical inference. I investigate how he drew, from the data summarized in the interindustry table, inferences on the American economy. To do so, I narrow the scope to one aspect of statistical inference, namely, the statistical determination of the model's parameters: I examine how Leontief inferred, from the data, some in-depth structural characteristic determinants of the national economy. This makes it possible to show how, in interwar applied economics, Leontief's statistical attempt, although unique in many aspects, echoed other parallel endeavors, offering a better understanding of the nature and significance of his direct induction approach.

---

4. For more conventional econometric issues, attention focused on his controversy in 1934 with Ragnar Frisch, the so-called Pitfalls controversy (see Morgan 1990; Boumans 2009; and Akhabbar 2019).

1. A Problem of Statistical Inference

To draw inferences with his interindustry device from statistical data, Leontief followed the same epistemic strategy as econometricians by stating a mathematical model. The model expressed the theoretical foundations of the statistical investigation as Leontief repeatedly advocated in favor of measurement with theory. In the introduction to *The Structure*, he warned "statistical economists" that "no stable analytical structure can possibly be built piecemeal without a predesigned plan and sturdy theoretical scaffolding" (Leontief 1941: 4). This is why his expression *direct induction* is in no way a case for measurement without explicit theory and mathematical modeling.

Leontief's "theoretical scheme" rested on the "economic theory of general equilibrium" (3) from which he derived a system of linear equations.[5] The model stated the static equilibrium of relative prices (P) and quantities (X) resulting from the "general interdependence" between all the industries and offering a "comprehensive view of the structure of the national economy as a whole." His framework, he underlined in *The Structure*'s subtitle, was "An Empirical Application of Equilibrium Analysis." Leontief opposed his theory-oriented approach to that of the "empiricists," who do not start from a theoretical model but from "the other end" by examining variables through a series of "correlation group[s]" on "separate samples." Although Leontief admitted that "few of these [empiricist] statistical studies are entirely devoid of theoretical background," he denied that "a string of partial correlations . . . can in some way represent a system of general interdependence" (Leontief 1941: 4). In contrast to the empiricist's data-driven modeling,[6] his theory-oriented approach aimed to bridge economic theory to statistical analysis by mobilizing mathematical and statistical tools. This was how Leontief (1936: 116) described his interindustry project as aiming to "fill in the 'empty boxes' of the theory of general equilibrium." In this respect, his so-called direct induction approach belonged to econometrics (Leontief 1948; see also Rothbarth 1943).

The Structure's content represents that view: the first part presented the data as summarized in the interindustry table; the second part presented the theoretical model to be employed to draw inferences; the third and last part

---

5. Although it can be interpreted as classical—a Ricardo-like model—I follow Leontief's designation of his model as being derived from general equilibrium theory. See also Neisser 1941.

6. See also Hendry's (1995) distinction between empirical modeling approaches.

only was about drawing statistical inferences on the national economy.[7] In such a framework, the main categories of inferences are the statistical determination of the model's parameters and the appraisal of the predictions derived from the model (alternatively, the forecasts) and of the hypotheses involved. One important constraint was the limitation in the data and their nature as "uncontrolled observation" from passive observation (Leontief 1941: 79). In a 1941 Harvard seminar, Trygve Haavelmo stressed the problem of finding "the numerical values of the parameters" and underlined that it is "important to consider whether the available passive observations can be used to draw inferences about these parameters" (1). The statistical determination of the parameters of a model's equations is a problem of statistical inference. Following a now-standard distinction in statistical inference between estimation and testing,[8] I narrow the scope to the former problem and leave aside the testing problems related to the hypotheses and predictions. Thus the issue is that of the statistical determination of the interindustry model's parameters by Leontief in *The Structure*.

In interwar econometrics, Leontief's reluctance to use the techniques of statistical inference based on the probability theory was not uncommon.[9] Consequently, little reference was made to "estimation"; instead, the problem was more often stated as that of the "statistical determination" of some coefficient or parameter.[10] This interwar terminology is consistent with the little use made of probability theory and would contrast with the statistical estimation of the parameters of probabilistic models, as later recommended by the Cowles Commission's econometricians. Indeed, and following Jacob Marschak's (1950) chapter "Statistical Inference in Economics," in the case of a nonprobabilistic model, "We assume the data to be measured exactly and to satisfy exactly the relations of theory. . . . The problem of estimation degenerates into that of determination." This, according to Marschak, characterized "certain 'prestatistical' problems facing the economic statistician" (6). In the interwar period, however, statistical economists did not consider the data free from errors but still often considered it ill-advised to employ probability theory.[11] Yet I show how

---

7. The book also contains appendices and two charts in a pocket. A supplement was made available on request.

8. See Haavelmo 1944: 66.

9. See Marschak 1938; and also Biddle 2017 and Morgan 1990.

10. Alternatively, the expressions statistical *measurement* or *derivation* were employed.

11. See Biddle and Boumans's introduction, this volume.

Leontief's interindustry method was historically related to works using probability-based measures of reliability and how he discarded them.

In econometrics, the statistical determination of the models' parameters requires one to mobilize statistical analysis. One can indeed consider with Leontief (1948: 392) that "the function of statistical analysis in application to econometric research is that of an intermediary between a general theoretical hypothesis and the directly observable facts." Leontief's closeness to logical positivist views of science shows in this reference to direct observation.[12] Here, I do not discuss the methodological foundations of Leontief's approach. I admit he considered the basic statistical information from which economists draw inferences "directly observable facts" or "direct observations." In this perspective, the time series of prices and quantities (for instance), from which the elasticities of supply and demand curves are inferred, are direct observations. The problem of the statistical determination of the elasticities of demand curves was one of the most important fields of application of econometric techniques. Leontief too contributed to this field. From the least squares method, Leontief (1929, 1932) had developed his own technique of statistically determining the elasticities of supply and demand.[13] In a comparison of the tools usually employed in econometrics to infer the numerical values of the parameters and those Leontief employed in his interindustry method, a discrepancy is found that needs to be explored.

The excerpt quoted above appeared in a book chapter Leontief wrote on econometrics. Reviewing developments in econometrics in the previous decade, Leontief (1948: 402) discussed mostly the Cowles Commission's structural econometric program as theorized by "Haavelmo and his school." He contrasted the latter with the previous works belonging to what he humorously called the econometrics' "*Sturm und Drang* period" (391). Although he ranked his own interindustry studies into econometrics, he made a clear-cut distinction between statistical inferences in conventional econometrics and his own approach to the problem as presented in *The Structure*: he characterized the former as *indirect*, describing it as "indirect induction" (402), and referred to the "indirect methods of probabilistic inference" (407), which he contrasted with the interindustry method assumed to rely more "on direct observation." This distinction was soon described by Leontief (1949, 1952) as that between "direct induction" ver-

12. About the connections between Leontief's methodology and logical positivism, see two congruent views in Akhabbar 2007, 2019; and Boumans 2012.

13. See also Leontief 1940.

sus "indirect induction" or "indirect statistical inference," that is, between conventional econometrics versus his interindustry studies. As a matter of example, in Leontief's view, the statistical supply and demand elasticities determined are *indirect statistical inferences* drawn with or without the help of the probability theory. Leontief contrasted this indirect induction with his interindustry inferences, whose characterization as "direct induction" needs to be clarified in terms of actual statistical practices.

Although Leontief's distinction emerged in a specific context, which included Haavelmo's probabilistic econometrics and Tjalling Koopmans's 1947 "measurement without theory" criticism of the empirical method of the National Bureau of Economic Research (NBER), I refer to his distinction in my examination of *The Structure*. Indeed, the statistical techniques employed by Leontief to determine the quantitative relations in his model exhibit little congruity with standard econometric procedures. For instance, the usual tools of cross-sectional and time series statistical studies were not mobilized, such as simple or multiple correlations, or regression methods. This would remain a characteristic feature of input-output analysis.[14] I argue that Leontief's distinction helps clarify this difference of approach.

In distinguishing between direct and indirect induction, I shall not put too much emphasis on the distinction between inference *with and without probability theory*, as the heated and troublesome discussions—that made Leontief refer to this period as the *Sturm und Drang* one—were not specifically related to the use of, for instance, *probable errors*, the latter being only one way (among others) to assess the reliability and trustworthiness of the numerical coefficients determined.[15] Yet Leontief's interindustry method emerged in the midst of the discussions of supply and demand equations' statistical determination once qualified by George Stigler (1939: 470) as scientific "frankensteins." In the presentations of his interindustry studies, Leontief repeatedly introduced his new framework as an alternative to this other approach. One path of studies would eventuate in the Cowles Commission's 1940s structural econometric program; the other path would turn into input-output analysis, a field where inference would conspicuously rely very little—and often not at all—on probabilistic inference (see Biddle 2017). Yet, in the interwar period, Leontief's emphasis was not on the use, or not, of probability theory. Instead, the problem, stated in terms of determination of the parameters, is that of get-

14. See Klein 1962: 129.

15. One of the most intense controversies is that between Frisch and Leontief, the well-known "Pitfalls" controversy of 1934 (Morgan 1990; Boumans 2009, 2012).

ting rid of the statistical techniques of correlation or regression (for instance) in favor of "direct" determination by specific sources of information. To examine how this view about the statistical determination of a model's basic parameters was implemented in *The Structure*, we need to introduce the theoretical model itself.

2. The Model, the Variables, and the Parameters: A Structural Approach

Just like standard econometrics, Leontief's approach starts from the introduction of theoretical assumptions and the formulation of a mathematical model. An analysis of the economy as a system of "general interdependence," the model attempts to connect all the sectors of the economy, businesses and households alike. Here I do not discuss the theoretical properties of Leontief's model but only its main characteristics to examine how it was employed to draw inferences from the statistical data. Although Leontief's interindustry model is well known, its 1937–41 versions differ in many respects from the later, more popular, Leontief-BLS approach (see Kohli 2001). In particular, the model's aims were different, as the original model was not directed toward economic policy.[16] In this respect, both the aims and method contrasted with another important and contemporaneous attempt to describe the "structure of the American economy" from a disaggregated perspective, namely, that of Gardiner Means's statistical studies undertaken for the National Resources Committee (NRC). The main aim of Means (1938: 1) and his group was to answer the following question: "Under prevailing technical conditions, what is the level of economic activity which would absorb practically all of the great army of unemployed?" The analysis was stated as a "pattern of resource use" defined as "an input-output pattern—a pattern showing the conversion of resources into useful goods and services" (20). The problem was tackled by an inductive statistical inquiry implemented industry by industry and covering the whole economy. The statistical method employed by Means was not the theory-based econometric approach Leontief favored but, instead, illustrates the empiricists' methods Leontief criticized in *The Structure*. And indeed, Means examined separately the correlations among factors of several industries without introducing some systematic scheme of general interdependence. In Sep-

---

16. This trait was severely criticized by Kenneth Boulding (1942).

tember 1938, Means—having expressed a strong interest in Leontief's interindustry table—[17]sent to Leontief his preliminary report for comments. Unsurprisingly, Leontief did not show a strong interest in Means's studies and did not participate in the associated debates on the ways to reach full employment.

In Leontief's original model, problems related to the level of economic activity and employment are irrelevant, as no absolute level or variations in outputs, employment, or prices can be studied: the model is strictly about relative prices and relative quantities. The latter aspect is one of the peculiarities of Leontief's first model. In this sense, the problem is really about the structure of production and consumption, prices and quantities, and not the absolute level of activity. In the model, the price of each commodity depends on the prices of all other commodities, the same for the quantities. A change in the consumption of one commodity could have consequences, directly or indirectly, on the prices and quantities produced of all the commodities. The whole economy is represented by n industries producing n homogeneous products. Importantly, in the theoretical model, the quantities are measured in physical units. Furthermore, each commodity is produced by one single industry, including labor and entrepreneurial services defined as part of households' output: commodity i is produced by industry i, and the households are the nth industry, delivering households services in a quantity X_n.[18]

The general interdependence in the economy is expressed by a set of n equations of prices and another for quantities. Leontief's equations express two equilibrium conditions assuming that, in each industry i, (1) the total physical quantity produced of one commodity (X_i) is equal to the quantity distributed and consumed by all the other industries ($\Sigma_j x_{ji}$) and (2) the output ($P_i X_i$) is equal to the outlays ($\Sigma_j P_j x_{ij}$).[19] A third set of equations describes the shape of the production and consumption functions. This is where the production function's technical coefficients are introduced and expanded, by analogy, to the households. In the sets of equilibrium prices and quantities equations, each side is divided by the correspondent output, to get ratios such as (x_{ij}/X_i), which is the quantity of j consumed to produce

17. Means asked Leontief for permission to publish in advance the interindustry table for 1929. It appeared in 1939 in Means's next volume, titled *The Structure of the American Economy*. The main title of Leontief's volume differed from that of Means only by the lack of "the" before "American economy" and the dates added (1919–29).

18. This is a "closed economic system" (Leontief 1941: 139).

19. Following Leontief's notation, x_{ij}, is the physical quantity of j used to produce the quantity X_i of i, i.e., the quantity of j consumed by the industry i.

one unit of i. This ratio is noted as a_{ij}. These coefficients are assumed independent constants and are the model's basic parameters. A simple linear relation between inputs and outputs, such as $x_{ij} = a_{ij}X_i$, is assumed. As Leontief (1941: 37) noted, "This is the same type of relation which was originally used by Walras in his first formulation of the general equilibrium theory." Like Léon Walras in the first editions of the *Eléments d'économie pure* (*Elements of Pure Economics*), Leontief considered these coefficients as part of the "data" and not of the "unknowns."[20]

To this framework, better suited to describe a stationary economy without saving or investment and without any possibility of productivity change, a series of coefficients are added. I consider only those that allow saving and investment, called saving or investment ratios, and noted $\boldsymbol{B}_i$. They are the ratios between an industry's output and its outlays. When introduced in the production function, we get $x_{ik} = (a_{ik}X_i)/\boldsymbol{B}_i$. These linear equations express the technical productive relations, the households' final consumption and willingness to save, and the willingness to invest in the various branches.

These three sets of equations are called by Leontief the "theoretical assumptions" of his model. From these, and given a numéraire, each relative price and quantity is deduced and expressed with regard to the model's constant coefficients only. Importantly, from this set of initial "theoretical assumptions," Leontief derived a set of final equations and coefficients describing the hypothetical reactions of the relative prices and outputs to some "primary changes," the "impulses" (34): for instance, with the households' services as a numéraire, he computed an industry i's output reactions to a "primary change of the investment and saving coefficients" of an industry k (80), as the elasticity formula $(dX_i/d\boldsymbol{B}_k) \cdot (1/X_i)$; the same with changes in technical or consumption coefficients. Leontief contrasted the initial *theoretical assumptions* above, the premises, to these *deduced* reaction equations. Accordingly, the model did not aim to describe only the economy at one moment in time as registered in the data; it aimed to infer beyond the data the expected reactions of the economy to impulses.

This approach calls for a few additional comments. First, the concern for such outputs' and prices' hypothetical reactions was common, in the interwar period, in the fields both of the econometrics of demand curves

---

20. Leontief (1941: 37) thus discarded more general production functions such as $F_i(x_{i1}, x_{i2}, \ldots, x_{in}) = X_i$.

and of business cycles. In this matter, the statistical determination of elasticity coefficients was a standard way to cope with such reactions. That was why Leontief (1941: 5) called his interindustry reaction functions *elasticities*, drawing an explicit comparison between supply and demand elasticities and his reaction functions.

Second, Leontief's distinction between the theoretical assumptions and the deduced reaction elasticities echoed the—although in inception and not yet stabilized in the 1930s— econometric conceptualization and terminology about structural relations and the relations determined by them, in particular as stated in the works of Ragnar Frisch, Tinbergen, and Haavelmo (see Biddle 2017; Boumans 2005, 2015; and Morgan 1990). In the 1940s, the Haavelmo-Cowles Commission econometric works would formalize the distinction between the structural and the reduced-form model. Leontief (1949, 1952) himself would then call his primary equations the structural equations of the model from which various results are derived, and call the basic parameters the structural parameters, or constants. In *The Structure*, although the terminology was not yet stabilized, Leontief established in a strikingly clear manner the distinction between the structural relations and the relations derived from them (the elasticities), as well as how the parameters (the "data") eventually determine the variables. Indeed, the model was introduced by distinguishing the "data" from the "variables" (or "unknowns"), such as the data "determine in their totality the magnitudes of all the dependent variables of the system"; thus the "data are those elements which are used as a basis of explanation" (34–35). In his model, the data are the coefficients (or parameters) to be statistically determined from the actual statistical information. These data, Leontief assumed, express the "structural properties of the empirically given system." There is a congruence with the vocabulary employed in several interwar business cycle studies, especially on the side of mathematical economists, by Frisch, Tinbergen, and Haavelmo.[21] According to Leontief, the structural characteristics determining the variables are "the technical and natural conditions of production and the tastes of consumers" (35). And these structural parameters are to be found in the "theoretical assumptions," the structural equations, from which are derived the reaction equations describing the prices and outputs elasticities.

---

21. See, for instance, the discussions of the three authors as reported in Phelps Brown 1937. These consonant terminologies indicate that Leontief's interindustry device was embedded in a larger network.

These distinctions are critical for the general strategy of statistical determination of the model's structural parameters. For instance, in conventional econometric studies of supply and demand, one usually did not attempt to determine the structural relations, namely, "the technical and natural conditions of production and the tastes of consumers," but to determine the derived supply and demand elasticities. In his interindustry method, Leontief radically shifted his strategy and drew the numerical values of the parameters not by estimating the elasticities (or reaction formulae) but by directly estimating the structural parameters in the structural relations. In modern terminology, direct would mean to estimate the structural parameters in the structural equations and not the parameters in the reduced-form equations. This approach, I argue, underlies Leontief's distinction between so-called direct induction by direct observation and indirect induction by the methods of indirect statistical inference.

3. The Statistical Determination of the Parameters

Given the theoretical scheme as formulated in his mathematical model, how did Leontief infer from his statistical data the numerical values of the structural parameters? And how does it relate to his distinction between direct and indirect induction? As stated above, the general strategy Leontief implemented was to directly draw the numerical values of his structural parameters rather than (indirectly) determining the coefficients in the derived reaction formulae (the elasticities). This is the first implication of the more "direct" approach to statistical induction. To better understand the significance of this strategy, we need to examine how Leontief practically inferred his parameters from the data.

In the original interindustry framework, the scope of this inferential problem depends on whether the empirical model is determined for a base year or not. I narrow my study to the former case and leave for further research the case where flows for different dates are considered. For a base year, the structural relations to be determined are the linear equations stated above. The parameters to be determined are the coefficients a_{ik} and the saving ratios. The main statistical device employed by Leontief to determine the structural parameters was his interindustry table. An obvious discrepancy appears in the use of the interindustry table as a device to determine the model's parameters: while the figures in the tables are in money units, the model is expressed in terms of physical units. Although this was an important issue when he attempted to compare flows at different periods of time (for 1919 and 1929), it had few consequences when dealing with one base year. In 1941, Leontief simply assumed that 1 million dollars of a product is 1 physical unit of that product. Therefore, the 6,153 million dollars of "Fuel and Power" produced in 1919 represent, by convention, 6,153 physical units of the industry's product (Leontief 1941: 72). This procedure allows one to draw directly from the statistical data summarized in the interindustry table some of the model's structural parameters in the required physical units. The ratios $\boldsymbol{B}_i$ are easily computed as the ratios between net outputs and net outlays. For example, for Households (industry 10), $\boldsymbol{B}_{10} = (55{,}447/43{,}516) \approx 1{,}274 > 1$, meaning that the industry is saving. Now, given the saving and investment ratios, the model's technical coefficients are directly determined according to the same ratio method. A coefficient's statistical measure is a *ratio* derived from one data point. As a descriptive statistic, it is the average input requirement for one unit of output. Leontief did not extend the discussion of how a measure is obtained further than the derivation of the ratio from the table. For a base year, each coefficient is derived as follows (Leontief 1941: 73–74):

> Since the magnitudes of all the elements on the right side of this equation $[a_{ik} = (x_{ik}/X_i) \cdot \boldsymbol{B}_i]$ are now given, the numerical value of a technical coefficient can readily be computed. For example: the coefficient a_{34} describing the use of fuel and power ($k = 4$) in the metals industry ($i = 3$) for 1919 equals $(398/14707)0.920 = 0.0249$.

This was how the basic coefficients were statistically determined.

The numerical value obtained from a descriptive statistic—the average input-output ratio—was directly used as a parameter in the model to infer beyond the data: the ratio was generalized into the linear input-output relation such that one could infer, for instance, by how much an input requirement would vary when the output varied.[22] In Leontief's analysis, it is not only presumed that, at one moment in time, parameters would remain stable even under hypothetical changes in inputs, outputs, or structural change in other parameters and in prices (4) but that their value would hold for some time and exhibit a certain degree of invariance (79).

22. For an interpretation of this linear relation as a *rule of inference*, see also Akhabbar 2007.

In John Maynard Keynes's vocabulary, this was an *inductive generalization*.[23] This inductive generalization needs to be examined further.

Let's draw some intermediary conclusions about the meaning of Leontief's direct induction approach to econometrics, as opposed to the other "indirect" approaches to statistical inference. I state tentatively two practical principles, which I elaborate on in the rest of this article: in *The Structure*, direct induction means (1) to determine directly the structural parameters in the structural relations—and not the coefficients in the equations derived[24] from these structural relationships; and (2) to infer the abovementioned parameters by a direct measure, such as the ratio method, instead of some "indirect" statistical technique such as some regression method.

These principles answer two important econometric questions: What parameters shall be statistically determined? And what statistical techniques shall be used to determine them? But they leave aside two other important questions: From what kind of data? And how to assess the reliability of the estimates? To get a better understanding of Leontief's direct approach, we need to answer all four questions. In 1931–41, Leontief did not elaborate on the choices he made, the scientific options he considered, the authors and works he reviewed to justify his framework, and the statistical method implemented. In the next sections, I attempt to answer these questions through a historical exploration of Leontief's options and choices.

4. Reliability Issues: Mechanical Objectivity and Expert Judgment

In *The Structure*, Leontief praised "the impersonal, quasi-mechanical methods of statistical analysis [that] often [enable the observer] to perceive the facts more objectively" (79). Statistical analysis would make possible some kind of mechanical objectivity that would free the investigator from the pitfalls of subjectivity and, in particular, of "[psychological] illusion." His interindustry framework, a disaggregated "picture" of the national economy, aimed at such a mechanical objectivity and was meant to avoid drawing "misleading inferences" (Leontief 1937: 127). In the main text, however, Leontief did not dwell on the reliability or accuracy of the numerical values he inferred for his basic parameters. The representativeness of the data in the table, or of the estimates he drew from it, was not a matter

---

23. About Keynes and statistical induction, see Biddle and Boumans, this volume.
24. The so-called reduced-form equations.

of discussion. With only one data point for each parameter, one could, however, wonder how the numerical values of the coefficients offer all together an accurate picture of the American economy in 1919 and how he could account for the measurement errors. Hans Neisser (1941: 610), one of the few commentators on Leontief's early interindustry studies, noted that the "acceptability of the results is . . . impaired by the absence of statistical reliability measures." Obviously, it was not Leontief's aim, at this stage, to consider measurement errors and to assess formally the reliability of his basic statistical estimates. The works gathered in *The Structure* resulted primarily from a tentative "experience" (Leontief 1937: 131) for illustrative purpose: it was a "laboratory test" (Leontief 1936: 116). This lack of reliability measures would, however, remain for econometricians a striking characteristic of interindustry studies. For instance, Gerhard Tintner (1952: 65), in one of the early econometric textbooks, underlined that "the failure to indicate the statistical reliability of [his] estimates is a serious shortcoming of Leontief's methods. No fiducial . . . confidence limits are given, and no significance tests are performed." We find the same in Lawrence R. Klein's (1953: 201) *Textbook of Econometrics*. Thus this feature of Leontief's method was more than a provisional stage, and its nature and significance need to be clarified.

Instead of producing reliability measures, Leontief justified and assessed the limits of his assumptions on the grounds of theoretical soundness and what appears to be nothing else but expert judgment. For instance, the very idea that investment in an industry is proportional for all the inputs consumed by this industry—apparent in the ratio—raised obvious concerns and was called by Leontief a "hardly warranted assumption." However, it was assessed as the lesser evil: "Lack of sufficient amount of empirical information, enhanced by certain mathematical difficulties, makes it impossible to treat this aspect of the problem with greater conformity to facts." Nevertheless, Leontief trusted his expert judgment in asserting that this assumption would be "likely to reduce the size of the errors"—although this size of errors was not estimated (Leontief 1941: 45).

The way Leontief assessed the credibility of his theoretical assumptions, by exercising his judgment, was similar in many respects to his justification in his econometric studies of supply and demand curves (especially 1929). In the latter, critical assumptions such as the constancy of elasticities along the curves and in time, and even more important, the independence of the curves' shifts, were justified on that ground. The same applies to the interindustry model and the justification of the constancy of technical coefficients and the nonsubstitutability of inputs, as well as the proportionality introduced by investment coefficients. About the former assumptions, while Leontief (1937: 113) offered mostly theoretical arguments, he recognized that they would "necessarily entail the existence of some discrepancy between our theoretical scheme and the actual industrial set-up that it is intended to represent." Leontief was nevertheless not keen to use the probabilistic tools of the theory of statistical inference to assess the discrepancy between the hypothesis and the data. Instead, he added conceptual arguments to mitigate the possible "disparity" of his "simplified scheme with the more realistic picture of our economic system" and eventually concluded that "the assumption of constant proportions is for all practical purposes entirely justified" (Leontief 1941: 39–40, 41).[25] Yet these justifications are important in the process of inferring from a data point (the numerical value of a coefficient) to how, hypothetically, input consumption would change if output changed.

Note that such exercises of expert judgment and the lack of mechanical statistical reliability measures were frequent in interwar econometrics.[26] Still, if we compare the statistical practices already mentioned above, to those implemented at the National Resources Committee (NRC) under Means's direction to study the structure of the American economy introduced above), we find some striking contrasts, especially in connection with the modern theory of statistical inference. Means did not use a mathematical model of the national economy, but he estimated structural relations between what he considered key estimates such as labor requirements and some industrial outputs or consumption. Acknowledging that their approach followed techniques developed at the US Department of Agriculture (USDA) by the Bureau of Agricultural Economics (BAE),[27] in Means's reports, the authors computed multiple correlation coefficients and trend equations to study eighty-one industries. For instance, the relationship between fuel consumed and railroad transportation of passengers was studied for the period 1920–32 by a linear equation, yielding the following: "Calculated fuel consumed = 28.0 − 1.66 (year–1926) + 0.1728 (net ton-miles) + 0.7774 (revenue passenger-miles)" (Means 1938: 99).

25. This problem of the testing of the hypotheses and predictions is beyond the scope of this article in which I focus on the statistical determination of the main structural parameters.

26. See Biddle 1999, 2017; Boumans 2015; and Morgan 1990.

27. Developed, in particular, by Mordecai Ezekiel, one of the BAE's leading economists (see Biddle, this volume). Ezekiel was also a member of the NRC's industrial committee.

Each such empirical relation was submitted to several reliability checks to assess its ability to make accurate projections beyond the sample period on which it was fitted. The data for 1920–32 were used to determine the empirical relations and that for 1933–36 were left for checking. In addition to graphical checks, the authors systematically computed the residuals to "indicate the closeness of fit" and "as an empirical test of the reliability of the formula for the years beyond 1932" (Means 1938: 89). By convention, for the extrapolated years, if the average residual was not greater than 5 percent, the relation was considered reliable. In addition to that, standard errors were computed and considered "a more satisfactory method" (89). Reliability of the estimates was stated from the comparison between the residuals and the standard error. However, Means warned that probabilistic interpretations of the standard error would not be attempted, "since the time series analyzed . . . do not constitute random and unrelated samples" (12).

As noted before, Means sent to Leontief a draft of this report. Although we do not have the comments Leontief sent, it appears from Means's answers that they concentrated on two points:[28] first, that some equations expressed relationships between variables as if one were independent from the other, while both would better be considered dependent variables; second, that the partial relations estimated to establish the required patterns of resource use did not guarantee any consistency. Both remarks can easily be related to Leontief's interindustry approach, as in his model all the variables are dependent variables and, in addition, general equilibrium equations guarantee the balance of resources and uses for all industries and commodities. Although Means agreed that the variables were not independent ones, he underlined that the relationships studied were statistical relations and involved no causality. However, he admitted, in his use of the least squares method, one variable had to be considered independent and the other the dependent one. As for the consistency of the patterns, Means agreed with Leontief and admitted that a more thorough look at consistency was reserved for future works. This discussion helps us understand Leontief's perspective. As a matter of statistical inference, it seems that Leontief was not impressed by the multiple correlations and the standard errors computed in Means's report. Instead, their discussion seems to replay the opposition, stated for instance by E. J. Working (1932) or Marschak (1938), between sample studies relying on inferential statistics

---

28. Means to Leontief, September–October 1938, HUG 4517, box 2, folder 1.

based on the theory of probability, and econometric approaches that did not usually rely on such inferential tools. In *The Structure*'s introduction, Leontief (1941: 4) discarded the "empiricist approach" based on series of correlations from separate samples, as it would never "represent a system of general interdependence." In this respect, Leontief's view stood close to that expressed by Working (1932: 255), who noted that what mattered was to understand the underlying "mechanism in operation" by stating a theory.[29] Leontief's approach thus stands in striking contrast to Means's line of work: not only because the former was based on a theoretical model while the latter relied on statistical models to draw inferences from data samples but also because only the latter attempted to employ probabilistic inferential techniques to assess the reliability of the estimates. Yet, as for the relation to the probability theory, NRC statisticians made an ambivalent use, since the standard error was computed without accepting the probabilistic assumptions associated with it. This led them to eventually discard the test of significance.

Another distinction between the two approaches was the nature of the data. Leontief proceeded to the statistical determination of his model for a base year and not from samples of historical data. Indeed, besides methodological and theoretical reasons, one reason for Leontief not to mobilize the same tools was that, for each interindustry coefficient, the sample of observations was limited to one measure: the one in the interindustry table. In this respect, the problem of the statistical determination of the equations in a general equilibrium framework had already been raised, especially in reaction to Henry L. Moore's *Synthetic Economics*, published in 1929, where he had attempted to work out a Walrasian econometric model. Leontief could not ignore this work and the subsequent discussions. For instance, Mordecai Ezekiel (1930) had highlighted the limitations of the statistical method proposed by Moore to determine his equations.[30] Taking the demand for cotton, Ezekiel noted that, in a general equilibrium scheme, it would depend on at least a hundred other prices, and since the reliability of the estimates depends directly on the number of independent observations in the sample, it would require one to use the whole history of production of cotton in the United States, inferring sup-

29. In econometrics, a similar analogy of the "mechanism of economic life" appears in Haavelmo 1944: 28. The question would be to know if this mechanism is to be considered a stochastic process (Haavelmo) or not (Leontief).

30. Ezekiel, an agricultural economist and statistician at the USDA, was one of Leontief's early supporters. Along with Means, Ezekiel was also a member of the NRC's industrial committee.

posedly constant coefficients from highly heterogeneous periods. This, according to Ezekiel, casts serious doubt on any future attempt to use time series and correlation analysis in this framework. Ezekiel recommended instead a more partial analysis where "even though the entire range of economic activity is not covered, it may be possible to solve a set of the simultaneous equations for the major commodities" (679). Such a partial approach was partly implemented by Means, in direct connection to Ezekiel and the BAE economists, to study the structure of the American economy. Although this feasibility problem should not be ignored, even in more favorable cases for the probabilistic theory of statistical inference, Leontief's (1948, 1971) postwar methodological stance shows that he considered the probabilistic approach to introduce statistical assumptions unlikely to be verified.

In 1931–41, Leontief gave little indication about why he did not rely— even in his other statistical works on supply and demand—on inferential measures based in probability theory. An exception was a comment read in December 1931 at an Econometric Society session titled "Quantitative Economics" and chaired by Irving Fisher. Commenting on a methodological discussion by Ezekiel of "statistical price analysis" and its relation to mathematical and economic theory, Leontief explained that "a peculiar technical characteristic of most of the available statistical methods is that they are really never quite adequate to our theoretical proposition" (quoted in Fisher 1932: 24). According to Leontief, statistical methods could only appraise "non-theoretical propositions" about a specific set of data, and therefore they say nothing about the general and conditional propositions of theory. Consequently, he noted, "The different reliability measures, standard errors and coefficient of correlation, I believe, are really relevant mostly to validity of this [kind of nontheoretical] arbitrary technical proposition" (24). It appears from Leontief's short but important methodological comment that he did not trust the modern theory of statistical inference (i.e., based on probability theory) to appraise the truth value of the theoretical propositions: it is useless for the econometric project to bridge economic theory and statistical data. As he noted, a statistical inquiry can neither prove nor disprove a general theoretical proposition, as one can always blame the specific mathematical relation tested, for instance, "if the linear correlation does not work we can try curvelinear [sic] correlation." This skeptical stance was also apparent in the "Pitfalls" controversy with Frisch, where Leontief (1934: 361) stated that "even the most perfect of statistical cross-checks could not possibly replace a critical analysis of the fundamental theoretical premises": the theoretician's expert judgment supersedes the tools of the modern theory of statistical inference. This comes as a confirmation of one of the meanings, tentatively stated before, of the practical significance of Leontief's direct induction econometric approach, and we can add a third principle that rules out probabilistic inferential techniques, as, for the usual economic data, he did not consider these techniques to be powerful tools to estimate and test empirical models. In his comment to Ezekiel, along with this skeptical view about the statistical determination and testability of economic theories, Leontief offered an alternative we need to examine further, some "ideal programme" of his own.[31]

5. The "Expansion of the Field of Direct Observation"

Leontief's 1931 comment would be echoed in his postwar methodological stance against probabilistic models in econometrics by asserting that the latter's statistical techniques would never compensate for inadequate data. In other words, gathering additional and better data should be preferred to increasing statistical sophistication (Leontief 1948, 1971). I contend that this methodological position, stated as early as 1931, was foundational to Leontief's interindustry project.

Leontief's comment sheds light on the interindustry studies he was preparing at the same period. Interestingly, the problem he put forward was not about the role of theory, as he acknowledged that "the very essence of a theoretical approach is to give us the possibility of ascertaining *the unknown facts that lie beyond our direct recognition*" (Leontief 1931: 23; italics added). Leontief's *direct induction* is not measurement without theory. Instead, Leontief considered the problem to lie in the information employed and how to use it. According to him, the right research direction was the search for additional data. When studying the supply and demand equations of a specific commodity, one should not be content with the market prices and volumes data. This approach was that of conventional econometric studies, just like his "simultaneous method" of 1929, which derived indirectly, from these market data, the supply and demand elastici-

---

31. I borrow from Frisch's expression as, in 1936, at an Econometric Society meeting in Oxford, Frisch stated his econometric "ideal programme" (1936).

32. About this simultaneous method and the history of the debates that led to the identification problem, see especially Morgan 1990.

ties.[32] To Leontief, the information to be secured should directly be about the fundamental determinants of supply and demand: additional data about consumption and businesses are necessary to statistically determine the "*structure* of the supply and demand schedules." This was clearly stated by him in a simple expression: "By *expansion of the field of direct observation,* we should be able to check our results" about these structures (Leontief 1931: 23; italics added). Affirmed as early as 1931, this was the core of Leontief's statistical method and doctrine, and it thus appears reasonable to consider his approach to statistical inference independent from the discussions with Frisch (and Marschak) during the "Pitfalls" controversy of 1934.

However, while rejecting the indirect approach of inferring the structural relations from the usual "set of facts" of "our price and quantity series," at the same period Leontief launched, at the NBER, a series of works on purely statistical relations of price-quantity variations. He studied inductively, without an explicit theoretical model, these price-quantity variations apparent in time series and measured by tools such as correlation coefficients. Interestingly, in this work published in 1935, Leontief made a distinction between these statistical covariation relations and the deeper and more stable underlying structural relations he assumed were determining their cyclical patterns. This distinction cannot but remind us of Frisch's contemporaneous distinctions, already stated in his propagation and impulse paper of 1933, where observable oscillations and cyclical variations had to be explained by less manifest structural relations as captured by so-called structural coefficients. Although Leontief's and Frisch's frameworks and methodologies were deeply different, they shared this general idea of statistical covariations determined by structural relations.[33] The problem was, then, to define a general strategy to infer the structural coefficients. In his comment to Ezekiel, Leontief made it clear that the strategy, which he would consistently follow with his interindustry approach, was to directly determine the structural relations: this confirms the first practical principle stated above.

Strikingly, this idea went against the strategy developed by Frisch in the 1930s—and fully implemented only in the 1940s by the Cowles Commission program on statistical inference—not to estimate directly the structural equations (the structural form model), but only the final equations

---

33. See also Boumans 2009 about the difference of timing and emphasis, in the 1930s, between Leontief's and Frisch's research agendas.

derived from it (i.e., the reduced form).[34] When Frisch (1936: 365–66) stated, *"Never try to fit to the data anything but a final equation"* derived from the "structural relations" (italics added),[35] Leontief (1931: 24) took the opposite path and aimed at "expanding our empirical investigation" to the very structural relations stated in the model.

Leontief's strategic choice to determine the structural relations from so-called direct observations had several important implications. In particular, since it was required, in addition, that the model's structural coefficients also find explicit correspondence with direct observations, those observations had to be independent from the economist's theory and be information close to or recognizable by, for instance, the engineers and technologists in the field. This was how Leontief discarded more sophisticated production functions. For instance, instead of an exponent to be determined by methods of indirect statistical inference, Leontief preferred coefficients defined as simple ratios that could be reduced to one measure that expresses—as I show—some technological constant. The metaphor, later popularized by Leontief, of input-output coefficients as ingredients of a cooking recipe is quite telling about this principle. It relied on a technological understanding of structural relations, assuming that they could be reduced to some necessary physical-cum-natural relation.

What relations and parameters shall one infer from the data? The structural ones, Leontief answered. It is now clear that this choice was the result of an explicit epistemic strategy—based on a distinction between statistical covariations of prices and quantities, and their underlying structural determinants—to deal directly with the latter. This, Leontief underlined, could not be done from the usual market price-quantity data only and thus required the *expansion of the field of direct observation*. Analysis in terms of general interdependence was already an answer to this, as "all the parts of the economic system are involved simultaneously" (Leontief 1935: 21), and therefore both the empirical model and the statistical data covered the whole national economy. But it was more than that comprehensive coverage, as it required specific data to study the "structure" of the economy. Furthermore, the reliability of the more direct inferences drawn from the "direct observations" collected depended heavily on the reliability of the

34. Furthermore, deduction, from "elementary equations and variables," of equations reduced, in a "final stage," to a "final equation," i.e., "one single equation containing only one variable," was called by Tinbergen (1940: 78), a "night train analysis."

35. This idea was considerably developed in Frisch 1938, where Frisch, however, also mentioned the possibility of cases where "the coflux relations are far from giving information about the autonomous structural relations" (418). See also, in section 1 above, the quotation of Haavelmo (1941).

data: Leontief's interindustry method of statistical inference is tightly intertwined with observation, as it attempts to reduce the former to the latter.

This *expansion of the field of direct observation* was the project Leontief launched in 1932 when he arrived at Harvard. Although Leontief extensively relied on the Census of Manufactures and the Census of Mines and Quarries, as he acknowledged in his statistical appendices, he had to collect additional data. Importantly, Leontief's table gathered more than the usual prices and quantities for each product: it required detailed cost data on intermediate consumption and labor and also households' consumption structure. Even for manufactures, the main data available in the censuses did not include interindustry flows of intermediate consumption, and Leontief had to refer to alternative sources. The multiplication of heterogeneous sources and the high degree of aggregation when sources were lacking make apparent that many data were not available and had to be estimated.[36] In such cases, we find in the appendices short descriptions of how they were estimated, and it appears that various means were used: terms employed by Leontief indicate different degrees of reliability in the estimates. When the figure was directly drawn from a published statistical table, only the source was mentioned. Otherwise, such indications appear, going from "estimated on [the] basis of," "estimated," "calculated," "estimated roughly," "very roughly estimated," to simply "on [the] basis of [a] statement in . . . ," or more radically "[any of these figures] can be determined with any degree of accuracy" and "[from] authoritative estimate" (Leontief 1936: 116–25). Again, the estimates' reliability was assessed on the basis of expert judgment and without use of the modern theory of statistical inference. Yet doubts about their reliability were not ignored, and Leontief (1941: 141) acknowledged—in the statistical appendices—that "in many instances different sources and different methods of indirect estimate had to be used." Such indirect estimates could come from answers to questions sent to industrialists and professional organizations. Again, in Leontief's terminology, "direct observation" is not immediate observation but the statistical data from which the inferences are drawn. He thus warned that "the purpose of this analysis is to show the meaning of [the interindustry table] if the numerical data contained therein are accepted at their face value" (21). This raises both the problem of the significance of Leontief's idea to determine directly the structural relations and also of the

---

36. Although the appendices are the main source of information available, they offer only a glance at the estimation process. *Estimation* is not employed here in the technical (probabilistic) meaning introduced before. It was, however, the term employed by Leontief in the appendices, introducing loosely some notion of uncertainty.

nature of the data employed for this statistical determination, that is, what Boumans (2009, see also 2015) called "expert observation."

6. Structural Investigations and Expert Observation

The methodological stance for the *expansion of the field of direct observation* was also a reason for Leontief to plead for maximum disaggregation to get the closest possible connection between the relation described— say between an input and an output—and the data.[37] For instance, instead of aggregating all the agricultural and food products into one industry, it could be disaggregated into many products. Obviously, the interindustry coefficients for, say, meats would be closer to direct observations of actual farming than those for the aggregated industry of agriculture and foods and even more if "Meats" was disaggregated further and if one could determine, for instance, the relation between corn fed and pork produced. It is already apparent in Leontief's 1937 article that he was aware of such issues. He then noted that agricultural studies were ahead in this respect and could be viewed as an ideal:

> The most direct way of obtaining the necessary information on this point would be that of *immediate observation*. Detailed studies of this kind can be found, for example, in the field of agricultural research in the form of numerous attempts at empirical verification of the "law of diminishing returns." The practical possibility of covering the entire field of agricultural, mineral, and industrial production with this kind of *specialized technological investigation* is so remote that at present it cannot be discussed at all seriously. (111; italics added)[38]

In the late 1940s, thanks to the success of input-output analysis, this possibility would appear to Leontief practically realizable and would be implemented for many industries. However, back in the 1930s, what were the agricultural researches Leontief referred to? As often was the case, Leontief did not make explicit references to works and authors, and we are left with our interrogations. The search leads us, again, to Ezekiel and the group of BAE statistical economists at the USDA.

37. Leontief (1937: 127) also expressed doubts about the reliability of the inferences drawn from index numbers.

38. See also Leontief 1971.

In the 1920s, at the BAE, Ezekiel and H. R. Tolley, in close collaboration with John D. Black, developed a statistical framework that aimed at improving the profitability of farms by examining in detail the contribution of each factor of production. As Leontief noted, it was expected that "farming is conducted under conditions of diminishing returns" (BAE 1924: 2). This excerpt is quoted from a BAE bulletin expressively titled *Input as Related to Output in Farm Organization and Cost-of-Production Studies*, indicating a common concern with Leontief's interindustry analysis of inputs and outputs in the American industries.

In these BAE studies, the problem was tackled from the perspective of the ratio of output per unit of input, examining the effect of input variations to determine the least-cost combinations of inputs. For instance, the effect of fertilizer on potato yield was studied with data on farms using different quantities of fertilizers. After statistical elimination of the effects of other factors and inputs, it was admitted that the potato output would grow, however, with diminishing increments. Two limitations in the method acknowledged by the authors were the use of passive observations and also that the estimations of the net effect of an input, considering the rest of the inputs remained unchanged, was necessarily contradicted by the fact that using more fertilizer requires more labor. In other words, "The various inputs do not vary independently of each other" (24). Leontief tackled this specific problem by assuming strictly complementary relations between inputs.

Almost twenty years before Leontief's works, this kind of analysis at the BAE (1924: 44) was coined an "input-output analysis." It was based on the statistical techniques of multiple correlation applied to samples from farm surveys. The probable error was systematically computed. Importantly, not unlike Leontief's studies, these cross-sectional studies viewed input-output ratios as primarily the expression of natural relations. Black, who moved to Harvard in 1927, was one of the originators and main supporters of this approach, as revealed in his textbook, *Production Economics*, first published in 1926. When Leontief arrived in the United States in 1931, with the support and guidance of Ezekiel, Black expressed immediate interest in the young economist. Leontief's first position was at the NBER in New York, but when he visited Harvard that year, on December 1931, Black took him to his classes.[39] Leontief was thus most probably

---

39. See HUG 4517, box 200, folder 3.

aware of Ezekiel's, Black's, and the BAE's works he referred to as *specialized technological investigations*.[40] Interestingly, these studies relied on the modern theory of statistical inference Leontief considered irrelevant to draw inferences from his own data (see Burnett, this volume).[41] Although he denied this approach the ability to (dis)confirm a theoretical proposition—like the "law of diminishing returns"— he had apparently considered these works an option to estimate statistical input-output relations. Yet the significance and the applicability of these studies to empirical general equilibrium was discussed and controversial at the time: the very meaning and existence of such structural relations, as well as the possibility to infer from them some estimates, was a matter of discussion.

The connection between such works and the Walrasian framework of constant *coefficients de production* had indeed already been established explicitly in 1928 and 1929 by Henry Schultz. This paved the way to further work in this direction. Indeed, H. Schultz (1929: 510), in discussing the theoretical foundations of the marginal productivity theory in a general equilibrium framework for its statistical study, noted: "If the expression 'input per unit of output,' which has recently been introduced by a group of agricultural economists, were confined to physical units only, it would be identical with the definition of a coefficient of production as given by [the Walrasian definition as the ratio between the output of a commodity and the quantity employed of a factor of production]."

Following Moore, H. Schultz's econometric project was then to implement the "statistical verification" of the Pareto-Walrasian marginal productivity theory. However, H. Schultz noted:

> The greatest difficulty in the way of a verification is the lack of reliable data from which to deduce coefficients of production. True, Federal and state agencies gather and publish cost-of-production data of various kinds, but they are generally useless for [the] present purposes. What is greatly needed is a series of well-planned experiments on the relation between input and output (coefficients of production) in various fields of production. The results of such experiments not only would throw a flood of light on problems of pure theory but also would be of great value to the industries concerned. . . . The data may be made to yield

40. See also Leontief 1929. Furthermore, in 1934, Leontief published a short survey on the Agricultural Adjustment Plan (Ezekiel was one of the fathers of this plan).

41. See also Biddle in this volume about the use by BAE economists of the theory of statistical inference and the mathematical theory of probability.

coefficients of production either of the Walrasian type . . . and corresponding to the average concept, i.e., to the agricultural economist's "input per unit of output"; or of the Pareto type, . . . and corresponding to the marginal concept. (529–30)

Leontief's statistical implementation of Walrasian "average" coefficients as simple ratios continued this idea. Furthermore, Leontief's (1948) praise of controlled experiment finds here a justification. In H. Schultz's project, such coefficients were expected to be, for many of them but not all, variable.[42] However, as noted before with Ezekiel's 1930 criticism of Moore's framework, and taking as an example the demand for cotton, the transferability of the partial statistical relations of agricultural input-output studies to a general equilibrium framework involving simultaneously hundreds of commodities raised lethal statistical inference problems when based on time series. Some of Leontief's methodological choices can be understood as an answer to these issues.

Although in *The Structure* Leontief did not aim to (dis)confirm any elaborated theoretical law, he probably stated the theoretical and the statistical problems he tackled as that of an empirical general equilibrium model using Walrasian coefficients of production as an implicit association to those previous works and discussions. Although they had been only tentatively attacked, Leontief's formulation of his empirical model cannot be viewed in splendid isolation. We can admit that when preparing his statistical estimates, Leontief considered the BAE techniques and the Moore-Schultz connection. These references show the scientific options Leontief probably considered, and the associated tools, namely, the econometric techniques employed to statistically determine theoretical relations and the inferential tools mobilized for the more inductive statistical approach of the Ezekiel-Black works (see also Ezekiel 1940). Yet the idea of his technical coefficients was explicitly embedded in and connected to such *specialized technological investigations*.

Interestingly, the BAE studies on input-output relationships were followed by few further works and raised informative issues about the belief in the very existence of such structural relations. According to Black (1940: 577), in the 1920s at the BAE, the view was that "input-output analysis is technology, and that economists should not spend their resources upon it."

---

42. H. Schultz (1929) endorsed Pareto's skeptical view on marginal productivity theory: unless very restrictive conditions are fulfilled, "the marginal-productivity theory fails" (512).

Only in 1935 was another "input-output research project" launched (578). These new studies generated new controversies—particularly between Black and Theodore W. Schultz[43]—on almost all grounds—theoretical, statistical, and methodological. The authors of these new studies (focused on dairy production) seriously considered the criticism on the irrelevance of the data (from passive observation) for their aims and the weakness of the statistical methods employed before. Instead, as suggested by H. Schultz, they ran controlled experiments in farms to study the relation between cow feeding and dairy production and inferred from the data collected "input-output curves." Again, this sheds light on Leontief's appreciative reference to such controlled experiments (1948). Still, even for such techno-biological relations, the possibility to find a "universal constant" was controversial, not only about how the inference was drawn—controlled experiment and use of the modern theory of statistical inference—but also whether the very constant sought existed.

T. W. Schultz (1939: 572) argued against these studies: "The quest for input-output constants . . . has been far from fruitful [because this] approach is inherently unrealistic." To him, this "quest" for "universal input-output constants" was comparable to that of the alchemists (584).[44] For T. W. Schultz, these ratios were the results of economic decisions made by entrepreneurs with respect to economic and technical expectations and to prices. Therefore, "The rates of transformation in most of agriculture are about as variable and changeable as prices. Input-Output rates change from year to year" (584). This was the exact opposite to Leontief's (1941: 41) view that considered he could infer from his data stable technical relations. Put in Frisch's vocabulary, with T. W. Schultz, these ratios were not structural parameters but confluent relations.[45] Nevertheless, in Leontief's perspective, such technological investigations were an important solution to the problem of the statistical determination of structural relations.[46]

43. See Burnett, this volume.

44. About statistical search for constants as alchemy, see also Keynes's critique of Tinbergen's econometric works (reproduced in Hendry and Morgan 1995).

45. However, neither Frisch nor Leontief (1941: 79) considered such technological ratios a universal constant but, instead, as holding "a certain degree of invariance over time." This question, however, is beyond the scope of this article. See also Frisch, Haavelmo, and Marschak's discussion in Phelps Brown 1937.

46. Ironically, coming from very different inferential traditions and divergent views on the statistical interpretation of input–output relations, Leontief and T. W. Schultz would eventually join against the "indirect" approach to statistical inference.

The "programme" Leontief outlined in December 1931 to explore directly the very "structure" of demand and supply relations was continued with the interindustry empirical model. Again, Leontief was not fully isolated. For instance, in the realm of neoclassical supply and demand equations, Stigler (1940) admitted that derivation of statistical cost curves would better be implemented that way, where "the economist must become a technician" (402). More generally, in 1935, Tinbergen had already stated that the statistical determination of the coefficients in econometric models could be performed in "two somewhat different ways . . . which may be called the structural and the historical method" (281). Just like Leontief emphasized the role of direct observation, Tinbergen (1938: 24) noted that "the structural method tries to measure immediately the constants appearing in the equations or to deduce them by reasoning in connection with direct measurement." We find here two concerns also important for Leontief, namely, that the inquiry is a cross-sectional study and not based on time series, and that it is an "immediate" or "direct measurement." We shall, however, keep in mind some nuances as cross-sectional structural studies—for instance, the Ezekiel-Black studies and experiments—did mobilize "indirect" probabilistic inferential techniques and the usual tools of regression and curve fitting. In other words, and because the problem at stake is logically an inferential one, "structural investigations" do not rule out by definition problems of statistical inference and associated probabilistic tools—unless they are discarded in principle. Furthermore, an important qualification and distinction between Tinbergen's definitions and Leontief's approach is that, while for Leontief the so-called structural relations were those determining upstream the supply and demand relations, this point was unclear in Tinbergen.[47] As far as basic structural coefficients are concerned, the specificity of Leontief's statistical approach rests on the three practical principles identified and from which it follows that one has (1) to directly determine the structural parameters in the structural equations, (2) to use "direct observation" and measurement, and not estimates from regression or curve-fitting tools, and (3) to rely on analytic appraisal and expert judgment to assess estimates' reliability while ruling out the use of probabilistic inferential techniques for the usual economic data.

Such structural investigations require specific data, and the lack of adequate data led Tinbergen (1935) to discard this approach. On the contrary,

---

47. See also Frisch's (1938) critique of Tinbergen's approach.

Leontief made the collection and organization of additional data the core of his econometric (interindustry) program. In his 1948 chapter, Leontief would consider the questionnaire method as part of his direct induction approach. According to Tinbergen (1940), although limited, the structural approach was, in economics, an "approximate" of the experiments of the natural sciences, just like the method of interview Gilboy, in particular, had implemented in 1932 to statistically determine sample demand curves (with no attempt to generalize beyond the sample).[48] Frisch, too, praised the interview method, as in 1938 he—quite allusively—expressed doubts about the possibility to systematically infer the parameters from passive observations, stating that "in economics the interview method is a substitute . . . for experimentation" (418; see also Boumans 2015). After 1948, Leontief would have Gilboy work with him. While Tinbergen favored the more standard indirect statistical techniques of the "historical method," such as multiple correlation analysis, Leontief defended the alternative strategy of structural investigations he had experimented with in the 1930s, the outcome of which was *The Structure*. In Leontief's perspective, the problem was not to infer empirical parameters from more sophisticated statistical techniques but, again, *by expansion of the field of direct observation* to infer from more and better data. Defined as a ratio or expressed as a technical data, a technical coefficient was closer to immediate observation than the parameters of a more general function: according to Leontief (1949: 213), his input-output magnitudes could be determined by simply "asking the ironmaster" and other experts or engineers. In continuation of Ezekiel, Black, and H. Schultz, this was how Leontief later became "the most pronounced advocate of expert observations in economics" (Boumans 2009: 49; see also Boumans 2016), this time, however, as a means for direct induction as he discarded the tools of indirect statistical inference.

7. "Direct Induction" beyond *The Structure*

I aimed to clarify Leontief's distinction between direct induction and indirect induction (indirect statistical inference) by considering the problem of the statistical determination of the interindustry parameters as a problem of statistical inference. In the latter problem, the econometrician uses the uncontrolled observations registered to draw inferences about the

---

48. See Maas, this volume.

parameters and their presumably accurate numerical values. As a matter of direct induction, to be able to establish a direct correspondence between the model's parameters and the observations, Leontief adjusted both the model and the data and sought to proceed to *the expansion of the field of direct observation*. To him, probabilistic inferential techniques were not useful. Only more and better cross-sectional data could help directly determine the model's structural parameters in a disaggregated framework. This was how he embodied the project of expansion of the field of direct observation in the development of the interindustry table.

An additional expansion considered by Leontief in *The Structure*, but not yet genuinely implemented, was the development of structural investigations. This was one of the aims of the creation by Leontief, in 1948, of the Harvard Economic Research Project (HERP). Interestingly, Gilboy would soon become HERP's (long-lasting) associate director. At the time, Leontief (1948: 398, 402) stressed that while his direct approach emphasized direct observation, controlled experiment, use of alternative sources of information, and also direct questionnaires, "the Cowles Commission econometricians [were] inclined to minimize the practical significance of this type of empirical study." Starting in 1949 with Anne P. Carter's and Hollis B. Chenery's Harvard PhD dissertations, this was how Leontief supervised works on the so-called technical and engineering production functions. In particular, he expected to reconstruct the technical coefficients "from below" (Leontief 1952: 7) by exploiting engineering data and also by developing "practical co-operation with psychologists and sociologists" (Leontief 1949: 225). Incidentally, also in 1948, and having taken a different path, Frisch, too, strongly affirmed the limitations of indirect inference of the structural parameters from the usual passive observations employed in econometrics. As for Leontief, he had consistently denied the modern theory of statistical inference the power to compensate for insufficient and inaccurate data, as he resisted the use of probability theory to assess the "risk" in employing estimates that were presumably accurate. Yet he developed other means to avoid *misleading inferences* by making strong choices under the label "direct induction." As Leontief later explained to T. W. Schultz, this was how he made the "decision to disaggregate as much as practically possible and to rely on long time series as little as possible." And, as a matter of odds, he added: "I know it is a gamble but who does not gamble cannot win."[49]

49. Leontief to T. W. Schultz, October 2, 1958, HUG 4517, box 25, folder 9.

References

Akhabbar, Amanar. 2007. "Leontief et l'économie comme science empirique: La signification opérationnelle des lois." *Economies et Sociétés* 39, nos. 10–11: 1745–88.

Akhabbar, Amanar. 2019. *Wassily Leontief et la science économique*. Lyon: ENS Editions.

BAE (Bureau of Agricultural Economics). 1924. *Input as Related to Output in Farm Organization and Cost-of-Production Studies*. Department Bulletin No. 1277, edited by H. R. Tolley, J. D. Black, and M. J. B. Ezekiel. Washington, DC: USDA.

Biddle, Jeff E. 1999. "Statistical Economics, 1900–1950." *History of Political Economy* 31, no. 4: 607–52.

Biddle, Jeff E. 2017. "Statistical Inference in Economics, 1920–1965: Changes in Meaning and Practice." *Journal of the History of Economic Thought* 39, no. 2: 149–73.

Black, John D. 1940. "Dr. Schultz on Farm Management Research." *Journal of Farm Economics* 22, no. 3: 570–80.

Boulding, Kenneth E. 1942. Review of *The Structure of American Economy, 1919–1929*, by W. Leontief. *Canadian Journal of Economics and Political Science / Revue Canadienne d'Economique et de Science Politique* 8, no. 1: 124–26.

Boumans, Marcel. 2005. *How Economists Model the World into Numbers*. London: Routledge.

Boumans, Marcel. 2009. "Observations of an Expert." Working paper, University of Amsterdam, March 30. SSRN, ssrn.com/abstract=1433806 (accessed June 30, 2020).

Boumans, Marcel. 2012. "Logical Positivism and Leontief." Working paper, University of Amsterdam.

Boumans, Marcel. 2015. *Science outside the Laboratory: Measurement in Field Science and Economics*. Oxford: Oxford University Press.

Boumans, Marcel. 2016. "Methodological Institutionalism as a Transformation of Structural Econometrics." *Review of Political Economy* 28, no. 3: 417–25.

Ezekiel, Mordecai. 1930. "Moore's Synthetic Economics." *Quarterly Journal of Economics* 44, no. 4: 663–79.

Ezekiel, Mordecai. 1940. "A Check on a Multiple Correlation Result." *Journal of Farm Economics* 22, no. 4: 766–68.

Fisher, Irving. 1932. "Quantitative Economics." *American Economic Review* 22, no. 1: 16–24.

Frisch, Ragnar. 1936. "An Ideal Programme for Macrodynamic Studies." In Phelps Brown 1937: 365–66.

Frisch, Ragnar. 1938. *Autonomy of Economic Relations: Statistical versus Theoretical Relations in Economic Macrodynamics*. Memorandum prepared for the Business Cycle Conference at Cambridge, England, July. Reprinted in Hendry and Morgan 1995: 407–19.

Haavelmo, Trygve. 1941. "The Elements of Frisch's Confluence Analysis." With Hans Staehle. Hectograph. Cambridge, MA: Harvard University.

Haavelmo, Trygve. 1944. "The Probability Approach in Econometrics." *Econometrica* 12 (supplement): 1–115.

Hendry, David F. 1995. "Econometrics and Business Cycle Empirics." *Economic Journal* 105, no. 433: 1622–36.

Hendry, David F., and Mary S. Morgan, eds. 1995. *The Foundations of Econometric Analysis.* Cambridge: Cambridge University Press.

Klein, Lawrence R. 1953. *A Textbook of Econometrics.* Evanston, IL: Row, Peterson.

Klein, Lawrence R. 1962. *An Introduction to Econometrics.* Englewood Cliffs, NJ: Prentice Hall.

Kohli, Martin C. 2001. "Leontief and the U.S. Bureau of Labor Statistics, 1941–54: Developing a Framework for Measurement." In *The Age of Economic Measurement,* edited by Judy L. Klein and Mary S. Morgan. *History of Political Economy* 33 (supplement): 190–212.

Leontief, Wassily W. 1929. "Ein Versuch zur statistischen Analyse von Angebot und Nachfrage." *Weltwirtschaftliches Archiv* 30, no. 1: 1–53.

Leontief, Wassily W. 1931. "Comments." In Fisher 1932: 23–24.

Leontief, Wassily W. 1932. "Studien über die Elastizität des Angebots." *Weltwirtschaftliches Archiv* 35, no. 1: 66–115.

Leontief, Wassily W. 1934. "Pitfalls in the Construction of Demand and Supply Curves: A Reply." *Quarterly Journal of Economics* 48, no. 2: 355–61.

Leontief, Wassily W. 1936. "Quantitative Input and Output Relations in the Economic System of the United States." *Review of Economic Statistics* 18, no. 3: 105–25.

Leontief, Wassily W. 1937. "Interrelations of Prices, Output, Savings, and Investment." *Review of Economic Statistics* 19, no. 3: 109–32.

Leontief, Wassily W. 1940. "Elasticity of Demand Computed from Cost Data." *American Economic Review* 30, no. 4: 814–17.

Leontief, Wassily W. 1941. *The Structure of American Economy, 1919–1929: An Empirical Application of Equilibrium Analysis.* Cambridge, MA: Harvard University Press.

Leontief, Wassily W. 1948. "Econometrics." In *A Survey of Contemporary Economics,* edited by Howard S. Ellis, 388–411. Homewood, PA: Richard D. Irwin.

Leontief, Wassily W. 1949. "Recent Developments in the Study of Interindustrial Relationships." *American Economic Review* 39, no. 3: 211–25.

Leontief, Wassily W. 1952. "Some Basic Problems of Structural Analysis." *Review of Economics and Statistics* 34, no. 1: 1–9.

Leontief, Wassily W. 1954. "Mathematics in Economics." *Bulletin of the American Mathematical Society* 60, no. 3: 215–33.

Leontief, Wassily W. 1971. "Theoretical Assumptions and Nonobserved Facts." *American Economic Review* 61, no. 1: 1–7.

Marschak, Jacob. 1938. Review of *Linear Regression Analysis of Economic Time Series,* by T. Koopmans. *Economic Journal* 48, no. 189: 104–6.

Marschak, Jacob. 1950. "Statistical Inference in Economics: An Introduction." In *Statistical Inference in Dynamic Economic Models,* edited by Tjalling C. Koopmans, 1–52. Cowles Commission for Research in Economics, Monograph 10. New York: John Wiley.

Means, Gardiner C., ed. 1938. *Patterns of Resource Use.* Technical Report, Industrial Section for the National Resources Committee, February. Washington, DC: NRC.

Morgan, Mary S. 1990. *The History of Econometric Ideas.* Cambridge: Cambridge University Press.

Neisser, Hans. 1941. Review of *The Structure of American Economy, 1919–1929*, by W. Leontief. *American Economic Review* 31, no. 3: 608–10.

Phelps Brown, E. H. 1937. "Report of the Oxford Meeting, September 25–29, 1936." *Econometrica* 5, no. 4: 361–83.

Rothbarth, E. 1943. Review of *The Structure of American Economy 1919–29*, by W. Leontief. *Economic Journal* 53, nos. 210–11: 213–16.

Schultz, Henry. 1929. "Marginal Productivity and the General Pricing Process." *Journal of Political Economy* 37, no. 5: 505–51.

Schultz, Theodore W. 1939. "Theory of the Firm and Farm Management Research." *Journal of Farm Economics* 21, no. 3: 570–86.

Stigler, George J. 1939. "The Limitations of Statistical Demand Curves." *Journal of the American Statistical Association* 34, no. 207: 469–81.

Stigler, George J. 1940. "Round Table on Cost Functions and Their Relation to Imperfect Competition." *American Economic Review* 30, no. 1: 400–402.

Tinbergen, Jan. 1935. "Annual Survey: Suggestions on Quantitative Business Cycle Theory." *Econometrica* 3, no. 3: 241–308.

Tinbergen, Jan. 1938. "On the Theory of Business-Cycle Control." *Econometrica* 6, no. 1: 22–39.

Tinbergen, Jan. 1940. "Econometric Business Cycle Research." *Review of Economic Studies* 7, no. 2: 73–90.

Tintner, Gerhard. 1952. *Econometrics.* New York: John Wiley.

Working, E. J. 1932. "Indications of Changes in the Demand for Agricultural Products." *Journal of Farm Economics* 14, no. 2: 239–56.

Politicizing the Environment: (In)direct Inference, Rationality, and the Credibility of the Contingent Valuation Method

Harro Maas

On March 5, 2020, *Food Safety News* reported that an "infamous" nitrate and phosphorus pollution litigation case was "finally going to get an ending." In 2005, the attorney general of Oklahoma, Drew Edmondson, had filed a lawsuit, *State of Oklahoma v. Tyson Foods, Inc., et al.*, against the upstream poultry industry for polluting the Illinois River Watershed. The case was heard without a jury by federal judge Gregory K. Frizzell between September 21, 2009, and February 18, 2010, but was then left without a decision in what the article described as a "judicial purgatory."

Edmondson had filed the case under CERCLA, the Comprehensive Environmental Response, Compensation, and Liability Act, better known as Superfund, to claim not only recovery and response costs for the environmental damage to a scenic tourist lake and river site but also costs due to loss of "existence" or "non-use" value, that is, value attributed to the mere existence of the natural resource. He argued that continued phosphorus pollution would damage Oklahoma's economic interests in tourism, an important industry to a poor state. But the state's popularity as a destination for outdoor recreation forced Edmondson's office to begin from a paradoxical situation: if environmental harm had really been done,

This article has been long in the making. Thanks to the participants of the *HOPE* conference 2020 for their comments, to the organizers Jeff Biddle and Marcel Boumans, and to Mary Morgan and Cléo Chassonnery-Zaïgouche for unwavering support and helpful comments. A great word of thanks should go to Steve Medema and in particular to Amanar Akhabbar and the referees of this journal for extremely helpful comments.

History of Political Economy 53 (annual suppl.) DOI 10.1215/00182702-9414889

then why did so many visitors continue to boat, swim, and fish in the watershed area?[1] It took the office of the attorney five years to prepare the case. When it started its preparations, the poultry industry responded with billboards along the highways touting the beauty of the area (with the implication being that it could not possibly be polluted) and the jobs the poultry industry brought to the region, to which the state and environmental interest groups responded with their own information campaign.

In this highly politicized and adversarial context, the state hired natural scientists to conduct studies on the pollution of the Illinois River basin, its pollution history and its possible remedies, that served as input for a contingent valuation study in use and nonuse values. The study was overseen by a Boulder-based environmental consultancy firm, Stratus Consulting. The primary instrument used by the study was a survey whose basic question was about a respondent's willingness to pay for a program to clean up and improve the water quality of the scenic lake and river site. The total value calculated from the survey would serve as input for the attorney general's damage claim.

Stratus Consulting engaged some of the leading experts in contingent valuation research, among whom were the environmental economists Richard C. Bishop and W. Michael Hanemann. The defendants in turn hired their own experts, among whom was the environmental and resource economist William S. Desvousges, to question the study's validity and outcomes. All three had been involved in, among others, the controversial contingent valuation studies on the Exxon Valdez oil spill of March 1989, though on different sides of the courtroom, Bishop and Hanemann for the federal government and State of Alaska, Desvousges for Exxon. When Hanemann in his out-of-court deposition was asked if he knew Dr. Desvousges and agreed with his opinions, he answered that "after the spring of 1989, [Desvousges] seemed to have a change of heart about contingent valuation. I think the summary is I agree with the old Bill Desvousges, but not with the new Bill Desvousges."[2]

1. Drew Edmondson was a Democrat who had assumed office in 1995 as attorney general and would stay on until 2011, when he was succeeded by the Republican Scott Pruitt. The Trump administration appointed Pruitt as director of the Environmental Protection Agency, from February 17, 2017, until July April 6, 2018, when he had to resign because of ethical misconduct. Edmondson was reelected without opposition as attorney general in 2006 and unsuccessfully ran for governor in 2010 and 2018.

2. Videotaped deposition of William Michael Hanemann, May 5, 2009, Case 4:05-cv-00329-GKF-PJC Document 2272-7 Filed in USDC ND/OK on 06/19/2009, p. 249.

My aim here is to situate this change of heart on the merits of the contingent valuation method historically. Contingent valuation went from being a rather innocuous method used in cost-benefit analysis to infer the demand and value of a recreational resource, to being a politically and judicially charged method for value claims in the adversarial context of complex environmental litigation cases. I situate the fulcrum of this transformation around the 1980s, but long before the Exxon Valdez oil spill. It is well expressed by one of the resource economists who stood at the cradle of the method itself, Marion Clawson. In a commentary for the *Environmental Professional*, the official journal of the major society for such professionals, Clawson (1980) complained about the "marked partisan politicizing of environmental, natural resource and conservation issues."

The politicizing of environmental issues went hand in hand with a shift in the use of contingent valuation survey questionnaires, from being a substitute for indirect inferences about the demand for recreation opportunities to being an instrument for value assessments about environmental harm. While the use of questionnaires for the first purpose was considered to hinge on assumptions about the rational responses of individuals to changes in costs that could be compared with indirect methods of inference to such responses, no such indirect method of inference was available for its second use. This, and the increasingly adversarial context in which the contingent valuation method came to be used, made that initial support for the use of survey questionnaires fade away. Not only did the quality of the instrument itself become increasingly questioned; so did the ability of respondents to give coherent responses to the questions asked. By contrast, proponents of the method of contingent valuation were convinced that any lack of rationality on the part of respondents and any flaws in the instrument itself could be repaired in a constant process of improvement. The different assessments of what can be inferred from a contingent valuation study and how its quality can be improved would bring environmental and resource economists to different sides of the courtroom.

How to Measure the Demand
for Outdoor Recreation?

As Spencer Banzhaf (2017) pointed out in this journal, the method of contingent valuation resulted from two strands of research that met in the 1970s. The first was empirical research on outdoor recreation, which had started to grow explosively from the 1950s on. The second strand of research aimed to find a money value for the sheer existence of a natural feature itself and fit with growing concerns of environmentalists at the end of the 1960s about questions of pollution and natural damage assessments. Both strands were in step with the importance attributed to cost-benefit analysis in US policymaking (Porter 1996).

In relation to the first strand of research, the method had been introduced quite innocuously as an alternative method to measure the value that individuals attribute to recreation sites. In the 1950s, resource economists developed the travel-cost method to help government agencies plan for the allocation of America's natural resources, be it for recreation, mining, or some other use. In view of the growing mobility in the 1950s afforded by rising automobile sales and the eventual completion of the interstate highway system, state agencies could reasonably anticipate a rapidly growing demand for outdoor recreation. There was therefore a need for a tool to put a value on the benefits of outdoor recreation for the purpose of rational planning of natural (and national) resources.

An important article in that effort was Clawson's "Methods of Measuring the Demand for and Value of Outdoor Recreation" of 1959. Clawson started from the observation that individuals and families incurred costs to travel to national parks. Demand for outdoor recreation in national parks could not be measured from market data because for all sorts of reasons there was no such market. Yet there were market-like data available that could give an indication of the demand of individuals (families) for the recreation opportunity. Clawson's idea was to infer this demand from travel-cost data. Such costs consisted of various items—gasoline, meals, lodging—which depended, among other things, on the composition of the household, the fuel efficiency of the car, and the distance traveled.

Clawson's idea was not completely new. In a 1947 letter to the US Park Service, Harold Hotelling had suggested calculating the demand for outdoor recreation from the average number of visits in different geographic zones and the average costs of travel. Even if Clawson may have been conversant with Hotelling's suggestion (Banzhaf 2010), his approach was markedly different. While Hotelling inferred demand from differences in travel costs to the recreational resource, Clawson argued that this was only half the story. In Clawson's terms, Hotelling would have only measured the value of the recreational experience but not the value individuals attributed to the national park itself as a recreation opportunity. As most national parks did not charge an entrance fee, the costs of travel only measured this last value at zero price for all visitors. To measure the value individual visitors attributed to the recreation resource itself, a second step was needed.

The ingenuity of Clawson's proposal was to use changes in travel costs and number of visits to make an inference to the demand function for the recreational resource itself. Clawson's procedure was to introduce a hypothetical: if an entrance fee was charged, how many visitors would refrain from visiting? By gradually raising the fee, it would be possible to uncover the whole demand curve for the recreational resource. Clawson (1959: 31) then also entered into a discussion about the total value of the recreational resource itself, but he was somewhat hesitant to use the total consumer surplus as such a measure because he considered its estimate "questionable in any situation."

By way of illustration Clawson used travel-cost data that could be easily obtained or calculated for four different national parks: Yosemite, Glacier, Shenandoah, and Grand Canyon. For Yosemite, Clawson used census data from 1950 and actual visits in 1953 from different counties inside and outside California that had been counted at the park's entrance. Clawson acknowledged the difficulties in the actual calculation, but these did not differ from ordinary statistical and econometric calculation and estimation problems. Hence the calculated travel costs might be imperfect, but they did give an indication of actual (average) travel costs incurred for different geographic distances to the national park. The statistical data needed were easily available, though imprecise, but they more or less hit the target: travel costs as a measure of the recreational experience. Clawson made similar calculations for the other parks.

Clawson then went on to his real target of interest: the estimation of the demand curve for the recreational resource itself or, better, the inference to the demand curve from the relation between travel costs and park visits. In an extensive discussion of Yosemite, Clawson explained how such a procedure could work. He included a large table, reproduced here as table 1, in which he relabeled the different geographic counties where visitors came from zones 1–5 for California and zones 1–6 for other states. The first two columns list actual visits and calculated travel costs. The subsequent columns show the expected drop in visits if a fee was charged of three dollars, five dollars, and so forth.

The expected drop in visits was read from the calculated relation between the number of visits and travel costs. It was Clawson's (1959: 26) "contention" that the newly plotted relation between (the remaining) number of visits and the entrance fee "approximates the true demand curve for the recreation opportunity itself." While Hotelling's proposal inferred demand for a recreational resource from differences in travel costs for individuals with identical preference schedules, Clawson's proposal depended on average comparability of preferences between different regions and on the assumption of a "rational" response to prices. That is, Clawson assumed that individuals would treat a price increase as they would treat any rise in costs. On that assumption the fall in demand for the recreational service could simply be read from the calculated relation between travel costs and the number of visits.

From Indirect Inference to Direct Survey
Measurement of Outdoor Recreation Demand

Clawson's two-step inference procedure to demand functions for recreation amenities became quickly referred to as "Clawson demand functions." It was taken up by the environmental and resource economist Jack Knetsch, who, just like Clawson, was affiliated with Resources for the Future. In 1966, Knetsch and Clawson published their jointly written and well-received *The Economics of Outdoor Recreation*. Knetsch would collaborate not only with Clawson but also with important resource economists such as John V. Krutilla and Robert K. Davis. Davis was particularly important for the introduction of questionnaires in measuring the value of environmental goods. In the 1980s Knetsch collaborated with Daniel Kahneman and Richard Thaler on their influential papers on the endowment effect. This last collaboration also gives an indication of the direction Knetsch's work would take. While starting as a moderate enthusiast of the possibilities of Clawson's measurement procedure, Knetsch would become increasingly skeptical that questionnaires could produce credible measurements of the demand for environmental goods.

In 1963, Knetsch published a succinct explanation of Clawson's measurement procedure. Clawson had mentioned the many different considerations that individuals could have in traveling or not traveling to a national park and the many practical difficulties this would cause in performing the actual statistical and econometric measurements and calculations. Knetsch briefly summarized those difficulties and considerations, but then put them aside by presenting a clear-cut hypothetical case from which the basics of Clawson's procedure could be readily understood. He then continued to draw some equally clear-cut policy conclusions. In contrast with Clawson, Knetsch provided only a theoretical sketch of the inference to "Clawson demand functions" from travel-cost data. Knetsch's data were hypothetical, but just like Clawson, Knetsch used his very simple example to show how one could use them to derive a demand function for the recreational resource. More clearly than Clawson, Knetsch made a distinction between money and time investment in outdoor recreation. While Clawson had been reluctant to give the consumer surplus a definite meaning, Knetsch argued that the surface below the Clawson demand curve measured the total consumer value of the recreational resource— that is, the total value of the recreational service, not of any other service the natural park might possibly provide to the public.

This different assessment of the consumer surplus follows almost directly from the different representations of the demand schedules in both papers. While Clawson started off from a textbook Marshallian demand function, his graphic plotting of his empirical estimates came nowhere near a graph that neatly cuts both axes so that a finite value could be calculated. Knetsch, by contrast, assumed a simple linear relation between travel costs and "consumer behavior" for three different cities; from that, he derived hypothetical demand data that he then plotted as a curve cutting both axes.

Knetsch perceived the relation between travel costs and park visits more explicitly than Clawson as a "proxy" for the nonexisting market transactions. He downplayed the analogy with an entrance fee in his "estimated demand curve" and considered it rather more generally a "cost reaction from general expenditure behavior." Knetsch stressed the *hypothetical* character of the derived demand curve, not because his data were hypothetical, but because the curve measured a hypothetical entity. Whether seen as a fee or otherwise, the procedure produced an "economically meaningful demand relation" that showed a consumer's willingness to pay for the recreational resource. "Actual payment may or may not be made, with this decision usually made on other considerations" (Knetsch 1963: 391–92). The consumer surplus, nicely defined by the demand curve cutting both axes, provided a measure of total benefits of the recreational "project" that could be used in cost-benefit analyses for planning purposes. Even though Knetsch used the same inference procedure to a demand curve as Clawson, his hypothetical example eliminated the messiness of statistical testing from incomplete and imperfect empirical data.

Knetsch's crisp concepts were taken up in a paper by Robert Davis. Like Knetsch and Clawson, Davis was a Harvard graduate, finishing his thesis in 1963 while at Resources for the Future. The interaction between Knetsch and Davis is apparent from Davis's comments on Knetsch's draft paper. In his thesis, Davis developed a different method to measure the demand for a recreational resource as a function of consumers' willingness to pay. Davis published a short version of his research in 1963 in *Natural Resources*, the same year Knetsch published his article in *Land Economics*.[3]

Like Knetsch, Davis had clearly been inspired by Clawson's 1959 article, but in his article (and thesis) he took a different direction. Clawson had stated that his method proposed to measure the demand for outdoor recreation "in the strict sense of the word 'demand.'" As he explained, this meant that his procedure measured "a willingness of users to pay measurable or definable sums of money for specified volumes of outdoor recreation" (Clawson 1959: 5). Willingness to pay appeared only once more in Clawson's text, when he explained how a monopolist should be able to "reap for himself" the consumer surplus by price discrimination, something he considered "probably but not always illegal" (31).

Knetsch also used the expression "willingness to pay" only twice, but in Davis's article it appears numerous times. And for good reasons. Even though the "strict sense" of the word *demand* may be "willingness to pay," in Clawson's and Knetsch's measurement procedures consumers are price takers who perceive a fee or a rise in costs and adjust their travel behavior accordingly. Clawson's and Knetsch's measurement procedures trace out consumer demand or, in Knetsch's (1963: 387) behavioristic terms, the "expression of consumer behavior," and from there infers consumers' willingness to pay for the recreation opportunity. But willingness to pay can also be registered without an effective behavioral response, that is, it can be registered merely from stated behavior, something Knetsch actually alluded to when he somewhat obscurely wrote that an "actual payment decision" is "usually made on other grounds" (392). This difference between stated and actual behavior would become important in judging the credibility of the contingent valuation method. For this reason, some environmental economists, such as Richard Bishop and Thomas Heberlein (1986), would consider willingness to pay as intended behavior and therefore still part of a respondent's attitude, not as an actual behavioral response.

Instead of following Clawson's two-step procedure in measuring the demand function, Davis measured the demand function *directly* from sur-

3. We can of course see these publications as economics "from the fringes," as Banzhaf (2010) has it in his excellent article on Clawson. But if we look at the place, Harvard, from which Clawson, Knetsch, and Davis received their PhDs, one might also say that the center is moving to the fringes.

vey respondents' expressed willingness to pay. Clawson's table 3 (here table 1) is instructive for thinking about Davis's alternative measurement procedure. Horizontally, Clawson listed the number of travels depending on costs and then added columns with gradually increasing costs, which Clawson thought of as entrance fees: three dollars, five dollars, ten dollars, and then twenty dollars. From these "fees" he calculated the decline in the number of visits for different geographic zones. Davis's procedure can be seen as suppressing the whole first stage—the collection of data on travel costs and so on—by directly asking respondents in a bidding game about their willingness to pay for the recreational amenity in which prices would go up until the respondent dropped out. That is, think of the above entrance fees as prices in a bidding game and do not infer the demand curve from actual data on travel costs and park visits, but ask respondents directly through a questionnaire how much they are willing to pay for a visit to the recreation opportunity. Just as one could derive the whole demand curve from Clawson's indirect measurement, so the whole demand curve could be measured directly with such a questionnaire. The consumer surplus would, then, give a total value estimate of the recreation opportunity, as Knetsch had suggested.

Davis's procedure measured demand "in the strict sense" of "willingness to pay," as stated by Clawson, but without the implied behavioral response. While Knetsch had emphasized the hypothetical nature of the derived demand curve, Davis's whole measurement procedure hinged on a hypothetical situation and hypothetical implied behavior. Davis emphasized he had tried to keep the hypothetical of the questionnaire to a minimum. He made sure to avoid using the word *fee*, as this could lead to "obvious biases," but also tried to avoid bias that might result from respondents' lack of time to state their bid.

> The hypothetical in the interviews was held to a minimum by not asking respondents to describe the magnitude of their response to price changes but only whether responses were positive, negative, or zero. A negative response to a bid meant the user would not come to the area at all. This is a realistic set of reactions for vacationists and week-enders who typically must spend all or none of their time on one area or at least have little opportunity to trade off a day or two between areas. Obvious biases were avoided by not calling the change in price a fee, by disassociating the interviewer with landowners and management agencies, and by structuring the interview so that respondents were not rushed into their decisions. (Davis 1963: 245)

Table 1 Estimated effect of raising entrance fees to Yosemite National Park, 1953

Area of origin	actual visits 1953 (1,000)	estimated costs per visit, pres. entrance fees $	Entrance fee raised by $3 per person		entrance fee raised by $5 per person		entrance fee raised by $10 per person		entrance fee raised by $20 per person	
			estimated visits (1,000)	added fee revenue ($1,000)	estimated visits (1,000)	added fee revenue ($1,000)	estimated visits (1,000)	added fee revenue ($1,000)	estimated visits (1,000)	added fee revenue ($1,000)
California zone 1	35	16.65	14	42	11	55	7	70	4	80
2	114	20.4	77	231	64	320	47	470	33	660
3	143	27.05	119	357	108	540	90	900	68	1360
4	119	29.05	111	333	102	510	86	860	67	1340
5	245	42.25	234	362	224	1120	208	2080	161	3220
subtotal	656		555	1665	509	2545	438	4380	333	6660
Other States zone 1	26	66.5	22	66	20	100	17	170	13	260
2	19	85	23	69	22	110	20	200	17	340
3	35	132.05	31	93	33	150	30	300	27	540
4	66	180	59	177	59	295	59	590	57	1140
5	40	227.5	42	126	41	265	41	410	39	780
6	51	284.5	48	144	48	240	48	480	45	920
subtotal	237		225	670	229	1100	215	2150	199	3980
Total	893		780	2335	729	3545	653	6530	532	10640

Note: I omitted Clawson's notes on the choices he made in calculating the figures in the table.

Source: Table 3 in Clawson 1959: 24–25.

Clawson had been clear about the fact that demand for outdoor recreation in national parks for all sorts of reasons was incomparable to a market situation, but this did not prevent him from using a fictional entrance fee as a frame of reference to infer to the demand function for the recreational amenity. Knetsch downplayed the idea of a fictional entrance fee and preferred to think of consumer behavior as simply responding to changes in costs. The impossibility of inferring the demand curve from normal market conditions was an "additional difficulty" that had, moreover, discouraged economists from paying adequate attention to outdoor recreation and similar "non-market goods" in the first place (Knetsch 1963). Why it was an additional difficulty was not clear, however, certainly not if one considers the difficulty of estimating a demand function from market data. Davis transformed the indirect measurement of the demand for a recreational amenity itself into a market situation. The questionnaire situation mimicked a market in which the respondent was placed in the role of a consumer and the interviewer "in the position of a seller who elicits the highest possible bid from the user for the services being offered" (Davis 1963: 245).

Thus, the problem to be solved went from being the indirect measurement of a demand function for which no market situation was assumed to being the direct measurement of willingness to pay in a questionnaire that mimicked a market. Clawson had assumed that the rationality expressed in actual behavior of visitors to national parks was equally present when individuals stated their willingness to pay for the recreational amenity in a paper market—a questionnaire. This a priori assumption had enabled him to make the inference to the demand function. Indeed, was this not the underlying assumption in any econometric effort to disentangle the laws of supply and demand? But rationality in Clawson's case meant little more than extrapolated behavior, while in Davis's case it was a cognitive claim about the ability of respondents to answer a questionnaire.

The Trouble with Questionnaires

Ever since the Wallis-Friedman (1942) critique of Louis L. Thurstone's (1931) measurement of indifference curves, economists have been uncomfortable with questionnaires.[4] In a contribution to an important 1986 conference volume on the CV method, a book that I discuss in more detail in the next section, V. Kerry Smith quoted from Deirdre McCloskey's *Rhetoric of Economics* (1983):

---

4. For an in-depth analysis, see Moscati 2018.

Economists are so impressed by the confusions that might possibly result from questionnaires that they abandon them entirely, in favor of the confusions resulting from external observation. They are unthinkingly committed to the notion that only the externally observable behavior of economic actors is admissible evidence in arguments concerning economics. (Cummings, Brookshire, and Schulze 1986: 162)

But if we look at the Clawson-Knetsch-Davis triad, the picture is more nuanced. Just like Clawson, many economists relied, and still rely, in their research on data gathered from questionnaires. The US Census, an important source of Clawson's data, is a case in point. And it is well known that the answers to census questionnaires are a source of "data trouble," certainly if they include questions about sources of income (Bouk 2018, 2020), but census data are used on a matter-of-fact basis by economists. Thomas Stapleford and Emmanuel Didier have detailed the efforts of labor and agricultural statisticians to circumvent well-known problems of deliberate deception and misreporting at the Bureau of Labor Statistics and the US Department of Agriculture. Yet the resulting data from their survey questionnaires were used as perhaps imperfect, but necessary, inputs in the empirical work of agricultural and labor economists (Stapleford 2012; Didier 2012). Smith (1986) gave the example of self-reporting from homeowners on the market value of their houses, which economists considered perfectly acceptable input in Hedonic Pricing calculations. Clawson showed himself well aware of the limitations of the available survey data, but these limitations did not prevent him from using those data for his statistical inferences to a demand function for recreational resources.

It is therefore not surveys or questionnaires per se that make economists feel uneasy, as McCloskey suggests, but a particular *kind* of questionnaire. That is, a questionnaire that asks about attitudes only, with no questions about actual behavior.[5] But it was precisely a questionnaire that comes close to an attitude survey that Davis proposed as an alternative to directly measure what the Clawson method measured indirectly. Respondents state, but do not wire, their contribution. The obvious question therefore was how Clawson's and Davis's methods of measurement compared to each other.

To answer that question, Knetsch and Davis wrote a joint paper that consisted of a combination of their 1963 papers to which they added an

---

5. Yet even this can hardly be maintained, as economists were up to their ears in the measurement of consumer and business attitudes for forecasting purposes. See Edwards 2012.

empirical travel cost study that they then compared with the results of Davis's 1963 survey. Originally published in 1966, the paper explains that the absence of a market mechanism for recreational goods, either because "we prefer it that way" or "because many kinds of outdoor recreation experience cannot be packaged and sold by private producers to private consumers," implies that "values" must be "imputed" to recreation services.

Their paper then goes on to explain both the travel cost method and Davis's questionnaire-cum–bidding game and compares the empirical results from a study on the Pittson area in northern Maine with Davis's results from a survey on the same area. They concluded that the results were remarkably close, even to such a degree that Davis's questionnaire method seemed more precise.[6] Searching for explanations, they suggested that "years of experience" in traveling to the recreational site could be seen as an "accumulation of consumer capital," which contributed to the "general economic consistency and rationality of the responses" (Knetsch and Davis 1966).

The authors expressed genuine surprise that the results of both studies agreed so closely,[7] and concluded that both methods could serve as "checks on each other in applied situations" (Knetsch and Davis 1966). There were of course some "rough spots" in both methods that needed to be "ironed out," but Knetsch and Davis (1966) believed both methods "to be worthy of a major research effort if benefit-cost analysis is to contribute its full potential in planning decisions affecting recreation investments in land and water resources." They also noted that a downside of Davis's questionnaire method was that it was substantially more expensive than the travel-cost method, which relied mostly on data that were easily available. If there was resistance to the use of questionnaires that measured something close to attitudes, this came from the costs of the method, not from principled resistance.

The surprising result of their comparison of methods was that a direct method of measurement could potentially be a substitute for an indirect method of inference. The travel-cost method used available data and made the inference on the assumption of a rational response of consumers to changes in costs. The questionnaire method created data and calculated the demand function on the basis of respondents' answers to valuation ques-

6. On the difference between accuracy and precision, see Porter 2007.

7. In fact, the survey results were reconverted to a representative sample for the Pittson area in terms of willingness to drive instead of willingness to pay, so that the authors speak at times of three instead of two methods to measure willingness to pay.

tions. Here the assumption was that respondents were able to provide coherent answers to questionnaires. Banzhaf (2017: 215) compared the answer of a respondent to a willingness-to-pay question in a questionnaire to a performative act in which a respondent "literally *speaks* economic values into being." This may be true for experiments in which things become real because you can spray them, but, as in fact Banzhaf continues to explain, nothing of the sort is the case for the pronouncements of respondents who only state but do not act on their answer. Because of this gap between words and deeds, the assumption of coherent and rational answers is more pressing in a questionnaire asking for a monetary value than the assumption of rational behavior in the travel-cost method. The close correspondence of outcomes between both methods was reassuring but still put the burden of proof on the questionnaire method, not on the travel-cost method. Credibility of the inference in travel-cost studies was exchanged for credibility of questionnaire responses in a hypothetical bidding game.

Measuring Nonuse Values of Environmental Goods

In his 1963 article, Knetsch wrote that an estimate of the demand curve on the basis of travel costs alone would in fact produce an underestimate "to the left of the true demand curve" because demand did not depend only on travel costs but also on travel time. By the end of the 1960s another source of bias in a value estimate of a natural resource had been suggested in the work of John V. Krutilla (1922–2003) in what Banzhaf (2019) has called the "environmental turn in resource economics." Krutilla grew up in Tacoma, Washington, in a Slovakian immigrant family. He left Tacoma to attend Reed College, from which he earned a bachelor's degree in economics. He then earned a PhD degree from Harvard in 1952. In 1955, he was one of the cofounders of Resources for the Future, with which he would remain affiliated until 1988. In an important paper, "Conservation Reconsidered," published in 1967 in the *American Economic Review*, Krutilla argued that the total value of environmental goods, such as national parks, transcends their use value, be it for recreation or other purposes. Even though not valued on the market, this nonuse value (as it came to be referred to in the 1980s) should be discounted in any cost-benefit evaluation. This value was concerned with concepts such as existence, bequest, heritage, and stewardship value, which did not all mean the exact same thing, but which according to Krutilla shared a public goods character. The value attached to the existence of a natural resource was nonrivalrous and nonexcludable, but that value represented nonetheless a true value to the public.[8] The question was: how to measure it?

Clawson, Knetsch, and Davis had of course also considered national parks as public goods. But in their articles, this was rather accidental and related to the way national parks were organized. It could have been otherwise, but for all sorts of good or bad reasons the task had fallen to the government. What they were interested in was the use of these parks and value estimates of the parks for recreation planning purposes. In contrast, Krutilla was interested in a different *kind* of value, the value that came not from actual use but from the sheer existence of the resource itself. This additional value had to be accounted for as well in questions of environmental planning.

Here, Davis's questionnaire method seemed to provide a natural solution. If it was possible to obtain coherent and rational responses to willingness-to-pay questions for recreation opportunities, why would it not be possible to obtain similar responses if asked for willingness to pay for the existence or improvement of an environmental good? In the early seventies, several resource and environmental economists tried their hand at this question. A landmark paper of 1974 by Alan Randall, Berry Ives, and Clyde Eastman on the valuation of environmental improvements (air visibility) at the spectacular Four Corners region, where Utah, Arizona, New Mexico, and Colorado meet, introduced the name and basic components of the CV method that are used today (Randall, Ives, and Eastman 1974). Their study consisted of a realistic and detailed sketch of the current situation, accompanied with photographs to explain the current and future situation, a plan for making the improvements, a willingness-to-pay question presented in such a format that the collection of the amount indicated in the response could be credibly expected to be collected (e.g., a special purpose increase in tax), control questions about a respondent's economic and demographic position (income, family composition), and questions about the respondent's understanding of the questionnaire. All these ingredients became refined over time and extended, for example, with a question that asked about (and revealed) sponsorship of the study, partly through criticism of this new use of the questionnaire method to elicit willingness-to-pay answers for environmental improvements.

8. For an extensive analysis, see Banzhaf 2019.

One such criticism was how to interpret the behavioral response in the questionnaire. Randall et al. (1974: 136) argued that respondents' willingness to pay was the behavioral response "of an underlying attitude: concern for environmental quality." In this context they discussed existing scholarship in sociology on how to conduct survey research to guarantee that respondents' answers to questionnaires will be "as reliable as possible" (136). Even if one agreed with Randall et al. that the expression of willingness to pay differs from the expression of an attitude, it is a response that, apart from a circle around a money value on paper, does not leave a behavioral trace. The difference is between actual and stated behavior, precisely the difference that Knetsch and Davis had discussed in their joint 1966 paper.

Clawson's indirect measurement procedure provided a check on Davis's questionnaire outcomes, a check that depended on actual data (however imperfect) about travels to national parks from which one could infer changes in demand. By definition there were no such data for the valuation of a public good like the *existence* of a particular national park. With a questionnaire we only observe stated behavior. Therefore, on the assumption of a properly constructed survey sample, the weight of evidence hinged on the coherence and rationality of respondents in their answers, on the credibility of the questionnaire, and on the credibility of the interview and survey procedures that had been followed.

And here emerged a clear crack in the profession. On one side there were those economists who did not think that respondents were able to rationally and coherently evaluate environmental improvement programs such as air visibility in the Four Corners region; on the other side there were those who put their trust in the rules and procedures of the questionnaire method itself to ensure a rational and coherent answer from respondents. This fissure would become explicit in a conference held in 1984. The conference was funded by the Environmental Protection Agency (EPA) and organized by the environmental and resource economists Ronald G. Cummings, David S. Brookshire, and William D. Schulze. Its purpose was to evaluate the merits of this newfangled method for evaluating money values of environmental resources.

Valuing Environmental Goods

Valuing Environmental Goods: An Assessment of the Contingent Valuation Method, the book from the conference, was published in 1986. It consisted of a thoroughly researched assessment by the conference organizers of the history and state of the art of the contingent valuation method, followed by commissioned comments by prominent environmental and resource economists that had been made at the conference. The state-of-the-art report had been circulated in advance to these contributors and to a "review panel" of economists with expert knowledge on public goods: Kenneth Arrow, Kahneman, Sherwin Rosen, and Vernon Smith.

Arrow was known of course for his work on social welfare, Rosen for his work on another method of valuation in cost-benefit settings, hedonic pricing, and Smith for public goods experiments, in particular for experiments testing for free riding and experiments that tested the Groves-Ledyard mechanism to elicit true preferences.[9] Kahneman, by contrast, was known among economists for his work on bounded rationality that emerged from his studies on biases in judgment and decision-making. Both angles, social welfare / public goods and individual rationality, show that the editors pitched the evaluation of the CV method as a weighing of pros and cons for the EPA's regulatory purposes against the ability of respondents to coherently answer questionnaire questions.

> For EPA regulations, such as air and/or water quality standards and regulations on hazardous waste disposal practices, costs may be amenable to estimation, but benefits attributable to a large part of these regulations are non-market, "public goods" in nature: cleaner air and water, a safer environment. Agencies such as EPA then have strong incentives and interests in identifying and developing means by which benefits attributable to public goods—such as environmental improvements—may be assessed. (Cummings, Brookshire, and Schulze 1986: 6)

The EPA was a product of the seventies. It was established by President Richard Nixon as a response to the growing environmental movement, with a mission to protect the environment and the health of citizens. Even though its first director, the Republican William Ruckelshaus, served only for a short time, he gained credit for making the EPA a nonpartisan agency.[10] He was called on by the Reagan administration in the spring of

9. E.g., Smith 1979, 1980, 1981. For a discussion of Smith's experiments, see Alvin Roth's introduction to Kagel and Roth 1995. I would like to thank Andrej Svorenčík for pointing me to this literature.

10. The Nixon administration first asked Ruckelshaus to serve as director of the FBI. Shortly thereafter, he became deputy attorney general, but he resigned when pressured by the Nixon administration to fire Special Prosecutor Archibald Cox. Ruckelshaus moved to Seattle to become a partner in a law firm.

1983 to again head the EPA; by then, the agency had become severely politicized. In a column for the *Environmental Professional* in the spring of 1980, Clawson, by then fellow emeritus at Resources for the Future, in clear reference to the EPA, complained that under President Jimmy Carter "virtually everyone" in the agency was "swept out" and replaced by "persons" from the "militant wings" of the environmental movement. He continued to observe that when Reagan took office in 1980, he "swept out the Carter people and replaced many of them with persons actively and prominently identified with opposition to environmental controls. Now the conservationists cry 'conflict of interest,' and the industry is, by and large, pleased" (Clawson 1980). When its director, Anne Gorsuch, was forced out of office by political scandals, Ruckelshaus was called back. He saw it as his task to restore confidence in the agency by hiring staff irrespective of political leanings or affiliations, solely based on their expertise.

The Cummings et al. report fits into this effort to regain trust by providing an unbiased and transparent assessment of the CV method, clearly displaying its pros and cons. But it also fits into the longer felt need within the EPA to search for a method that might be able to support its mission to protect the environment and public health, for which other methods of valuing public goods, such as the travel-cost method or hedonic pricing, were ill equipped. In their introduction the editors wrote that the travel-cost and hedonic pricing methods might work for some environmental goods, but that for most "regulatory concerns" of the EPA, such as air and water quality and environmental safety issues, contingent valuation was "the only game in town" (Cummings, Brookshire, and Schulze 1986: 7). Hence it was important to get a grip on the possibilities and pitfalls of the CV method to see if it could be successfully used for the EPA's regulatory purposes, the valuation of environmental and health concerns.

When CERCLA passed Congress in 1980, an additional legal layer was added to the discussion about the CV method. While Cummings et al. emphasized the use of contingent valuation as a method to estimate the environmental *benefits* of CERCLA, they listed loss of nonuse or passive use values as one of the components of environmental *harm* and contingent valuation as one of its methods of measurement. An assessment of the merits of the CV method was thus needed not only to measure the benefits of investments in the environment but also for practical liability purposes.

That same year, 1980, the EPA commissioned the environmental economists Robert C. Mitchell and Richard T. Carson, then also affiliated with

Resources for the Future, to develop an exemplary contingent valuation survey. Their survey asked respondents to state their willingness to pay for different levels of improvement of the national water quality ranging from activities like boating, fishing, and swimming to its use as drinking water. The survey included the option to revise an earlier willingness-to-pay bid after being shown how much someone with specified economic and demographic characteristics already paid on average to improve water quality. To counter anchoring response bias, the questionnaire presented bid choices on cards.

An initial report and an extensive survey pretest were published in 1981 and 1984. These served as the basis for Mitchell and Carson's (1989) handbook on the use of CV surveys to value public (environmental) goods, published in 1989, to which their EPA questionnaire was added as an appendix. A survey method that initially had been developed for the rather innocuous purpose of valuing tourist sites for recreation planning purposes, and had been experimented with in exploratory papers by Randall, Cummings, Brookshire, Schulze, Ralph d'Arge, Knetsch, and others, thus promised to become a method to produce value assessments of environmental benefits and harm in a regulatory and legal context.

Pushback: Are Respondents Rational?

Not all resource economists were happy with this development. When shifting from environmental benefits to costs, questionnaires should in principle change from questions about willingness to pay for benefits to willingness to accept compensation for environmental harm, and the differences between both answers should, on theoretical grounds, be expected to be small. However, empirical results showed differences that were, according to some critics of the method, all over the place.

In a joint 1979 study, Irene M. Gordon and Knetsch reviewed the evidence on differences in willingness to pay / willingness to accept measures (which they referred to as compensation required) and searched for possible explanations. From Resources for the Future, Knetsch had in the meantime moved to Simon Fraser in Burnaby, close to Vancouver, with which Gordon was also affiliated. This would in addition facilitate his collaboration with Daniel Kahneman, who had become a professor of psychology at the University of British Columbia in 1978.

Gordon and Knetsch started from the observation that, theoretically, willingness to pay and willingness to accept could diverge because of income effects. Another possible explanation could be that willingness-to-pay answers were budget constrained, whereas there was no such constraint on willingness to accept or, in their words, demand for "compensation." Empirical studies found, however, differences on the order of four times or even "a variation of 20 to 1, clearly not a small difference." Their reestimates of the data used in one of the original studies suggested that it would be difficult to explain such large differences from income effects alone. To illustrate their concerns, they drew a diagram with extreme indifference curves that could explain the large gap between willingness to pay and willingness to accept bids. But such indifference curves would lead to inconsistent preferences at different income levels. Gordon and Knetsch (1979) were very cautious not to dismiss survey results "completely," but even when it would be possible to "solicit honest replies to fully understood answers," better evidence on an individual's responses might be gained from responses in "observable behavior" in "realistically constrained" experimental settings instead of an individual's "answers to surveyor's questions."

Gordon and Knetsch thus mainly worried about the reliability of respondents' answers to questionnaires and less about the quality of questionnaires themselves. In his collaboration with Kahneman, Knetsch would further question the ability of economic agents to evaluate the value of environmental goods. Results would be first presented in Kahneman's comments at the 1984 EPA conference on the valuation of environmental goods and further developed in their work on the endowment and warm glow effect (Kahneman, Knetsch, and Thaler 1990, 1991; Knetsch 1989; Kahneman and Knetsch 1992). Beginning in the mid-1980s, Knetsch's increasing skepticism of the CV method would be eclipsed by Kahneman's more vocal criticism.

The preliminary results Kahneman presented at the 1984 conference were concerned with a telephone survey among residents in Ontario about their willingness to pay for improving the water quality of one or all lakes in Ontario for fishing. The choice for a survey on water quality was not incidental, given the publication of Mitchell and Carson's exemplary valuation study for the EPA. The structure of the questionnaire was clearly informed by the work of Amos Tversky and Kahneman (1983) on the conjunction fallacy, that is, the difficulty subjects have distinguishing between parts and wholes. Kahneman showed three nearly identically situated demand curves they had calculated from the survey data for two different lakes and for all the lakes in Ontario, from which he drew the conclusion that individuals could not distinguish between the contribution to only one or all lakes, thus violating standard microeconomic rationality assumptions. This result would resurface in many studies critical of the method of contingent valuation and would become referred to as the embedding or scope effect. Skeptics of these results, such as Mitchell and Carson, would rebuff similar studies as that of Kahneman and Knetsch that offered respondents near or perfect substitutes so that it would have been surprising to find large differences in willingness-to-pay answers.

Kahneman emphasized that "as an outsider" to economics, he did not share the economists' assumptions that individuals would have more or less well-formed preferences even for ordinary consumption goods let alone for nonmarket goods. Rather, Kahneman expected that such preferences, if there were any, were articulated on the go and primed by the scenarios and specific wording of the questionnaires. He feared this problem would only be aggravated for questionnaires that asked for a willingness to pay for commodities which he could only perceive as "ideological values" such as "clean air and nice views" (Cummings, Brookshire, and Schulze 1986: 192). He recommended that any use of the CV method should be tested on its anchoring effects and that these tests should be sufficiently strong "to elicit the anchoring effect in all its beauty" (193). Implicitly referring to Mitchell and Carson's exemplary study for the EPA, Kahneman added that there was unfortunately "sad news for anyone who thinks that the bidding card will eliminate the problem [of anchoring]. Several recent studies by Jack Knetsch and Robin Gregory have confirmed the highly predictable result that the bidding card is susceptible to anchoring biases for the simple reason that the range of values on the card provides information" (192).

Kahneman echoed concerns that motivated the state-of-the-art report itself. The report consisted of substantive discussions of reasons and causes of bias in survey research, lessons to be learned from experimental economics and cognitive science and decision theory, but its final chapter discussed the range of questions to which the contingent valuation method could be usefully applied. Cummings et al. compared a selection of studies on the contingent valuation method, the travel-cost method, and hedonic pricing with respect to their "accuracy." They argued that these three different methods should be considered as measuring devices just like measuring instruments in the natural sciences. Lacking an absolute scale, the only way to compare these different instruments was to compare them under "reference operating conditions" that would specify the conditions under which the measurement should be made. These conditions would thus circumscribe the range of use within which one could expect results from different measurement procedures that were within the same range of error. Just as the quality of measurements in "scientific applications" depended on conditions such as "temperature, atmospheric pressure, etc.," so did the quality of the CV method depend on four reference conditions that might enforce coherence in measurements. These conditions effectively limited the application of the CV method to goods that could also be measured with the travel-cost method or hedonic pricing. Outside this scope, any pronouncement on the credibility of the measurements produced with contingent valuation would be preliminary at best.

Assuming that, within the range of +50%, value estimates derived from indirect market methods include "true" valuations by individuals, these results suggest that CVM values may yield "accurate" estimates of value in cases where individuals have had some opportunity to make actual previous choices over that commodity in a market framework. These studies do not demonstrate that people are capable of providing market like values using the CVM for commodities which are not already being traded in existing markets, at least to a limited or indirect degree. In this latter regard, examples include such "commodities" as existence and option values for preserving an environmental asset over which people have no experience in making prior choices. (Cummings, Brookshire, and Schulze 1986: 102)

The four "reference operating conditions" they selected focused on the role of a respondent's understanding of and familiarity with the artificial commodity on offer.

1. Subjects must understand, be familiar with, the commodity to be valued.
2. Subjects must have had (or be allowed to obtain) prior valuation and choice experience with respect to consumption levels of the commodity
3. There must be little uncertainty.
4. WTP, not WTA, measures are elicited. (Cummings, Brookshire, and Schulze 1986: 104)

A graphical explanation underscored that the editors limited the range of applicability of contingent valuation surveys to goods that were as close

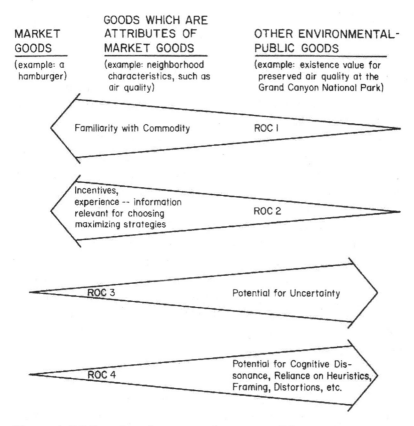

MARKET GOODS	GOODS WHICH ARE ATTRIBUTES OF MARKET GOODS	OTHER ENVIRONMENTAL-PUBLIC GOODS
(example: a hamburger)	(example: neighborhood characteristics, such as air quality)	(example: existence value for preserved air quality at the Grand Canyon National Park)

Figure 1 ROCs and market, nonmarket commodities.

Source: Cummings, Brookshire, and Schulze. 1986: 108, fig. 6.2.

to ordinary consumption goods in ordinary markets as possible (see figure 1). The first two reference operating conditions pointed their arrow toward "market goods." The third and fourth pointed theirs toward "other environmental-public goods." But as the third and the fourth conditions were formulated in negative terms, the reading of figure 1 was that there was less room for uncertainty and less potential for "cognitive dissonance" if respondents had more familiarity and more experience with the pricing of the good on offer, as was the case with ordinary market goods. In short, because respondents were familiar with market goods, they were better placed to state their true preferences because they better understood the commodity they were supposed to evaluate.[11] Unfamiliarity with the amenity on offer became almost identical with a respondent's inability to provide coherent answers to the CV questionnaire.

The editors listed the "existence value for preserved air quality at the Grand Canyon National Park" as an example of a public good that would be more difficult to evaluate in money terms than the "air quality" in a city like Los Angeles, which in turn was more difficult to evaluate than a hamburger. Thus, if respondents were confronted with a willingness-to-pay question for a hamburger, it could be reasonably assumed that they would be able to make up their mind in a "maximizing" fashion that could "elicit true, market like" preferences (Cummings, Brookshire, and Schulze 1986: 103). The editors thus considered the "accuracy" of CV research higher if it treated everyday consumer choices in the market than if it was concerned with consumer preferences for environmental public goods. In other words, Davis had introduced a credible method, but not for the evaluation of willingness to pay for public goods like the improvement of water or air quality in environments with which respondents were not familiar. Familiarity was identified with familiarity with market goods. But just as families from the 1960s on became increasingly familiar with outdoor recreation, thus building up "consumer capital" in evaluating the value of nature, so, one could imagine, could respondents to CV questionnaires be educated to understand and evaluate CV studies on nonuse values.

This was exactly the line followed by Mitchell and Carson in their 1989 handbook and EPA exemplary water quality study of the early 1980s. They argued that coherent and reliable answers from respondents could be secured if proper care was spent on the different elements of a CV questionnaire—its scenario, its wording, pretesting and survey procedures—and if transparency was secured about the survey's sponsor. They stressed the importance of the actual setting in which the questionnaire was held. In-person interviews that would take the appropriate time to explain the environmental amenity on offer, including visual aids, would help respondents understand and evaluate the public good on offer. Instead of the reference operation conditions of Cummings et al. that limited the applicability of CV surveys, Mitchell and Carson finished with a set of guidelines that would guarantee the quality of the questionnaire and extend its use to environmental issues beyond what respondents were familiar with from daily market behavior.

11. There was broad agreement among all participants that strategic overbidding to increase the supply of a public good was a minor issue because it did not show up in the data.

Rules of Inference, Framing,
and Respondent's Rationality

Valuing Environmental Goods was published in 1986, Mitchell and Carson's handbook in 1989. In the meantime the stakes had been raised by a decision from the DC court of appeal in a lawsuit filed by the State of Ohio against the Department of the Interior (DOI). The lawsuit asked the DOI to change its guidelines for environmental damage assessment to no longer give priority to assessment at market prices. Reluctantly, the DOI included contingent valuation as an equally valid method and confirmed the inclusion of nonuse (passive use) values as part of recoverable environmental damage.

The shift from benefits assessments of tourist sites for planning purposes to the assessment of environmental damage in a legal context changed the CV method from an innocuous alternative to the travel-cost method to a method that could be used as a weapon by federal and state agencies (and others) to enforce public protection against environmental harm. With the grounding of the Exxon Valdez in March 1989, it was clear that contingent valuation would be used by federal and state government agencies to obtain a value estimate of environmental harm done that would include nonuse values. As this episode has been covered in detail, also in this journal (Banzhaf 2017; Maas and Svorenčík 2017), let me just observe that to the dismay of many economists the blue-ribbon panel that was installed by the National Oceanic and Atmospheric Agency (NOAA) and chaired by Nobel laureates Kenneth Arrow and Robert Solow articulated a set of guidelines for CV studies that came very close to those formulated by Mitchell and Carson. These guidelines should serve as some sort of quality guarantee for the use of CV studies in regulatory and legal cases. The economists Elizabeth Hoffman and Brian Binger and the environmental attorney Robert Copple warned that these guidelines were turning "economic fiction" into "legal fact" (Binger, Copple, and Hoffman 1994: 1029). The experimental economist Glenn Harrison (2002) feared that future contingent valuation studies would strategically aim to comply with the panel's guidelines, which he considered to "lack any logic and empirical foundation," and he advised researchers in contingent valuation "to ignore it completely and think the important issues through on first principles." In the 1992 Exxon-sponsored conference that took place just before the hearings of the NOAA's blue-ribbon panel, William Desvousges had warned that with the stakes raised, it was no longer only undershooting but also overshooting environmental damage claims that could hurt social welfare: "This concern is critical in NRDAs [natural resource damage assessments] that may result in substantial monetary settlements or expensive litigation efforts. Neither substantially overestimating nor underestimating damages improves social welfare because all members of the public ultimately share the burden of either type of mistake" (Desvousges et al. 1993: 92). For Desvousges, and many economists in the mainstream, contingent valuation studies that included nonuse value estimates tried to do more than they were able to, with harmful welfare consequences.

We have seen that scientists, lacking first principles, searched for rules to guide them in their research. But there is a difference between the kinds of rules formulated by Cummings et al. and the rules articulated by Mitchell and Carson / the NOAA panel. In explicit comparison with measurement practices in the natural sciences, the reference operating conditions of Cummings et al. aimed to secure comparability between different measurement procedures and thus to secure convergence of measurement results. If their comparison between measurement in physics and economics holds water, the historical example should be the one discussed by Hasok Chang in his *Inventing Temperature* (2004); there, Chang discusses the iterative measurement procedures of the nineteenth-century French physicist Jules Regnault, who, lacking an absolute temperature scale, carefully compared the measurements of different types of thermometers to search for a satisfactory temperature scale.[12] In our case the comparison between different measurement procedures for willingness to pay should result in a credible willingness to pay value and hence a credible total value for the amenity on offer, neither overshooting nor undershooting true values too much.

The reference operating conditions of Cummings et al. limited the credibility of his assumption in reference to the situation with which economists felt comfortable: common market goods. If too far out of the range of the known, rationality could not be guaranteed, and no trust could be put in the measurement procedure. The range was determined by the limits of application of two of the three measurement procedures Cummings et al. considered: travel costs, hedonic pricing, and contingent valuation. Travel costs and hedonic pricing were restricted to what could be seen as market-like situations with which respondents to contingent valuation

---

12. I would like to thank Marcel Boumans for reminding me of the relevance of Chang's work.

questionnaires were familiar. Contingent valuation potentially could be applied to situations outside this range, but how to establish its credibility? How could one know whether respondents would provide coherent answers to questions about situations with which they were unfamiliar?

The difference with Regnault's problem situation is that in a social science like economics, measurement procedures hinge on assumptions about the rationality of subjects who can talk. Mitchell and Carson tried to use this difference by providing a set of rules that were basically taken from standing practices in survey research. Use focus groups, and pretest to make sure the questionnaire is unambiguous. Use support materials to help respondents understand the situation about which they are asked. Use an interview procedure that gives respondents sufficient time to digest the information and think about their answers. Include control questions to check if respondents understood the task and their own answers. Coherence, and hence rational responses, are sought through ongoing improvements to the questionnaire and the conditions under which the actual interview is conducted. But all such precautions will not remove the concerns of psychologists and economists who have reasons to doubt the ability of respondents to coherently answer a question. We have seen how Knetsch became increasingly skeptical and then teamed up with Kahneman and Thaler to further explore the biases in an individual's decision-making.

This leads me to two final observations. The first is about biases in decision-making that are taken as well-established facts, such as the endowment effect. Even when replicated, such facts also hinge on experimental and questionnaire procedures, and as recent research from Charles Plott and others suggests, if the experimental protocol is changed, the endowment effect becomes less pronounced or even vanishes (Plott and Zeiler 2005, 2007, 2011; but see Isoni, Loomes, and Sugden 2011). Similarly, the work of the cognitive psychologist Gerd Gigerenzer has shown that some of Kahneman and Tversky's strongest results regarding biases in decision-making vanish when the wording of questions is changed (most famously perhaps in Gigerenzer 1991). This does not mean that earlier results regarding decision-making have been refuted, but it becomes difficult to attribute them unequivocally to irrational agents or to imperfect questionnaires—a classic Duhem-Quine situation.

This brings me to my second observation. The rules of Cummings et al. and of the blue-ribbon panel were designed to reach closure about the applicability of a new method of inference to economic value, and one might say that that is what scientific rules are for: they guarantee a procedure for the establishment of a scientific fact. But as observed by Sheila Jasanoff (1992), in an adversarial context, rules achieve the exact opposite.

State of Oklahoma v. Tyson Foods is a good example. At a substantial cost, Stratus Consulting conducted a total value CV survey (i.e., a survey measuring use and nonuse value) for the plaintiff in support of its claim that Oklahoma had suffered substantial environmental losses due to nitrate and phosphorus pollution. To measure the money value of these losses, the survey outlined a recovery scenario that first explained the environmental decline since the early 1960s, then explained a program to restore the Illinois River Watershed to this earlier condition, then explained the payment mechanism, and then asked how much a survey respondent was willing to pay to clean up the pollution, followed by some demographic control questions, control questions on the respondent's understanding of the questionnaire, and information about the sponsor of the survey (the State of Oklahoma). A preliminary intercept study was conducted to get a "feel" for the situation; focus groups and pretests were held to ensure that the initial situation and the environmental amenity on offer were well understood. Two different surveys were conducted to make sure that respondents could coherently distinguish between the costs of a partial and an extended cleanup of the Illinois River Watershed. All of this was undertaken to make sure that respondents understood the question and that the survey outcome would provide a credible value assessment. But instead of reaching convergence on a credible value, defendants pointed out design errors and the poor statistical performance of the survey and hence the unreliability of the value estimate of environmental harm that resulted from the survey. Instead of accepting all the steps in survey research as black boxes, defendants opened them up and questioned the decisions that had been made in the design and conduct of the survey. In adversarial situations, rules do not create closure. Without an absolute scale, any inference based on rules remains open to dispute, and former colleagues watch each other from different sides of the courtroom.

References

Banzhaf, H. Spencer. 2010. "Economics at the Fringe: Non-Market Valuation Studies and Their Role in Land Use Plans in the United States." *Journal of Environmental Management* 91, no. 3: 592–602.

Banzhaf, H. Spencer. 2017. "Constructing Markets: Environmental Economics and the Contingent Valuation Controversy." In *The Age of the Applied Economist: The Transformation of Economics since the 1970s,* edited by Roger E. Backhouse and Béatrice Cherrier. *History of Political Economy* 49 (supplement): 213–39.

Banzhaf, H. Spencer. 2019. "The Environmental Turn in Natural Resource Economics: John Krutilla and 'Conservation Reconsidered.'" *Journal of the History of
Economic Thought* 41, no. 1: 27–46.

Binger, Brian R., Robert F. Copple, and Elizabeth Hoffman. 1994. "Use of Contingent
Valuation Methodology in Natural Resource Damage Assessments: Legal Fact and
Economic Fiction." *Northwestern University Law Review* 89, no. 3: 1029–1116.

Bishop, Richard C., and Thomas A. Heberlein. 1986. "Does Contingent Valuation
Work?" In *Valuing Environmental Goods: An Assessment of the Contingent Valu-
ation Method*, edited by Ronald G. Cummings, David S. Brookshire, and William
D. Schulze, 123–47. Totowa, NJ: Rowman and Allanheld.

Bouk, Dan. 2018. "The National Data Center and the Rise of the Data Double." *Historical Studies in the Natural Sciences* 48, no. 5: 627–36.

Bouk, Dan. 2020. "Error, Uncertainty, and the Shifting Ground of Census Data."
Harvard Data Science Review 2, no. 2: 2–9.

Clawson, Marion. 1959. "Methods of Measuring the Demand for and Value of Outdoor Recreation." Reprint no. 10. Washington, DC: Resources for the Future.

Clawson, Marion. 1980. "Politicizing the Environment." *Environmental Professional*
2: 223.

Cummings, Ronald G., David S. Brookshire, and William D. Schulze. 1986. *Valuing
Environmental Goods: An Assessment of the Contingent Valuation Method.*
Totowa, NJ: Rowman and Allenheld.

Davis, Robert K. 1963. "Recreation Planning as an Economic Problem." *Natural
Resources Journal* 3: 239.

Didier, Emmanuel. 2012. "Cunning Observation: US Agricultural Statistics in the
Time of Laissez-Faire." In *Observing the Economy: Historical Perspectives*, edited
by Harro Maas and Mary S. Morgan. *History of Political Economy* 44 (supplement): 27–45.

Edwards, José M. 2012. "Observing Attitudes, Intentions, and Expectations (1945–
73)." In *Observing the Economy: Historical Perspectives*, edited by Harro Maas
and Mary S. Morgan. *History of Political Economy* 44 (supplement): 137–59.

Gigerenzer, Gerd. 1991. "How to Make Cognitive Illusions Disappear: Beyond 'Heuristics and Biases.'" *European Review of Social Psychology* 2, no. 1: 83–115. doi.
org/10.1080/14792779143000033.

Gordon, Irene M., and Jack L. Knetsch. 1979. "Consumer's Surplus Measures and the
Evaluation of Resources." *Land Economics* 55, no. 1: 1–10.

Harrison, Glenn W. 2002. "Contingent Valuation Meets the Experts: A Critique of
the NOAA Panel Report." Mimeo.

Isoni, Andrea, Graham Loomes, and Robert Sugden. 2011. "The Willingness to Pay–
Willingness to Accept Gap, the 'Endowment Effect,' Subject Misconceptions, and
Experimental Procedures for Eliciting Valuations: Comment." *American Eco-
nomic Review* 101, no. 2: 991–1011.

Jasanoff, Sheila. 1992. "Science, Politics, and the Renegotiation of Expertise at EPA."
Osiris 7: 194–217.

Kagel, John H., and Alvin E. Roth. 1995. *The Handbook of Experimental Economics.*
Princeton, NJ: Princeton University Press.

Kahneman, Daniel, and Jack L. Knetsch. 1992. "Valuing Public Goods: The Purchase of Moral Satisfaction." *Journal of Environmental Economics and Management* 22, no. 1: 57–70.

Kahneman, Daniel, Jack L. Knetsch, and Richard H. Thaler. 1990. "Experimental Tests of the Endowment Effect and the Coase Theorem." *Journal of Political Economy* 98, no. 6: 1325–48.

Kahneman, Daniel, Jack L. Knetsch, and Richard H. Thaler. 1991. "Anomalies: The Endowment Effect, Loss Aversion, and Status Quo Bias." *Journal of Economic Perspectives* 5, no. 1: 193–206.

Knetsch, J. L., and R. K. Davis. 1966. "Comparison of Methods for Resource Valuation." In *Water Research*, edited by A. V. Kneese and S. C. Smith, 384–89. Baltimore: Johns Hopkins University Press.

Knetsch, Jack L. 1963. "Outdoor Recreation Demands and Benefits." *Land Economics* 39, no. 4: 387–96.

Knetsch, Jack L. 1989. "The Endowment Effect and Evidence of Nonreversible Indifference Curves." *American Economic Review* 79, no. 5: 1277–84.

Maas, Harro, and Andrej Svorenčík. 2017. "'Fraught with Controversy': Organizing Expertise against Contingent Valuation." *History of Political Economy* 49, no. 2: 315–45.

Mitchell, Robert Cameron, and Richard T. Carson. 1989. *Using Surveys to Value Public Goods: The Contingent Valuation Method*. Washington, DC: RFF.

Moscati, Ivan. 2018. *Measuring Utility: From the Marginal Revolution to Behavioral Economics*. New York: Oxford University Press.

Plott, Charles R., and Kathryn Zeiler. 2005. "The Willingness to Pay–Willingness to Accept Gap, the 'Endowment Effect,' Subject Misconceptions, and Experimental Procedures for Eliciting Valuations." *American Economic Review* 95, no. 3: 530–45.

Plott, Charles R., and Kathryn Zeiler. 2007. "Exchange Asymmetries Incorrectly Interpreted as Evidence of Endowment Effect Theory and Prospect Theory?" *American Economic Review* 97, no. 4: 1449–66.

Plott, Charles R., and Kathryn Zeiler. 2011. "The Willingness to Pay–Willingness to Accept Gap, the 'Endowment Effect,' Subject Misconceptions, and Experimental Procedures for Eliciting Valuations: Reply." *American Economic Review* 101, no. 2: 1012–28.

Porter, Theodore M. 1996. *Trust in Numbers: The Pursuit of Objectivity in Science and Public Life*. Princeton, NJ: Princeton University Press.

Porter, Theodore M. 2007. "Precision." In *Measurement in Economics: A Handbook*, edited by Marcel Boumans, 343–56. Amsterdam: Academic Press.

Randall, Alan, Berry Ives, and Clyde Eastman. 1974. "Bidding Games for Valuation of Aesthetic Environmental Improvements." *Journal of Environmental Economics and Management* 1, no. 2: 132–49.

Smith, V. Kerry. 1986. "To Keep or Toss the Contingent Valuation Method." *Valuing Environmental Goods: An Assessment of the Contingent Valuation Method Edited by RG Cummings, DS Brookshire, and WD Schulze*. Totowa, NJ: Rowman and Allanheld.

Smith, Vernon L. 1979. "Incentive Compatible Experimental Processes for the Provision of Public Goods." *Research in Experimental Economics* 1: 59–168.

Smith, Vernon L. 1980. "Experiments with a Decentralized Mechanism for Public Good Decisions." *American Economic Review* 70, no. 4: 584–99.

Smith, Vernon L. 1981. "An Experimental Comparison of Three Public Good Decision Mechanisms." In *Measurement in Public Choice*, 57–74. Springer.

Stapleford, Thomas A. 2012. "Navigating the Shoals of Self-Reporting: Data Collection in US Expenditure Surveys since 1920." In *Observing the Economy: Historical Perspectives*, edited by Harro Maas and Mary S. Morgan. *History of Political Economy* 44 (supplement): 160–82. doi.org/10.1215/00182702-1631824.

Thurstone, Louis L. 1931. "The Indifference Function." *Journal of Social Psychology* 2, no. 2: 139–67.

Tversky, Amos, and Daniel Kahneman. 1983. "Extensional versus Intuitive Reasoning: The Conjunction Fallacy in Probability Judgment." *Psychological Review* 90, no. 4: 293.

Wallis, W. Allen, and Milton Friedman. 1942. "The Empirical Derivation of Indifference Functions." *Studies in Mathematical Economics and Econometrics in Memory of Henry Schultz*, edited by O. Lange, F. McIntyre, and T. O. Yntema, 175–89. Chicago: University of Chicago Press.

Contributors

Amanar Akhabbar is associate professor of economics at ESSCA School of Management in Paris. His research interests are the methodology and the history of economics and, in particular, the case of quantitative and interindustry economics. In 2019, he published *Wassily Leontief et la science economique*, elaborating on Leontief's economic epistemology in its historical context.

Jeff Biddle is professor of economics at Michigan State University. His research interest is the history of economics in the United States during the twentieth century, and his recent work has focused on the development of empirical methods in economics. He is the author of *Progress through Regression* (2021), a history of the Cobb-Douglas production function regression as an empirical research tool in economics.

Marcel Boumans is Pierson Professor of History of Economics at Utrecht University. His main research focus is on understanding empirical research practices in social science from a combined historical and philosophical perspective. He is particularly interested in the practices of measurement and modeling and the role of mathematics in social science. Because models are not complete as sources of knowledge for sciences outside the laboratory, additional expert judgments are needed. This is the topic of his most recent monograph *Science Outside the Laboratory* (2015). His current research project "Vision and Visualisation" explores how expert judgments (views) are made and how they could be validated, particularly in those research practices where visualizations are built or used.

Paul Burnett is a historian of science and oral historian with the Oral History Center at UC Berkeley. He joined the Center in 2013 from the Science and Technology Studies Program at St. Thomas University in New Brunswick, Canada, where he was an

History of Political Economy 53 (annual suppl.) DOI 10.1215/00182702-9414903

assistant professor. He completed his PhD at the Department of History and Sociology of Science at the University of Pennsylvania in 2008, where he developed his research on the politics of expertise—how scientists and experts establish their credibility, and how people choose between different kinds of expertise to try to solve social, political, scientific, and technical problems. He is currently completing a book about the agriculture group at the University of Chicago Department of Economics.

Laetitia Lenel is a postdoctoral researcher at the history department of Humboldt-Universität zu Berlin. Her book project explores the transatlantic history of business forecasting in the twentieth century. In 2020, she coedited a volume on the history and current state of economic forecasting.

Harro Maas is a professor in history and methodology of economics at the Centre Walras-Pareto for the history of economic and political thought at the University of Lausanne. He succeeded Craufurd Goodwin as the series editor of Historical Perspectives on Modern Economics. He has written on changing methods of observing, modeling, and visualizing the economy in the nineteenth and twentieth century. His book on the Victorian polymath Stanley Jevons with Cambridge University Press (2005) was awarded the Joseph Spengler Best Book Award 2006 by the History of Economics Society. His edited volume (with Andrej Svorenčík) of a witness seminar on the emergence of experimental economics with Springer (2016) received the Best Book Award in the History of Economics from the European Society for the History of Economic Thought (2018). With Mary S. Morgan he edited *Observation in Economics, Historically Considered* (2012) and with Hsiang-Ke Chao a special issue of *East Asian Journal in History of Science, Technology and Society*, on diagrammatic reasoning in the sciences (2020). Among his recent publications are, again with Andrej Svorenčík, "'Fraught with Controversy': Organizing Expertise against Contingent Valuation" (2017), and "Monitoring the Self: François-Marc-Louis Naville and His Moral Tables" (2020). This last article is part of his current project "Moral Accounting Matters" funded by the Swiss National Science Foundation (grant no. 100011_188931) that aims to historicize current theories and practices of consumer governance.

Mary S. Morgan is the Albert O. Hirschman Professor of History and Philosophy of Economics at the London School of Economics; she is an elected Fellow of the British Academy and an Overseas Fellow of the Royal Dutch Academy of Arts and Sciences. She has published widely on social scientists' practices of modeling, observing, measuring, and making case studies, and has long-standing interests in tracing how social science research is used to effect change in the world. Her current team project has been investigating the functions of narratives across the natural, human, and social sciences.

Boris Samuel is a researcher at the French National Research Institute for Sustainable Development (IRD) / Paris Diderot University. His research examines statistical and macroeconomic practices to analyze the social and political trajectories of African countries. With Kako Nubukpo, he wrote "The Neoliberal Turn and the Consolidation of a Transnational Bureaucracy: A Research Note on Economists and Statisticians in Francophone West-Africa," for the August 2020 issue of *Actes de la recherche en sciences sociales*. He has coordinated several special journal issues on quantification in Africa, in particular "Reason and Imagination of Planning," *Politique Africaine* no. 145; and with Béatrice Hibou, "Macroeconomics from Below," *Politique Africaine* no. 124.

Thomas A. Stapleford is associate professor in the Program of Liberal Studies at the University of Notre Dame. He is the author of *The Cost of Living in America: A Political History of Economic Statistics* (2009) and coeditor of *Building Chicago Economics* (2011), and has published a range of essays on the history of empirical economics, the history of American capitalism, and the history and philosophy of science more broadly.

Aashish Velkar is a historian at the University of Manchester, UK. He is the author of *Markets and Measurements in Nineteenth-Century Britain* (2012) and has published a range of essays on histories of measurements, standards, and economic nationalism in Britain and India.

Index

History of Political Economy 53 (annual suppl.) DOI 10.1215/00182702-9663331
Copyright 2021 by Duke University Press